Ways of the Rivers

Ways of the Rivers: Arts and Environment of the Niger Delta

MARTHA G. ANDERSON and
PHILIP M. PEEK, Editors

With contributions by

E. J. Alagoa

Martha G. Anderson

Lisa Aronson

Kathy Curnow

Henry John Drewal

Joseph Eboreime

Joanne B. Eicher and Tonye V. Erekosima

Sonpie Kpone-Tonwe and Jill Salmons

Philip E. Leis

Keith Nicklin

Philip M. Peek

Kay Williamson and E. E. Efere

UCLA Fowler Museum of Cultural History

LOS ANGELES

The Fowler Museum is part of UCLA's School of the Arts and Architecture

Lynne Kostman, *Managing Editor*
Patrick Fitzgerald, *Designer*
Daniel R. Brauer, *Production Manager*
Don Cole, *Principal Photographer*
David L. Fuller, *Cartographer*

UCLA Fowler Museum of Cultural History
Box 951549, Los Angeles, California 90095-1549

Requests for permission to reproduce material from this volume should be sent to the UCLA Fowler Museum Publications Department at the above address.

Printed and bound in Hong Kong by
South Sea International Press, Ltd.

Distributed by the University of Washington Press,
P.O. Box 50096, Seattle, Washington 98145.

Front Cover: Detail of figure 1, page 24.

Pages 2-3: The Ofurumo masquerade.
Photograph by Martha G. Anderson, Ondewari, 1992.

Page 36: Detail of figure 3.17a.

Page 130: Detail of figure 6.1.

Page 220: Detail of a side view of figure 9.23.

Back Cover: Figure 6, p.27.

This book was made possible with
major support from:

National Endowment for the Humanities,
dedicated to expanding
American understanding
of history and culture

National Endowment for the Arts

Jill and Barry Kitnick

Additional support has been provided by:

Yvonne Lenart Public Programs Fund

Ethnic Arts Council of Los Angeles

Manus, the support group of the UCLA Fowler
    Museum of Cultural History

Charles and Kent Davis

Tom and Diana Lewis

Herbert M. and Shelley Cole

Library of Congress Cataloging-in-Publication Data

Ways of the rivers : arts and environment of the Niger Delta /
Martha G. Anderson and Philip M. Peek, editors ; with
contributions by E.J. Alagoa... [et al.].
        p. cm.
        Includes bibliographical references (p.).
        ISBN 0-930741-90-0 (soft)
        1. Niger River Delta (Nigeria)—Social life
        and customs. 2. Niger River Delta (Nigeria)—
        Environmental conditions. 3. Arts—Nigeria—
        Niger River Delta. I. Anderson, Martha G., 1948– II.
        Peek, Philip M.

DT515.9.N55 W39 2002
306'.09662—dc21   2002018929

List of Lenders to the Exhibition

American Museum of Natural History, New York
The Art Institute of Chicago
Dr. Richard and Jan Baum
Brooklyn Museum of Art
Herbert and Shelley Cole
Charles and Kent Davis
Joanne B. Eicher
Fred Feinsilber
Toby and Barry Hecht
W. and U. Horstmann
Indiana University Art Museum, Bloomington
Indianapolis Museum of Art
Iris & B. Gerald Cantor Center for Visual Arts,
      Stanford University
Jill and Barry Kitnick
Krannert Art Museum and Kinkead Pavilion,
      University of Illinois, Urbana-Champaign
Jay T. and Deborah Last
Mr. and Mrs. J. Thomas Lewis
The Menil Collection, Houston
The Museum of Fine Arts, Houston
National Museum of African Art, Smithsonian
      Institution, Washington, D.C.
North Carolina Museum of Art, Raleigh
Bruce Onobrakpeya
Peabody Essex Museum, Salem
Robert B. Richardson
Eric Robertson
Mr. and Mrs. Richard Rogers
John B. Ross
Seattle Art Museum
Mr. and Mrs. Edwin Silver
The University of Pennsylvania Museum of
      Archaeology and Anthropology, Philadelphia
John and Enid Van Couvering
Dr. Leon and Fern Wallace
Walt Disney-Tishman African Art Collection

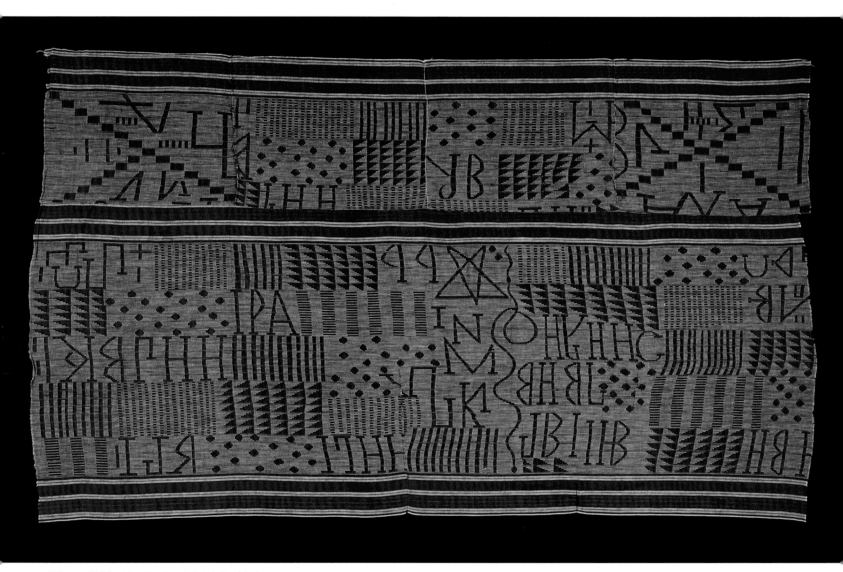

*Wrapper. Kalabari Ijo. Cut-thread cloth (pelete bite).
By Osonta John Bull. L: 203.8 cm. FMCH X84.600;
Purchased with Manus Funds. The Kalabari collect,
display, and wear a wide variety of textiles, including
many manufactured in Europe and Asia (see chapter
10 of this volume). Pelete bite, or "cut-thread" cloth, is
created primarily by Kalabari women who painstakingly
lift and snip threads in woven cloth imported from India
to create intricate, openwork patterns.*

**To
Roy Sieber
who taught us
how
to swim.**

— Martha G. Anderson and
Philip M. Peek

Contents

Part 3: Arts and Identity

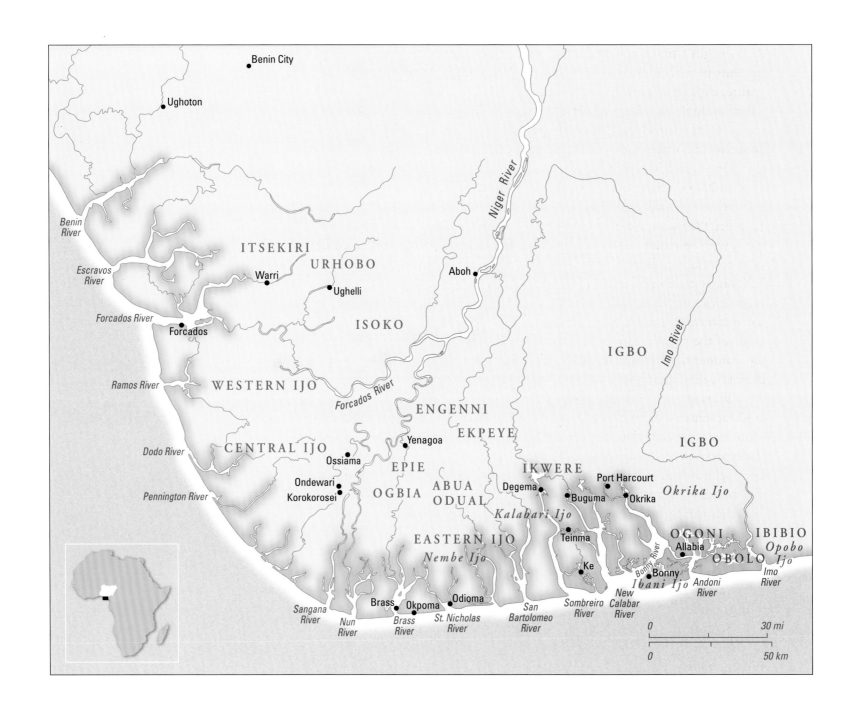

Foreword

As we begin a brave new millennium, our relationship to the environment presents us with some of our most critical challenges. How do we regard nature, exploit its resources, and succeed or fail to preserve it? How will the use of natural resources immediately affect political, religious, and economic transactions around the globe? These are urgent, central, and universal concerns of contemporary life. Yet, they are also concerns that have defined lifestyles, forged identities, and shaped cultural practices for centuries.

In Nigeria, where the Niger Delta occupies an enormous area crisscrossed by rivers, tributaries, swamps, and lagoons, water has always been far more than a simple element of nature. Water is synonymous with life itself, with spiritual sustenance, with wealth and prosperity, and especially with communication and identity. For years, the waterways of the Niger Delta have connected and divided people, serving as conduits and obstacles, repositories of riches and realms of danger. The ambivalence associated with these contrasting potentialities is made manifest through the arts, cultures, and ethos of the many peoples inhabiting this aqueous region. In this challenging environment, peoples of the Delta experience a dynamic confluence and a dramatic divergence of ideas, memories, histories, and art forms.

Ways of the Rivers is the first publication dedicated to the complex cultural matrix of the Niger Delta. It is also one of the few studies of African art to examine the relationship of culture to environment and to explore the expression of an entire region as opposed to a single ethnic group. It has long been acknowledged that ethnic entities are arbitrary categories and that lived experience constantly defies such invented boundaries and demarcations. Whether through trade, intermarriage, warfare, migration, or political consolidation, ethnic groups constantly interact with one another—identities shift according to historical circumstances and social transformations. The Niger Delta offers a rare glimpse into the complexities of intercultural dynamics, while presenting some of Africa's most remarkable visual and performance arts within their broader contexts.

Sculpture from the Niger Delta is among the largest and most dramatic on the African continent. From fantastic horizontal headdresses depicting sharks, sawfish, crocodiles, and pangolins to awe-inspiring spirit figures armed with weapons and potent medicines, Delta arts are anything but understated. Instead, they are astonishing in their aesthetic and symbolic assertiveness, as when *ivri*, "emblems of adamance," raise individuality, willpower, and inner strength to remarkable heights. At the same time, some of Nigeria's most exquisite small-scale works in bronze using lost-wax casting have been found in the Delta. Women's arts are equally important, as witnessed in the performative richness of initiation rites, stunning accoutrements, and regal commemorative sculptures of mothers and prominent women. Textile arts—also the domain of women—articulate many experiences in the region, as seen in masquerade ensembles, "dressed" funeral rooms, and the evocative garments of Delta people. Even ephemeral genres such as puppetry achieve narrative mastery. These dynamic arts have been created to meet the particular needs of specific moments, and some are no longer produced. Yet many continue into the present, and others are invented, as with the work of such famous contemporary artists as Sokari Douglas Camp and Bruce Onobrakpeya. Their work is a testimony to the resilient ideas and creative genius of the Delta peoples.

The Niger Delta encompasses a profusion of ethnic groups, including Ijo, Isoko, Urhobo, Ijebu, Ogoni, and Itsekiri peoples. The subject matter of Delta arts also ranges widely—from the pirates, missionaries, and merchants who served as middlemen in earlier trade networks to playful water spirits who emerge as masks during annual festivals. The present book explores this artistic scope and range with the interdisciplinary research of African, European, and American anthropologists, archaeologists, art historians, historians, folklorists, and linguists, each of whom has dedicated years of study to a particular region, ethnic group, or cultural phenomenon in the Niger Delta. Only through this tapestry of perspectives can we begin to grasp the complexity of the Delta and its historical and art historical dynamics.

This project began in the mid-1990s under the creative tutelage of former Fowler Museum director Doran H. Ross. The Fowler's extensive holdings of Niger Delta arts combined with strong scholarship on the region made the prospect of an exhibition most promising. Drs. Martha Anderson of Alfred University and Philip Peek of Drew University were invited to be guest curators because of their profound understanding of this remarkably complex region. We are most appreciative of their many insights and efforts and their leadership in organizing the publication and accompanying exhibition. We also thank the many scholars whose important research is published here, much of it for the first time. *Ways of the Rivers* has been developed with the assistance of generous grants conferred by the National Endowment for the Humanities and the National Endowment for the Arts, for which we are very grateful. The project has also has been supported by a gift from Barry and Jill Kitnick—an early groundbreaking show of important Niger Delta artworks was organized in 1976 by Barry Kitnick for his former gallery, Gallery K. Additional support has been provided by the Yvonne Lenart Public Programs Fund, Ethnic Arts Council of Los Angeles, Charles and Kent Davis, Tom and Diana Lewis, and Herbert M. and Shelley Cole. A project as ambitious as *Ways of the Rivers* could not have come to fruition without the contributions of these individuals and organizations.

We also extend our warm thanks to the lenders to the exhibition (please see the List of Lenders to the Exhibition on p. 5), whose works bring to life the remarkable artistry of Niger Delta peoples. By making their works accessible to a broad public, such lenders are integral to furthering the educational mission of the Fowler Museum and UCLA more generally. A number of friends and institutional colleagues provided special assistance as the exhibition was being organized: Kathleen Bickford Berzock, Theodore Celenko, Charles Davis, Woods Davy, Richard Faletti, Barry Hecht, Manuel Jordan, Chris Mullen Kreamer, Alisa LaGamma, Pamela McClusky, Rebecca Nagy, Diane

Pelrine, Eric Robertson, Enid Schildkrout, William Siegmann, and Cherie and Edwin Silver.

As always, the remarkable staff of the Fowler Museum is to be congratulated for its commitment to the project's realization. Sarah Kennington, assisted by Farida Sunada, oversaw the exceedingly complex loan arrangements with tireless energy and absolute dedication. Jo Hill, Fran Krystock, and Anna Sanchez have seamlessly coordinated the conservation and collections requirements of the works in the exhibition. David Mayo and his installation team have once again created a breathtaking visual experience for an exhibition that sensitively and dramatically evokes the ethos of the Niger Delta world. Martha Crawford has conceived a spirited graphic voice for the exhibition. Betsy Quick, Alicia Katano, and Ilana Gatti have developed exciting family and public programs that will engage our audiences in the spirit of the Delta. Amy Hood has been an effective spokesperson for the project in the form of publicity and promotion. Lynne Brodhead and Leslie Denk have successfully led the efforts to bring the project the financial support it required. Marylene Foreman, Allison Railo, and Betsy Escandor have ably overseen the financial and administrative dimensions of the project.

A book of this scale has demanded the coordinated efforts of a talented team. Lynne Kostman has done a heroic job of editing all the essays, working with the authors, and securing photographs and permissions. For the book design we are grateful to Patrick Fitzgerald, who has created a visually appealing format, and to Danny Brauer, who has supervised the book's production and printing. Don Cole has brought his nuanced eye to photographing the many works reproduced in this volume.

Finally, our sincere thanks go to Martha Anderson and Phil Peek, whose commitment and steadfast dedication to this project have been present every step along the way. Like the watery currents of the Niger Delta, they have flowed with the vagaries of exhibition development with patience and flexibility and have been responsive to our needs and concerns. It has been inspirational to learn about the Delta from them firsthand and to witness the realization of their vision and dreams for this far-reaching project.

On behalf of the Fowler Museum, we are most honored to be the organizers of this exceptional project and hope that this volume will stand as proof of the sensitivity and strength with which the peoples of the Niger Delta have coped and cared for their environment over time. As multinational interests present new threats and challenges to Delta communities, we hope this book will serve to underscore their resilience, receptivity, and cultural brilliance.

Marla C. Berns   *Mary (Polly) Nooter Roberts*
Director   Deputy Director and Chief Curator

Preface Cultural Identity in the Multicultural Niger Delta

PHILIP E. LEIS

> I have learned to wear many faces.
> —Okara 1978, 18

In the Niger Delta, masks and other products that might fall under the rubric of "art" were part of a social fabric whose complex interweave provided the various contexts in which these objects must be understood. Depending on the circumstance, the same object could be venerated, feared, played with, or ignored. A sculpture could symbolize its owner's character, as in the case of the *ivri*,[1] or, as with the *oru*, be seen as having an identity of its own. A mask could be part of an elaborate scenario, beginning with the costuming of the dancer and followed by a performance involving special dance steps, songs, acting, and drumming; this could continue for several days (Clark 1966) or, as with the Kalabari, form part of a cycle of performances lasting over a period of years (Horton 1960, 29). An emphasis on context, however, raises the question of whether the objects are properly defined by an ethnic reference—the Isoko *ivri* or Ijo *oru*—or whether the similarity of the objects in form and function contributed to the definition of an ethnic identity. We propose in this book that the objects were critical in the historical process of both defining and being defined by the Delta populations.

A. *Ivri. Isoko. Wood. H: 69.2 cm. Walt Disney-Tishman African Art Collection. Photograph by Jerry L. Thompson. Among the Isoko, men and women can acquire personal sculptures known as* ivri *to help them to control their assertiveness (see interleaf D). War leaders, however, serve larger* ivri *to increase and maintain their aggressiveness in order to safeguard their communities.*

An individual's identity is commonly understood as dependent on context: an Ijo, for example, in New York is seen as, and may identify himself as, an African; in Ghana, the same person is a Nigerian; in Nigeria, an Ijo may be known as such; in the Niger Delta, it depends on where the person resides and to whom he is talking. We also know that constructing an identity is much more complicated than stipulating a geographic point of reference. The ways in which an Ijo blends or mixes African and European cultural traditions while living in London for decades offer another dimension to identity. History is yet another facet, and a particularly confounding one when migration and state formation are added to the question of identity. The national boundaries drawn in Africa by European colonial powers a century ago ignored indigenous ethnic sentiments; the internal boundaries first drawn within the countries, such as the tripartite division of Nigeria, are frequently seen as having exacerbated them.[2]

As Nigeria has aged from a newly created country, divided into Northern, Eastern, and Western Regions in the early part of the twentieth century, to a nation of thirty-six states at the end of the century, the relevance of an ethnic constituency has accentuated the significance of an ethnic identity. Whether the multiplication of Nigerian states can satisfy the needs of the various ethnic

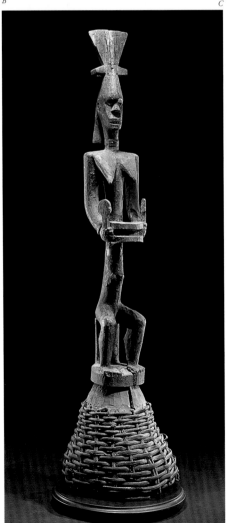

B   C

groups—enfolding them within a national identity—as opposed to becoming a point of conflict threatening national stability itself is a question for Nigeria's future. The Nigerian case, furthermore, illustrates that the problems inherent in studying questions of identity are not cultural ones alone. The British domination of the Niger Delta began in 1891 with the formation of the Oil Rivers Protectorate. The "oil" in the name referred to palm oil. The Biafran Civil War in the late 1960s highlighted a replacement for the region's most valuable natural resource. The central government formed a new kind of protectorate based on oil, but this time the oil was petroleum, and the cultural consequences of being an Ijo or an Ogoni or one of the other Delta populations became increasingly more significant than during the colonial period.

Nigerian census data are notoriously inaccurate. In an attempt to gain an accurate and politically acceptable count, while avoiding the strife that resulted from earlier efforts, the census of 1991 excluded questions revealing ethnic, linguistic, or religious affiliation. Some of the populations in the Niger Delta, defined by the primary language spoken, were roughly estimated in the early 1990s to be: [3]

Ijo	1,779,000
Isoko/Urhobo	546,000
Itsekiri	510,000
Ogoni	500,000

Ijo speakers occupy the major portion of the Delta, flanked on the far west by Ijebu-Yoruba; on the western and northwestern borders of the Delta, by the Itsekiri, Urhobo, and Isoko; on the north and northeast by the Igbo, and on the east by the Ogoni and Ibibio. The Itsekiri speak a Yoruba language but appear to be culturally closer to Benin; the Urhobo and Isoko speak dialects of Edo, yet are culturally distinct from the Itsekiri, and to some extent from each other; and Ijo speakers have a language dissimilar to the others, yet share cultural and social features with the Itsekiri, Urhobo, Isoko, Igbo, Ogoni, and their other neighbors. (See the appendix to this volume for a fuller discussion of linguistic diversity in the Delta.)

Much as identity shifts with context, the similarities and differences within and among these various populations depend on the degree of focus. When telescoped, individuals see themselves as being quite different from others living in the region. Ijo living in a Central Delta village have said they can hear the nuances of speech among people in their own clan who come from neighboring communities. Dialects spoken by the Ijo in the east and west are mutually incomprehensible. Ijo in the southern part of the Delta stress the mother's descent group; those in the northern part, the father's. Women in the latter area practice clitoridectomy; those in the former do not. When the focus is broadened, it is difficult to delineate one linguistic group from another on the basis of social and cultural features. Art styles suggest a possible means of classification (Anderson 1983, 232–60), but Ijo living near the mainland tend to share more cultural features with their neighbors, such as the symbolic importance given to the "right hand" among the Western Ijo, Itsekiri, Urhobo, and Isoko, than with the Central Ijo. As Peek observed in noting the similarity in masquerades between the Urhobo and the Nupe, who live toward the northern end of the Niger Valley, above

D

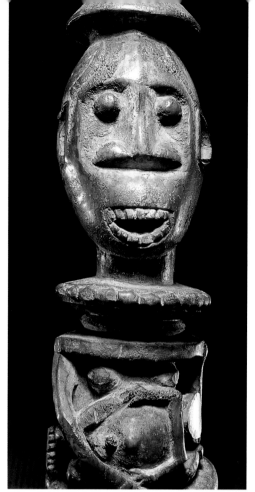

E

the confluence of the Niger and the Benue, cultural similarities extend well beyond the Delta (1983, 41).

With a wider perspective, the differences become more a variation on a theme than the basis for drawing sharp boundaries around ethnically defined populations. In many ways the physical qualities of the Delta seem to be a figurative reflection of the difficulties confronted in identifying the peoples living there. The boundaries between mainland and Delta have shifted over time, the rivers and streams leading from the Niger to the sea are intermeshed, as are the mangroves whose branches and roots are so intertwined as to become indistinguishable from each other. This imagery could, of course, have been applied to the human occupation of the Delta long before the economic and political developments that gave rise to the ethnic categories recognized in Nigeria today. The geographical dimensions of the Delta, however, are far more than metaphoric in their ability to shape the social and cultural development of the people living there. The area is made up of a seemingly endless number of islands that change in size and type of resources from the small sandy stretches of beach where the Delta meets the sea, to the islands in the mangrove swamps that are inhabitable only prior to the flooding during the rainy season, to the large islands that form the headlands. This island environment provided the kind of isolation that led to adaptive variation within historically related peoples, and the waterways were also the pathways for trade and social intercourse that produced cultural convergences among peoples of different provenience.

Whatever analytical problems might arise in the attempt to bring conceptual order to a region where every island was an opportunity for establishing a new "frontier" (Nzewunwa 1980, 244), or a "frontier of opportunity" (Dike 1956, 20), it must be understood that the peoples of the Delta did not need European explorers, colonial administrators, or

B.   *Detail of figure C.*

C.   *Female water spirit headdress. Ijo. Wood, plant fiber, metal alloy, and pigment. H: 73.7 cm. Charles and Kent Davis. Ijo headpieces can take the form of humans, animals, or composite creatures, and two or more types can appear in the same masquerade. The elegant female on this headdress was probably the wife or daughter of the central character in a masquerade play. Her own extravagant headgear suggests prestige, as do her seated posture and the objects she holds in her hands.*

D.   *Ceremonial staff with figures. Seventeenth to eighteenth century. Ijo. Ivory with traces of pigment. H: 77.5 cm. Charles and Kent Davis. A Western Delta provenance has been suggested for this unique object, which bears certain hallmarks of Ijo style but suggests influences from neighboring cultures, including Benin. The finial forms an elaborate hat for a maternity figure "enthroned" above a kneeling male retainer who bears a flintlock pistol. Both wear ruffs, a fashion introduced by early European traders. The imagery and the use of ivory connote wealth and prestige, and the excellent condition of the staff indicates that it probably adorned an important shrine (Nicklin 1995, 391).*

E.   *Detail of figure E.*

*F.   Water spirit headdress. Eastern Ijo. Wood.
L: 31.1 cm. Walt Disney-Tishman African Art
Collection. L2001.11.2. Photograph by Jerry L.
Thompson. Although it takes the form of a human face,
this mask would have been worn on top of the head in
màsquerades honoring water spirits. Eastern Ijo groups
shared similar mask types and masking societies, but only
those of the Kalabari are well documented. The bulging
eyes of this example most closely resemble those seen on a
Nembe Ijo example, but the carving is much more
delicate and refined (Horton 1965a, fig. 60).*

*G.   Post from a meeting house. Urhobo. Wood.
H: 191.6 cm. FMCH X81.1569; Gift of William Lloyd
Davis and the Rogers Family Foundation. The Isoko and
Urhobo make posts for their meeting houses in a similar
style, but they offer different reasons for doing so. The
Isoko claim that their posts serve a decorative function,
but for the Urhobo, they reportedly serve as ancestral
images (eshe). The crocodiles and other reptiles on Urhobo
posts refer to animal counterparts of the ancestor who
travel between the worlds of the living and the dead
(Foss 1976, 20).*

H.   Back view of figure G.

scholars to tell them who they were. The Itsekiri, for example, as Ayomike points out, did not have "to await the Portuguese or the British to give them the acceptable variant of the name of their homeland" (1990, 19). The Ijo say they called themselves Izon (Truth) before their name was mispronounced by early European traders (Okara nd, 1). Who the Delta peoples eventually became, however, is a matter of identity formation.

Notions of primordiality and cultural conservatism on the one hand and of inventiveness and cultural convergence on the other are two major ways of thinking about identity formation. The former stress descent, the latter collaterality. In the first instance, an ethnic group is defining its boundaries by reference to descent from a common ancestry (blood ties) and to a natural, or innate, shared tradition of customs and beliefs. In the second, the boundaries are based more on opposition to surrounding populations, and the cultural differences within a population are fused within a re-created history. An ethnic group discovers itself by assimilating different past populations with an eye toward legitimating its history on a par with that of present-day neighbors. Just which of these points of view applies to a particular population will depend on its history and the historical data available. A newly defined ethnic group, by the very nature of the opposition that creates it, may quickly arrive at a self-definition that insists on its primordial status. In theory, then, cultural identities can be formed in different ways; in practice the processes blend and can be hotly contested.

One of the remarkable features of cultural identity is that seemingly similar peoples may see themselves as being different, and conversely, peoples defining themselves as having one culture may be more different from each other than they are from those that they see as belonging to other ethnic groups. We have no simple answer as to why this occurs, particularly where populations are on intimate contact with each other, even intermarrying. The Delta peoples provide us with a good example of how conservatism and cultural change can operate at the same time and thus suggest one type of resolution.

The now generally accepted thesis that most African societies were not sharply delineated in ethnic terms until the imperatives of colonial administration called for them to become political entities (Lentz 1994) fits particularly well for the Delta peoples. None of the presently identified ethnic categories were organized in a single political entity before European contact. The so-called invention of tradition has worked as much to divide populations, or to keep them divided, as it has to create a sense of a primordial shared history among autonomous communities.

The peoples of the Delta, analogous to the habitat they occupied, were many separate yet connected parts that constituted a whole. As long-term occupants they illustrated the dual cultural processes of divergence and convergence. Their linguistic affinities reveal that the Ijo, the Itsekiri, and other groups had separate root origins. The differences within each resulted from a long period of

I. *Face bell. Lower Niger Bronze Industry. Copper alloy. H: 15.9 cm. Charles and Kent Davis. Face bells, which are found in a wide variety of styles, may have served either as spirit emblems or as insignia for rulers. The grotesque features of this head, which has a frog emerging from its mouth and snakes crawling across its cheeks, suggest the ability to command dangerous, supernatural powers. Similar motifs appear in the art of Ife, Owo, and Benin.*

separation due to migration, contact with other populations, and adaptation to the historic and environmental conditions of the Delta. The process of migration also brought different populations closer together through trade, markets, intermarriage, and transmission of beliefs and objects.

The earliest accounts indicate that Europeans were using names and stereotypes to identify a population. The ways the populations themselves came to use these ethnic identifications were not unique to the Delta. What may be unique was the use of figures, masks, and other objects in formulating the process of cultural change within a context of cognatic descent groups and multiple forms of marriage. New settlements gained and retained their history by reference to the spirit objects, such as Egbesu in the Central Delta, carried by the eponymous founder of a community. A community's moral authority rested in the belief that the object had historical significance; it legitimated a descent group's claim to the land, rivers, and lakes. In this the scope of authority extended to the level of clan organization. Spirit objects, however, were of the present and not just the past. As explanations for the vagaries affecting human life, they could become powerful objects, gaining a following that would incorporate the local community without its necessarily having to defer to the clan spirit object.

J. *Pangolin masquerade headdress. Egbukere Ekpeye. Wood, paint, metal, cloth, rope, and nails. L: 105.4 cm. The Museum of Fine Arts, Houston; Museum purchase with funds provided by Baroid Corporation in honor of their Nigerian employees at "One Great Night in November, 1990," acc. no. 90.499. Animals that defy categorization, cross boundaries, or behave in unexpected ways often serve as mediators with the spirit world. None is more unusual than the pangolin, or scaly anteater, a creature that looks like a fish or reptile but climbs trees and gives birth like a mammal. The Ekpeye link pangolins with smithing, a process that involves transformation. Their pangolin masks appear at celebrations of renewal and transformation.*

The importance of individual choice reflects the relationship between ethnic identity and the identification of spirit objects with ethnic groups. The spirit objects referenced an ethnic category as part of stereotyping that apparently began in the disputes that gave rise to the migrations into the Delta and continue to the present day. The unique identity of each object, however, acted as a reference point to provide the historic grounding and the everyday rationale for dealing with individual and communal problems.

The separation of carved object and the spirit that occupied it was not unlike human development. Each person was unique, yet the process of enculturation and intercultural transmission diminished differences between peoples of similar or different orgins. Similarly, each *oru* was unique, identified with a name and with powers and tastes unique to it. One was known for the ability to heal or to help a woman overcome her barrenness; another, for killing thieves. Yet the style of carving and the commonality in the rituals performed, including song and dance rhythms, resulted in a dynamic fusion of artistic representation that both identified a cultural tradition and crossed ethnic lines.

K.   Crocodile masquerade headdress. Delta peoples. Wood, fiber, and pigment. L: 215.3 cm. Indiana University Art Museum, 72.116.2. Photograph by Michael Cavanagh and Kevin Montague © Indiana University Art Museum. Because the crocodile moves freely between land and water, it serves as a mediator between different realms, but its popularity as a masquerade character has more to do with its role as a dangerous predator. Much to the delight of the audience, performers armed with machetes often convey its ferocious nature by chasing people around the arena. In addition to headdresses like this one, numerous others with composite features incorporate voracious-looking crocodile snouts.

Acknowledgments

This exhibition, like most, has had a lengthy history, one replete with twists and turns to rival even the most meandering of the Niger Delta's many creeks. When we approached Doran Ross, the former director of the UCLA Fowler Museum, about working with his institution six years ago, he responded "Great idea!" Apparently he had forgotten that he had asked us to consider organizing a Niger Delta exhibition nearly a decade earlier. Construction of the Museum's present facilities, however, prevented us from moving forward at that time.

This delay was to prove fortuitous: it allowed sufficient time for our ideas to develop and for additional fieldwork to take place. In 1991, we had the good fortune to meet with several colleagues who had worked in and near the Delta—including Jill Salmons, Keith Nicklin, and Perkins Foss—while attending a planning meeting for a book on Nigerian art in Geneva. Our conversations there—including one that most appropriately took place aboard a boat on the lake—convinced us of the importance of looking at the region as a cultural complex and spurred our interest in organizing an exhibition. When we announced meetings of the newly formed Niger Delta Arts and Cultural Heritage Interest Group at the African Studies Association meetings in 1993 and 1994, Eli Bentor, Kathy Curnow, Henry Drewal, Joanne Eicher, Philip Leis, and Rosalinde Wilcox, indicated their interest in working with us. We also corresponded with E. J. Alagoa, who represented a group of scholars based in Nigeria, including Kay Williamson, E. E. Efere, Robin Horton, F. N. Anozie, Abi Derefaka, Sonpie Kpone-Tonwe, and Joe Eboreime. Several others—Lisa Aronson, Ekpo Eyo, John Picton, Herbert M. Cole—joined us at planning meetings in New York in 1995 or New Orleans in 1998. We were also able to discuss the project with Tonye Erekosima in Washington, D.C., in 1995 and subsequently. Elisha Renne, Roberta Sumberg, Judith Gleason, and Nancy Neaher Maas also met with us at various stages of the project and generously offered photographs for use in the book and the exhibition.

From these roots a mighty mangrove grew. We want to thank all of the authors and others who contributed essays, photographs, and ideas. Their collegiality and their willingness to devote time to this project have been exceptional. We would also like to specially thank Abi Derefaka and F. N. Anozie, Eli Bentor, Kathy Curnow, and Rosalinde Wilcox for contributing essays to a special issue of *African Arts* dedicated to the Niger Delta, which is being published to complement this volume and the accompanying exhibition. Barry Hecht is also deserving of our thanks for his role in helping us track down specific works of art.

The skilled and congenial staff of the UCLA Fowler Museum has given us an immense amount of support over the years, and we thank all of those who have worked behind the scenes for their intelligence, creativity, and enthusiasm. Our special thanks must go to Doran Ross, who encouraged and guided us through the first stages of this monumental project, to Polly Nooter Roberts, the Museum's deputy director and chief curator, who pulled the exhibition together and saw it to conclusion, and to the current director of the Museum, Marla C. Berns, who has given support and encouragement in the final stages of the project. The book and the exhibition simply could not have come to fruition without their seasoned expertise, enthusiasm, and dedication. We join Marla and Polly in thanking the exceptional staff of the Fowler Museum for their extraordinary efforts.

In addition, we must also acknowledge all those Delta artists, past and present, whose works inspired us in the first place. No exhibition should be solely a memorial to the past. We sincerely hope these wonderful works will inspire other Niger Delta artists. We offer further thanks to all those who hosted us during our various travels in the Delta and answered all those strange questions. We hope our versions of their answers do justice to the vast body of knowledge that was shared with us. It is our sincere wish that this volume may inspire others to pursue further studies of this extraordinarily rich and diverse part of the world. Finally, we offer thanks to family and friends who wondered at and were wearied by our obsession with the ways of the rivers. We hope all those who aided us along the way are as pleased as we are with the results of that collaboration! Our thanks to all. Bon Voyage!

Martha G. Anderson

Philip M. Peek

Notes on Orthography

As will become almost immediately apparent in the course of reading this volume, the Delta is from a linguistic standpoint an incredibly dense and complicated region. A glance at the appendix and the map that introduces it will confirm this impression. The Ijo (Ijaw) group, for example is made up of seven separate languages, and one of them, Izon, has close to thirty inherently intelligible dialects. The work of Kay Williamson and E. E. Efere is thus truly pioneering. Because there exists such a plethora of languages and dialects within this geographically small region, and because systems for standardizing orthography have not been established in each and every case, we have refrained from indicating diacritics and tone marks for words taken from the many languages of the Delta. A sense of proper orthography may be gleaned from the appendix by Williamson and Efere, specifically from figure X.10, "Words for 'Mangrove' in the Niger Delta." Unlike the languages of the Delta proper, Yoruba, the language spoken by peoples living to the west of the Delta has been long studied and its orthography systematized. Diacritics and tone marks therefore appear within the context of chapter 6 of this volume by Henry John Drewal, which compares the masquerades of the Ijebu-Yoruba to those of the Niger Delta.

Introduction Charting a Course

MARTHA G. ANDERSON and

PHILIP M. PEEK

I believe the great swamp region of the Bight of Biafra is the greatest in the world, and that in its immensity and gloom it has a grandeur equal to that of the Himalayas.

       —Mary H. Kingsley 1897 [1965], 95

The country may be described as one in which Nature is at her worst. From the slime and ooze of the soil up to the devitalising heat and humidity of the atmosphere, it leaves its mark on the people in an enervating and demoralising influence.

       —Major A. G. Leonard 1906 [1968], 51

Although the Niger Delta is possessed of great natural beauty, not many Europeans—or Delta inhabitants for that matter—have shared Mary Kingsley's inspiring assessment of the region. Unfortunately, it is the perspective of Major Leonard that more Europeans would have endorsed. As the world's second largest delta—its largest inhabited delta—the region continues to make a profound impression, for better or for worse, on those who enter it.

The intricate maze of islands and waterways that run through the Delta initially baffled Europeans who took several centuries to "discover" that the rivers they had been trading in formed the end of the mighty Niger (figs. 2–4). As only a handful of these Europeans ever ventured more than a few miles from the major rivers and creeks, they knew remarkably little about the Delta's peoples. Thus, although the Portuguese arrived in the Delta as early as the fifteenth century, Europeans did not reside in Isoko country until the 1920s, and only a handful have ever lived in the villages near the Delta's center. Due to widespread fears of water travel, many Nigerians, including government officials, continue to avoid the area today.

For centuries, peoples with diverse cultural traditions have lived in the Delta side-by-side, sharing an environment dominated by water and subject to floods, tides, and tropical downpours. Because resources vary from one part of the region to another, people have long used the rivers as avenues of commerce; and some later served as middlemen in the overseas trade. Most groups maintained their own languages, but the cultural exchanges that accompanied economic transactions often generated comparable customs and art forms. Instead of dividing people, the Delta's many waterways have helped to create cultural confluences among them.

The arts of the Niger Delta include some of the largest wood sculptures and most vibrant masquerade traditions in all of sub-Saharan Africa (fig. 1). Delta residents have responded to their world by incorporating their unique environment in their celebrations, even to the extent of performing in canoes

1. Bush spirit figure. Ijo. Wood and pigment. H: 218.5 cm. Private Collection. The Ijo associate the rivers that border their villages with wealth, fertility, and trade, but they regard the surrounding forests as perilous places, fraught with dangerous animals and violent spirits. When enshrined, powerful bush spirits such as this one can protect villages from being invaded by enemies, hostile spirits, disease, and other malevolent forces.

2.   This nineteenth-century illustration by William
Allen depicts a cortege including the artist himself, the
famed explorer Richard Lander, and King Boy of Brass
accompanied by many canoes. The procession is shown
traveling through the Delta to meet King Obi Ossai of
Aboh, who had earlier kidnapped the Lander brothers
(see chapter 2 of this volume) and had agreed to make
reparation consisting of "two bullocks, ten goats, and
four hundred yams" (Allen 1840, 9).

3.   View of boats on Erohwa Creek in Isokoland.
Photograph by Philip M. Peek, 1971.

4.   This photograph taken from space dramatically
illustrates the numerous waterways that traverse the
Niger Delta. Photograph courtesy of NASA.

5.   Paddle with two figural carvings. Ogoni. Wood.
L: 119.4 cm. Brooklyn Museum of Art; Gift of Mr.
and Mrs. Lee Lorenz, 1993.179.5. In the Niger Delta,
paddles can serve as spirit emblems, shrine furnishings,
and dance props as well as equipment for propelling
canoes. A head wearing a pith helmet (or bowler hat)
adorns the handle. The female, who perches above the
flaring paddle holding a mirror (?), probably represents
a maiden fresh from the type of initiation rites often
referred to as the "fatting house."

6.   Sawfish headdress. Delta peoples. Wood, paint,
and mirror. L: 69.3 cm. North Carolina Museum
of Art, Raleigh; Purchased with funds from various
donors, by exchange, 85.1. The imposing size of the
sawfish and its long, wicked-looking snout account for
its popularity in masquerades performed throughout
the Delta. The artist who carved this elegant example
exaggerated the length of its toothed rostrum and
streamlined its body. Although large, undocumented
examples are often assigned to the Ekpeya and Abua,
others, including the Itsekiri and some Ijo groups, make
similar headpieces on the same scale.

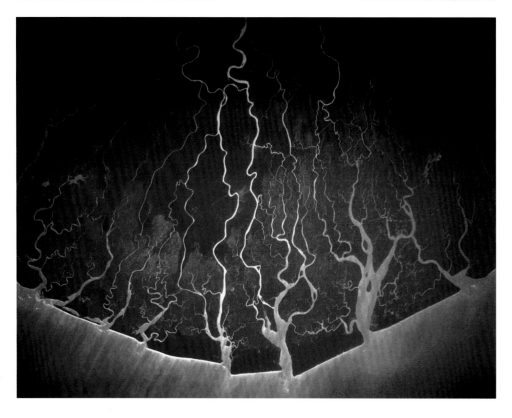

on the water. Paddles and canoes feature prominently in their art and rituals (fig. 5). The Delta peoples share beliefs in water spirits and bring them to life in masquerades as fantastic aquatic beings (fig. 6). Over the decades shrines have reflected the "foreign" origins of these spirits and emphasized their prosperity by incorporating a range of trade items from bronze bells (fig. 7) to plastic dolls. In contrast, images of ancestors and of forest spirits—brandishing weapons and sporting European-style top hats—recall the warrior societies that once operated throughout the region and evoke the fabulous tales of wealthy merchant princes and daring pirates that continue to circulate (fig. 8).

The history of European contact with the peoples of the Niger Delta— albeit fascinating in some respects—is replete with horrible ironies. On the one hand, Delta entrepreneurs remained successful in controlling trade arrangements until the latter part of the nineteenth century when the British broke the hold of local middlemen. On the other hand, by the late sixteenth century the Portuguese had secured a monopoly on supplying slaves to their own plantations in Brazil and those of the Spanish in the Caribbean. With the primacy of this trade in human beings, the section of the Guinea Coast containing the Delta became known as the "Slave Coast." Millions of people were forcibly taken from their homelands to work on plantations in the Americas. When the British, who later dominated the region, sought to replace trade in slaves with trade in palm oil in the nineteenth century, the Delta region became known as the "Oil Rivers." Tragically, beginning in the 1960s, petroleum replaced palm oil as a chief commodity, enslaving people in a different way. Delta inhabitants must now confront the oil spillage and other environmental damage that have wreaked havoc on fishing and farming in the region. Paradoxically, while oil companies have threatened the Delta's delicate ecosystems with their modern drilling technology—garnering vast profits in the process—the region's inhabitants have been left without even the most basic amenities. Recently, protestors held oil workers captive demanding fresh drinking water as their ransom. Throughout all this adversity, the extraordinary people of the Delta continue to adapt to rapid change while maintaining a variety of distinctive artistic and political traditions.

5.

6.

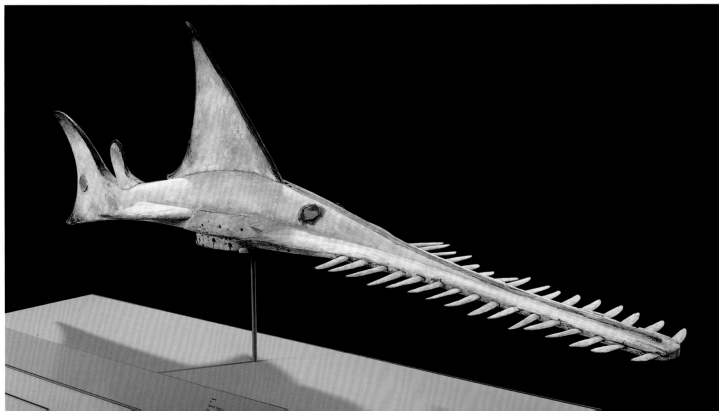

7. Face Bell. Ijebu. Bronze. H: 85 cm. W. and
U. Horstmann. These large bell-shaped heads share
some characteristics of Benin bronze work but more
strongly demonstrate Yoruba stylistic features, such
as large eyes. A number have been located in the
Ijebu-Ode area of Yoruba country where they serve
primarily as status symbols and may be worn.

8. Masquerade headdress. Ijo. Wood and cording.
H: 65 cm. Anonymous Loan. Shrine images and
figures surmounting masquerade headpieces often
model towering hats. A popular trade item in the
nineteenth century, top hats still survive as status
headgear among Ijo males living in the Central and
Western Delta. Although he resembles bush spirit
images, this figure, who grasps a smaller figure in
one hand, represents a water spirit, as do all Ijo
masquerade headdresses.

Land and Peoples

The Niger Delta as we know it today began to be formed in the early Tertiary period, about sixty-five million years ago (see Anozie and Derefaka, forthcoming). It is presumed that people have lived there for the past five millennia, although this has yet to be substantiated by archaeological evidence. The first peoples to arrive probably occupied the tropical forests on the Delta's northeastern edge, then gradually moved further south into the freshwater swamps, finally reaching the mangrove swamps near the coast by about 800 C.E. Those who settled in the coastal saltwater region lived primarily by hunting, fishing, and trading with their inland neighbors; those living in the freshwater regions of the interior combined fishing with hunting and farming.

The actual Delta comprises an area defined by the Forcados River to the west and the Imo River to the east. Often, however, neighboring riverain and coastal areas are included in discussions of the region. The Niger Delta's coastal boundaries are thus often considered to coincide roughly with the furthest limits of Ijo settlement, reaching from Opobo in the east nearly to Lagos in the west. The northern boundary falls above Aboh, an Igbo town on the Niger River at the head of the Delta. Many Delta traders, however, routinely traveled as far north as Idah near the confluence of the Niger and Benue Rivers. The Ijo established fishing villages as far east as Cameroon (see Wilcox, forthcoming).

Although Ijo speakers predominate, the region is ethnically diverse; its inhabitants represent a number of different language groups, and each of these groups, in turn, contains several distinct languages, most of which are not mutually intelligible (see the appendix to this volume). Finally, many languages are further subdivided into dialects. Because of this exceptional diversity, many Delta inhabitants will speak two or three Nigerian languages in addition to English or Pidgin English. Populations range in size from the Ijo speakers, who numbered about one million in 1963 (at 2 percent of the population in the less reliable 1991 census, they sometimes claim to be the fourth largest ethnic group in Nigeria), to the Obulom, Ogoi, Defaka, and other small groups whose languages are confined to single communities.

Theoretical Issues

Any discussion of the Niger Delta and its peoples raises a number of theoretical issues. The most obvious of these is the question of environmental determinism. This approach, which few would support today, was given considerable credence in nineteenth-century anthropology. In the mid- twentieth century, Reverend John W. Hubbard, an Anglican missionary who spent years studying the Isoko and Urhobo peoples, maintained that we "cannot understand their history until we have a thorough knowledge of their land and its geography" (1948, 2). As if to underscore the importance of environment, he began his study with a river journey to the Isoko and Urhobo regions. Certainly, the Delta's distinctive environment creates boundaries for human beings; but cultural behaviors within these ecological parameters differ tremendously. Although a model of environmental determinism does not serve to explain the rich diversity found in Niger Delta cultures, any study must consider the important role that the region's unique topography played in encouraging certain historical developments, such as trade.

9.   A woman paddles a canoe loaded with fish traps near the Western Ijo town of Ossiama in Oiyakiri clan. Photograph by Martha G. Anderson, 1992.

10.   Young boys fishing along the waterside at the Central Ijo town of Korokorosei in Olodiama clan. Photograph by Martha G. Anderson, 1992.

11. *Water spirit mask. Eastern Ijo. Wood. L: 33 cm. Krannert Art Museum and Kinkead Pavilion, University of Illinois, Urbana-Champaign; Faletti Family Collection 2001-11-1. This mask closely resembles the one that appears as figure F in the preface to this volume. Its protruding mouth and bared teeth, however, add a more animalistic dimension. Details such as scarification also differ. Assuming that these masks represent the same character, variations could indicate that they come from different Eastern Ijo groups or from rival "houses" within one group.*

The various theories proposed to explain migration into the Delta—all of which tacitly assume that no one would "normally" seek to live in such an environment—constitute another area of debate. The "refuge area" thesis, for example, asserts that people would only migrate into the Delta to avoid greater harm threatened or experienced elsewhere. Traditions concerning the irrational demands of an *oba* of Benin or the fear of an avenging army are, for example, cited as the cause for people fleeing into the Delta. Given the warrior ethos cultivated by some peoples within the Delta (see chapter 3 of this volume), it is not improbable that a group may have provoked its own expulsion. The prominent Nigerian historian E. J. Alagoa, however, stands among those opposed to such migration theories.

A further issue for consideration is the cohesion of multiethnic communities, significant because the Delta peoples seem to demonstrate the variable applicability of any theory of human behavior. While they have managed to maintain peaceful, cohesive communities for long periods of time, they have waged savage war against each other as well. Contemporary events provide dramatic proof of such pendulum swings. On one hand, terrible interethnic violence has occurred within the city of Warri, while on the other, enthusiastic conventions of Delta peoples continue to strive for a stronger, unified political voice.

Most sociopolitical units among Delta peoples are small in size and diverse in origin. Large-scale ethnic identification is very recent, and Delta communities still function primarily at a village-group, or "clan," level. While the term *clan* might not be correct technically, it continues to be used by the people living in the region. Most Delta communities owe their origins to a procession of many different groups arriving over long periods of settlement; yet these same communities ascribe to common historical traditions that serve to unify them and accept titled leaders who trace descent from different ancestors. Therefore, while Delta peoples are extraordinarily autonomous (*acephalous* is the most frequently used term), they also demonstrate an exceptional capacity for incorporating and fusing social units.

Issues of commonality and independence surface within the sphere of art as well as in the sociopolitical realm. Today, few of those engaged seriously in the study of African art would argue for the existence of discrete style areas, but neither can they dismiss the likelihood of common forms occurring among neighboring peoples—nor would that preclude the existence of radically different artistic features among those same peoples. Surely the internal variation within any single people's artistic production demonstrates an enormous possible range as well (figs. 11, 12).

Thus the Niger Delta is more than an exceptional physical environment, more than a long-term victim of the vagaries of world trade, more than a matter of complex social organizations, and more than an artistic corpus striking for its homogeneity in certain respects and its uniqueness in others. It is perhaps best conceived of as a conceptual framework. Its inhabitants exist within a unique fabric of cultural resemblances and cultural differences. Thus, there is perhaps more "mutual intelligibility" within the arts than among spoken languages, more similarities among dress and diet than among social structures. For example, virtually all peoples treated in this volume have comparable masquerade complexes: people invite the water spirits to join them on land and, in turn, often join the water spirits in their realm (figs. 13, 14).

12.   *Elephant masquerade headpiece. Ijo or Ijebu-Yoruba. Wood and pigment. L: 74.9 cm. FMCH X85.326; Anonymous Gift. The skull-like features and flat surface of this horizontal headpiece suggest an Ijo origin, but Henry Drewal assigns it an Ijebu-Yoruba provenance. The Ijebu openly admit to borrowing water spirit masquerades from their Ijo neighbors, but they have modified them and introduced new forms. The idea of transforming the lower part of the face into an elephant's trunk and tusks that terminate in hands has not been documented among the Ijo. It may be a Yoruba innovation.*

This volume is unique among studies of African art in that it is devoted to a definable geographic area, as opposed to an individual ethnic group or a whole nation. This approach has broad implications because it permits study of a puzzling dynamic of human cultures, an inquiry into a simultaneous need to be both alike and different within what we often term a culture area. Countless migrations into the Niger Delta over thousands of years ensure that ethnic identity has always been a critical dynamic, affecting both the interactions of Delta peoples and their relationships with outsiders. As Philip Leis has aptly suggested (see the preface to this volume), "In many ways the physical qualities of the Delta seem to be a figurative reflection of the difficulties confronted in identifying the peoples living there. The boundaries between mainland and Delta have shifted over time, the rivers and streams leading from the Niger to the sea are intermeshed, as are the mangroves whose branches and roots are so intertwined as to become indistinguishable from each other" (fig. 16).

13

14

15

16

Identity

Contiguous ethnic groups are never as different from each other as they believe themselves to be. Nevertheless, as is readily observed, the Igbo are clearly more Igbo than the Yoruba. What accounts for the difference? Exploring the dynamics of cultural complexes introduces an important perspective to the study of African art. This volume and the accompanying exhibition seek to demonstrate aspects of those entangled influences—including style—that provide some sort of distinction among cultural groups.

We begin with the premise that the arts reflect ethnic identity and that both their content and form will be used to demonstrate change, affiliation, and difference. A cultural complex is composed of a myriad of elements, any and all of which may be altered. A masquerade, for example, involves masks, music, costume, dances, and songs; it occurs at a certain time in a certain place for specific reasons. This enumeration could continue, but the point is that any of the above-listed elements can be transformed.

This volume is an attempt to contribute to ongoing discussions concerning elements of cultural identity. In this capacity it will touch upon: images and representations that contribute to identity; identity as enacted in core complexes that vary among cultures within a region; the different uses and manifestations of cultural borrowing; and ways in which intergroup relationships are defined. Masquerades and shrine arts will provide the basic framework for exploring these issues.

While the arts provide an excellent area within which to investigate cultural change, it is extremely difficult to predict the direction, intensity, or even the type of change that might occur. Often, distinctive traditions occur in some areas of life but not in others; for instance, people may carefully protect differences in a style of dress or the meaning of a masquerade dance but not find similarities in food patterns threatening. Groups can justify cultural borrowings as divine interventions or corrections of the errors of others, or they can consciously manipulate tradition by establishing and touting similarities, a strategy often employed in the quest for political prestige. Several Isoko clans have used the traditions surrounding their *ivie* (priest-kings) either to affirm or deny links to the powerful Benin Kingdom to the north. Culturally similar groups living in multiethnic settings may express ambivalent or even contradictory attitudes toward borrowing. The Itsekiri, for example, accuse their Urhobo rivals of copying their dress and dance styles, while ironically asserting their own distinctiveness by using masks that openly imitate Ijo types. People do not exist in a vacuum; they are always conscious of themselves in relation to others—affirming or denying cultural similarities or differences in order to accomplish specific goals.

By examining a range of art forms that reflect cultural borrowings, as well as distinctive traits, this volume focuses on cultural authentication—the process by which traditions derived from outside of a group are validated by the authority of political or religious leaders. As groups adjust new elements—whether borrowed from distant or closely similar cultures—to make them conform to local aesthetics and beliefs, they often obscure their origins. The Kalabari, for example, have submitted European hats to radical changes in both style and meaning, transforming them into "traditional" headgear worn by prominent men (fig. 17).

13. *This trio of* umale *(water spirit) masquerades typifies those of Itsekiri urban social clubs. The spirit in this case is Okpekuru, which is also the name of the fish on the headpieces. Photograph by D. Anthony Mahone, Warri, 1994.*

14. *In this masquerade performed by the Omo Ologbara Cultural Society, an Itsekiri social club, two performers independently rotate while dancing beneath a headpiece featuring figures in canoes. Photograph by D. Anthony Mahone, Warri, 1994.*

15. *Face mask. Urhobo. Wood and pigment. H: 45.7 cm. Walt Disney-Tishman African Art Collection. Photograph by Jerry L. Thompson. This finely carved mask depicts Omotokpokpo, or "Girl with youthful body," one of the minor water spirits who are said to attend the great Oworu (Ohworu) as she travels upriver from the Ijo region. The girl's crown and hairdo (which may include the two "horns") identify her as a bride. Her scarification conforms to the markings once worn by the Urhobo. Unlike the horizontal Ijo headpieces that inspired the Urhobo water spirit festival, this mask was worn over the face (Foss 1981, 146).*

16. *"Mangrove swamp in the delta of the Niger." Gleaner Pictorial Album 1: 23, fig. 1. Illustration courtesy of the Church Mission Society, London.*

Modern political realities have heightened awareness of ethnic differences while simultaneously promoting a sense of regional identity. Some of the Delta's residents, like the Ijo, have only recently stressed their ethnic unity, electing to heighten the awareness of themselves as a group out of political necessity. Notions of identity do not always coincide with language. For example, the prosperous Kalabari Ijo downplay their relationship to poorer, more rustic Ijo subgroups living to their west; conversely, the latter consider numerous other Delta groups to be Ijo, even though they speak different languages. The sense of a regional identity rests partly with a shared resentment of political domination by larger mainland ethnic groups; it was this that led Delta peoples to lobby together for the creation of Bayelsa, Delta, Rivers, and other bordering states. More recently, rivalries among riverain groups and hopes for a larger share of the national wealth have prompted calls for further subdivisions, but Delta men still express their regional identity by wearing distinctive garments called *dons* (a term that may be derived from the Portuguese honorific), which play on the style of Victorian boiled shirts introduced by nineteenth-century British traders.

With this history of fission and fusion, the Niger Delta serves as a microcosm of the ethnic and political tensions the nation of Nigeria has suffered since achieving independence. It has now become axiomatic in African studies to observe that anti-imperialism seldom translates into nationalism once independence is gained. Nigeria has repeatedly provided examples of the difficulties involved in attempting to unify diverse ethnic groups. From its earliest incarnation as a federation of three states, or regions, through a vicious civil war, to its present configuration of thirty-six states, Nigeria seems to have always been at war with itself. Within this tragic, larger canvas, the peoples of the Niger Delta were perhaps more acted upon than actors in their own right. Invaded over the centuries by foreign armies and traders, raided for slaves, and later exploited for mineral oil, this beleaguered area has remained much neglected in terms of social services and the material improvements associated with other oil-rich areas of the world such as Bahrain and Kuwait. While the Delta peoples have sought after political unity as a means to survive the politics of larger ethnic groups, poverty, abuse, and frustration have led to interethnic conflicts as recently witnessed in Warri.

17.   *A young man wearing a hat known as an* ajibulu.
Photograph by Joanne B. Eicher, Buguma, 1988.

Overview of the Volume

The foregoing comments cannot hope do justice to the richness of Niger Delta cultures or the complexity of the region's social problems. The essays that follow, however, will more closely examine the Delta, its history, its ecology, its peoples, and its art from a variety of perspectives. Our contributors take us from several hundred years ago to the present, from the lagoons at the western edge of the Delta eastward to Cameroon and northward to the margins of the Delta and mainland.

Part 1 will treat different dimensions of the critical history of trade, pre-European and European, that have aided in defining cultural groups and supporting various artistic enterprises. The essays in part 2 consider the physical environment within which the Delta peoples live and its impact upon them. Finally, in part 3, we examine issues of art and identity within the context of a number of Delta peoples.

This volume is organized broadly in terms of ethnic groups, and although differences in language, historical experience, and local ecology correspond to substantial variations in worldview, sociopolitical organization, and subsistence pattern, a number of similar cultural features cut across these lines. The inhabitants of the Delta share what we will term a "water ethos." This ethos manifests itself in shrines, masquerades, and rituals associated with water spirits. By means of short illustrated interleafs, we also hope to provide a sampling of the many art forms and cultural complexes that exist within this wonderful watery world.

18.   The amananaowei, *or town chief, attending a demonstration of the local funerary rites. Photograph by Martha G. Anderson, Ossiama, Oiyakiri clan, Western Ijo, 1992.*

19.   Professor E. J. Alagoa (center) with his wife and other members of his family during the Itoru Bamo (Chalking) ceremony held at his inauguration into his father's chieftaincy. Photograph by Elisha Renne, Nembe, 1995.

Part 1: Early History, Trade, and Contact

Chapter 1

Lower Niger Bronze Industries and the Archaeology of the Niger Delta

PHILIP M. PEEK and

KEITH NICKLIN

Background — *Philip M. Peek*

The Niger Delta has been inhabited for hundreds of years, but very little archaeological research has been carried out in the region to date. The first major site survey was conducted only about thirty years ago, and it has been supplemented by relatively few investigations since (Anozie 1988). Although one might not expect such a swampy region to yield much in the way of archaeological finds, even the limited surveys carried out thus far in various sites throughout the Delta have provided much intriguing information. Significant terra-cotta artifacts have also been recovered from several shrine renovation sites in Isoko country (Peek 1980). These brief studies have established that the earliest habitation in the Niger Delta dates back to at least the eighth century C.E. at Ke in the Eastern Delta, while other sites scattered throughout the Delta offer evidence of tenth to twelfth century dates with even earlier living sites on the mainland bordering the northeastern Delta.[1] The variety of artifacts recovered from even the earliest habitation sites offers ample evidence of the broad range of economic and ritual activities pursued by Delta peoples. It should be noted here that in addition to the evidence derived from archaeological investigation, the study of historical linguistics is valuable in aiding us to trace the migration and interaction of Delta peoples (see the appendix to this volume).

Surely among the most intriguing of Nigeria's many artistic traditions is the loosely grouped body of objects commonly known as the "Lower Niger Bronzes," a designation originated by William Fagg (fig. 1.3). The pieces placed in this category range from the delicate "hunter" (Fagg 1960, no.15) to far less refined objects encountered in small shrines throughout Southern Nigeria and the Niger Delta. This category of artifacts provides fertile ground for speculation about past life in the Delta (figs. 1.2, 1.4). It must be noted, however, that these pieces form a grouping primarily because they do not fit within more defined traditions. The thinking is that if bronze objects are not from the court of the Benin Kingdom (figs. 1.5, 1.6) or do not belong among those found at Igbo-Ukwu or are not part of the Yoruba Ogboni bronze traditions, then they must be "Lower Niger Bronzes." The variety of forms, styles, alloys, and contexts incorporated within this category should, however, be ample warning that they cannot possibly be products of a single tradition.

Although it seems to have been assumed heretofore that there could not be any workshops—other than those remarked above—producing sophisticated bronze works, experience now assures us that the technical skills and accomplishments of Nigerian peoples should not be underestimated. It is far more likely that, as I found among the Isoko, at least a basic knowledge of bronze casting existed in many locations throughout Southern Nigeria. It has also been presumed that bronze casters in Benin working "on the side"

1.1   Face mask. Lower Niger Bronze Industry. Copper alloy. H: 21.9 cm. National Museum of African Art, Smithsonian Institution; Museum Purchase, 86-12.5. Photograph by Franko Khoury. This small maskette resembles certain Kalabari Ijo wooden masquerade headdresses. One Nembe Ijo masquerade actually uses bronze headpieces, but faces similar to this one more often serve as spirit emblems in water spirit shrines. The motif on the forehead suggests a bird with its head and neck bent to the side. Miniature bronze faces, often worn around the neck or on bags, are found throughout Southern Nigeria.

1.2   Hippopotamus. Before 1850. Middle Benue
River, possibly Abakwariga people. Copper alloy.
L: 20.9 cm. The Menil Collection, Houston, no.
Y 801. Photograph by Hickey-Robertson, Houston.
Like other powerful aquatic and amphibious animals,
the hippopotamus is a popular character in Delta
masquerades. Miniaturized forms such as this frequently
decorate shrines and were imported into the Delta.

1.3   Vessel with chameleons. Circa 1668–1773
(TL dating). Lower Niger Bronze Industry. Copper
alloy. H: 22.2 cm. National Museum of African Art,
Smithsonian Institution; Museum Purchase, 85-16-1.
Photograph by Franko Khoury. This unique vessel
arrived in England shortly after the Benin Punitive
Expedition of 1897, but it does not conform to
Bini style. Because of their ability to change color,
chameleons often signify transformation. They are
also used for ritual communication between the
human and the spirit world.

1.4   Quadruped. Nineteenth century? Lower Niger
Bronze Industry. Copper alloy. H: 22.9 cm. Brooklyn
Museum of Art; Gift of Mr. and Mrs. John A. Friede
76.20.6. Delightful creatures such as this one, which
may be modeled after a leopard or a hippopotamus,
have carefully executed decorative patterns that offset
the blunted face and limbs. A number of these
unidentifiable forms have been reported throughout
the Delta, usually in the shrines of local deities.

1.2

1.3

1.4

1.5 Plaque with crocodile head. Benin. Sixteenth or seventeenth century. Brass. H: 40.7 cm. Collection of Jay T. and Deborah Last. Plaques depicting aquatic creatures, such as this one, decorated the pillars of the oba's *palace in Benin City and testify to the close associations of Benin with local rivers and the Delta.*

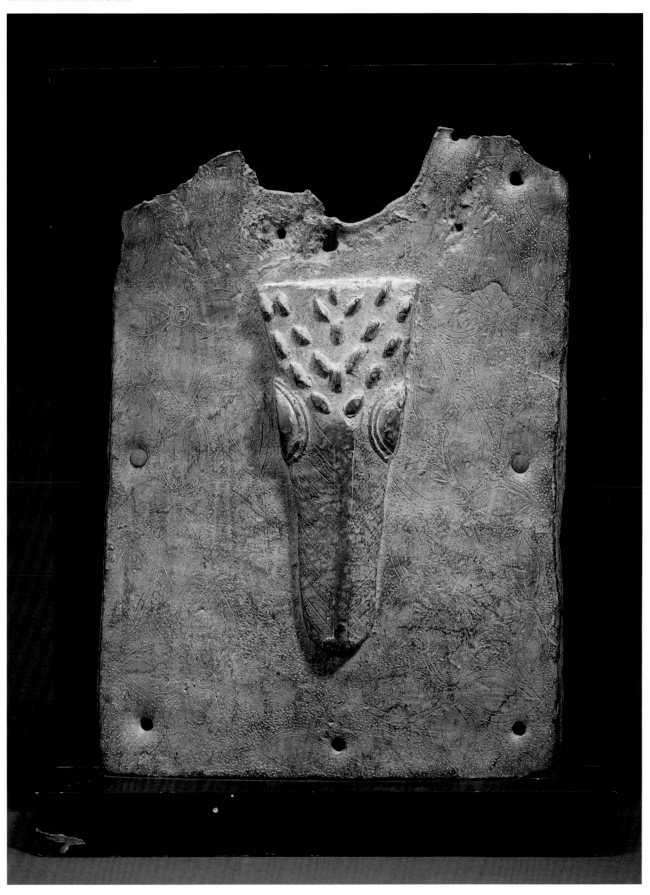

or perhaps even escaping the control of the *oba* of Benin altogether and moving elsewhere created the "Lower Niger Bronzes." We do know that there were "official" bronze casters working in Udo and that some of the larger of the "Lower Niger Bronzes" originated there. Too often, however, poorly cast pieces from Benin have failed to be accepted as such and have instead been considered the lesser efforts of incompetents working elsewhere, though we have no proof of this.

Use, function, and meaning are still problematic areas for us when considering this group of bronzes. For example, the shapes we are accustomed to calling "bells" (fig. 1.9) may not have been bells per se. Many lack clappers and may well have been used as gongs. Also, some that are clearly bell shaped (figs. 1.7, 1.8) have attachments along the side suggesting that they were worn. Of note, in 1971 I photographed a priest wearing a crudely carved animal hung with many ancient bronzes (fig. 1.10). The priest assured me that this had replaced a leather bag. This wearing of bronze objects intended to jangle as the priest walked along is a tradition that has been recorded among a number of Igbo groups (Nzimiro 1972) and in the Cross River area (Nicklin 1982). Many bronzes are found in and on shrines and were most likely struck like gongs during services.

1.6   Plaque with mudfish. Sixteenth or seventeenth century. Benin. Brass. W: 20 cm. Collection of Jay T. and Deborah Last. Depictions of mudfish in Benin court art were indirect references to royalty and the wealth of Olokun, god of the waters.

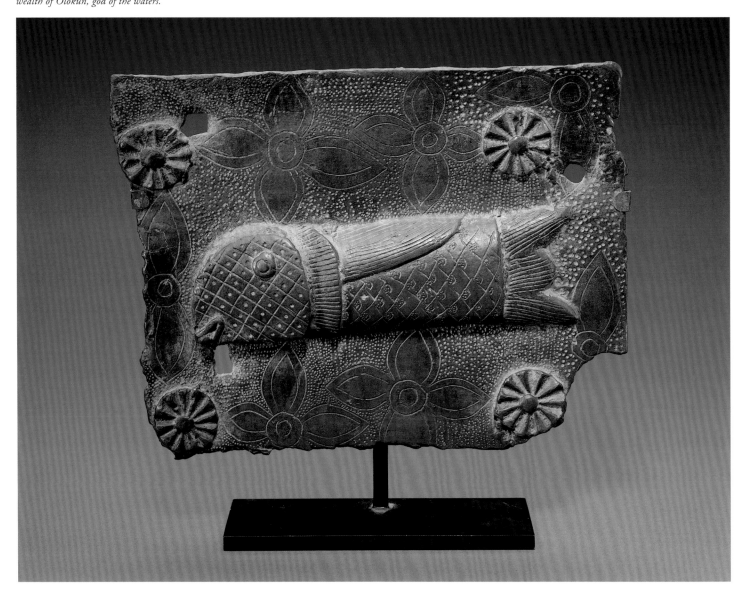

1.7 Bronzes belonging to a priest of Akawa. Photograph by Philip M. Peek, Uzere, 1966.

1.8 Two bronze "bells" found in Ole. Photograph by Philip M. Peek, 1971.

1.9 Forcados-style bell. Lower Niger Bronze Industry. Copper alloy. H: 15.1 cm. National Museum of African Art, Smithsonian Institution; Museum Purchase, 85-1-7. Photograph by Franko Khoury. This is one of the most common bell-shaped head forms. As an indication of the popularity of the form, some were apparently produced in molds in England for trade in the Niger Delta. These can be identified by a seam where the two halves have been attached (as opposed to the seamless cire perdue method used in Nigeria). Some of the iconographic elements remind one of the bronzes of the Yoruba Ogboni Society.

1.10 Isoko priest with bronze objects. Photograph by Philip M. Peek, Erohwa, 1971.

Nancy Neaher (1979b) conducted a full comparative study of bell types a number of years ago (figs. 1.11, l.12), later complemented by the work of Carol Lorenz (1982). Neaher argued for the prominence of Awka blacksmiths, who traveled throughout much of the territory where the bronzes have been found, as the creators of these objects (1976b). While the skills of Awka smiths are undeniable, the techniques of smithing and of metal casting are rather different. One might more profitably link terra-cotta traditions to bronze casting given that the special clays used for cores and to encase the wax models would be better known to terra-cotta workers than to blacksmiths. In fact, one might as likely speculate about links to the beautiful molded Olokun shrine pottery tradition given the assumed associations with Benin. But we need not go so far afield because many terra-cotta fragments have been found throughout the Delta. In 1975, E. J. Alagoa reported in detail on terra-cotta "masks" found at Ke in the Niger Delta. By means of samples obtained nearby these were dated to between the tenth and the seventeenth centuries (Alagoa 1975b).

Another basic category of Lower Niger Bronzes includes objects that are replicas or skeuomorphs (fig. 1.13). The Andoni leopard skull (see

1.11 Hippopotamus bell. Lower Niger Bronze Industry. Bronze. H: 12.7 cm. Collection of Toby and Barry Hecht. The prevalence of the hippopotamus in the Delta has led to its being known as the "river horse."

1.12 Elephant bell. Lower Niger Bronze Industry. Bronze. H: 10.2 cm. Collection of Toby and Barry Hecht. Despite the elephant's prominence as a symbol of leadership in many parts of Africa, the hippopotamus is represented far more frequently in the Niger Delta. Nevertheless, elephants remain a royal symbol in Benin City, and ivory horns are still used as status symbols throughout the Delta.

fig. 1.24, below) is obviously an example of this, but objects have been found throughout Isoko country as well that appear to be bronze copies of the most sacred shrine fixture, the *ovo* (figs. 1.14–1.16). There are similar examples of stylized Igbo *ofo* and Ijo *ovuo* in bronze as well. Replication in bronze of special ritual and prestige items seems to be an ancient tradition in Southern Nigeria.

Small bronze masks have been found in widely separated communities (see fig. 1.1). At first these were thought to be insignia linking the ruler who wore the object to the *oba* of Benin. While this is probably the case for the *ata* of Idah, it is less sure for the *eze nri* and seemingly baseless for the masks found in Isoko country. Periodically bronze and terra-cotta objects are found in fields and in ponds by Isoko farmers and fisherfolk. People will also report seeing such ancient works in bush areas, often in *aho* (bad bush) where "bad deaths" were cast in the past, an association that Nicklin encountered as well (see below). Sometimes such materials are taken to shrines found in all communities dedicated to Eri Anwan, the ancient spirits, because these wondrous objects are associated with both the ancients and the spirits. Other times, excavations for the foundation of a new house will reveal bronzes and

1.13 Leopard skull. Lower Niger Bronze Industry. Bronze. L: 17.8 cm. Collection of Toby and Barry Hecht. Numerous Delta shrines, especially in men's meeting houses, display real leopard skulls, the leopard being widely associated with leadership and warfare. Bronze versions with delicate decorative additions, such as seen on this example, were also displayed in shrines. Some bronze skulls found buried in the area east of the Delta appear to have served as emblems of chiefly rank, among them a tenth-century example found at Igbo-Ukwu.

1.14 Bronze ovo *lying with* ovo *sticks in an ancestral shrine. Photograph by Philip M. Peek, Okpe, 1971.*

1.15 Ovo or ofo. Isoko or Urhobo. Bronze. L: 23 cm. FMCH X91.416; Gift of Peter J. Kuhn. This enigmatic form (see also figs. 1.14. and 1.16), seemingly spoon-shaped, is actually a replica of the ovo *twigs (*Detarium senegalense Gmelin*), bundles of which are essential ritual items for all Isoko, Urhobo, and Western Igbo, as well as some Ijo groups. Called* ofo *among the Igbo and* ovuo *by many Ijo peoples, these ancestral representations frequently assume elaborate abstract forms. Some have zoomorphic or anthropomorphic features in addition to delicate geometric decoration.*

1.16 Ovo. Isoko or Urhobo. Bronze. L: 21 cm. Private Collection. This ovo *in the form of a stylized animal is decorated with floral motifs on its upper body.*

1.17 Bronze figure found in Ole. Photograph by Philip M. Peek, 1971.

1.18 Terra-cotta objects from Oteri village. Photograph by Philip M. Peek, 1971.

terra-cottas. I recorded the fruits of several such accidental finds in 1971 (figs. 1.17, 1.18). In a survey of bronzes found in several Ijo shrines, Robin Horton reports that origins are usually attributed to the "water people," thus reflecting the "wealth from the waters" theme found throughout the Delta (1965b).

There has been dispute over the years as to whether or not the objects under discussion are truly bronzes. Because the technical skill involved remains the same, I would rather discuss these works as bronzes than brasses. Until there is full metallurgical analysis, we really do not know (witness the revelation that many Ife "bronzes" are nearly pure copper), and frankly the valuing of bronze over brass should not hinder us. Another facet of the larger puzzle is that we know several types of "Lower Niger Bronzes" were cast in England, presumably Manchester. On some bell-heads, a telltale seam can be found that indicates a wooden mold, as opposed to the cire perdue method used in Nigeria.

At present we lack a proper metallurgical analysis of most of the bronzes that are available in museums and collections, as well as a full formal study of them. The following essay by Keith Nicklin and an earlier article (Nicklin and Fleming 1980) reveal how much can be learned by close analysis of a single group of bronzes (see also Curnow forthcoming). And, tragically, there has been no further field study of these extraordinary pieces. This leads us to raise a critical reminder. This puzzle of the Lower Niger Bronzes, as with so many in Nigerian history, has not been addressed due to the tragic internal problems that Nigeria as a whole has suffered. Archaeological and art historical research seldom finds favor with military dictatorships, and a people rightly concerned about matters of basic health and safety can hardly enjoy the fruits of academic study. But without such research, we only perpetuate our ignorance of the exceptional history of the Niger Delta. Hopefully, the changed situation in Nigeria will permit these and other important topics of study to be pursued.

The "House of Skulls" Revisited:
New Light on the Lower Niger Bronzes[2]—*Keith Nicklin*

In September of 1904 at the instigation of the chiefs of Bonny and Opobo, Captain A. A. Whitehouse, then acting commissioner of the Eastern Division of Southern Nigeria, burnt to the ground a so-called "veritable Golgotha… at Allabia, the principal town in the Andoni [Obolo] country" (Aldred 1949, 39).[3] Whitehouse reported that at least two thousand human skulls were counted in the shrine prior to its destruction. The contents of a nearby "fetish house," mainly artifacts of bronze, iron, ivory, and pottery, as well as a ship's bell from a Dutch slaver and a length of drain pipe of European manufacture, were forwarded to the British Museum. Whitehouse published an account of the "necessary measures" that were his duty to perform in order to put down the "baneful influence upon the surrounding villages" of Andoni human sacrifice and cannibalism (1905, 410).

The late nineteenth and early twentieth centuries saw the most aggressive phase of British imperial expansion, witnessing a series of punitive expeditions that in each case brought about the violent subjugation of a Southern Nigerian people. These included: Ediba, 1895; Benin and Oron, 1897; Ekuri, 1898; Aro Chukwu, 1902; Uzere's Eni oracle, 1903;

Akparabong and Obolo, 1904. We now know from N. C. Ejituwu's excellent book (1991) that in looting and torching the Andoni "House of Skulls," Whitehouse had in fact desecrated and destroyed the Oko-Yok-Obolo, or high altar of the tutelary deity of the Obolo monarchy. We also know from the same source that there is no evidence of cannibalism among the Obolo and that a powerful prohibition on an Obolo "first strike" on their enemies permitted only defensive warfare. The human skulls in the Oko-Yok-Obolo were those of enemies who were virtually certain to have taken Obolo heads should the opportunity have arisen.

Almost ninety years later, in the company of Dr. Ejituwu, I visited Agwut-Obolo (Allabia) to find that the reconstituted Oko-Yok-Obolo still dominates Obolo sociopolitical life and that annual tribute is still paid to the "national deity" (fig. 1.19). I now proceed with a description of the "Andoni hoard" held by the Ethnography Department of the British Museum, London, in the light of an extensive literature on the Lower Niger Bronzes and my own fieldwork in the Eastern Delta and elsewhere in southeast Nigeria.

1.19 The shrine, Oko-Yok-Obolo, or "House of Skulls," at Agwut Obolo (Allabia). Photograph by Keith Nicklin, 1992.

1.20 Seated male figure, possibly a representation of Yok-Obolo, the tutelary deity of the Obolo (Andoni) people. Bronze with piassava repair. H: 29 cm. Trustees of the British Museum, 1905.4-13.60. Removed from Agwut Obolo (Allabia) in 1904.

1. Seated Male Figure

This copper-alloy casting (fig. 1.20) represents a seated man bearing a horn in his left hand that extends, mouth uppermost, from the shoulder to the side of the abdomen. The protuberant umbilicus and circumcised penis are prominently depicted. The right arm of the figure is missing and a broken part of the head is held in place by a local repair consisting of piassava fiber. The figure appears in this condition in a photograph taken in Nigeria of the contents of the Andoni "fetish House," published by Whitehouse (1905, facing p. 412).

When considered in terms of the known corpus of eastern Nigerian bronzes, this piece in its overall style, especially with regard to the rendition of the nostrils and lips, most closely resembles the figure of a "hunter" said to have been collected at Benin in 1897 (Fagg 1960, no. 15). In both pieces the relative proportions of head, trunk, and lower limbs are similar. In fact, Fagg (1960, 16) maintains that the Andoni male figure is "surely related to the hunter." Accordingly, in his *Nigerian Tribal Images* exhibition held in Britain in 1960, Fagg identified elements of a so-called "hunter style" in this piece along with several others chosen to represent his then newly coined "Lower Niger Bronze Industry." According to Peek (1980, 62), the treatment of mouth, herniated umbilicus, and thick legs of an Isoko bronze seated figure (H: 15 cm) also bears stylistic similarity to that of the Andoni figure in question.

Fagg (1960, 16) maintains that the "ladder-like design" marking the spine of the "hunter's" antelope and bordering his eyes is "a fairly reliable diagnostic" of Lower Niger Bronze Industy style. A similar mode of relief decoration appears both on the pendant suspended from a beaded (?) necklace and on the convex side of the horn held by the Andoni figure. This instrument probably represents a side-blown ivory horn or a representation of this type of object cast in metal. A side-blown ivory horn with incised diagonal pattern (BM. 1905.4-3.65) and a sizeable portion of a bronze object of the same kind with relief decoration in the form of a lizard on the convex side (fig. 1.21) are included in the Andoni "hoard." The ladder relief decoration is repeated in the form of scarification marks on the cheeks and temples of the figure considered here, a feature of facial adornment found on some wooden masks and figures of the stylistically transitional northern Igbo and Benue Valley areas of eastern central Nigeria (see Nicklin 1995, 387).

The Andoni figure is seated on a cylindrical stool with a broad circular top and base. This would appear to be a representation of a box-stool comprising "two discs of wood…joined by nesting bark cylinders" of the type called *akpa* by Igala (Sieber 1965, 81, fig. 2). This in turn relates to the form of seat called *ekpokin* depicted on Benin plaques (Fagg and Fagg 1960, no. 155). A more elaborate version with a smaller round-topped cylinder for each foot, all built upon a flat wooden base, is employed by the Igala chief of Eteh as both throne and container for royal regalia (Sieber 1965, figs 2–4; 1980, 138–39). The wooden box-stool is thought to be the prototype for the seat and container of sacred objects shown in some Benin plaques (a cast-brass copy of which is illustrated in Von Luschan 1919, figs. 323–25A and 666) and the stone and terra-cotta stools of ancient Ife, wooden forerunners of which, called *apere*, are still in use in present-day Ife (Willett 1967, 82–84).

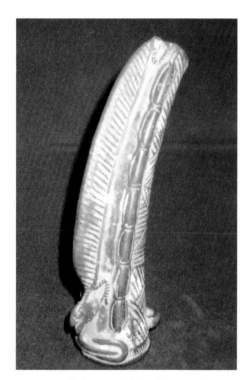

1.21 Part of a bronze side-blown horn with line patterns in relief and a stylized lizard, also in relief, along the convex side. Trustees of the British Museum, 1905.4-13.64. Photograph by Frank Willet. Removed from Agwut Obolo (Allabia) in 1904.

Ethnographic examples of cylindrical, lidded wooden stools covered with animal hide were recorded by Nicklin in the 1970s. These were used as containers of chiefly regalia among the Yakur of the Obubra area and the Etung of Ikom, both in the Cross River region. A bronze figure seated on a box-stool has been attributed to the Mbembe of the Obubra area (Loudmer and Poulain 1975, no. 86). Comparable examples are also known from the Niger Delta region itself. For example, Horton (1965b, 64) describes a brass object "shaped like a miniature stool in which top and base are joined by a cylinder" among a group of *pere* title insignia at the northwestern Delta settlement of Akugbene, east of Forcados. He notes that this is a metal version of a "personal cult-object common in the area but generally made of wood"; both are called *bra kon*. Of note, also included in the Andoni hoard (BM.1905.4-13.69) is a "[c]ylindrical stool of wood and bark, round which is fastened by a rope of plaited leaf, a number of goat skulls" (BM Register: 1905.4-13.69). According to Whitehouse's inventory (BM Eth. Doc. 209), the stool is stained red with camwood and was found in "the women's Juju House."

The Andoni figure illustrated here is depicted wearing a conical cap that in general form may be compared to the headgear of the "hunter" and also to that of a kneeling bronze female figure holding a bowl, which has been attributed to the same workshop, if not the same hand, as the "hunter" (see Nicklin 1989, 41). The site of this workshop is not known. The male figure also wears three bracelets, or a triple bracelet, on the left forearm and a pair of anklets, probably representing metal or ivory ceremonial regalia. A number of penannular rings, some of which could have been worn, exist in the Andoni hoard.

Despite the fact that the piece in question is described in the Whitehouse inventory as "One Copper Nude Figure of an Ijo Native" (BM Eth. Doc. 209), it is actually depicted with a multistranded waistband bearing a series of sausage-shaped attachments at the sides and rear. Both the neck pendant and the waistband attachments appear to be charms. One significant example of the importance of a charm worn on the body is provided by the "special necklace" presented to King Jaja by the *obara*-Yok, the high priest of Obolo, as a seal of the Obolo-Opobo Treaty of 1869. This charm was known as the *nfi*, or "dust," of Yok-Obolo (Ejituwu 1991, 137; Alagoa and Fombo 1972, 31). These ornaments as well as the elaborate headgear and regalia (box-stool, decorated horn) are all indicative of high ritual or secular Oboto office. Citing a local informant, Ejituwu (1991, 168) identifies our seated bronze figure as the image of none other than Yok-Obolo, the "national deity" of the Andoni, who call themselves Obolo.

Yok-Obolo means "The mask of Obolo." As apical ancestor Yok-Obolo represented the soul of the people. His symbol was the monitor lizard, *uta*, and his messenger the vulture, *edene*; to harm either of these creatures was an abomination. The Obolo ruler and war leader was the *okan*-Obolo; his regalia included an ivory horn, *odu*, and a number of giant manillas, *ekwe*. He was installed in office by the high priest, *obara*-Yok, acting in concert with *oru*, the council of kingmakers, and its executive arm, *ofiokpo* (Ejituwu 1991, 56–57).

2. Carnivore Skull

The British Museum Register lists a "cast bronze model of a leopard's skull, ornamented with spirals and lines in relief" (fig. 1.22). The piece in question is damaged to the extent that the canine teeth and posterior part of the skull are missing. This breakage reveals the hard-clay core invested by a skin of metal, a technological feature typical of a small copper-alloy object cast by the cire perdue method. Following the sagittal crest of the bronze skull is a notched line in relief, possibly a skeuomorph of cordage, bordering a series of spiral motifs following the same axis. Spiral motifs also adorn the jaw, zygomatic arch, and posterior portion of both sides of the skull, and a diagonal row of inverted chevrons appears on the anterior part of the orbits. The piece has been TL dated to 1665 C.E. +/- 40 (Nicklin and Fleming 1980, 105).

Although this object is listed by Whitehouse (BM Eth. Doc. 209) as a "Copper Tortoise," it has justifiably been compared by Cyril Aldred (1949, 38–39) to a complete, somewhat stylized and slightly elongated bronze representation of the cranium of a leopard (fig. 1.23) held by the Royal Museum of Scotland, Edinburgh. This was acquired by a former administrator of Southern Nigeria, Major W. Birrell Gray, and presented to the museum by his widow, without any indication of its actual origin.

On the basis of the obvious resemblance between the two bronze carnivore skulls, Aldred ascribed the Edinburgh piece to the Andoni. Had the latter been looted in 1904, however, it would have appeared in the Whitehouse inventory referred to above, which it does not. Nonetheless,

1.22 Stylized carnivore skull. Bronze. L: 17 cm. Trustees of the British Museum, 1905.4-13.61. Removed from Agwut Obolo (Allabia) in 1904.

1.23 Stylized bronze carnivore skull from Southern Nigeria. Bronze. L: 19 cm. © The Trustees of the National Museums of Scotland, reg. no. A.1946.967, neg. no. 7467. Presented to the Royal Museum of Scotland, Edinburgh, in 1946.

it is likely to have been acquired in the course of one of the other punitive expeditions conducted by the British in southeastern Nigeria in the late nineteenth and early twentieth centuries, for example, that led against Udung Uko, near Oron, by Whitehouse and Hill in 1897 (Uya 1984, 88–89).

The two bronze skulls described above are similar to one found in the shrine of the guardian spirit Kaloruwei at the coastal Nembe town of Okpoma, east of Brass in the Central Niger Delta (Horton 1965b, 80, pl.3). This piece (L: 19 cm) is also richly decorated with spiral motifs and was said by one of Horton's informants to be very much like an item in a shrine called Ogoni at the nearby Nembe village of Odioma. This bronze was said to have been used as a masquerade headdress, along with others made of the same metal (Horton 1965b, 82). A further carnivore skull (L: 19 cm) with spiral decoration, lacks provenance and is held by the Nigerian Museum, Lagos; it is illustrated by Neaher (1976a, fig. 34).

Brass replicas of a leopard and of a crocodile, together with five ivory and wooden carvings of dog, leopard, and human skulls, constitute the *sacra* of the Otusi shrine at Aro Chukwu in eastern Igboland (Ekejiuba 1967, 12). According to F. I. Ekejiuba, this shrine is dedicated to the head of the Aro heroes and his ancestors, and the leopard and crocodile are royal totems (1967, 13). Dogs are associated with the group of Aro who combined hunting with agriculture and in the mythical past brought the people to their present site in Aro Chukwu.

The best-known eastern Nigerian bronze carnivore skull is a realistic representation of a leopard (L: 24.2 cm) mounted on a copper rod, from the royal burial chamber at Igbo-Ukwu, near Awka in Igboland. This archaeological site yielded radiocarbon dates of around the ninth century C.E. (Shaw 1970). The cranium and mandible of the Igbo-Ukwu leopard skull are cast in a single piece. While the Igbo-Ukwu and Andoni bronze carnivore skulls have been unambiguously identified as leopards, the same is not true of that from Okpoma, which, according to Horton (1965b, 80) has possible dog and hyena affinities. Moreover, the Okpoma bronze skull was observed placed alongside two natural skulls of a "small forest cat," which also suggested to Horton possible prototypes for the caster. Of relevance in this respect is an item (BM 1905.4-13.50) in the Andoni hoard, comprised of a leopard and a goat skull lashed with cane to a wooden staff, which also has two manillas attached.

1.24 Stylized carnivore skull, with one canine tooth missing. Bronze. L: 16.50 cm. Trustees of the British Museum, 1905.4-13.62. Photograph by Frank Willett. Removed from Agwut Obolo (Allabia) in 1904.

3. Stylized Carnivore Skull

Also in the Andoni hoard is a "more conventionalised" bronze leopard skull (fig. 1.24; BM Register 1905), described by Whitehouse as a "Copper Alligator" (BM Eth. Doc. 209). The clay core of this object has been given a TL date of 1680 C.E. +/- 40 (Nicklin and Fleming 1980, 105). This piece is virtually identical to a bronze carnivore skull (L: 17 cm) from Uya Oron, on the west bank of the Cross River estuary (Nicklin and Fleming 1980, 104–5). The object in question, called *ukiang* by the local people, was unearthed in 1974, together with three manillas, a bronze torque, four iron spear blades, and three iron sword blades. According to Chief Okon Uwe Akan, then the *ofong afaha ibighi* at Uya Oron, these are the grave goods of Ntuk Idim Uma, founder of Urue Ntuk Idim ward of Uya Oron.

On the upper and lower surfaces of both castings, following the long axis, is a series of parallel notched lines, possibly a skeuomorphic representation of cordage. Horizontal lines of skeuomorphic cordage decoration also occur on the double-looped arches on either side of the castings. The main body of either side of the casting, the canine teeth, and the twin knobs at the base of the posterior of the skulls, are decorated with fine parallel lines, suggestive of skeuomorphic wrapping with wire. The prominent canine teeth of the castings are decorated by the reversed spiral motif.

A bronze (L: 20 cm) of similar stylized carnivore type, but differing in decorative detail, is given a Lower Niger/Cross River provenance in a volume of studies of African metalwork (Brincard 1982, 122, fig. H 13).

4. Decorated Bell

This bell (fig. 1.25) is registered as "cast bronze with lattice and rope patterns in relief." It is tubular in form, slightly everted at top and mouth, with an integral suspension loop at the top; it is decorated with skeuomorphic cordage. Three small loops, one above the other at one side, are similarly decorated. This piece falls into the category of "Lower Niger Bronze Bells" described by Carol Lorenz (1982, 52–53; 120, fig. H 8). According to Lorenz, the side lugs may have been for the attachment of crotals or to provide alternative means of suspension. She also maintains that the shape of this type of bell is related to segments of Benin *uxuhre* staves or elements of the Igbo and southern Edo *ofo* trees, bronze copies of which occur in some Southern Nigerian ancestral shrines.

A similar cylindrical bell (H: 18 cm), with two side loops is reported from Isoko by Peek (1980, 64, pl. 11; also see fig. 1.8, above), who compares its "delicate almost 'filigreed'" decoration with an Igbo-Ukwu bell (Shaw 1970, 2: pl. 86) and a piece from Sagbama in the Northern Delta (Horton 1965b, 85, pl.9). Peek also describes three similar bells, less finely decorated from Isoko (1980, 62, fig. 6, 64, fig. 12). The bells and other bronze objects found in shrines of major Isoko clan deities represent "points of accumulation for wondrous and beautiful objects" (1980, 66). Peek advances a convincing case for the former existence of indigenous Isoko casters, while also acknowledging that itinerant Igbo smiths did reach Isokoland in the past and that some "bell-shaped forms" originated from Benin City.

1.25 Bell with lattice and cordage patterns in relief and loops at top, side, and base. Bronze. H: 20.3 cm. Trustees of the British Museum, 1905.4-13.63. Removed from Agwut Obolo (Allabia) in 1904.

5. Manillas

The fact that there are over fifty items in the Andoni hoard that, broadly speaking, may be classed as manillas reflects their prominence in Obolo culture (figs. 1.26a,b). According to Ejituwu (1991, 67) copper-alloy manillas, known as *ekwe*, introduced by Portuguese traders, were modeled on Obolo prototypes: the spiral manilla (*ajara*) was modeled on the raffia bracelet worn by old women, while other forms replaced shell neck ornaments. The small penannular manilla came to be the standard unit of exchange, with others equivalent, respectively, to four, twenty, and one hundred times this amount. As elsewhere in the Niger Delta, for example in Ogoniland (Kpone-Tonwe 1997), manillas served not only as currency and means of accumulating wealth but also as status symbols.

Ejituwu (1991, 62) draws attention to the presence of manillas in Obolo shrines where they serve to "concentrate" requisite "spiritual forces." Nicklin's fieldwork conducted in 1992 confirms that the Obolo still preserve manillas in shrines of the ancestors, Isi Ebikan, and that they are worn or carried in funerary processions: spiral manillas are worn around the wrist or ankle and large penannular ones around the neck. A large "twisted" manilla looted by Whitehouse (1905, 414–15) is said to have had offerings made to it by women at the second, sixth, and ninth months of pregnancy. It is also described as the "ram's horn" manilla and was believed to excite the passions of a woman laying her hands on it and to impart strength to the mother-to-be.

It was also customary for large "King" and "Queen" manillas (Grey 1957, 58) to be placed in the graves of prominent elders. This is interesting in view of the fact that the bodies of Obolo dead had to be brought before

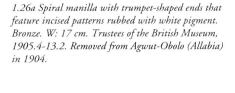

1.26a Spiral manilla with trumpet-shaped ends that feature incised patterns rubbed with white pigment. Bronze. W: 17 cm. Trustees of the British Museum, 1905.4-13.2. Removed from Agwut-Obolo (Allabia) in 1904.

the shrine of Yok-Obolo prior to receiving appropriate burial goods for interment by members of an immigrant Ibibio group at their settlement at Anyamboko (Ejituwu 1991, 58). It was various bronze objects, including manillas, poking through the soil in these waterlogged cemeteries, that gave rise to the Southern Ibibio saying, "If you wish to get money quickly, go to the burial ground of the Andoni" (Jeffreys 1930).

Ejituwu (1991, 6) maintains that since ancient times the Obolo have operated a taxation system bringing wealth to the holders of high office at the spiritual home, the site of the Yok-Obolo shrine, formerly at Egwede and later at Agwut Obolo, the "Sanctuary of the Obolo." It is here also that at the annual festival held in honor of the national deity, the Ekwe Yok-Obolo, or sacred manillas, are paraded and displayed (fig. 1.27). Ejituwu (1991, 63) also points out that in the nineteenth century, the Obolo were the principal suppliers of manillas and "other brass works" to the whole Niger Delta. This situation owed much to the early establishment of trade with the Portuguese at the seaboard Obolo settlements of Asarama and Ilotombi, before the expansion of neighboring city-states, especially Opobo.

The large spiral manilla illustrated here and removed from "The House of Skulls" by Whitehouse (see figs. 1.26a,b) has been described by Nigel Barley (1995, 399) as being of a genuine bronze—rather than brass—of remarkably high copper content. This piece, like a smaller one in the same group (BM 1905.4-l3.3), is treated with lines of punched decoration, inlaid with kaolin.

*1.27 Manillas and torques (*ekwe*) to be displayed at the Ntin festival held in September at Agwut Obolo in honor of Yok-Obolo, the Obolo tutelary deity. The sword blade (spearhead?) is called* ogeh ifop. *Photograph by Keith Nicklin, 1992.*

1.26b Another view of the manilla shown in figure 1.26a. Trustees of the British Museum, 1905.4-13.2.

6. Swords

Both of these bronze swords (fig. 1.28), described by Barley (1995, 339) as "almost Art Nouveau" in style, are double-edged with grips of coiled copper wire. The blades have a central rib along their length, broaden out toward rounded tips, and are blunt, indicating a ceremonial rather than a utilitarian function. Horton (1965b, 88) maintains that a "beaten twisted and repoussé" sword at the Kalabari village of Teinma, slightly east of Degema, "resembles a similar instrument in the Andoni hoard," despite the fact that the Kalabari example is pointed. The two Andoni swords are similar in form to a sword from the Benin Punitive Expedition of 1897, which has a twisted copper-alloy ring pommel and is described by Augustus Pitt-Rivers (1900 [1976], 74, pl. 37, fig. 284–85) as "unusual" for Benin.

The blade of the larger Andoni sword has lines of geometric decoration that appear to have been cold-worked. A similar mode of indented decoration is present on the bronze head of an Andoni spear (BM 1905.4-13.56), several similar spearheads from the Oron area held by the National Museum Oron (Nicklin 1999, 61), and sword blades of various shapes from Benin (Pitt-Rivers 1900, pl. 28, fig. 198–99, pl. 48, fig. 376–77). A pointed sword blade or spearhead, called *ogeh ifop*, was seen by Nicklin in 1992 among the Ekwe Yok-Obolo at Agwut Obolo (see fig. 1.27). In addition, a long spearhead of copper "of fine workmanship and great age" was reported by P. Amaury Talbot (1923, 309) at the Oron town of Inua Abassi, situated at the mouth of Widenham Creek. According to Whitehouse (1905, 415) the swords and spears in the "House of Skulls" were "emblems of war and invoked for success before setting out on an expedition."

1.28 Two double-edged swords with grips of coiled copper wire and chased decoration, with transverse bars of white pigment. Bronze. L (of longer sword): 68.7 cm. Trustees of the British Museum, 1905.4-13.58-59. Removed from Agwut Obolo (Allabla) in 1904.

Discussion

Despite the singular appearance of the face on the seated male figure (see fig. 1.20)— which suggests an affinity with wood, especially mask, sculpture—in overall stylistic configuration it is closest to the famous bronze "hunter," epitome of the Lower Niger Bronze Industry (Fagg 1960, 16). As pointed out above, it also bears some resemblance to an lsoko bronze seated figure (Peek 1980, 62; see fig. 1.17, above). Probably from the same, unknown, workshop as the hunter are two other superlative pieces: a bowl supported on a pedestal comprising "figures of monkeys squatting, with arms twined through legs, on mudfish" (Fagg 1963b, pl.63a), and a kneeling female figure holding a bowl (Nicklin 1989, 40–4l). Although the monkey bowl and the kneeling female figure were found in Benin and given a sixteenth-century date, Fagg himself asserts that the Lower Niger Bronzes, "formerly attributed to Benin… have a grotesque and imaginative character inconsistent with a Benin City origin (1960, 16)."

Denis Williams (1974, 255) suggests an Ijebu origin for at least some elements of the Lower Niger Bronze idiom, pointing out that a "multitude of shared iconographic motifs" supports such a connection. Certainly, the ladder-like design motif, one of the most diagnostic traits of the Lower Niger Bronze Industry (according to Fagg) and prominent in respect of the Obolo seated male, is commonly found on Ijebu paired *edan* staffs and bracelets of the powerful Yoruba Ogboni institution. The same motif also adorns Forcados as well as Isoko "bell-heads" (see fig. 1.9, above), a genre known as *omo* in Yorubaland, where, especially in the Ijebu area, such objects are the exclusive property of prominent chiefs (Drewal 1995, 414). Perhaps the best-known example of an Ijebu bell-head is the Avbiama bell, collected at Benin, in the National Museum Lagos (Williams 1974, 257–58, fig. 200). All this evidence would seem to point toward the former existence of an important export trade in bronze castings from Ijebu in a number of directions, not least across the Delta from west to east. Such a conclusion is supported by the existence of a close style relationship in women's weaving between the southwestern Yoruba town of Ijebu-Ode and the southern lgbo village of Akwete on account of predominantly west to east cloth trade in previous centuries (Aronson 1980b).

Prominent among the Andoni hoard are two bronze representations of carnivore skulls, one more naturalistic than the other, Horton (1965b, 80) likens one of them (see fig. 1.22) to a bronze carnivore skull at Okpoma and describes a certain "stark realism," if the relief work is ignored. However, while the stylistic affinities of the more naturalistic of the two Andoni bronze carnivore skulls point west, those of the more stylized piece (see fig. 1.24) point in the opposite direction. The latter piece is so similar to the bronze *ukiang* from Oron as to suggest the work of a common hand. Reference should here be made to the present-day cordiality between the Oron and the Obolo, emanating from a widespread belief that the Obololand of today was once shared with the forefathers of the Oron people, after their common migration from "Rombi" or "Ramby" in the Rio del Rey area of what is now Cameroon (Nicklin 1999).

The close similarity of the two highly stylized bronze carnivore skulls could be accounted for either by trade between the respective areas or the activities of itinerant smiths who are known to have operated throughout eastern Nigeria until the early years of the twentieth century. The candidates posited by Neaher (1979a) for such an extensive itinerant smithing role are Igbo smiths from Awka, Abiriba, and Nkwere. However, it is also known that the Aro people were highly successful slave traders and purveyors of religious artifacts in metal to the peoples of the same region, dominating a complex system of overland routes focused upon their famous oracle, the Ibiniukpabi, or "Long Juju," situated in the heart of their homeland at Aro Chukwu (Northrup 1978, 114–44). Aro influence was curtailed when a British column blew up their oracle in 1902.

Ejituwu (1991, 62–63) admits that since the Obolo have no such traditions, the "Andoni Bronzes" may have been imported from "some neighbouring area with a well-developed brass-casting tradition." He suggests that they might have been made by the Ohafia people of the Bende Igbo area, representatives of whom are said to have once resided with the Obolo. Ohafia oral history suggests that this occurred in the fifteenth century and that when they departed they retained the Obolo mode of tattooing the body (Ejitwu 1991, 109).

Interestingly, Ejituwu (1991, 63) remains open as to the origin of the Obolo bronzes, mindful of Peek's evidence for the Isoko, another Delta people, conducting their own copper-alloy casting of religious artifacts. Although both Ibibioland and the Cross River forest region to the north and west of the Palm Belt were subject to the activities of itinerant Igbo smiths and the Aro traders, there were also indigenous blacksmiths and brass casters among the Yakur of the Middle Cross River and the Enyong Ibibio of the Lower Cross River respectively (Nicklin and Fleming 1980; Fleming and Nicklin 1982). It is by no means inconceivable that at least part of the Obolo corpus originated at either of these sites, especially given the central location of Oron in the Cross River estuary, in relation to Obolo and Enyong. Further, a distinctive mode of decoration suggestive of wrapping in copper wire is present in respect of the stylized carnivore skulls of Obolo and Oron on the one hand and two bronzes that are attributed to the Middle Cross River on the other. Of the latter, one is a seated male figure from the Mbembe people and the other a representation of a human head from Akouaya (Loudmer and Poulain 1975, nos. 86, 88). Yakur, Mbembe, and Akouaya (Akwaya) are situated close together in the Obubra area.

The heterogeneity of the Lower Niger Bronze Industries material— exemplified no better than among the Obolo corpus—would seem to be the outcome of all of the factors discussed here, including the importation of bronzes into the Delta region from sites such as Ijebu-Ode outside the Delta proper and output by both local and itinerant smiths, as well as by the Aro, who traded metal goods made by their own smiths as well as those manufactured by others. This considerable passage of goods and personnel carried metal casting concepts across the far reaches of the Niger Delta and its contiguous areas. Northward this traffic penetrated the Benue Valley, and so it is not surprising to find decorative spiral motifs on an Imborivungu Tiv pipe resembling those on a carnivore skull representation from the Niger Delta or Cross River.

The Obolo-Opobo Treaty of 1869, which established King Jaja's role as an Obolo suppliant, provides a rather recent example of a political relationship between two different groups being ratified by the exchange of ritual property.

The occurrence of Benin bronze regalia in various parts of eastern Nigeria, such as the pendant mask of the *ata* of Igala, no doubt reflects the efforts of that kingdom to extend the reach of its hegemony. However, the close resemblance of a round-ended sword found in Benin to a pair of swords from Obolo could be explained by importation from Obolo or elsewhere, just as well as by Obolo marking its vassalage to Benin by placing sacred goods from Benin at the altar of the Obolo national deity.

Despite the difficulty of being able definitely to ascribe a site of production to individual Lower Niger pieces, there is considerable appreciation among some Africanists of the high aesthetic value of many of the bronzes. While Williams (1974, 257) wrote of work of "extreme individuality and masterly technical achievement… from Andoni to Forcados," Fagg (1963b) went as far as to say that the bronzes implicated in "The Lower Niger Bronze Industry mystery" represent "the very pinnacle of Nigerian artistic achievement" and "if the source… of the antelope-hunter can be identified, prove more important than Ife itself."

Interleaf A
Exploration, Trade, and Colonization

Martha G. Anderson

Beginning in the late fifteenth century, Duarte Pacheco Pereira and other early European visitors to the Niger Delta published fascinating accounts of their travels. Delta inhabitants living along the coast, however, kept foreigners from venturing far upstream in an effort to retain control of lucrative trade routes. As a consequence, early European travelers to the Delta failed to realize that they had entered branches of the fabled Niger River. More than thirty men would ultimately die trying to solve the "riddle of the Niger." Finally, and somewhat accidentally, in 1831 John and Richard Lander succeeded in tracing its lower course from the interior, when King Boy Amain of Brass—an alleged scoundrel and certain opportunist—escorted them to the coast in hopes of collecting ransom from an English vessel moored in the Brass River (Gramont 1975; see chapter 2 of this volume).

Soon after, Captain (later Admiral) William Allen recorded the Delta's magnificent scenery in words and images (fig. A.1) As commander of the HMS *Wilberforce* and expeditionary surveyor on Laird and Oldfield's expedition of 1832, he undertook his drawings "to delineate the features of the country, and the manners of the people." By combining the tradition of "pictorial views" with that of exploratory cartography and experimenting with the idea of multiple scenes within a single "diorama," he set an important precedent for the expeditionary and ethnographic photographers who followed (Ryan 1997).

Early visitors often commented on the flourishing trade conducted along the Delta's waterways. Internal trade routes, established long before the Portuguese arrived at the coast, provided an important foundation for the Atlantic trade. The Delta lies at the eastern end of what was the notorious "Slave Coast" of West Africa, where the deplorable traffic in human lives began in the late fifteenth century and continued long after the British outlawed it in 1808 (Curtin 1967; 1970; Lovejoy 1981; Alagoa 1986; Manning 1986; 1990). In 1827, a British captain counted sixteen to twenty slaving ships at Bonny, the most important trading center in the Delta at the time (Dike 1956, 98). The center of the Delta proved even more difficult to police, and the slave trade persisted into the twentieth century in that region (fig. A.2).

In the nineteenth century, the British attempted to promote "legitimate trade" in palm oil as an alternative to trading in slaves. The region proved to be so well endowed with this product that traders began calling it the "Oil Rivers." The length of time required to collect palm oil encouraged European settlement, which ultimately promoted colonization. At the peak of the palm oil trade in the 1860s, Bonny had 350 resident Europeans, but mortality rates were staggering. Of the 278 Europeans living in New Calabar, 169 died during a single outbreak of yellow fever, an epidemic that claimed many African lives as well (Jones 1963). Yet many Delta residents speak wistfully of this era, for it brought prosperity to communities that had previously been shut out of the trade by coastal middlemen (figs. A.3, A.4).

Beginning with a naval blockade aimed at stamping out the slave trade, Britain began to interfere increasingly in the internal affairs of the region. In the mid-1880s, intent on protecting its financial interests from piracy and other threats, it established a protectorate, later known as the Oil Rivers Protectorate, which became the Niger Coast Protectorate in 1893 (fig. A.5). Following amalgamation with Lagos into the Colony and Protectorate of Southern Nigeria in 1906, it united with Northern Nigeria to become part of the Colony and Protectorate of Nigeria in 1914. During this period, the British advanced their agendas—undermining the authority of local deities and opening the area to legitimate trade—by mounting a series of punitive expeditions, plundering shrines, deporting unruly leaders, and persuading local leaders to sign treaties.

The colonial government adapted itself to the riverain environment of the Delta, and, following the pattern set by traders, established administrative headquarters in hulks moored near Delta communities (fig. A.6). The *George Shotton*

A.1 Illustration from William Allen's Picturesque Views on the River Niger Sketched during Lander's Last Visit in 1832–33 (1840). This scene, one of four "Views on the Nun Branch of the River Niger," may depict "Kiambli" (Ikianbiri or Ekiambiri) in Bumo clan, the same small Ijo village of nine dwellings—"square with gable ends"—that Allen would describe in the account of his second voyage up the Niger in 1840. On that journey, he remarked that in general "[t]he houses were well-built, of clay, and in good order. The inhabitants a fine athletic race" (Allen and Thomson 1848, 1: 180).

A.2 "Shipping slaves in West Africa twenty-five years ago." Gleaner Pictorial Album 1: 5, fig. 6. Photograph courtesy of the Church Mission Society, London. This illustration depicts slavers operating at Lagos in the mid-nineteenth century.

hulk stationed at Bonny served as "consulate, treasury, customs-house, hospital and prison" until the first permanent consulate was built there in 1904 (Chadwick 1938). Watercraft continued to be the most convenient mode of transportation for European, as well as local, residents for many decades, and they remain essential to those conducting trade or governing in many parts of the region today.

A.3   Mr. Powis, a trader,
photographed in his quarters,
New Calabar, 1897. Photograph
© Trustees of the British Museum.
Powis was killed in a diplomatic
expedition to Benin later the same
year. Note the decorative paddles
on the walls.

A.4   Two Europeans and a
number of African assistants
standing in a large corrugated-iron
store or warehouse. Photograph
reproduced by permission of the
Syndics of Cambridge University
Library. The location is tentatively
identified as Opobo based upon
the fact that the name is written
on one of the supporting girders of
the building.

A.5   Captain F. J. Bartwell with Chief Young Briggs (to his right) and other chiefs of Abonnema, 1897. Reproduced with the permission of Unilever PLC (from an original in the Unilever Archives), box 25, folder 2, no. 51. As Philip Allison (1988, 104) observed, "Young Captain Bartwell, The Vice-Consul, appears perfectly confident of his ability to deal with the venerable local Kalabari chiefs, who, in turn, are also no doubt confident of their ability to deal with Captain Bartwell."

A.6   Chief Dore's canoe and the government hulk, Sapele, 1896. Rhodes House Library, MS. Afr. R239 No. 2. Photograph © Bodleian Library, Oxford, U.K. In the early days, palm oil traders, like their slave-trading predecessors, lived aboard dismasted sailing vessels known as "hulks" and stored their oil in cask houses on shore to await shipping. This hulk has been demasted and fitted with a tin roof, much as the palm mat roof has been added to the canoe to shelter its occupants from the elements. Philip Allison (1988) identified Chief Dore, correctly spelled Dogho, as an Itsekiri chief who would rescue survivors of the Benin Massacre a year after this photo was taken. Dore was also the rival of Nanna of Itsekiri (see interleaf C).

A.7 *Masquerade headdress. Ijo.*
Wood and pigment. L: 86.5 cm.
FMCH X86.1099; Gift in memory
of Barbara Jean Jacoby. Photograph
by Denis Nervig. This unusual
water spirit headdress incorporates
two imported marks of status,
a European cannon and a bowler
hat. Well-dressed Delta gentlemen
wear bowler hats even today, and
many villages throughout the region
still display antique cannons.

A.8 *Thomas Ona (Odulate).*
Boat with figures. Wood and
pigment. L: 44.5 cm. FMCH
X95.46.2A–L; Estate of William
A. McCarty-Cooper. Photograph
by Denis Nervig. Ona produced
charming portraits of colonial
officials for a largely Western
clientele. He worked in a typically
Yoruba style but carved each
element separately, then combined
them into scenes like this one—
an imperious British district officer
being paddled about the creeks
in a canoe. Although Europeans
sometimes suspected they were being
caricatured, Ona claimed to be
more interested in portraying
emblems of rank and authority
(Willet 1971, 143, fig. 132;
Thompson 1976, ch. 17, 1–2).

A.9 *Ceremonial manilla. Bronze.*
H: 17.1 cm. Collection of Toby
and Barry Hecht. The manilla,
a type of metal currency introduced
to West Africa by the Portuguese in
the fifteenth century, continued to
circulate in southeastern Nigeria
until the British suppressed it in
1949. Smaller, plainer manillas
were bartered and larger, more
ornate examples continue to be
employed in shrines and ceremonies
(Baker 304–10).

A.10 *A variety of manillas.*
Manilla at upper right and center
three: FMCH X86.939, FMCH
X86.948, FMCH X86.938,
FMCH X86.941—all Gift of
Steve Nelson. Two large manillas
at left and cluster of three at lower
right: FMCH X65.9010, FMCH
X65.9017, FMCH X65.8264,
FMCH X65.8266, FMCH
X65.8265—all Gift of the
Wellcome Trust.

A.7

A.8

A.9

A.10

Chapter 2   From Middlemen to Missionaries

E. J. ALAGOA

Introduction

This essay will examine external influences on the cultures of the Niger Delta, focusing on Nembe (fig. 2.1), one of the Ijo city-states of the Eastern Delta, which also include Elem Kalabari, Bonny, Opobo, and Okrika. The title "From Middlemen to Missionaries," however, reflects a change in roles that also occurred in the Itsekiri kingdom of Ode-Itsekiri, or Warri, in the Western Niger Delta and the Efik state of Old Calabar, or Calabar, on the Cross River estuary to the east of the Niger Delta.

Prior to the arrival of western European explorers and traders on the Guinea Coast in the late fifteenth century, each of the Niger Delta city-states had developed political, social, and economic systems capable of sustaining trading activity across the length and breadth of the Delta, as well as into the hinterlands (Alagoa 1970; 1971). Further, each had established its own trading areas. The Itsekiri of the Western Delta, for example, traded in the Edo hinterland and interacted mainly with the Urhobo communities; while the Ijo states of Nembe, Elem Kalabari, Bonny, Opobo, and Okrika operated among the Igbo and related communities, as well as among the Ogbia, Abua, Ogoni, and Ibibio; and the Efik of the port city of Calabar on the Cross River influenced the entire valley of that waterway, ranging over areas outside the Niger Delta.

As the major centers of population and power on the coast, the city-states of the Delta ultimately became the focal points for the transatlantic slave trade and for the exchange of products such as palm oil, which was traded from the late eighteenth through the nineteenth century (Dike 1956). They were natural bases from which explorers, traders, missionaries, and colonizers operated. Assuming the role of intermediaries, the coastal city-states received trade goods from across the Atlantic and exchanged them for local produce from the hinterlands, which they in turn supplied to European visitors. This transfer of material goods from the West for the products of Africa (slaves, ivory, palm oil, etc.) eventually extended to the transfer of immaterial goods. From the end of the nineteenth century through the beginning of the twentieth century—paralleling the British colonial occupation—Niger Delta middlemen were the first to receive Christian missionaries and would assume the role of purveyors of Christian doctrines and Western education to neighboring communities.

The Slave Trade

The first Europeans to visit the Niger Delta in the late fifteenth century, the Portuguese, were basically traders following on the heels of those who had undertaken the great voyages of discovery (Ryder 1959). In West Africa, they named sections of the coast according to the trade goods they found to be most abundant there, thus the "Ivory Coast," the "Gold Coast," and the "Slave Coast," which included the Niger Delta. In the Western Delta, the Portuguese concentrated on the Itsekiri kingdom of Warri. They

2.1   Royal ancestor figure. Nembe Ijo. Wood. H: 83.8 cm. University of Pennsylvania Museum of Archaeology and Anthropology, AF 5122. King Ockiya of Brass, a wealthy nineteenth-century Nembe Ijo ruler, commissioned a number of figures to represent his family and his ancestors (see fig. 2.12). Although he may have borrowed the idea of royal portraiture from Benin, the figureheads of European ships seem a more likely inspiration given the naturalism of these carvings. This female figure, who at some point lost her arms, may once have been "dressed" like those depicted in figure 2.12.

considered it to be a principality affiliated with Benin, which they had reached in the 1480s. In the Eastern Delta, they designated the combined estuaries of the New Calabar and Bonny Rivers the Rio Real (Royal River), and this area became the center of their activities with the city-states of Bonny and Elem Kalabari. They did not make immediate contact with the city-state of Nembe, situated about twenty miles up the Brass River (which the Portuguese called the Rio Bento). It was not long, however, before the rulers of Nembe were doing business with the visiting traders at the estuaries of the Brass and the neighboring Nun River in the territory of the Akassa people, another coastal Ijo group. From the sixteenth through the nineteenth century, the Portuguese, Dutch, British, and French traded at these rivers and to some extent also at locations in Andoni (Obolo) territory to the east of Bonny.

The Europeans were initially restricted to the coast under the direction of the local rulers. The Delta traders went up river in canoes, which, according to Duarte Pacheco Pereira, were "the largest in the Ethiopias of Guinea," and brought down to the visitors "slaves, cows, goats, and sheep" (1937, 131–32). Although there are no surviving examples of these large trade canoes, canoes built specifically for the protection of the trade are now displayed at regattas, and are favorite subjects for modern artists (figs. 2.2, 2.3). Slaves and local produce were sold to the Portuguese in exchange for "copper bracelets [manillas], which [were] greatly prized—more than those of brass" (see figs. A.9, A.10). Around 1508 the rate of exchange was eight to ten "bracelets" per slave, for which the coastal middlemen would have traded fish or locally manufactured salt. The trading chiefs of Nembe, like their counterparts in the other trading city-states, built huge canoes manned by members of their "houses," or trading corporations, to go up the Niger as far as Aboh, Onitsha in Igbo country, Idah in Igala country, and beyond. They also exploited the agricultural produce of neighboring Ijo communities in the freshwater Delta, including the Central Delta Ogbia, Odual, and Abua.

During the period of the slave trade, contact between the coastal middlemen and Europeans was limited. The visitors built shore collection centers, or barracoons, in which slaves were kept for them to pick up on visits that were as short as they could possibly make them. Some barracoons and shore buildings may still be seen at Akassa on the Nun River estuary.

The Palm Oil Trade

Direct contact between the European traders and the local middlemen became closer after the end of the slave trade and the effective establishment of the palm oil trade in the second half of the nineteenth century (fig. 2.4). Traders moored hulks (*oliki*) close to shore on which they could live for short periods before eventually seeking permission and land from their hosts to construct "factories," warehouses, businesses, and living quarters (figs. 2.5, 2.6). Abandoned *oliki* could still be seen stuck on the sands off Twon on the Brass River until a few years ago when they were swept away by shore erosion.

In the Nembe area, the British established "factories" at Twon on the Brass River during the reign of King Forday Kulo (r. 1800–1832). In the following years, they entered into a series of formal treaties to end the slave trade and slavery, and to set up rules to regulate the palm oil, or "legitimate,"

2.2 Photograph of a Brass war canoe, circa 1911. John Holt Collection. Liverpool Public Libraries, neg. no. 229/2.

2.3 A war canoe at the funeral of Chief Koki. The canoe is paddled by forty young men (twenty seated on each side). Photograph by Barbara Sumberg, 1993.

2.4 "The anchorage off the Town of Bonny River." Illustrated London News *(June 22, 1850: 436)*

2.5 Photograph of a trading hulk. Rhodes House Library, MS. Afr. R 239 No. 6. Photograph © Bodleian Library, Oxford, U. K.

2.6 Sampling palm oil in Bakana, 1896. Reproduced with the permission of Unilever PLC.

2.2

2.4

THE ANCHORAGE OFF THE TOWN OF BONNY RIVER.

2.3

2.5

2.6

trade. Joint judicial authorities, known as courts of equity, were set up to adjudicate cases involving Europeans and Delta peoples. Regulations for determining prices and the manner in which "trust" goods were to be received in advance by chiefs (who would exchange them in the hinterlands for palm oil) were agreed upon. The visiting traders, known as "supercargoes," formed close partnerships with local chiefs, established liaisons with local women, and took the sons of the local nobility to Europe to be educated. Formal dinners attended by chiefs and supercargoes were organized on board trading ships or at the "factories" on land. At Bonny, for example, there developed a formal ceremony referred to as "breaking trade," which involved a visit to the ship by the king to determine price, "followed by a dinner given by the ship's captain to the king, and reciprocated before the ship sailed by an invitation to dine ashore extended by the king to the ship's captain and officers" (Jones 1963, 94).

European exploration in West Africa at this time focused on determining the source of the River Niger, a quest in which the Niger Delta state of Nembe played a unique part. In 1830, King Boy Amain of Brass bought the British explorers Richard and John Lander—who had been captured by King Obi Ossai of Aboh—out of the king's hands, carried them down to the Brass and Nun River estuaries, and handed them to their countrymen trading there. It was ironically thus that the Lander brothers were able to determine the Niger Delta to be the termination of the great River Niger. This episode marked the beginning of a firmer relationship between the British and the rulers of Nembe. The progress of contacts is recorded in formal treaties dating from this year, in the exchange of gifts, and in the interior of the *okpu* (ancestral house) raised to the memory of King Boy Amain (r. 1830–1846) in Nembe (Alagoa forthcoming; Alagoa 1975a). It has also been recently commemorated in murals painted by the artist Geoffrey Okolo in Nembe City Hall (fig. 2.7). The event is memorialized as well in the proverb "*Kobai ene/Beken'owei bagha*," which may be translated, "Procrastination/Did not kill [saved] the white man." This suggests that the manner in which the king managed to rescue the explorers from being sacrificed by his own Nembe compatriots was by refusing to bring the issue of their disposal up for prompt deliberation.

2.7   A segment of Geoffrey Okolo's mural in Nembe City Hall that commemorates the rescue of the Lander brothers by King Boy Amain in 1830. Photograph by W. Ofongo, 1998.

The Establishment of Colonial Rule

The case of Nembe will serve to indicate the steps by which the British colonized the Niger Delta and its hinterland. The transition from the slave to the palm oil trade had enabled Britain to create a naval force based at the island of Fernando Po (present-day Equatorial Guinea). This squadron, aimed at destroying the slave trade, enforced treaties with other European powers, patrolled the coast to seize slave ships, released recaptured slaves at Freetown in Sierra Leone, and entered into treaties with kings and chiefs of local states to ban slave trading and to protect Christian missionaries and European traders.

In the Nembe area, the process was initiated by a "treaty offensive and defensive" signed by King Boy Amain and Lieutenant Colonel Edward Nicolls, superintendent of the base at Fernando Po, on May 14, 1834. Later, on November 17, 1856, a comprehensive "code of commercial regulations," or "comey treaty" (*comey* referring to the duties paid to local Niger Delta rulers), was signed by King Kien of Ogbolomabiri and King Arisimo of Bassamiri, representing the Nembe Kingdom, and Thomas J. Hutchinson, the British consul for the Bight of Biafra (now Bonny) and the Island of Fernando Po. As of 1849 British authority on the coast had become formalized; no longer was it represented by a transient naval officer, but by a substantive consul. The treaty of 1856 also represented a code prepared by the supercargoes on the Nun and Brass Rivers and sanctioned by the British political authorities on the coast. The first article of the treaty required the contracting kings and chiefs to give up the slave trade for "legitimate trade." Succeeding articles specified the sums to be paid as duties, or comey, to the kings of Nembe, the payment of other dues ("custom bar," "pilotage"), the terms on which the supercargoes may "give goods out on trust," the collection of debts, respect of the local totem (the African/royal python), and the settlement of disputes. Other treaties and conventions followed in quick succession, confirming the abolition of the slave trade and of slavery or providing additional protection for British traders and missionaries. The institution of courts of equity—on which the trading chiefs sat with the supercargoes to settle disputes—in all the ports of the Niger Delta provided the British one means to gradually subvert the sovereign legal authority of local rulers. Beginning in the 1880s the European scramble for African lands was in progress, and all earlier treaties and relationships were exploited to the end of colonial control.

Gradually, sole British rights to trade and influence crept into treaties and conventions. Along the River Niger and the Central Delta, the Royal Niger Company (later the United Africa Company) was given a charter to establish such influence beginning in 1879. The company proceeded to establish a sphere of monopoly trade running along the Niger from Lokoja to a depot at Akassa on the Nun estuary. In the 1880s, the exercise of a trade monopoly excluding Nembe from its traditional trading areas for export and subsistence food supplies to the immediate north and west constituted a major source of irritation. The establishment of a British consulate at Twon on the Brass River in 1891 was not sufficient to overcome local feelings of resentment. At the same period, the British authorities (the Royal Niger Company and the British consul) systematically began to revise earlier trade and friendship treaties, making them treaties of "protection," and to convert the courts of equity into full-scale instruments of British legal and political control.

It was in this atmosphere of tension that the Nembe people launched a surprise attack on the Akassa base of the Royal Niger Company on January 29, 1895, in an attempt to stem the tide of British imperialism. Naturally, the British retaliated, destroying towns, seizing cannons, and exacting fines. These events heralded the formal establishment of British colonial rule starting from the Niger Delta and ranging up into the Nigerian hinterland. In the Western Delta, Nanna of the Itsekiri was removed in 1894 (see interleaf C), in Nembe King Koko was deposed in 1895 (fig. 2.8), and Oba Ovonramwen of Benin was seized in 1897. For the rest, it was "pacification" through punitive expeditions, such as the destruction of the Eni oracle of the Isoko, the deportation of King Ibanichuka of Okrika, and the setting up of the structures of colonial rule.

It became clear to all Niger Delta communities that resistance by armed struggle was futile. Accordingly, individuals served their own interests, following the British colonizers into the Nigerian hinterland as interpreters, guides, and so forth. They thus adopted a strategy of survival through collaboration. The collaborators did not garner any special favors from the colonial rulers. It was rather a case of individuals utilizing the good fortune of earlier contacts to acquire literacy, Christian education, and knowledge of the ways of the new rulers so they could enhance their own status. They were in demand as intermediaries for local communities and for the colonial rulers. In the twentieth century then, residents of the Niger Delta city-states who had been middlemen in earlier centuries became missionaries of the new colonial order, carrying religion, education, and other elements of the new culture into adjoining territories.

As the British moved through the Niger Delta and pacified new areas in the hinterland, they created "native courts" and "native authorities" out of existing institutions and promoted local elite—in accordance with a system of indirect rule—who were directly controlled by British district officers, commissioners, and others. These structures gradually penetrated deeply into the political and social systems of Delta communities. The schools that came with the Christian missions under the protection of the colonists made an even deeper impression on the mental and spiritual life of the peoples, to some extent alienating youth from their traditions and culture. Yet while colonial rule was designed to create new men, new cultures, and new societies, it never fully achieved the aims of its founders, and some of the changes it set in motion only took root during the postcolonial period, after 1960. Thus the peoples of the Niger Delta and other Nigerian communities lived through the colonial period with a great many of their cultural values and institutions intact. They mastered ways of surviving the impositions and pretensions of their colonizers and ultimately succeeded in bringing about revolutionary change.

The Role of Religion in the Process of Colonization

The Portuguese were the first to send Christian missionaries into the Niger Delta, specifically to Warri from the offshore islands in their control. These early efforts, however, did not meet with success. In the late nineteenth century, British Protestant missions, operating from bases in Sierra Leone,

2.8 *A segment of Geoffrey Okolo's mural in Nembe City Hall that includes a portrait of King Frederick William Koko (r. 1889–1898) who fought the British in 1895. Photograph by W. Ofongo, 1998.*

attempted to establish strongholds on the West African coast in the wake of the movement to halt the slave trade. In the Niger Delta, the first secure Anglican mission was established at Bonny in 1864 by Bishop Ajayi Crowther, a liberated slave; this was accomplished at the invitation of King William Dapa Pepple (Alagoa and Fombo 1972). Bishop Crowther, his son Archdeacon Dandeson Crowther, and other missionaries from Sierra Leone who had formerly been slaves followed this initial success with additional missions: one on the Brass River at Twon in 1868, founded at the request of King Ockiya (r. 1863–1879); one among the Kalabari in 1874; and another among the Okrika in 1880. King Ockiya's two sons, Anthony Ofieafate Ockiya and Daniel Ogiriki Ockiya, themselves became pastors and missionaries. Reverend Daniel Ockiya (1874–1954) translated the Bible, the Book of Common Prayer, and hymns into Nembe and preached the gospel to neighboring Ijo and Ogbia communities, following the footsteps of Nembe traders who had built places of worship at market sites. As he himself remarked, "When the word of God had taken a stronghold on the Nembe, Brass Christians, they carried it wherever they went. The traders carried it with them to their different trading centers. They built places of worship where they worshipped every Lord's Day" (Ockiya 1988, 77).

As the pioneer Nembe missionary, Daniel Ockiya provided the tools with which others could spread the Anglican church through most of the new Bayelsa State of Nigeria. Thus this Christian denomination virtually attained the position of church of the establishment. Bonny, Opobo, Kalabari, and Okrika Christians performed a similar function in parts of the Rivers State and along the Imo River valley in Abia State. At Bonny, Nembe, and other locations in the Niger Delta, and at Calabar, prefabricated churches were built (figs. 2.9, 2.10). Local artisans learned church design and construction from Sierra Leonian and other craftsman and thus aided in spreading a tradition of Christian architecture through the region of southeastern Nigeria (fig. 2.11).

2.9   *"Converts of Brass conveying their new church to Nembe on the Niger."* Gleaner Pictorial Album *1: 27, fig. 8. Photograph courtesy of the Church Mission Society, London.*

Change and Continuity
Politics and Society

Colonial conquest presented a fundamental challenge to the worldview of Niger Delta communities. British officials directly controlled the local chiefs they pressed into their new government institutions. The local political leaders became the tax collectors of the colonial administrations. The change at the top of the political system was therefore clear, and every symbolic and substantive step was taken to drive home the message that the states and kingdoms of the Niger Delta had lost their independence to the British sovereign. Interestingly, this time of change witnessed particularly long periods of interregnum; it was as if the communities hesitated to appoint new rulers to replace their last independent kings. Thus at Nembe, King Koko, who died in 1898, was only replaced by the first king to assume the title under colonial rule, Reverend Anthony Ockiya, in 1926. Similar delays occurred among the Itsekiri, Okrika, and other communities. At the local level, however, communities continued to govern themselves using age-old institutions such as the "house" system employed in the Eastern Delta city-states of Nembe, Kalabari, Okrika, Bonny, and Opobo—a system that has persisted in a variety of forms to the present. Indeed, members of the modern educated elite take pride in assuming chieftaincy titles within this traditional "house" system as a means of establishing their relevance to their communities and credentialing themselves as grassroots leaders.

The Economy

The change in the economic system brought about by colonial rule was extremely traumatic as it deprived Niger Delta communities of their profitable status as middlemen. The result of colonial "pacification" of the Nigerian hinterland was to open it directly to the full influence of external trade and the world economy. This in turn leveled opportunities between the coastal and the hinterland communities, and it eventually turned the scales against the coastal communities with their comparatively low population levels. The introduction of British currency in place of local units and methods of exchange—actively promoted through the enforcement of taxation as an engine of wage-labor and a cash economy—proved one of the most radical measures to be instituted by the colonial regime.

Christianity

The Christian missions profited from colonial rule, depicting the victory of British arms as evidence of the superiority of the Christian god over local gods. The destruction of such cults as that of Aro Chukwu, which the colonial authorities accused of slave trading and other offenses, served to drive home this object lesson. The missions entrenched themselves in local communities by building not only churches but also educational institutions, including technical and crafts schools. As noted earlier, they also embarked on the translation of the Bible and liturgy into local languages through the creation of local orthographies and the training of local clergy. The observation of basic rules such as the keeping of the Sabbath, wearing of European dress, and prohibitions against participating in traditional dances, festivals, and so forth, separated Christians from other members of society.

2.10 "St. Clement's Church Bonny (from a Sketch by Archdeacon Dandeson Crowther)." Gleaner Pictorial Album 1: 28, fig. 11. Photograph courtesy of the Church Mission Society, London.

2.11 St. Luke's Anglican Pro-Cathedral Church, Nembe. This modern structure replaced an imported prefabricated original. Note the monument over the grave of the Reverend Daniel Ockiya in the foreground. Photograph by W. Ofongo, 1998.

Despite this, certain practices, such as polygamy, belief in divination and witchcraft, and traditional means of combating and treating disease, have been difficult for Christians to overcome. Indeed, many converts continue to be accused of consulting diviners and participating in traditional practices officially disapproved of by the Christian church. It has also been difficult to transform the Ijo idea of God as mother into the Christian concept of God the father. As a result, the translators of the Bible and other Christian texts into Ijo dialects, especially into Kolokuma, have had an extremely difficult task.

The example of King Constantine Ockiya is particularly instructive of the ways in which Christianity has and has not become integrated in the lives of Delta peoples. As noted earlier, King Ockiya invited missionaries into Nembe and assisted them in establishing a thriving mission, but he himself did not make a personal commitment to Christianity. He only formally received baptism on his deathbed and was given the Christian name Constantine, after the emperor who made Christianity the established religion of the Roman Empire. The king had, however, given up the figures representing his personal gods to the missionaries before his death (fig. 2.12). At his demise, both Christians and traditionalists claimed the right to perform rites. In the end each group carried out a separate funeral.

The memorial symbols to be found at the *okpu* erected over his grave exemplify the effort to reconcile two systems of belief (fig. 2.13). Outside the mausoleum stands a life-size portrait erected to his memory by his European trading partners. Inside, the following symbols attest to his personal effort to modernize his people while remaining faithful to those traditions that he thought viable: holes used for pouring libations to an ancestor; a bottle of spirits as evidence of previous libations; the skull of a ram as evidence of previous sacrifice; a metal cross symbolizing the Christian faith; a wreath and glass case with artificial flowers, part of the Christian tradition; two paintings of ensigns on the wall—one depicting a cross, the other a talking drum and a traditional board for playing draughts.

2.12 Bishop Ajayi Crowther with companions standing beside three ancestral images belonging to King Ockiya of Brass, 1877 or 1878. Photograph courtesy of the Church Mission Society, London.

Just as members of the king's lineage have continued to offer libations at his *okpu*, they have also maintained a shrine (*opu osain*) that he had kept for the protection of the health and well-being of the general public. It consists of a large clay pot mounted on three wooden supports in which certain protective medicines would have been prepared for public use at times of epidemics and so forth. This is kept in a low hut with walls of corrugated iron sheets and palm frond roof.

Funerals continue to be an area where traditional practices compete with Christian ones. Opinions vary as to how far Christians should go to accommodate local traditions. Adherents of Christianity no longer carry out the rites of *ikpataka* divining (Alagoa 1968; Horton 1968) in which a coffin or bamboo frame is used to pronounce the cause of death and other matters, nor do they engage in *aka kara*, or symbolic filing of the teeth of the deceased, or the rites of *otiti paan*, the chanting the name of the deceased to send the spirit to join the ancestors. Nonetheless Christian funerals in Nembe still involve the rites of *tiripaga*, or the public display of the corpse at a city square for the purpose of collecting the financial or material contributions of all citizens in a demonstration of kinship affiliation and solidarity. Nembe funerals are also gradually adopting the Kalabari custom of decorating the funeral parlor with expensive new cloths as well as heirlooms from old cloth boxes. Modern artists are also now commissioned to make large portraits for display at the sites of funerals. Coffins have changed from being plain bamboo structures (*ikpataka*), to costly works of art. Cement, marble, or brass sculptures representing the dead are also gradually appearing on grave sites in Nembe (fig. 2.14).

2.13 Life-size portrait of King Josiah Constantine Ockiya (r. 1863–1879) commissioned by his European trading partners at the okpu *commemorating the king and his son Anthony Ofieafate Ockiya (r. 1926–1957). Photograph by W. Ofongo, 1998.*

2.14 Bronze portrait bust at the grave site of Chief Theodore Idibiye Francis Ogiriki, grandson of the Reverend Daniel Ogiriki Ockiya and a professor of medicine. Photograph by Elisha Renne, Nembe.

Expressive Culture

The design and construction of churches throughout the Niger Delta and into the hinterlands attest to the missionary influences and contacts among peoples of the Niger Delta and with neighboring communities (see fig. 2.11). The spread of Western formal education, including schools of arts and crafts, has produced a growing number of professional and semiprofessional artists working outside the traditional canon. Accordingly, realistic sculptures of local leaders and recent ancestors are becoming common and exist side-by-side with the traditional forms of symbolic art used in shrines and by the masquerade societies, such as in the distinctive Kalabari Ekine and the ancestral *duein fubara,* or foreheads of the dead.

A comparison of the works of two Nembe artists Geoffrey Okolo and Jackson Waribugo with works given to Bishop Ajayi Crowther by King Ockiya in 1877 (see fig. 2.12) suggests that the naturalistic style of the two modern artists derives from an older tradition, one that persists despite their exposure to European conventions. An exhibition brochure published in 1977 by the Rivers State Council for Arts and Culture describes Geoffrey Okolo (1925–1996) as having "studied commercial design at the Nigerian College of Arts, Science and Technology, Zaria (now Ahmadu Bello University), and gained a Diploma in Fine Arts." Okolo's artistic legacy is exemplified by a remarkable mural depiction of the history of Nembe that covers three walls in the Nembe City Hall (see figs. 2.7, 2.8).

The same brochure described Jackson Waribugo as having been "born in Brass [Nembe] in November 1945, and [having] studied sculpture and metal casting at the Academy of Fine Arts in Carrara [Italy]. Though a specialist in monumental sculpture, Waribugo also produces wooden walking sticks and decorative wooden busts." Waribugo's monumental sculptures are to be found in the Hotel Presidential, the Diete-Spiff Sports Complex, the Rivers State Council for Arts and Culture, and the Isaac Boro Park—all in Port Harcourt. He has also been commissioned to create sculptures of important persons in various cities of the Eastern Delta, including the figure of King Amakiri in Buguma, and others at Nembe, Okrika, and Opobo (fig. 2.15). Waribugo has not only depicted historical personages, such as the war hero Isaac Boro, but also gods and goddesses, such as the figures on the lawn of the Hotel Presidential (fig. 2.16).

It must be noted that serious local and international threats exist to the survival of the cultural heritage of the Niger Delta and to the full flowering of the creative talents of its artists. Poverty disposes youths to pillage community artistic treasures for sale on the Western art market. Local religious zealots also pose a serious threat. In the 1920s and 1930s, the Garrick Braide Protestant movement of the Eastern Niger Delta led to the destruction of many works of art in shrines and ancestral homes. Several Niger Delta pieces now in British museums were moved there by colonial officials such as P. A. Talbot during this period. Recently, the last civilian governor of Rivers State, Mr. Rufus Ada George, destroyed a number of public monuments on the grounds that they were pagan and promoted immorality. On this basis Waribugo's *Mangrove Giant,* an elemental male figure wrestling with a crocodile, displayed at the entrance to the Alfred Diete-Spiff Stadium in Port Harcourt was removed, reported destroyed, and replaced with a sculpture depicting two hands holding up a map of the Rivers State that is certainly devoid of

2.15 Jackson Waribugo's sculpture of the late Chief Joseph Ayibatonye Alagoa at Tombi, Nembe. Photograph by W. Ofongo, 1998.

the evocative power of the original. Similarly, a figure depicting a traditional warrior by Waribugo in Isaac Boro Park was destroyed, leaving only figures representing modern military men bearing guns (fig. 2.17). Ironically, the first military ruler of Rivers State, Commander Alfred Papapreye Diete-Spiff, was Jackson Waribugo's patron and provided the support for his training in Italy. Unfortunately, the Nigerian government has historically failed to institute effective policies to preserve cultural values and property or to inspire creative energies. Residents have received little assistance from their postcolonial governments in terms of protection of the environment or of the cultural heritage.

Conclusion

This has been but a brief sketch of the cultural history of the Niger Delta from the period of the first transatlantic contact until the present. Perhaps what is most remarkable is the length of time following the initial contact with Europeans in the late fifteenth century that the Niger Delta city-states were able to retain their control of trade with the hinterlands. Ironically, it was the British Empire's establishment of a squadron to combat the slave trade and slavery that ultimately provided a means for Europeans to gain control of trade within the Delta and to submit it to colonial rule. Despite this history, the peoples of the Delta, whether functioning as middlemen or missionaries, have been able to retain much of their unique traditions and worldview.

2.16 Jackson Waribugo's sculpture of a concourse of gods and goddesses on the lawn of the Hotel Presidential, Port Harcourt. Photograph by W. Ofongo, 1998.

2.17 All that remains of Jackson Waribugo's figure of a traditional warrior, which stood in Isaac Boro Park, Port Harcourt. Apparently, it was one of the sculptures destroyed at the orders of Governor Ada George of Rivers State. Photograph by W. Ofongo, 1998.

Interleaf B
Privilege and Power: Merchant Princes of the Eastern Delta

Martha G. Anderson

Many Delta peoples acquired chiefs only after the British implemented their policy of "indirect rule" in the late nineteenth century. Under this policy, the British recognized priests of clan deities, acclaimed warriors, successful traders, and signatories of treaties as political leaders. In the saltwater zone along the coast, competition for control of lucrative trade networks, which intensified with the arrival of Europeans, had already resulted in the emergence of small city-states headed by influential rulers. Among the Eastern Ijo, the most powerful chief to preside over a group of trading concerns became known as its *amanyanabo,* meaning "owner of the land" or "king."

Merchant princes of the Eastern Delta, such as Pepple of Bonny, Jaja of Opobo, Amakiri of Kalabari, and Koko of Nembe, flaunted their considerable wealth and employed Machiavellian tactics in their attempts to outmaneuver competitors. (This behavior also occurred on occasion in the Western Delta; see interleaf C on Nanna of Itsekiri.) During the latter part of the nineteenth century, however, many of these colorful leaders made the mistake of trying to outsmart the British, who sent one after another into exile. Nigerians now acknowledge these leaders as heroes who resisted imperialism, but their actions were also motivated by financial considerations. Some of these men amassed great wealth. A mid-nineteenth-century British visitor to Bonny described King William Dappa Pepple (the seventeenth ruler of Bonny and its fourteenth crowned head) as "a great dealer in palm oil and a very cunning trader." Though his fortunes suffered during the seven years he spent in exile for trying to provoke a war with the neighboring Kalabari, his annual income was rumored to exceed fifteen thousand pounds (fig. B.1).

The emphasis on trade led to a complicated system in which status based on royal descent competed with status based on achievement in the form of financial success (fig. B.2; Jones 1963, 57–62). The amazing social mobility that resulted allowed anyone who demonstrated outstanding business savvy and leadership ability—including "bought slaves" and one or two enterprising women—to assume political power. In fact, slaves ruled the majority of Ijo canoe houses. King Jaja of Opobo, who rose from slavery to rule a house in Bonny, even founded his own "kingdom" with the backing of British traders. By 1888, however, the British found that Jaja had become troublesome, so they sent him to the British West Indies where he died in 1891. His son, Prince Frederick, who was educated in London, succeeded him as *amanyanabo* of Opobo in 1893 (fig. B.3).

Among the Eastern Ijo, the idea of erecting memorials seems to have developed in response to these greater social distinctions, for such sculptures were made only for high-status individuals. Several Eastern Ijo groups, including the Okrika, Nembe, and Kalabari, make, or once made, memorials to commemorate the dead. The fact that their more egalitarian relatives to the west do not share this tradition suggests fairly recent innovation, as does the variety of forms found among these eastern groups.

For a relatively short time, the Okrika Ijo placed ritual pots, or *odu,* on ancestral shrines to commemorate high-status women, as well as male leaders. (Opuogulaya 1975). Talbot (1932 [1967]) judged the type of pot used for this purpose, which was adorned with human faces, to be relatively new when he visited the area early in the twentieth century. The Kalabari Ijo claim that they used stools, called *osisi duein,* as memorials, prior to introducing ancestral screens, or *duein fubara,* about two centuries ago (figs. B.4–B.6) The latter represent the heads of trading concerns known as "war canoe houses," but like Central and Western Ijo carvings made for bush spirits, they portray their subjects as warriors with markings that designate status in the *peri* warrior society (cf. fig. B.7). On the screens, the Kalabari leaders—flanked by followers to indicate their importance—are depicted with numerous indicators of status and authority, including war paint, skulls, weapons, and European hats. Most of the central figures, and occasionally secondary figures, wear their favorite masquerade headpieces, attesting to the importance of attaining rank in local Ekine or Sekiapu masking societies (see interleaf H).

King Ockiya, a nineteenth-century Nembe Ijo ruler promoted his dynasty by commissioning figures to represent his ancestors (see chapter 2 of this volume). Using a technique common in southeastern Nigeria but unusual in Africa on the whole, the carvers attached separately carved limbs to the torsos. The naturalism of these figures contrasts with the abstract style that typifies most Ijo carvings and may have been inspired by the figureheads of European ships, as William Fagg

has suggested (1963a, 76). The latter were a familiar sight at trading depots along the coast, and at least one example, salvaged from a decaying hulk, survived to grace the offices of a colonial headquarters in the region in late 1930s (Chadwick 1938). When King Ockiya later converted to Christianity, he surrendered his ancestral figures to Bishop Crowther (see fig. 2.12).

B.1   "King Peppel [Pepple] of Bonny-Town" as portrayed in the Illustrated London News *(June 22, 1850: 437). The author of the article notes that, "King Peppel is about 32 years of age, having ruled nearly ten years." King William Dappa Pepple embraced Christianity during the five years of his exile that he spent in Britain and established a mission in Bonny on his return.*

B.2   Chief Young Briggs, a Kalabari leader, seated in a wheelchair, 1902. Reproduced with the permission of Unilever PLC (from an original in the Unilever Archives), box 25, folder 2, no. 55. Though they sometimes employed "indigenous" emblems and fashions to legitimize their authority or advance their political agendas, many Delta chiefs also adopted European (or European-inspired) fashions and incorporated imported items as status symbols.

B.3 *An Opobo ruler, probably Frederick Sunday Jaja (1873–1915), also known as Obiesigha, the son of the famous King Jaja, shown with his retainers. The prince and two flanking figures (one of whom may be Shoo Peterside, Chief of Opobo) wear European dress. The others wear a mixture of European and African garments. The horned object held by a youth seated in front of Prince Frederick has not been identified. Photograph reproduced by permission of the Syndics of Cambridge University Library.*

B.4 *Kalabari ancestral screen. Photograph by Nigel Barley, Buguma, 1987.*

B.5 *Drawings of an Okrika pot and a Kalabari stool (Talbot 1932 [1967], facing p. 244).*

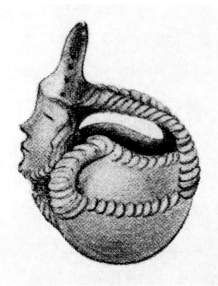

B.6   Ancestral screen. Kalabari Ijo. Wood, metal, and pigment. H: 162.5 cm. Charles and Kent Davis. Unlike most Kalabari sculpture, ancestral screens were designed for visual impact. Their construction shows knowledge of European joinery techniques, learned from ships' carpenters during centuries of trade. The rectangular format of the screens has led to speculation about the influence of Benin plaques, European prints, and even photographs (Barley 1988). Like numerous others, this screen shows the central figure wearing the headdress of Alagba, an important masquerade character. Versions of the masquerade owned by different canoe houses vie for attention when they appear every seventeen years. (See also interleaf H.)

B.7 *Chief Will Braid and soldiers, Bakana, 1899. Reproduced with the permission of Unilever PLC (from an original in the Unilever Archives), box 25, folder 2, no. 58. Kalabari Chief Davies to the left and Chief Will Braid to the right are surrounded by supporters bearing rifles. Kalabari trading concerns were known as "war canoe houses," and the Kalabari continued to share the warrior ethos with the Central and Western Ijo.*

B.9 *Kalabari* amanyanabo *and Benin chiefs at opening ceremonies of the*
Buguma Centenary. Photograph by Joanne B. Eicher, 1985.

B.8 *Chief's hat (*ajibula*). Kalabari Ijo. Made by Chief Johnny West. Cloth,*
feathers, ram's beard, mirrors, foil paper, plastic. H: 46 cm. Collection of
Joanne B. Eicher. Kalabari men don top hats, bowlers, and fedoras as
expressions of power and prestige, but only chiefs wear hats as flamboyant this
one. Kalabari hatmakers began with a European model and added layers of
material and meaning to create the ajibula, *a distinctive and "traditional" art*
form. The concentric circles—used in conjunction with plastic baubles, fringe,
and foil—are a Kalabari symbol (Arnoldi and Kreamer 1995, 51).

Interleaf C
Nanna of Itsekiri, "Merchant Prince of the Niger Delta"

Joseph Eboreime

C.1   Nanna of Itsekiri going into exile. Reproduced with the permission of Unilever PLC (from an original in the Unilever Archives), box 25, folder 2, no. 17. Nanna is shown here wearing a Hausa robe, quite different from the normal Itsekiri dress. It would have been considered exotic and certainly was very costly.

In defining themselves in the post-independence era, the Itsekiri people, who inhabit the mangrove swamp at the far west of the Niger Delta, have focused upon a variety of symbols. One of the most important icons of their identity is Nanna of Itsekiri (fig. C.1), the nineteenth-century merchant prince of the Niger Delta who defied the British and acquired enormous wealth through his monopoly of the palm oil trade.

Unlike the Urhobo, Isoko, and Ijo, by the fifteenth century the Itsekiri had developed a strong monarchical system centered around an *olu* (king). By the late 1500s Portuguese Catholic missionaries had been successful in converting the Itsekiri monarchs to Christianity. Olu Atuwatse I—the son of the first Catholic *olu*, Sebastião—went to Portugal for ten years to receive an education and returned with a high-born Portuguese wife (P. C. Lloyd in Bradbury 1957, 181). Atuwatse's son, the future Olu Antonio Domingo, married a half-Portuguese woman from San Tome. These close associations with the Portuguese proved crucial in affording the Itsekiri protection as they gradually extended the bounds of their kingdom (Kathy Curnow, personal communication).

By the mid-nineteenth century, however, following the death of Olu Akengbuwa and several of his heirs, the *olu*'s throne was left vacant. Wealthy traders moved quickly to fill the power vacuum, and the most powerful among them assumed the position of *gofune*, or governor, of the Benin River. Under the new system of leadership, the Itsekiri continued to expand their trading territory. Having forced the European firms from Ode-Itsekiri in 1873, they established their own trading posts and beaches up the Warri River connecting with the Urhobo and Benin interior for trade. While the Urhobo resented these incursions, they were unable to combat the powerful Itsekiri war canoes (P. C. Lloyd in Bradbury 1957, 181).

In the late nineteenth century a rich and powerful trader named Olomu became the *gofune*. Before his death in 1883, Olomu chose his son Nanna to succeed him. An incredibly skillful trader, Nanna became *gofune* in 1884. The same year, he signed a treaty with the British, promising to protect their interests. Ultimately, however, Nanna came to feel that the British were cheating him on the price of palm oil, and in 1886 he decided to boycott them. This led to war, and Nanna, a brilliant strategist, successfully held the British off for three months—even using submerged barbed wire to snag their ships. When the British shelled Nanna's base of operations at Ebrohimi along the Benin River, it is reported that they captured 100 cannons, 445 blunderbusses, 640 dane guns, and over 1,000 flintlock rifles and cap guns, in addition to revolvers (Ayomike 1992, 34). They are also said to have freed over 10,000 of Nanna's slaves and to have destroyed many of his personal effects (Ayomike 1992, 34). Despite this destruction of property, Obaro Ikime indicates that

C.2   Robes belonging to Nanna of Itsekiri. Collection of the Nanna Palace Museum. Photograph by Joseph Eboreime.

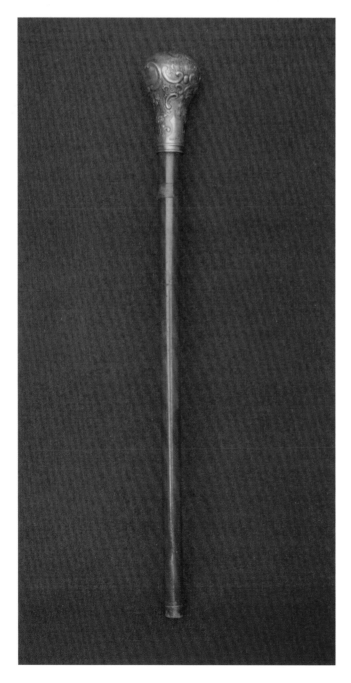

most of Nanna's remaining goods were sold for over £6,500 to settle trade debts (1969, 165). When Nanna was finally captured by the British, he was tried and exiled to Ghana.

It was not until 1906 that Nanna was allowed to return to Itsekiriland, settling in Koko. He called his section of the settlement "New America," modeling it after Ebrohimi. There, along with his sons, who had trained as carpenters in Ghana, he built a Mediterranean-style home. Nanna died in 1916. His home, now known as the Nanna Palace Museum, was declared a national monument in 1990. The museum houses many of the luxury items that Nanna collected during his lifetime (figs. C.2–C.6).

Acquiring European goods was a long-standing tradition among the Itsekiri elite (fig. C.5). Nanna's collection contains many items that would have been typical of those amassed by high-ranking chiefs. Among them are long white robes with red sashes resembling those worn by Catholic clergy, *eberen* swords, oil lamps, chandeliers, embroidered Nupe or Hausa robes (see fig. C.1), Victorian vases, staffs, brass pots, glazed pipes, water filters, gold rings, tobacco containers, silver trays, chinaware, epergnes, large stoneware jugs, clocks, tankards, crystal decanters, pendants, pleasure canoes, prestige and utilitarian paddles, silver and golden beds, giant iron pots, ladles, cannons, and cannon balls. Both the *olu* and chiefs wore many cloths imported from India and Europe. There are sufficient European objects dating from the eighteenth and the nineteenth century to warrant the inclusion of an antique show in the annual Coronation Anniversary held at Warri and Ode-Itsekiri (see chapter 7 of this volume).

C.3   A hat belonging to Nanna of Itsekiri. Collection of the Nanna Palace Museum. Photograph by Joseph Eboreime.

C.4   The staff of office presented by the British to Nanna. Collection of the Nanna Palace Museum. Photograph by Joseph Eboreime.

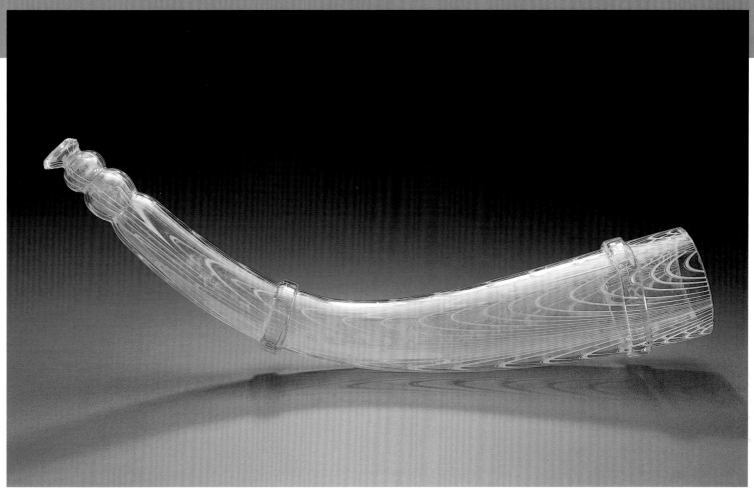

C.5 *Trumpet. Murano, Italy. Late seventeenth or early eighteenth century. Glass. L: 43 cm. FMCH X97.26.1; Anonymous Gift. Glass trumpets such as this one were traded into West Africa, along with glass canes, from the seventeenth through the nineteenth century. They became the property of important merchants and chiefs.*

C.6 *A brass container inscribed "Nanna Oloma." Collection of the Nanna Palace Museum. Photograph by Joseph Eboreime.*

Chapter 3 Bulletproof: Exploring the Warrior Ethos in Ijo Culture

MARTHA G. ANDERSON

LAGOS, Apr 21 [1997] (IPS)—Violent communal feuds in the oil-rich Delta region in south-eastern Nigeria are threatening the economic lifeline of the West African nation—its petroleum industry....

"We seek the assistance of the Navy each time we want to, move," Bassey Asanga, Administrative Manager of Chevron, one of the leading oil companies operating in the area, told reporters one day after the captain of a merchant boat was kidnapped in the area....

Fred Etete, an executive director of [Diesel Power Nigeria Limited], confirmed at the weekend that efforts to obtain the release of Apoh, whose captors are believed to be of the Ijaw [Ijo] ethnic group, were continuing....

Market women who use the waterways to transport their fish and other wares have reportedly been attacked by youths. "They just do what they want," one of the attacked vendors told the independent newspaper, the 'Guardian', at the weekend. "They have no control, they smoke hemp and drink ogogoro (a locally brewed gin)."

"The drunken youths are always armed," she added....

A chemical engineer who works on Forcados island off the coast of Warri told IPS on Monday in a telephone interview that "the situation is chaotic...every day there are reports of attacks on the waterways."

Asked if the navy had not secured all areas, the engineer said: "How much can the navy do when these youths are so unruly? They grew up in this delta, know the waters like the palm of the hands and are fantastic swimmers." [Oyo 1997]

Recent news reports of youths terrorizing market women and disrupting oil production in the creeks near Warri recall a long string of advisories issued by European visitors to the Niger Delta. Beginning with Duarte Pacheco Pereira (1937, 140–43), who in 1505 published an account of his late fifteenth-century visit to the region, they almost invariably describe peoples living west of the Nun River as hostile, intractable, piratical, and warlike. Though the need to justify colonization may color foreign reports of incessant warfare in the region, as J. Okoro Ijoma suggests for the neighboring Igbo (1983), Delta residents tend to accept—and even promote—an image of themselves as warriors. Long after local warfare ceased, the Ijo (the term used to refer to the Central and Western Ijo throughout this chapter) often describe themselves as a bold, independent, and contentious people, and attribute these qualities to their warlike past.

The ethnographic record confirms that the Ijo and their closest neighbors—including the Isoko, Itsekiri, and Urhobo—were warlike peoples. Though their frequent saber rattling seldom led to open warfare, they expressed this attitude in everything from speech to dress. An Isoko war leader, for example, added a feather to his bonnet to denote each of his kills

3.1 Bush spirit. Ijo. Wood. H: 172.1 cm. FMCH X79.476; Gift of William Lloyd Davis. A quintessential Ijo "warrior," this bush spirit is protected by "bulletproofing" medicines contained in his calabash necklace. Placed at the edge of a Delta village, he would have protected it against human and supernatural invaders.

(Peek 1986). The egalitarian Ijo, who did not recognize a central authority even at the village level, professed allegiance to clan war gods. They not only sited their villages with an eye to defense but barricaded them with sculpted sentinels, raffia curtains, and potent medicines, methods some communities still employ to deter supernatural invaders. Numerous references to aggression persist in the region today: in Ijo shrines, where bush spirits take the guise of proud warriors; in masquerades, where youths dare armed maskers to attack them; and in rituals, where diviners—regardless of gender—employ military tactics to deal with militant spirits. Indeed, nearly any examination of Ijo expressive culture calls for a discussion of "warfare," a term used here to describe a variety of combative behaviors ranging from fistfights to piracy.

This chapter argues that the warrior ethos provides a model for Ijo art and ritual, as well as an ideological basis for warfare and other forms of aggression (fig. 3.2). General discussions of Ijo warfare and trade at the end of the nineteenth century establish the context for stories about Iyo, an Ijo warrior, and Bibikeala, his "pirate" counterpart, whose activities encompass this period. As biased, embellished, and legendary as these tales may be, they reveal a magical side of combat often overlooked by more formal histories (Ogot 1972; Reyna 1990). A summary of the Ijo worldview, which follows, turns the tables by focusing on war-related imagery in bush spirit shrines. It provides an appropriate backdrop for an eyewitness account of a ritual conducted by a female diviner in the 1960s, long after Iyo and Bibikeala had

3.2   A ceremonial "war party" participating in a festival for Egbesu, the war god of Kolokuma clan. The men are threatening to attack the author if she does not meet their demands for illicit gin. Photograph by Martha G. Anderson, Olobiri, 1978.

died. This story confirms that Ijo women shared the heroic ideal that the warrior ethos engendered. Though they did not engage in actual warfare, women could attain considerable status by serving as "ritual warriors." More importantly, this tale captures the sense of awe and wonderment with which the Ijo regard the universe far better than the most systematic analysis of their worldview.

Ijo "Warfare" and the Warrior Ethos

According to numerous oral histories, piracy, slave raiding, and assaults on strangers once made travel along the Delta's waterways so treacherous that the Ijo regarded trading as a dangerous activity to be undertaken by only the bravest of men (Amangala 1939, 15; P. Leis 1962, 7). Older inhabitants of the area still speak of a time when conflicts between villages made even local excursions risky, for small-scale wars continued to erupt well into the twentieth century despite a number of aggressive—and downright brutal—British attempts to pacify the region. In fact, residents of a particularly factious community recall that simply walking from one end of town to the other once required courage, for wards comprised of tight-knit kin groups—the units that waged war—engaged in civil infighting as well as intervillage hostilities. Feuding sometimes became so entrenched that villages incorporated buffer zones to ease tensions. In more extreme cases a disaffected ward or faction moved to the opposite side of a river or resettled further away.

Local accounts provide few details about specific conflicts but paint a broad picture of Ijo "warfare." Unlike the great African states of Songhai, Zulu, and Dahomey, the Ijo had no standing armies, nor did they fight wars of conquest and expansion. Even intervillage hostilities, or *sowoi bi*—the type of fighting that most clearly merits the term *war*—resemble the ceremonial feuds waged by the Dani of New Guinea more closely than modern mass warfare (Heider 1970). Although—unlike the Dani—opponents stopped short of halting combat to keep their feathered headdresses from being spoiled by rain, conventions did require them to balance losses by providing young girls to replace their victims. Thus, sporadic raids and sorties usually resulted in only a few deaths on either side before opponents formed covenants (*ovuo*) to end fighting (Owonaro 1949, 72–73; Freeman n. d., n. p.).[1]

Gauging the frequency and duration of fighting proves more difficult. A history of Olodiama clan (Freeman n. d., n. p.) lists six covenants honored by the town of Ikebiri and notes two casualties suffered in another, perhaps later war; but it does not indicate how much time these events spanned nor how long each lasted. Moreover, some of the violence Ijo chroniclers recount falls outside these parameters, including intravillage animosities and raiding. The latter could lead to warfare but appears to have had a life of its own. In addition to practicing piracy (*aru sara*, or "to spoil the canoe"), a few pugnacious warriors turned fighting into a full-fledged career by plundering villages with war parties composed largely of slaves. They seem unlikely to have formed covenants or honored conventions such as those requiring restitution. Present-day inhabitants of the area recall several specific types of raiding, including *ogun gbin* (to stage a surprise attack on a town); *toru koro* (to go to a distant area and kill people on the rivers); and *ninibiraba* or *ninikon* (to kill passersby with weapons).

If the Ijo fought as regularly as they would have us believe, what provoked them to do so? Competition to control lucrative trade routes might explain why warfare escalated nearer the coast among groups that became directly involved in the overseas trade, but it does not adequately account for infighting among those living in the interior. E. J. Alagoa supplies a more plausible motive by linking common motifs in origin myths—like fleeing from enemies, migrating to avoid war indemnities, and squabbling over shares of a communal hunt—to "the obvious need for a thin spread of population to exploit the meager resources of the environment" (1972, 189–90). Local histories, however, tend to offer personal grievances—ranging from failure to offer compensation for accidental deaths to refusal to pay adultery fees or gambling debts—as grounds for most subsequent hostilities. Nevertheless, economic factors alone do not account for warfare, for wars seldom resulted in the acquisition of land, property, or significant wealth.[2] Of the several types of African warfare identified by Georges Balandier, the Ijo fit most closely with the groups who regarded "war and hunting as supreme trials to prove the real quality of a man" (1974). Much like the Bete of Côte d'Ivoire, they fought to demonstrate their strength and courage, not to annihilate their opponents.

Though not as aggressive as Ijo men, Ijo women occasionally fight each other, abuse their husbands, and band together to punish men for mistreating their wives. In former days, they played a limited role in warfare. Though wives often served as peacemakers out of a desire to keep their husbands' wards from fighting their own families, they ultimately supported their spouses and occasionally even assisted them by handing them weapons in battle (N. Leis 1964, 223–24). Women danced processional war dances (*ogele*) and sang war songs before men set off to fight. The lyrics of their songs often echo the insults they hurled at warriors to make them angry when facing their enemies. They scolded their husbands for being boastful at home, challenging them to demonstrate their prowess in the battlefield. When a war party returned from a successful foray, they joined in the celebration.

The Ijo themselves often complain that the volatile disposition of their people as a whole—whether located in their ethos or their very nature—predisposes them to conflict, noting that their ancestors were so highly combustible that even insults once sparked wars. G. I. Amangala offers a typical, if somewhat backhanded, example of this approach by marveling that the "general temperament" of a clan located near Warri "is quite different from any [other] Ijaw clan," for "They hate court palaver and fights and are seldom seen in courts for cases and disputes" (1939, 9). S. K. Owonaro, on the other hand, explains the Ijo's quarrelsome behavior by invoking the type of "origin myth" promoted by literary Ijo of his generation. He contends that Oduduwa, the Yoruba deity credited with fathering the mythic progenitor, Ijo, cursed his son "to receive no respect from his children who should be stubborn, obstinate and unruly as he (Ijo) had been to his father." He adds that Oduduwa "further proposed that warfare and strife should hunt Ijo where-ever he should go" (1949, 1–5).

Ultimately, however, most Ijo attribute their ancestors' warlike behavior to a desire for the acclaimed *peri* title, a distinction clan war gods bestowed on men for killing either human beings or animals—such as leopards, hippopotami, manatees, and sharks—that the Ijo consider to be like human beings. *Peri* provided the primary means for men to gain status in an essentially egalitarian society, as did similar titles honored by neighboring groups, including the Urhobo, Isoko, and Igbo. Among the Ijo, the intangible rewards clearly outweighed the tangible ones, for recipients simply earned the right to drink with their left hands, wear special costumes, which differed from clan to clan, and perform a special *peri* "play" at the funerals of other titleholders. English-speaking Ijo sometimes refer to this event as the "fit-confessing ceremony," for each participant proclaims his "fitness" for the title by raising his right arm and issuing a distinctive cry at the waterside; Alagoa considers the term "feat-confessing" more apt (personal communication, 1998).

Profit would seem to constitute a clear and sufficient motive for other forms of aggression, including piracy and slave raiding, as Obaro Ikime (1967, 68) has suggested. Ironically, he compares the Ijo to desert dwellers who "have always raided settled peoples in the more fertile plains next to them." The Ijo, however, seldom emphasize this aspect of raiding. Owonaro (1949, 86), for instance, grounds raiding in the same ethos as warfare by noting that piracy was "considered an act of valour in those dark days," whether or not it resulted in material gain. One Delta resident put it more simply by observing that in a culture that applauded acts of bravado, "Everyone wanted to be a hero." The quest for the acclaimed *peri* title alone seems to have inspired one "champion warrior" from Ikebiri to ambush and kill seven men as they traveled along the rivers, thereby touching off the war mentioned above (Freeman n. d., n. p.).

Philip Leis, one of the very few anthropologists to have worked in the region, identifies several factors that fostered the Ijo's warrior ethos, including their ecological setting and their colonial experience, which almost certainly intensified fighting and may well have stimulated migration (personal communication, 1998). He sees it as a manifestation of Ijo individualism, which is inextricably linked to their acephalous, nonunilineal form of social organization. He notes striking differences between the Ijo and other African societies that might be described as warlike, including the Nyam-Nyam of Cameroon, whose warrior ethos focuses on land and chieftaincy rather than the self. He also finds them different from the Yanomamo of Brazil, for whom warfare "predicates the form of socialization and dictates the style of inter-community relations." In fact, the Ijo's rugged individualism and personality types remind him more of Americans.

A Warrior

Owonaro paints the mythic progenitor, Ijo, as the consummate warrior, "a stalwart man of exquisite physique…very powerful, warlike and brave," who "gallantly fought with his father in many a battle to subdue their enemies." He reminds his readers that it was through "acts of valour, courage and power coupled with intelligence and amazing personality" that Ijo "became very important and respectable in the city [of Ile-Ife]" (1949, 3). Although his myth bears all the hallmarks of a modern invention, it encapsulates the ideals Ijo warriors undoubtedly aspired to achieve (fig. 3.5).

Drum titles chosen by later Ijo warriors—like Odiyen (Mighty man) and Aguda (Twist someone)—indicate their desire to convey an impression of formidable strength and barely contained aggression, but fighting obviously

3.3 *Bush spirit. Ijo. Wood and white pigment. H: 170.2 cm. FMCH X84.496; Gift of Edgar F. Gross. Ijo warriors went off to battle looking much like this figure, equipped with weapons, medicine gourds, and war paint for protection and often wearing imported headgear to proclaim their status.*

3.4 *Bush spirit, Ijo. Wood and white pigment. H: 139.7 cm. FMCH X81.1564; Gift of William Lloyd Davis and the Rogers Family Foundation. This figure has lost its weapon, but its medicine gourd and white "chalk" markings—believed to possess supernatural properties—show its readiness to fight.*

3.5 *Man dressed as warrior at the Kolokuma Egbesu festival. Note the top hat, medicine gourd, and "war paint." Photograph by Martha G. Anderson, Olobiri, 1978.*

3.6 *The bush spirit Osuwowei (Rain man) shown with one of his remaining medicine pots. He formerly had seven. Photograph by Martha G. Anderson, Umbugbene, 1979.*

demanded the aid of supernatural powers as well as physical prowess. Residents of Olodiama clan report that whenever warfare threatened their villages, their war god, Egbesu, turned into a leopard and set off to kill the enemy in advance of the war party. The Ijo credit renowned warriors with similar capabilities. They say many transformed themselves into animals, while others camouflaged themselves as natural objects. According to local histories, Zala of Okpotuwari turned into a young palm tree, and Oguru of Ayama changed into the footprints of animals. The most successful warriors reportedly also commanded a body of magical knowledge called *atamgba* and a type of magical speech known as *aunbibi,* or "unknown language," because it is unintelligible to ordinary Ijo. Command of this language enabled them to accomplish miraculous feats simply by uttering a few words and thus endowed them with tremendous power.

The Ijo regarded courage as "both a personality characteristic and an achievement," for it could be acquired by various means (N. Leis 1964, 213). In addition to using slaves as human shields, warriors fortified themselves with a veritable arsenal of charms and herbal concoctions. Many of the gourds (*atu*), belts (known variously as *egbe*, *gbinye*, and *ideri*), and other items that adorn figure carvings (fig. 3.6) probably represent "bulletproofing medicines," like the smoking pot one celebrated warrior suspended from his neck to devour enemy bullets and the fans others used to deflect them.

Recipe for a Traveling Medicine

An anonymous informant collected the following recipe from a native doctor in Ibeni in the 1960s.

Libate at the trunk of a tree known as *inyanyanga*, which is used for carving canoes. It has compound leaves with a midrib. Take fourteen leaves [an auspicious multiple of seven] and dry them. Collect one hundred and one bees. You can find dead ones in palm wine. Burn the leaves and bees in a new clay pot adding seven seeds of alligator pepper. While burning, libate, telling the medicine it should be active. Open the mouth and remove the seeds from a type of calabash called *atu*. Grind the medicine into a powder and put it inside the calabash. Cork it tightly and keep it hanging inside the house so it won't touch the floor.

Put it in your pocket whenever you travel. If danger threatens, run or paddle away. If people or spirits pursue you, take some of the powder, put it on your palm, and blow it at them, telling the bees to go out and fight. They will be afraid when they see it, because in even a little bit of powder, one hundred and one bees will go out and sting them until they scatter. Run or paddle until you get out of harm's way, then whistle and wait until one bee comes and flies around. Beat it. When it falls, quickly put it back inside the calabash. When the calabash is corked, all the bees you've set loose will disappear, and you can go on your way.

Spirits in shrines also wear medicine gourds, but the recipes for medicines are specific to each shrine.

Charms of this sort could also render people invisible, seek out or ensnare enemies, and destroy them. Warriors also visited shrines to splash herbal concoctions onto their bodies from medicine pots (called *osain,* a term that denotes the Yoruba god of medicine) both to prepare for battle and to cool down afterward. Like the neighboring Isoko (Peek 1976b), the Ijo report killing diviners who established war shrines, simultaneously preventing them from divulging secrets and equipping others with the same power.

Stories about Iyo, a renowned warlord from Ossiama in Oyakiri clan, still circulate throughout the Central Delta. When two friends failed to join him, as promised, in waging war on a nearby town, he formed his own village. The touchy warrior decreed that his family and slaves speak the dialect of a town in a neighboring clan on pain of death; even today, residents of his village talk like people from Amassoma. The following account, given by a great-grandson, draws on information collected from family members (including an elderly granddaughter's childhood memories of Iyo) and a more unusual source. Iyo appeared to his great-grandson in dreams and told him to put drops into a young boy's eyes; when he did so, the boy became possessed and revealed things about his famous ancestor.

Before Iyo mounted his war boat, he slept on a trash heap for seven days—the number the Ijo consider most auspicious—in order to keep his enemies' spirits and charms from finding him and driving him mad. He bathed

3.7 Iyo's great-grandson preparing to launch a reconstruction of Iyo's war canoe. Photograph by Martha G. Anderson, 1992.

himself and the slaves he selected for battle with medicines from numerous pots, each with its own name. A small calabash endowed him with amazing powers; it ensured that nothing—not even gunshots—would harm him or anyone who accompanied him into battle. He tied it to the tip of the flag on his canoe so that it touched the surface of the water (fig. 3.7).

Iyo performed several types of divination in preparation for combat. When he pointed his middle finger toward an oak tree across the river from his village and commanded it to fall using "unknown language," it would fall and then tell him how the war would go. He also put a penny in a saucer, set it on the bow of his canoe, and spoke magical words to it. If the saucer fell inside, the canoe would cut itself free and jump like a speedboat toward the town he was fighting.

Everyone hid whenever Iyo returned from war because he would kill the first person he saw—a wife, son, daughter, or slave—for his medicine pots. If no one appeared, he would call out a name, and that person had to come forward to be slaughtered. He usually brought back many captives and sacrificed most of them for his gods as well. He poured the blood into his medicine pots and threw the bodies into a part of the bush where only he could go.

All his magic and medicines could not prevent Iyo from losing an occasional battle, but they did allow him to escape relatively unscathed. According to one tale, the irascible warlord once went to Ogboin clan to fight people as fearsome as he was. Realizing they would defeat him, Iyo told his slaves to hold each other's waists, then he beat the ground with a handwoven towel; together they turned into a long line of egrets and flew off. When his adversaries rushed to the water to cut the charmed flag from his canoe, the boat started to move as if it had an engine, traveling so fast it had already landed by the time the "egrets" returned to his village.

Iyo may have acquired some of his charms and medicines from herbalists, but the Ijo hold that success on such a grand scale can be achieved only by fostering personal relationships with powerful spirits. Though warriors usually look to bush spirits for support, Iyo's descendants attribute his awesome abilities to water spirits who emerged from a "whirlpool" (*ifiyou* or *ofiyou*) and pulled him underwater while he was bathing at about the age of ten. When he emerged three days later—a number the Ijo consider auspicious— he told his parents to send him to train with a powerful sorcerer in another community, but water spirits continued to instruct him on every aspect of war through dreams. He lived to a ripe old age, dying in 1942 when he was estimated to be ninety.

Overseas Trade and Piracy

Pereira (1937, 131–32) and other early European travelers described the huge canoes that had plied the Delta long before they visited; these were used for carrying fish, livestock, slaves, cassava, salt, pots, cloth, and other products from east to west and north to south. When foreign merchants arrived at the coast, groups living in the adjacent saltwater region, who relied heavily on trading to procure agricultural produce, began collecting "comey," or customs duties, from them and acting as their middlemen in order to guarantee a share of the profits. Their canoes (See fig. 2.2) left the coast loaded with imported brassware, implements, alcohol, and firearms to be traded first for slaves and later for palm oil (Alagoa 1964, 1970).

In order to maintain their position, Nembe (or Brass, as the British called them) Ijo middlemen, who dominated trade along the Delta's central artery, the Nun River, designed their canoes to discourage competition from foreign traders and withstand attacks from inland neighbors. Suitably impressed, the Lander brothers describe an "extremely large and heavily laden" vessel that they saw in the 1830s:

> It is paddled by forty men and boys, in addition to whom there may be about twenty individuals, or more…so that the number of human beings will amount to at least sixty…it is furnished with a cannon, which is lashed to the bow, a vast number of cutlasses, and a quantity of grape and other shot, besides powder, flints, etc. It contains a number of large boxes or chests, which are filled with spiritous liquors, cotton, and silk goods, earthenware, and other articles of European and other foreign manufactures; besides aboundance of provisions for present consumption, and two thousand yams for the master of a Spanish slaver, which is now lying in the Brass River…in this canoe three men might sit with ease abreast of each other. It has been cut out of a solid trunk of a tree, and draws four feet and a half of water, being more than fifty feet in length. [Lander and Lander 1832 (1965), 258–59]

Though the Portuguese began trading at Nembe in the fifteenth century, the slave trade only gained importance in the region during the second quarter of the nineteenth century when other ports were blockaded. Even then, middlemen dealt largely with mainland suppliers. The region's relatively brief heyday—lasting only half a century—did not begin until the "legitimate" trade in palm oil became significant (Alagoa 1964). By the 1850s Samuel

3.8 Shrine object. Isoko. Wood, pigment, cloth, clay, plant fiber, partial human skull, cowrie shells, broken ceramic vessel. L: 120.7 cm. FMCH X84.49a,b,c; Gift of John L. Ross and Mary M. Penn. Photograph by Denis Nervig. This unusual vessel suggests a canoe, but the addition of a carved head at one end and "legs" at the other transforms it into a human torso. Three of the figures mounted on the rim appear to be males sporting Western-style helmets; the other three seem to be females wearing elaborate coiffures. The cargo, a partial skull, might commemorate a military victory. In the 1930s, James Welch reported that warrior shrines displayed vessels containing skulls (1937, 270).

Crowther counted seventeen Nembe canoes near one Ijo village and estimated he had seen a hundred altogether along the Nun, some carrying six puncheons, or large casks, of palm oil (Crowther and Taylor 1859, 12). By 1895, however, more profitable conditions could be found on the eastern and western fringes of the Delta, and trade on the Nun declined (Alagoa 1964, 62).

Foreign travelers reveal almost nothing about life inside the villages they passed along main thoroughfares and still less about those located on more remote waterways. They had little direct contact with local inhabitants during this period and hardly any dealings of a friendly nature, as Alfred B. Ellis remarked: "Very little is known of this part of Africa beyond the actual coast line and the Niger river, up which steamers ascend for some hundreds of miles. Between Benin and the Nun mouth the numerous western outlets have not even been surveyed, and we find on the Admiralty charts 'natives hostile and cannibals.' In that portion of the delta the inhabitants will hold no friendly intercourse with the white men" (1883, 114–15).

By all accounts, including their own, the Ijo did their best to promote a reputation for piracy. Frustrated by Nembe and Itsekiri middlemen, who operated further to the west, they attacked nearly every expedition that set out to explore the Niger and raided many of the vessels that plied its arteries for trade. In 1823, after pirates audaciously mounted a second attack on a brig he commanded, Captain John Adams termed the Ijo a "predatory race" who not only plundered the cargoes of foreign boats, but sometimes murdered their crews (1823 [1966], 117–18). Nearly sixty years later, Adolphe Burdo echoed these sentiments; he predicted that if a steamer were to run aground on a sandbank, "the crew would assuredly be massacred and the cargo pillaged" (1880, 108). Casualties of the period include one of the famous Lander brothers, killed by a piece of copper bolt fired on his expedition as it traveled along the Nun in 1834 (Hamilton 1862, 23), and a young British officer named Pennington, "treacherously murdered" by "Creekmen" while surveying the coast in 1846 and memorialized by the river that still bears his name (Burton 1863, 2: 246).

In light of these and other incidents, the British, who sought to control trade in the Delta, found it advisable to equip boats like the *Sultan of Socotoo* (named for Sokoto, a Nigerian caliphate) with armor made of iron screens and even resorted to mounting firework displays to fend off pirates (Dike 1956, 206). In 1886 the Royal Niger Company finally broke the hold of coastal middlemen and established trading depots upriver. By 1889 it had entered into more than a hundred treaties along the Lower Niger and established dozens of factories in the region. Nevertheless, agents from Sierra Leone presided over these depots, and Ijo living inside the Delta continued to have little contact with Europeans (Mockler-Ferryman 1892, 32). As late as 1926 British administrators labeled them a "truculent group" that had "never really been conquered" (Ikime 1967, 75).

A Pirate! A British Account

Soon after the turn of the century, the British tried to consolidate their position in Southern Nigeria by suppressing slave raiding and trading—illegal since 1807 but still carried on in out-of-the-way spots like the Central Delta—by encouraging legitimate trade, by abolishing the "juju" hierarchy, and by opening the country to "civilization."[3] In order to further these objectives, they launched a series of military offensives, including two that targeted one of Iyo's contemporaries—a "pirate chief" named Bibikeala.

Bibikeala's downfall began in February 1902, when colonial officials sent troops up the Nun to put a stop to murders and piracy so that trade could "be opened up again." Later that month, Major Hodson, stationed at Sabagreia (Seibokorogha) in Kolokuma clan, requested urgent assistance after a group of chiefs called to "palaver" with him arrived to make a "warlike demonstration" in their canoes, "calling on the whitemen to come out and fight." By October, reports describe a state of unrest so acute that "life and property are rendered unsafe and trade is practically stopped." They identify "Egbeddi" (Igbedi) on Wilberforce Island, home to the warlike chiefs who confronted Hodson, as the principal trouble spot and recount a particularly egregious crime a party of men from that village had committed several months earlier when they ascended Taylor Creek, beheaded the occupants of a canoe, then toured the countryside showing off their trophies and proclaiming that they intended to settle all their disputes in like manner.

British authorities demanded that the murderers surrender and return the severed heads for proper burial. They warned all towns engaged in piracy to make restitution or face punishment but focused on the apprehension of "Bibi-Cala," a "native of Egbeddi" and one of its "chiefs," charging him with several acts of piracy against Nembe traders. Captain D'Oyly, who responded to the call with fifty-two men, set fire to Igbedi and two nearby towns. His troops inflicted forty casualties and suffered only one loss. Because they failed to capture the alleged criminals, they disarmed "the countryside" by destroying twenty-five thousand firearms—a remarkable number considering that they left villagers armed with dane guns.[4]

By implementing a series of punitive expeditions like this one, the British claimed to have brought six thousand square miles under control, but piracy continued to plague them. Bibikeala may well have considered himself invincible after escaping unscathed, for by the following year, colonial officials once again accused him of various crimes. They launched a more ambitious campaign, stating his capture as their primary objective. By trying the troublesome pirate for sundry murders, they hoped to show an influential "juju" in the area to be powerless against the government and thereby encourage the Ijo to bring their disputes to the new native courts.[5]

On September 19, 1903, a contingent blocked the creeks surrounding Wilberforce Island while troops toured the vicinity, harassing and pressuring inhabitants to turn Bibikeala over for justice in the event that a reward of sixty pounds failed to secure their cooperation (figs. 3.11a,b). Nearly two weeks later, the crew of one of the smaller vessels spotted a lone man paddling a canoe by moonlight: "After a brief struggle the runaway was secured, and it was seen that it was no less a personage than *Bibi-Cala* himself." Four hundred-and-thirty-one men equipped with five heavily armed launches—three armored and two steel canoes—had finally succeeded in capturing the infamous pirate.

A Pirate? Local Accounts

The British may have branded Bibikeala an outlaw, but Owonaro provides a distinctly Ijo perspective on his conduct by referring to him as "a war chief of a high local fame who attacked some Brass Traders." He adds that "He could

3.9 *Figure with staffs, possibly a bush spirit. Ijo. Wood, cloth, and feather. H: 122 cm. Collection of Robert B. Richardson. The planklike body of this figure recalls Kalabari Ijo ancestor memorials, but the geometric shape of the mouth suggests an origin further to the west.*

3.10a,b *Bush spirit. Ijo. Wood and chalk. H: 153.7 cm. Art Institute of Chicago; Gift of the Richard and Barbara Faletti Family Collection, 2000.321. Photographs by Jerry L. Thompson. This elongated figure resembles an example photographed in the south Central Ijo region in the 1950s. The white stripes suggest the chalk markings worn by warriors. The bared teeth may be intended to indicate powerful speech and an assertive personality.*

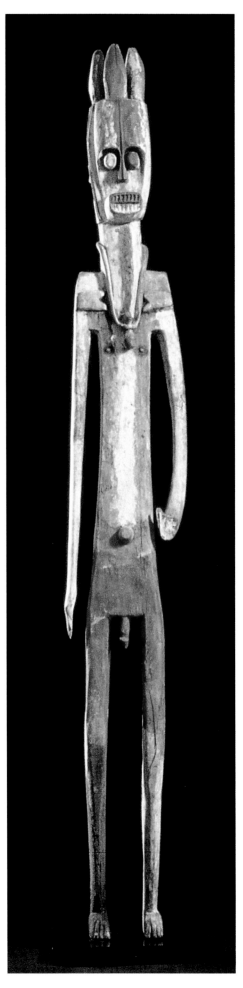

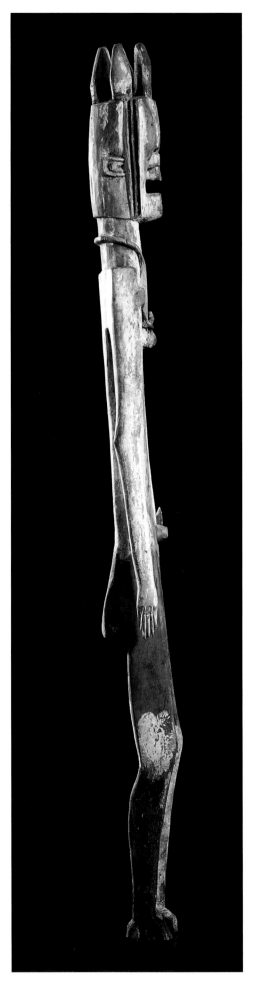

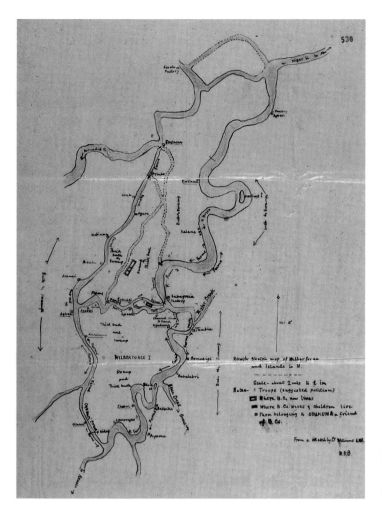

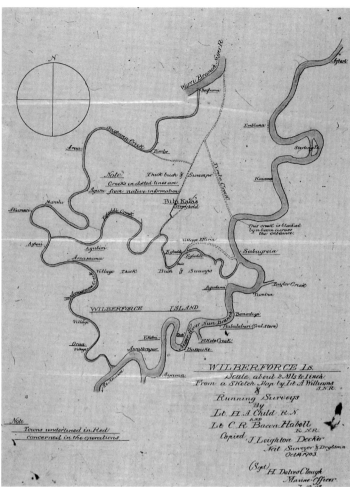

3.11a,b Two archival maps from the "Bibi-Cala"
expedition: (A) a rough sketch map of Wilberforce
Island and (B) Wilberforce Island drawn from sketch
map with "Bibi Cala's Stronghold" indicated along
a bush creek. Public Record Office, Kew Gardens,
Richmond, Surrey, England, CO 520 20 96089.

not have been captured but considering possible punishment of innocent people by the force he rowed out of the creeks, and as it was not humanly easy to submit oneself for death, he was caught by the people of Kaiama and handed over to the members of the force and was executed" (1949, 113–14).

In an unpublished manuscript based on family recollections and local legends, Bibikeala's grandson, J. E. I. Bebeke-ola, portrays his notorious ancestor as a victim of circumstance, claiming his admittedly bloody career began with a desire to right a wrong committed against his family. While Bibikeala was still a youth, his father's trusted slave ran off during a trading expedition to Aboh, the Igbo town that controlled trade on the Niger River above the Delta. When he grew older, Bibikeala pledged to wage a lifelong war against the Igbo village held responsible for the loss unless it returned the missing slave or offered compensation for his loss. After several forays into the Aboh region to set fire to villages, capture slaves, and generally wreak mayhem, Bibikeala became caught up in a byzantine chain of events that began when a Nembe trader residing in Igbedi accidentally committed adultery by glimpsing the "private parts" of his host's wife. The incensed husband, Poweigha, promptly retaliated by seizing the trader's goods. Soon afterward, Bibikeala innocently traveled to the Nembe area to engage in legitimate trade, but on his arrival, the "adulterer's" father confiscated his property as compensation for the items Poweigha had taken from his son. On returning to Igbedi, Bibikeala sought revenge by attacking Poweigha who, in turn, shot both him and his son. A shrine priest called on to settle the dispute convinced Poweigha to pay half of Bibikeala's losses and instructed the latter to recoup the rest from Nembe traders.

Bibikeala and four supporters set out in a canoe, pausing to libate in the river to ensure the success of their mission. When they reached a likely spot, they hid until they heard the oars of a "big Brass trading canoe." "Using all tactics of piracy," they stoned the front paddler with a bottle of "dangerous chemicals [potent medicines?]" and stormed the canoe. The traders and crew jumped overboard; the captain resisted, but the buccaneers pushed him overboard and took control of the vessel. Following further adventures, they arrived home to celebrate the capture of a canoe several times larger and much better stocked than the one Bibikeala had lost by sharing looted "J. J. Peters gin" with their townspeople.

J. E. I. Bebeke-ola adds that his grandfather once sent a severed hand, leg, and head from three different victims to another renowned warrior simply to impress him with his own power. Tales like this may or may not be true, but they probably have some basis in fact, for people as far away as the Isoko area, where his townsmen sometimes traded, still speak of "Bibi-Cala" with awe (Peek, personal communication, 1995). Nevertheless, his descendant describes him not as a pirate but as a strong man who protected Igbedi from pirates—a savior to some, if clearly a menace to others.

Stories, songs, and commemorative names kept Bibikeala's memory alive until, some eighty years later, when his spirit grew restless and began to cause trouble for his family in order to demand the funeral rites his execution had denied him. His descendants performed a type of burial known as *feun duwei* (air dead), in which the spirit of the deceased is called to a crudely carved stick that then serves as a substitute for the corpse; publicly vindicated, Bibikeala could finally join his ancestors in the land of the dead.

Bibikeala's Power

Both Iyo and Bibikeala seem to have had ties to a town called Odi in Ogboin clan and might even have met there. Even if Iyo had only heard of Bibikeala's exploits, he would certainly have wanted to know where his piratical counterpart got his power. Information gathered in preparation for their second expedition convinced the British that Bibikeala headed a secret society to which all the local chiefs belonged. A. A. Whitehouse, the Political Officer assigned to the second expedition, found it "quite certain" that he was "a great 'Medicineman,'" adding, "There is no doubt that Bibi Cala has been able to carry on his career of crime for such a long time, through fear of the 'Fetish' or Juju that he is believed to possess." Kolokuma Egbesu, the war god responsible for awarding *peri* titles in Kolokuma clan, might fit the description of such a "juju," but his shrine is located in Olobiri, not Odi, as the intelligence reports indicated. According to his grandson, Bibikeala and his comrades sang war songs and called on "the war gods of their fathers" prior to their sorties; unfortunately, he only mentions Egbesu by name.

When an Amassoma chief accompanied Whitehouse to Bibikeala's camp, they found, "only a few small Idols and a few bits of wood and Iron stuck in the ground covered with the dirty bits of cloth and filth." Nevertheless, Whitehouse observed that his companion seemed, "greatly impressed, and on no account would he touch the objects." He noted, "This place was destroyed when the village was fired." The numerous carvings Whitehouse later presented to a museum in Liverpool suggest that laying waste to shrines like this one may not have involved destroying the images they housed. Unfortunately, museum records simply note that he collected them during the raid on Wilberforce Island.[6]

Though their disparate styles suggest the figures may come from villages scattered along the expedition's circuitous route, it is tempting to think that at least some of them once stood in Bibikeala's shrine. The centerpiece of the collection—the janiform figure Eckhart von Sydow chose to represent a quintessentially Ijo style (1954, 55, fig. B)—even looks the part of a pirate/warrior (fig. 3.12). Though it might represent another spirit Bibikeala served, it could not be one of the "few small idols" Whitehouse saw at his "stronghold," for it stands nearly seven feet tall. The rarity of pieces dating from this period adds to its importance. A summary of beliefs about bush spirits (*bou orumo*, the bush or forest spirits, or *bouyou*, the bush people) provides the likeliest grounds for speculation about its function and meaning, for neither *suwo oru* ("gods from above," including clan war gods) nor most water spirits (*bini oru*) require figurative images. Moreover, shrines for bush spirits often have close ties to war.

Bush Spirits

The Ijo hold that human beings befriend, marry, and even bear children with nature spirits while awaiting birth in the creator's realm. These spirits may later follow their human friends or family members to earth in order to demand offerings or images (fig. 3.13). In addition, people can encounter nature spirits in the forests and rivers surrounding their villages. The Ijo claim that both good and bad spirits reside in the environment, just as good and bad people exist in the world. They acknowledge this distinction by presenting offerings of good food (farina with oil or split and roasted plantain) to good spirits and bad food (farina without oil or plantain neither split nor roasted) to bad spirits. Similarly, they use their left (or "bad") hands to throw offerings for bad spirits away from their bodies to prevent them from coming close and causing trouble.

A song sung in Olodiama clan admonishes, "Beware of the bush, the bush is a difficult place," for the Ijo believe the forest to be fraught with supernatural dangers as well as physical ones. People take precautions when working there, fearing that a spirit startled along a bush path might strike them deaf and dumb, cause them to give birth to a deformed child, or kill them on the spot. They must be particularly careful not to disturb certain types of vines and termite mounds and to avoid areas reserved for spirits. Nevertheless, the latter can lay claim to any part of the forest and assume the form of any plant or animal; simply cutting down the wrong tree can have catastrophic consequences for an entire family. Women even try not to call loudly to each other when working on their farms to avoid drawing the spirits' attention (N. Leis 1964, 73).

Although the Ijo say bush spirits resemble them more closely than water spirits, they often describe them as ugly, unkempt creatures. Many also exhibit physical abnormalities; as one diviner explained, the most powerful people in the bush are disfigured or disabled, for these conditions make them proud and extremely irritable. When presenting offerings to the forest,

3.12 The large raffia-skirted janiform figure in the Whitehouse collection as illustrated in Sydow (1932, pl. 2). Similar images now wear cloth skirts. The feathers probably indicate his warrior status. Photograph courtesy of the Board of Trustees of the National Museums and Galleries on Merseyside (Liverpool Museum).

3.13 Woman with an image representing a bush spirit companion. A diviner told her that she befriended the spirit while living in the creator's realm before birth. Photograph by Martha G. Anderson, Korokorosei, 1991.

diviners call on "the lame," "the blind," and "the deaf in the bush" (Wata Agama, personal communication, Korokorosei, 1979). Some of the songs sung at rituals abuse spirits "who cannot stand firm," as diviners imitate their ungainly movements; others portray them as uncouth misfits, so independent and diffident that they transgress Ijo ideals. One warns, "The bush holds many grudges; the bush is a different town (or world)"; another compares dealing with the forest to cutting fruit from young palm trees that have many shoots growing along their trunks; a third notes that the most warlike individuals, like Iyo, dance the war dance alone and stand alone like the raffia palm because their roughness prevents others from getting close to them.

Bad implies strong, as well as evil, and when evil spirits are truly nasty, enshrined spirits have to project qualities like ruthlessness and volatility to convince followers of their ability to protect them, if no longer to lead them in war. Priests frequently speak of the dangers involved in serving such touchy and vindictive masters, but their complaints only enhance the spirits' reputations. As a song sung for a bush spirit enshrined in Olodiama clan announces, "Dirimobou is bad; therefore he is a good spirit," recalling the explanation Bibikeala's descendant offers for his piratical behavior.

Spirits tend to rise and fall as people perceive their strength to wax and wane, but a number of shrines founded before or during Iyo and Bibikeala's lifetimes survived until the 1970s, and some continue to attract followers. Though the original carvings deteriorated long ago, their replacements often wear top hats, recalling the era when trade flourished in the region. Surprisingly, they depict bush spirits as warriors with no apparent physical abnormalities aside from multiple heads, which indicate clairvoyance, vigilance, and superhuman powers rather than anomalies. The figures proudly carry weapons, display medicines, and wear war paint to indicate their readiness to fight; they dress in dark colors to signify strength and indomitability. Though some now emphasize their ability to bring children and promote prosperity, warriors once visited their shrines to consult divination ladders and treat themselves with medicines before setting off to fight.

These spirits drink with their left hands, as only *peri* warriors can do. Their songs are often war songs, including two sung at Azama in Apoi clan for Benaaghe, whose image recalls the Whitehouse figure. One uses the metaphor of a fishing expedition to chide him not to be lazy when the time comes for war; the other tells how Snail, who lacks hands and feet, prepares for war by asking to be covered with a leaf to hide him from his enemies. His ploy recalls the medicines and shape-shifting strategies Ijo warriors employed to avoid detection.

The contradictory image of the bush spirit as social pariah and stalwart defender reflects the ambivalence Ijo sometimes express toward warriors of the past and, by extension, toward their own collective temperament. They not only regret that the bold and independent qualities they prize make them exceptionally argumentative and quick to resort to physical violence but readily acknowledge the dangers highly combative individuals pose to society. For example, people admire the physical prowess displayed by wrestlers but sanction those they deem to be overly aggressive. Interestingly, they suspect bush spirits of causing this behavior in order to prompt their human friends

3.14 Multiheaded bush spirit surmounted by an animal. Ijo. Wood. H: 203.2 cm. Collection of Toby and Barry Hecht. Multiheaded figures can represent a variety of bush spirits, but seven-headed examples may depict Tebesonoma, or "Seven heads," a character in the Ozidi narrative, which is performed throughout the Central and Western Delta. The animal surmounting the figure may be a leopard. Men earned warrior titles by killing leopards, sharks, and other powerful animals, as well as by taking human lives.

3.15 Multiheaded bush spirit surmounted by an animal. Ijo. Wood. H: 167.6 cm. FMCH X81.1568a,b; Gift of William Lloyd Davis and the Rogers Family Foundation. The detachable headdress worn by this four-headed figure supports a four-legged animal, which in turn dominates a smaller quadruped. The predator may be a leopard, an animal symbolically linked to warfare, or a dog. The latter are thought to accompany spirits as "guides."

3.16 Man with a carving representing his bush friend. When he behaved too aggressively in the wrestling arena during his youth, diviners determined that a spirit he had befriended in the spirit world before birth wished to join him on earth. Photograph by Martha G. Anderson, Ikibiri, 1978.

to acknowledge relationships formed in the creator's realm. Providing an earthly receptacle—a carving in this case—brings the spirit under control and restores the wrestler's behavior to socially acceptable standards (fig. 3.16). Likewise, providing a shrine for a temperamental bush spirit channels its aggressiveness into protecting the community, much as carvings called *ivri* do among the neighboring Isoko and Urhobo (Foss 1975; Peek 1986).

A story about an exceptionally brutal man who lived in Korokorosei in the early twentieth century suggests that the Ijo may have resorted to extreme measures to neutralize the power of individuals who posed a serious threat to society. In 1978, older residents of Korokorosei described an enormous man named Yasara or Iyasere as so powerful, demanding, and destructive that not even ten or twenty men could restrain him. This is almost certainly the same Yesere Otongbolo mentioned in a history of Olodiama clan (Freeman n. d., n. p.). If so, it confirms accounts of his unusual size by terming him "a very huge man of giant stature," and clarifies local standards for gigantism by adding that he was "more than six feet in height." The author portrays Yesere as a Samson-like figure. Captured by Chief Nangi of Ekeu in Bumo clan, he reportedly broke his chains, knocked down walls, ran through a forest, and swam across a river to safety, despite being handcuffed. This remarkable deed so impressed Chief Nangi that he reportedly sent his former captive a case of gin; nevertheless, Korokorosei residents say his own townspeople considered Yesere so dangerous that they conspired to kill him. They tricked him into going fishing, then ambushed him along a path that leads to a sacred lake.

Interestingly, although Ijo living west of the Nun River do not commemorate the dead with sculptures, Yesere's executioners carved a figure to keep his spirit from troubling them. Moreover, they placed it alongside the path he took out of town, renamed him Ogbongo, and "married" him to a previously acknowledged bush spirit named Ipogholi, who presides over a sacred lake behind the town. By doing so, they transformed a reputed sociopath into a protective spirit, for the Ijo typically post carved images around their villages to keep evil forces at bay. Although the figures had deteriorated by 1978, people continued to leave plantain and fish for the spirits on their way home from the bush (see chapter 4, this volume). Surprisingly, in light of Yesere's stature, they estimate that the figure was only four feet tall.

Three Bush Spirit Shrines

Odewei of Korokorosei in Olodiama clan provides a good example of the way enshrined bush spirits combine the idea of social misfit with a military image. Though his last priest—who died in 1979—emphasized the help the spirit offered in hunting, fishing, and bearing children, a song sung for the shrine's medicine pot offers a grim but reassuring message for those seeking its protection. It calls on the pot to come out of the bush "to crush the dead and the spirits." Warriors once slept at the shrine and washed with its medicines before setting off to battle.[7]

According to his priest, Odewei began as a small figure on the lid of the medicine pot but demanded a real carving when he became powerful himself (fig. 3.18). Though his image portrays him without apparent physical defects, one of the songs sung for him asks, "What sort of an awkward looking man is

3.17a,b   Multiheaded bush spirit surmounted by an animal. Ijo. Wood, pigment, glass, metal, and nails. H: 169 cm. Private Collection. The white coloring on this figure—possibly a warlike bush spirit known as Tebesonoma—may denote his status as a titled member of the peri *warrior society. This figure's glass eyes enhance its aura of supernatural vigilance and vitality.*

he?" Another repeats the abuse "*yangaba, yangaba*," which may be translated as "rough" or "twisted body," again and again, comparing his ungainly movements to those of someone who suffers from yaws. A third berates him for refusing to share food and drink with his family and calling on them only in time of war. These songs are war songs; their lyrics echo insults the Ijo once hurled at warriors to incite them to fight. War paint, weapons, charms, dark clothing, and even the name of the infant carved on his wife's back— "War canoe will never have bad luck"—underline his preparedness for war.

Two shrines from neighboring villages amount to variations on the same themes. Isobowei of Olugbobiri uses the guns displayed in his shrine when he goes out to fight and wears a medicine gourd and native belts to protect himself from gunshot (fig. 3.21). The feathers that ornament his image shake to warn people when trouble approaches. His name, which may be translated as "Man from the Isoko/Urhobo area," identifies him as the slave of the shrine's medicine pot and endows him with certain personality traits, for the Ijo say that slaves, like the disabled, tend to be touchy and bear grudges. His wife's diminutive size belies her contentious nature, for her name, "What is in the mind of a small woman," reflects the Ijo belief that short people are strong-minded. Olugbobiri residents claim that veterans of the Biafran conflict came from far-off towns to thank Isobowei for protecting them in battle.

Members of his shrine in Ikebiri report that Edisibewei once lived in Benin but became lost after his townsmen tricked him into carrying a sacrificial canoe into the forest. He wandered about the Delta until reaching a section of the Ikebiri bush known as Dirimobou, where the presiding spirit overpowered and enslaved him. Dressed for battle (fig. 3.20), he supports a small war canoe manned by two figures: one, called "Black magic will not hurt me," loads a gun; the other, "Diviner from Ufe," not only fires it but uses it to communicate with Edisibewei, who is deaf, by drumming on the canoe. The names of the figures who flank him—"Not marrying a woman in vain" (emphasizing his wife's readiness to support him) and "Mashing something to cause it to spoil" (indicating that his companion can render people soft and weak like rotten fish simply by touching them)— reinforce the image of a forceful spirit prepared to battle anyone who stands in his way. Some say Edisibewei went off to fight in the Biafran war and never came back, but people working in Dirimobou still run the other way whenever they hear a pounding noise or a kingfisher, for both might announce his return.

Although the imposing figure Whitehouse collected during the "Bibi Cala" expedition probably functioned in a similar setting, a much wider range of possibilities may exist, for the Ijo tend to be secretive about powerful shrines. A shrine associated with Iyo underlines how problematic attempts at reconstruction can be. His stature as a warrior might lead us to expect a monumental image like Isobowei's—a spiritual doppelganger of sorts—but the shrine (fig. 3.19) consists of two diminutive figures, a miniature canoe, and assorted utensils, one of which represents a medicine pot Iyo used for human sacrifices. The scale of the carvings—said to conform to the originals— suggests they may be personal spirit companions maintained after Iyo's death because of his exceptional power. The priestess, a great-granddaughter of Iyo's, identifies them as water spirits, both called Nezeri, and presents offerings to

3.18   *Odewei, a bush spirit associated with success in warfare and hunting. He is shown with his wife, who carries a child on her back, and a pangolin, which guides him. Photograph by Martha G. Anderson, Korokorosei, 1978.*

3.19   *Nezeri, a water spirit shrine originated by the great warrior, Iyo. Photograph by Martha G. Anderson, Ossiama, 1992.*

3.20   *Edisibewei, a bush spirit, accompanied by his supporters. Photograph by Martha G. Anderson, Ikebiri, 1978.*

3.21   *Isobowei, a bush spirit accompanied by his wife and equipped with weapons. Photograph by Martha G. Anderson, Olugbobiri, 1978.*

3.18

3.19

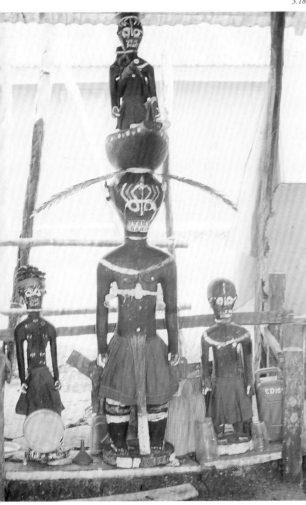

3.20

3.21

3.22   Bou seimo, *a rite held to spoil the power of the bush spirits. Photograph by Martha G. Anderson, Korokorosei, 1979.*

them at the waterside (*bini kamain aiye*) during the shrine's annual renewal.[8] She says the husband goes to war while his wife waits at home, but songs sung for the shrine do not include war songs.

A Diviner

Acting on instructions from the spirit world, Ijo diviners sometimes advise people to acquire carvings and serve shrines, but often they prescribe herbal remedies and rituals instead. Not surprisingly, references to warfare and violence abound in rites for bush spirits. Those performed to compensate the bush after someone has killed a spirit (*bou gbee*), those designed to spoil the power of bush spirits when they retaliate against someone for various transgressions (*bou seimo*; fig. 3.22), or those aimed at "unlocking" a womb when spirits indicate their need for appeasement by delaying delivery (*okoko pogholo*): all feature herbal medicines and other materials from the forest and involve negotiating with spirits to end hostilities, beating them back, or spoiling their power.

Although most of the diviners who conduct these rites are women, the pattern of confrontation and mediation they employ often parallels the behavior of Ijo men in warfare. In 1978 a diviner claimed that an expedition she led into the forest to restore a man's eyesight was "just like going to war," because she had to confront hostile bush spirits, who were retaliating against her client for killing two spirits living in trees he felled near a sacred lake. She also compared herself to a referee in a wrestling match, for she had to mediate between antagonists. She wore an amulet empowered by a prominent water spirit to protect against attacks by angry spirits (fig. 3.23), and other water-spirit followers made necklaces from leaves to remind the bush of its covenant with the water. Following the same conventions that govern warfare, they replaced the trees with saplings.

Rituals for water spirits, who contrast markedly with bush spirits in both appearance and behavior, seldom call for such aggressive measures. They can materialize as anything from fish to sewing machines to beautiful, fair-skinned mermaids. Although they can be troublesome, many are thought

3.23   *A diviner wearing an amulet to protect her from angry bush spirits while performing a rite (*bou gbee*) to compensate them. Photograph by Martha G. Anderson, Korokorosei, 1979.*

3.24 Janiform hermaphroditic bush spirit. Ijo. Wood. H: 113 cm. FMCH X81.1567; Gift of William Lloyd David and the Rogers Family Foundation. This remarkable janiform figure wears a type of medicine gourd that usually connotes masculine aggression around its neck and on its upper arms. It could simply represent a spirit as a hermaphrodite but recalls as well the powerful female diviners who stand poised between two worlds, ready to wage war against hostile spirits.

to bestow children and prosperity; nevertheless, the Ijo sometimes invoke powerful enshrined water spirits to punish criminals by slaying members of their families and occasionally credit evil spirits living inside the rivers with killing people on their own initiative.

Residents of Ondewari in Olodiama clan tell a remarkable story about a diviner named Queen, who visited the area in the 1960s to battle evil spirits from both realms. Like most diviners, Queen derived her ability to redress problems with the spirit world from a personal relationship with a powerful water spirit. She claimed that when she was a young girl, spirits pulled her into the water while she was bathing and kept her there for seven days; legends involving underwater sojourns are common throughout the Delta, and many Ijo diviners report having made similar journeys as children. In 1992, an Ondewari man related Queen's story as she had told it:

> I realized that I was in another world. Ekine, a great water god of Seibiri [now called Opuama, in Bumo clan], sent his child to bring me to him. He appeared in the form of a python and took me to a house of bells…. There, the water spirit, who was now in human form, spoke to me, saying, "You are a virgin. I saw you and took you. I want you to work in my name to destroy any evil god, whether inside the water or on land. When anyone needs your help, go and do the work in my name." He gave me nine herbs, nine powers from among his powers. Accordingly, I returned to the world to work with these nine powers [nine being a multiple of three and hence auspicious]. [Levi Yeiyei, personal communication, Ondewari, 1992]

Queen grew up to become a famous diviner. Tales of her phenomenal ability to survive underwater spread throughout the Central Delta; rumor holds that Urhobo, Yoruba, and even Hausa people came to consult her and take her to their towns to work for them. Ondewari residents say that Queen was already an old woman in 1963, when a delegation traveled to her home at Anyama in Tarakiri clan to consult her about an alarming number of premature deaths.[9] After Queen assured them that she would kill the evil spirits responsible with a small knife Ekine had given her, they agreed to pay her eight hundred *naira*, a sum equivalent to well over a thousand dollars at the time and one that demonstrates substantial faith in a diviner's ability in a part of the world where people earn very little money.

Attributing inspiration to nature spirits allows Ijo diviners a great deal of latitude in organizing rituals. Queen's unusually ambitious program incorporated new ideas and combined familiar ones in new ways. She drew on purification rites, fishing festivals for sacred lakes, and a variety of ceremonies performed to address problems with nature spirits; she even borrowed the notion of an agreement that individuals seal with the creator before birth and elaborated it into a contract governing the entire community, for one of the songs she taught people to sing begs the creator to recall the words "Ondewari spoke in the other world" (*zibe bari*) and to replace the bad destiny it chose with a more favorable one.

At nighttime, Queen instructed adult women to gather naked with their fishing baskets. They began fishing upriver and moved downstream, catching all types of fish—sea fish, bush fish, and river fish—in abundance. When they reached the other end of town, Queen told them to dance up to the ancestors' arena, carrying their catch and singing songs. They piled the fish in a huge heap, then cooked and ate them out-of-doors. Three days later, at daybreak, Queen told the men to dress in white—the color Ijo associate with purity, wealth, and the spirit world in general, as well as the shade water spirits favor—and ordered them to bring seven canoes equipped with drums. She took her place in the center with three canoes at each side, then boasted: "When going toward Ossiama, there's a spirit in the water at a place called Burukana. That god is Ibezige. He's the greatest god in the entire area. I'll go down into the water to kill that god. I'll stamp him to death." According to area residents, this spirit would kill a toothless infant if it merely touched the water; it was so powerful that small babies and uncircumcised boys would die of diarrhea even if currents only carried their bodily wastes to that area.

The canoes traveled to the boundary with Ossiama, their drums beating. Queen told the men to paddle as if they were going to war. She kept cutting the water with Ekine's knife in her right hand and spraying it into the air with a small broom he had given her in her left. As she became possessed, the river became rough. When the canoes reached Burukana, Queen announced that she would go down into the water to fight the spirit as she had done in her youth, but people begged her not to because of her age, so she invoked him instead, then waited until he came near the surface of the water and stabbed him to death. He emerged in the form of a giant stingray, four fathoms (eight yards) wide.

At a place called Okyapou, Queen battled another spirit blamed for killing newborn babies and their mothers. When she stabbed him, he turned into a shine nose, or croaker—"a great, mighty fish"—and floated on the water. The party moved on to a sacred bush called Ibozu Kumo, where Queen declared, "There's an evil spirit here as well [but] it's on land, not in the water." When she stabbed this one, it turned into a monkey and ran three miles into the forest before it died. She revealed that evil spirits lived there, too, and slaughtered them with her knife. Now, no forbidden place remained up to the boundary with Oporoma.

The men returned to their canoes. Whenever they reached a place where she detected a wicked spirit, Queen cut the water with her knife until blood poured out, showing it had died. Some spirits turned to fish, some to pieces of wood. They were floating all over the river. Finally, Queen ended the expedition at an island that separates the gods of Ondewari from those of Olugbobiri.

On returning to Ondewari, Queen became possessed and began moving up and down the streets. There was turbulence everywhere. When people reported hearing footsteps roaming about, Queen informed them that evil spirits filled the entire area; she ordered the men to clear grass and trees behind the town and kill all domestic animals, as well as a duiker, an iguana, a pangolin, and other wild animals that turned up inside people's houses. Queen told people not to eat the wild animals, though they could eat domestic ones they had owned before she started her job. Later, she warned that bringing sheep or eagles inside the town would spoil everything she had done.

After a few days, most of the trees near the waterside withered off, indicating they were evil spirits. Heaps of fish sat in the arena, and dead fish filled the river. People even saw sharks and stingrays floating there, along with Niger perch and many other types of fish. Queen warned residents of nearby towns not to eat them, but others passing by tried to take them. The gills might be flapping, but the flesh would be rotten. This continued for seven days.

Queen had not finished her work, as she learned when an evil spirit pulled her into the water one day as she was urinating from a canoe. People had to struggle to drag her back inside. She revealed that a spirit who had survived her campaign by traveling to a far-off town had returned home to discover his family and friends dead. No evil spirit remained to explain what had happened, so he went to the boundary between Olugbobiri and Olugboboro to consult a spirit named Kighebuboghe, who reported: "I learned a certain woman killed all the gods and wanted to go see for myself. When I reached the boundary, she was still there, so I couldn't go in, but I heard the news." The other god swore, "I'm going to kill her," but Queen determined to kill him instead. The canoes paddled back to the spot where he had tried to drown her. When Queen stabbed him, he turned into a great shine nose and floated on the water. That was the last god she killed (fig. 3.25).

Having cleansed the town, Queen told people to bring newborn babies to the river and bathe them there. She announced that she must stay in Ondewari for seven years and pledged that if any child died during this period, she was not a good native doctor. During the time she spent there, no child died in either the town itself or its two offshoots. After seven years

3.25 A map of sacred places in the area around Korokorosei, which includes some of the area Queen cleansed of evil spirits. Drawn by Israel Kigibie.

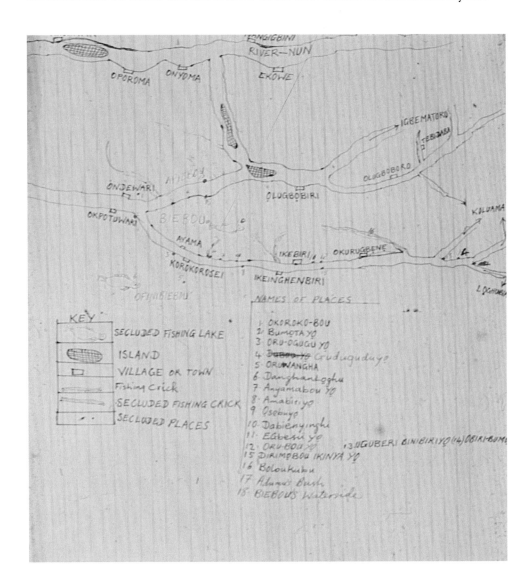

had passed, people took a newborn to wash her at a spot in the river where bathing small infants was formerly forbidden. The child grew up, married, and bore three children. None died.

Queen also set up three medicine pots inside the town. Both she and the man to whom she revealed the recipes have died, so the town can no longer perform the annual renewal festival properly, and evil spirits could return. About ten years after she left, residents hired a diviner from Apoi clan to cleanse the town because people had drowned while diving for water snails; nevertheless, they claim that no forbidden places remain in the river, and report that Ondewari has continued to progress.

Modern-Day Warriors and Pirates

Though hardly typical, Iyo, Bibikeala, and Queen typify different aspects of the same ethos. Queen may well be the most exceptional of this group—in addition to being the most powerful—for even elderly residents of Olodiama clan cannot recall hearing of another diviner as intrepid as she was. Neither of the precedents cited for her campaign—a covenant formed by neighboring Okpotuwari to stop a bush spirit from clubbing children to death and a janiform figure erected near a section of the Ondewari forest to keep bush spirits from disfiguring them—comes close to the scale of her seven-year stint in Ondewari.[10]

On hearing tales of Queen's exploits, one Ijo listener regretfully observed, "There is no one like her again"; but others have continued to battle evil spirits, disease, and witchcraft, for beliefs about witches (*founyou*) have become increasingly prominent since being introduced to the area around 1950 (P. Leis 1962, 55; N. Leis 1964, 202). A man called to Korokorosei from the saltwater region after an alarming number of untimely deaths in the early 1980s, advised townspeople to cut down certain fruit trees because evil spirits had gotten into them. A female diviner from another clan visited the town in 1991 to open it up to development, particularly oil production, by suppressing witches and evil spirits blamed for blocking its progress. Within a six-week period of that year, a Korokorosei diviner performed three *seimo* to deal with problems attributed to bush spirits. Queen's successors also include two Christian prophets, who periodically attempt to subdue evil spirits. One (fig. 3.26) also conducts "crusades" at area villages, where he not only heals the sick but also casts out demons and elicits witchcraft confessions.

Iyo and Bibikeala have also spawned numerous counterparts. The captain of a coastal fishing vessel recently confided that attacks by speedboats have become so rampant around the Benin, Escravos, and Calabar Rivers that "experienced sailors now avoid those seaways like the fabled Bermuda triangle" (Aimienmwona 1997, n. p.). Though the Ibibio and other coastal groups participate in these raids, seven suspected "sea pirates" apprehended near an Ijo village on the Delta's western fringe in 1997 carrying "two bags of assorted charms," as well as weapons, were probably Ijo (Ukadike 1997, n. p.). Bands of Ijo smugglers have also trafficked along the coast for decades, using their knowledge of the Delta's myriad waterways to carry "illicit gin" and illegally imported goods to markets on the mainland. (At least one Central Delta woman has engaged in this dangerous line of work, according to N. Leis 1964, 114.)

3.26 A prophet in the Church of Zion. He conducts crusades at villages throughout the region. Photograph by Martha G. Anderson, Ikebiri, 1992.

3.27 *Jackson Waribugo's sculpture of Isaac Adaka Boro in Boro Park, Port Harcourt, Nigeria. Photograph by W. Ofongo, 1998.*

3.28 *A titleholder demonstrating the* peri *play as performed at Ossiama. The man inherited his title from a relative. Photograph by Martha G. Anderson, Ossiama, 1992.*

Others have found a more respectable arena for their talents in military service. Many of the Ijo soldiers who fought in the Biafran War invoked spirits and employed war medicines, but Isaac Boro provides the best example of this ethos. Although he had previously been dismissed from the police force for misconduct, Boro went on to become a student activist and revolutionary leader. While fighting for the creation of an independent Niger Delta Peoples Republic during the "Twelve Day Revolution" of 1966, he engaged in piracy and employed military tactics gleaned from his elders (Boro 1982, 96–123). Captured, condemned to death, then pardoned by General Gowon, the Nigerian head of state, Boro fought for the federal side in the Biafran War, earning the rank of major before dying in battle in 1968. A statue commemorating this native son of Kaiama—a town in Bibikeala's clan—now stands in Port Harcourt, the heroic image of a modern-day warrior (fig. 3.27).[11]

Conclusion

Fifty years ago, Owonaro described his people as "faithful, honest and brave," but noted that the same "recalcitrant habit," which made them "rather refractory and sometimes difficult to control in gatherings," also confounded attempts at unity (1949, 71). An anthropologist who visited the Central Delta in the late 1950s observed signs of progress in one village, where a few "strong-willed men ready to suffer countless insults" had finally managed to accomplish several communal projects (N. Leis 1964, 217). Nevertheless, long after the arena for settling conflicts had shifted to law courts, another found that Ijo parents continued to instill the principle of retaliation and encourage physical bravado by scolding their children for failing to fight when justifiably provoked to do so (P. Leis 1962, 101–2, 121).

Most Ijo have turned to churches for power and protection, but many communities recall their warlike past by mounting ceremonial war canoes to honor clan war gods and visiting heads of state. Some still dispatch war parties to confront individuals held responsible for accidental deaths and launch sacrificial war canoe effigies to combat epidemic disease. Although a handful of titleholders continue to conjure up visions of men like Iyo and Bibikeala by performing the *peri* play (fig. 3.28), the prospect of intervillage warfare now seems remote. Still, a few would-be warriors seem determined to revive the bad old days. Press reports estimate that more than a hundred people died in the violence that rocked the Warri area in 1997 following a controversial decision to move governmental headquarters from an Ijo community to an Itsekiri one. The following year, a band of Ijo "warriors" attacked a boatload of Urhobo mourners accompanying a corpse to a funeral, marched thirty captives to a shrine, then reportedly sacrificed them "before the image of a local goddess" (AFP news release, March 19, 1998).

In reporting this incident as the "March Massacre," Reuters News Agency described the Delta as "an impoverished region riven by community rivalry and ethnic hatred which boils over in sporadic clashes" (1998), but ethnic violence of this scale has largely been confined to the Warri region. A growing number of Delta residents now realize that they must join forces with their neighbors if they wish to improve their lot. Having won the campaign for greater self-determination with the creation of several Delta states, they now face a more difficult battle. Exploitation of the region's vast reserves of oil has not only failed to bring its residents prosperity, but caused environmental damage that threatens to upset their already precarious way of life.

This situation has inspired a new generation of warriors, who combine timeworn traditions with modern-day tactics. In September 1998, chalk-painted, but media-savvy youths from Akassa clan consulted their newly revived war god, Egbesu, before hijacking two Agip workboats to protest oil spills and high unemployment and to demand a greater share in the wealth oil from their region has generated (Reuters 1998). One boasted to a reporter, "I'm not afraid [of government soldiers]. If they use a gun to shoot me, I am not afraid of them. What I believe is that a gunshot will not kill me" (Andersson 1998).

A year later, in early November 1999, the killing of twelve police officers by a band of armed youths had tragic consequences for the town of Odi, where the murders occurred. Unlike the Egbesu Boys, the perpetrators had no clear political agenda. Although townspeople branded them hooligans, federal troops retaliated against Odi by demolishing all but a church, bank, and clinic, and killing as many as two thousand, mostly unarmed, residents. Graffiti left behind by the soldiers suggests that they saw themselves as staging a punitive expedition. Some of the soldiers expressed their desire to punish all Ijo people for crimes committed by a gang of outlaws, while others took jabs at Egbesu:

We go kill all Ijaw people with our gun.
Learn a lesson. Visit Odi.
Na you get Oil? Foolish people.

Idiot, why Egbesu no save una!
Where is the Egbesu power?
Shame on your juju (Egbesu).
Silence. No noise. Egbesu is dead.
Say No to Egbesu. Yes to soldier.
Who get power pass, soldier or Egbesu?
Wetin happen here? Na Egbesu battle. Who win?
Na we— Nigeria Soldiers.[12]

3.29   *War canoe motif on T-shirt designed for the Kolokuma Egbesu Yam Eating Festival. Photograph by Martha G. Anderson, Olobiri, 1978.*

Interleaf D
Forms of *Ivri*

Philip M. Peek

The *ivri* is one of the best known of Delta art forms to the extent that it appears in the form of an Ijo *ifiri* on the back of the thousand CFA banknote, which is used in the Francophone countries of West Africa (figs. D.1, D.2). *Ivri* were also among the earliest sculptures from Southern Nigeria to appear in several important collections, generating much vivid art historical speculation. Leon Underwood's query as to whether an *ivri* represented "ferocious speed or swift ferocity" (1947, 43) still reverberates. Conjecture aside, the *ivri* (or *iphri* according to some Urhobo orthographic systems) and its association with violence affects the lives of Delta peoples even today. John Agberia (1998) reports that *ivri* images are still prominent and have been employed in contemporary urban ethnic violence in Warri and elsewhere. This is hardly surprising given that the warrior ethos of Delta peoples has formed the subject of novels—among them Elechi Amadi's *The Great Ponds* (1969)—as well as receiving attention in recent news reports detailing the kidnapping of Shell Oil workers (see also chapter 3 of this volume).

The "*ivri* complex" (image types, behavioral correspondences, and so on) is found throughout much of Southern Nigeria. G. I. Jones reports broad use of these images with the Western Igbo utilizing the "Ivhri cult and its figures with their Edo and Ijo neighbors" (1989a, 47). While some have linked it directly to the Igbo *ikenga* (fig. D.3) and the Edo *ikegobo* as a "cult of the hand" (fig. D.5; see Vogel 1974), among the Isoko, Urhobo, and Western Ijo, the *ivri* assumes a different nature. First of all, for the Isoko other images and concepts replace the elements represented by the Igbo *ikenga*, such as the *obo* (right hand) and *oma* (spirit double), while the Ijo also distinguish between *ifiri* (by most accounts derived from the Isoko *ivri*) and *bra kon,* or *amabra*, which stands for the right hand. For that matter, the Igbo themselves have the *okpossi* (representing one's personal *chi*, or "spirit"; fig. D.4) and *ofo*

D.1 Ifiri. Western Ijo. Wood. H: 64.8 cm. The Metropolitan Museum of Art, The Michael C. Rockefeller Memorial Collection, Purchase, Matthew T. Mellon Foundation Gift, 1960. (1978.412.404). Photograph by Schecter Lee. Photograph © 1986 The Metropolitan Museum of Art.

D.2 A 1000 CFA banknote, used in Francophone West Africa, showing an image of an Ijo ifiri *resembling that in figure D.1.*

D.3. Ikenga. *Igbo, Awka region. Wood and pigment. H: 74.3 cm. FMCH X65.3807; Gift of the Wellcome Trust.*

D.4 Okpossi-*related figure. Igbo. wood. H: 74.3 cm. FMCH X65.9035; Gift of the Wellcome Trust.*

D.5 Ikegobo. *Edo (Benin). Wood. H: 22.2 cm. FMCH X68.458.*

D.6 Oma *figures. Isoko. Wood and cloth. H: 26–27.3 cm. FMCH X67.611,614,615; Gift of the Wellcome Trust.*

D.9 Ivri. *Isoko. Wood. H: 95.3 cm. FMCH X81.1563; Gift of William Lloyd Davis and the Rogers Family Foundation.*

D.7 *Igbo* ikenga, *Isoko* obo *(for a woman), and Isoko* ivri. *Photograph by Philip M. Peek, 1970s.*

D.8 *Isoko* ivri *and Igbo* ikenga. *Photograph by Philip M. Peek, 1970s.*

D.10 *Emede clan* ivri *and elders. Photograph by Philip M. Peek, 1965.*

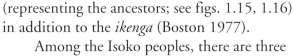

(representing the ancestors; see figs. 1.15, 1.16) in addition to the *ikenga* (Boston 1977).

Among the Isoko peoples, there are three types of personal shrine images: *oma* (fig. D.6), which represents the "spirit double" that resides in the other world; *obo* (fig. D.7), which symbolizes the right hand and personal endeavor; and *ivri* (figs. D.7–D.9), which stands for personal determination and "adamance" (Peek 1981; 1986). The various peoples of Southern Nigeria have slightly different notions of the components of individual personality, but all agree that these various aspects can be affected through ritual and personal effort. Among the Isoko, for example, someone exhibiting excessive stubbornness or anti-social behavior must serve his or her personal *ivri* to lessen these traits. On the other hand, larger *ivri,* which are served by the Igbu (warrior society) and *iletu* (war leaders) of the community, function

D.11 Ivri. *Urhobo. Wood. H: 59.7 cm. FMCH X80.693; Anonymous Gift.*

D.12 Ivri. *Urhobo or Isoko. Wood. H: 54.6 cm. FMCH X81.1561; Gift of William Lloyd Davis and the Rogers Family Foundation.*

to increase and maintain their owners' aggressive tendencies (fig. D.10).

Perkins Foss reports a slightly different perspective regarding the meaning and function of the *ivri* (or *iphri*) among the Urhobo (figs. D.9, D.12). Historically, these images were related to the slave trade, an observation first recorded by Reverend John W. Hubbard in the 1930s. Documented Urhobo *ivri* share a feature not found among Isoko examples: a sort of superstructure of wooden slats with loose raffia fronds attached to the backs of the images (fig. D.13). Informants called these fronds "wings." Foss has suggested that this feature may be a link to Ijo ancestral screens (Foss 1975, 143, pls. 62–67).

As a carving, the *ivri* is best known for its striking formal features. Most notable is the prominent fanged maw, apparently that of a quadruped (fig. D.14). Often there are projections ranging upward from the sides, and frequently the larger images support a central warrior figure, perhaps accompanied by attendants. Unfortunately, there is no consensus as to the meaning of any of these features. An animal seems to be the source of the imagery, but there is no agreement as to what type, and one finds arguments for leopards, hippos, and elephants. While the open mouth with prominent teeth may symbolize aggressive speech (Peek 1986), the emphasis on large incisors certainly reminds one of a leopard.

Scholars, including most recently Agberia (1998), have found their informants far more concerned with the function of *ivri* than the form; therefore, while there is little consensus as to what exactly the *ivri* represents, all associate it with aggression and protection from violence. Consistency of form is clearly of secondary import as demonstrated in the Isoko town of Ivrogbo where the community's *ivri* took the form of a woven basket.

The "*ivri* complex" seems to be an Isoko variant within a larger complex of dramatic images related to behavioral elements (see fig. A in the preface to this volume). While one can link one or two formal features, such as the prominent Isoko "tail," with the projection on an Edo *ikegobo* image (Bradbury 1961), or the weapons with those carried by the human elements of the *ikenga,* one must also

D.13 Urhobo ivri *with a backing screen. Photograph courtesy of Jean Borgatti.*

D.14 Ifiri. *Ijo. Wood. H: 94.3 cm. FMCH X87.1313; Gift of Elizabeth Lloyd Davis.*

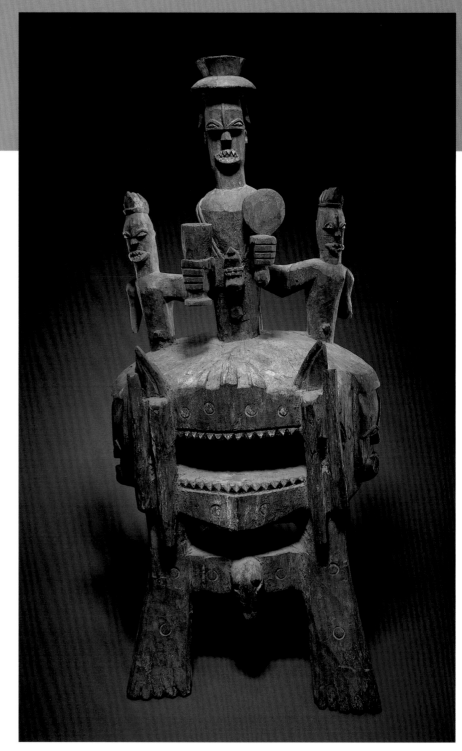

consider associated beliefs and practices. Thus, we might just as rightly question a link to the Edo practice of "Making the Father" (Baker 1954, facing p. 129) in which an image very like the *ivri* is carried on the head, as we have seen in the Isoko clan of Uzere (fig. D.15). *Ivri* that belonged to former *ivie* ("priest-kings"; sing. *ovie*) of the clan are memorialized by their display during celebrations of Eni, the major clan deity (figs. D.16, D.18).

In terms of the relationship of *ivri* traditions and Delta peoples, the Western Ijo acknowledge that they borrowed the *ivri* form from the Isoko, and while there have been several studies of Urhobo

images, we know nothing of apparently similar forms among Western Igbo peoples (Jones 1989a).

There is no question that the functions served by these images remain important. In the early 1970s, I photographed a rather unique *ivri* in the Urhobo town of Ughelli (fig. D.17) and was told that it was for a woman "because women are like men now!" Styles change as evidenced by the wondrous chartreuse *ivri* from Uzere (fig. D.19). *Ivri* continue to be carved and served because, as with people everywhere it seems, images (as well as weapons) of aggression are retained even in times of peace, if only to act as deterrents.

D.15 The ivri *of the* ovie *of the Uzere is carried around the town to cleanse the community during the annual ceremonies for Eni, the senior clan deity. Photograph by Philip M. Peek, Uzere, 1965.*

D.16 Pairs of ivri *that belonged to a former* ovie *displayed in front of the family compound. Photograph by Philip M. Peek, Uzere, 1965.*

D.17 *On the left, a Urhobo* ivri *for a woman; on the right, a Urhobo* oma *for a man. Photograph by Philip M. Peek, Ughelli, 1965.*

D.18 Ovie *of Uzere with the* ivri *of Eni, the senior clan deity, and regalia. Photograph by Philip M. Peek, 1971.*

D.19 *"Transitional"* ivri *from Uzere clan. Photograph by Philip M. Peek, 1965. This* ivri *is presently in the collection of the Phoebe Hearst Museum of Anthropology, University of California, Berkeley.*

Interleaf E
The Urhobo

Martha G. Anderson

E.1   Male shrine figure. Urhobo. Wood and pigment. H: 130.8 cm. FMCH X76.1856; Gift of Mrs. W. Thomas Davis, in memory of W. Thomas Davis. Accoutrements such as beads worn low on the shoulders, a top hat, and thick ivory cuffs emphasize this spirit's position as a titled leader, rather than suggesting military power and aggression. In contrast, the medicine gourd worn prominently on the chest demonstrates the figure's possession of powerful, herbal medicines that guarantee his invincibility in battle.

E.2   Female shrine figure. Urhobo. Wood and pigment. H: 125 cm. FMCH X91.338; Gift of Helen and Dr. Robert Kuhn. Females may appear as secondary figures in male-centered shrines focusing on military prowess or as primary figures in female-centered shrines focusing on procreation. A nursing mother often represents the "wife" of a male spirit. The crownlike headgear worn by this figure gives her a regal appearance, and traces of red pigment may allude to her status as a new mother.

The Urhobo people are estimated to number nearly half a million. They speak an Edo language similar to that of the neighboring Isoko and have associations with the Bini, Igbo, and Ijo as well. Their rich artistic traditions reveal the influence of all of these groups while demonstrating a remarkable degree of consistency in form, style, and meaning. The Urhobo share the fascination of other Delta peoples with the watery environment of the region, and they stage water spirit festivals, including those that pay tribute to Ohworu (or Oworu, see interleaf I).

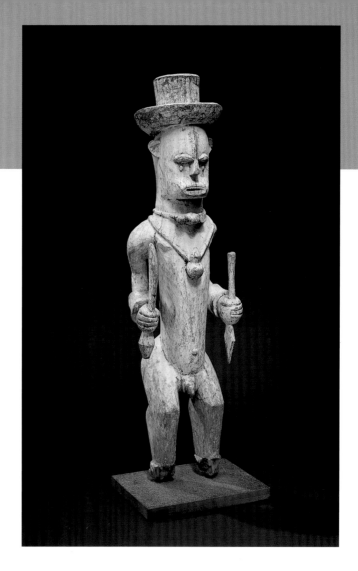

In sculpting symbols of aggression known as *ivri* (or *iphri;* see interleaf D), as well as monumental images of warlike beings (Foss 1975; 1976), they also embody the region's warrior ethos. Like the neighboring Ijo and Isoko, the Urhobo enshrine hoards of sacred objects that include Lower Niger bronzes (see chapter 1 of this volume).

The Urhobo honor both ancestors and nature spirits with their figurative sculptures. Figures dedicated to specific ancestors who played a prominent role in founding a lineage, village, or clan (*eshe*) preside over communal meeting houses. Standing at the center of the hall, aligned with its physical and spiritual axis, an *eshe* carving provides an image of leadership and a moral compass for those who gather to deliberate affairs affecting the larger community. People who engage in dangerous occupations, such as warfare and hunting, may present the *eshe* with offerings in the process of seeking its protection. Conversely, the ancestors, who look out for and guard against antisocial activity, inflict illnesses on those who practice sorcery or witchcraft. Wrongdoers must confess their misdeeds before the figure of their esteemed ancestor if they wish to recover.

Eshe images take a variety of forms, all of them massive. Most shrines focus attention on an isolated carving, emphasizing the power of an individual clan leader, sometimes joined by his immediate ancestors. Like Ijo bush spirit images, many *eshe* carvings are janiform, giving them an air of supernatural authority and heightened visual command of their surroundings. Elaborately carved columns or pillars can incorporate a variety of human and animal images (see preface, fig. G.), alluding to the collective leadership that prevails at the lineage level, as well as conveying concepts associated with various motifs. In some cases, groups of sturdy images suggest ancestral power proportional to their number.

E.3   Male shrine figure. Urhobo. Wood and pigment. H: 101.6 cm. Private Collection. Urhobo style emphasizes broad shoulders and a thick chest; these traits are often accentuated by a necklace riding around the shoulders. Also typical are a broad forehead with prognathous jaw, an elliptical mouth placed rather low on the face, and oval eyes.

E.4   Female shrine figure. Urhobo. Wood and pigment. H: 138 cm. Private Collection. This figure is probably not a central shrine image or a "wife" because she lacks a child and has only modest power and prestige emblems. Kaolin suggests purity and otherworldliness. Like her warlike male counterparts, however, this figure conveys an impression of energy.

128

Instead of focusing on an honored individual ancestor, groups of figures depicting nature spirits (*edjo*) form dramatic displays in shrines. The Urhobo associate *edjo* with magical powers manifested in the environment and credit them with empowering semi-mythic, village-founding warriors to perform heroic feats. Many *edjo* inhabit particular creeks or sections of the forest, but others are thought to float about in the air. Villages can honor several *edjo*, but they reserve full artistic treatment—including extensive shrine ensembles and lavish festivals—for the *edjo* who is acknowledged as "the spirit of the town," whose actions concern the entire community. Diviners may advise clients to serve an *edjo* who is inflicting them with maladies or misfortunes in order to satisfy his demands for attention.

E.5 Male shrine figure. Urhobo. Wood and pigment. H: 152.4 cm. Collection of Dr. Richard and Jan Baum. Urhobo figures have multiple facial keloids. This figure, who probably attended a male "warrior," strikes a military pose.

E.6 Maternity figure. Urhobo. Wood and pigment. H: 121 cm. Private Collection. This female figure cradles a child, perhaps attesting to the ability of a central male spirit to bear children. Her elaborate headgear and ornaments indicate prestige.

E.7   Male shrine figure. Urhobo. Wood and Pigment. H: 62.2 cm. Collection of Toby and Barry Hecht. This warrior wearing a top hat recalls similar Ijo images of bush spirits, but his features conform to Urhobo style.

E.8   Male shrine figure. Urhobo. Wood and pigment. H: 122 cm. FMCH X64.999; Museum Purchase. This eye-catching figure depicts a seated male wearing an unusually elaborate crown. His red—presumably coral—accessories present a striking contrast with his body and stool, which are painted a pale green. Peoples throughout the region associate coral with water and wealth, and the Urhobo further associate it with the court of Benin. Reportedly found near Benin City, this figure dates from about 1879.

Not all *edjo* have figurative images. Some assume the form of natural materials, such as roots or sticks, or metal objects, which may range from Lower Niger Bronzes to scraps found while fishing or farming—all of which are believed to have supernatural origins. A few *edjo* appear as mud sculptures (see interleaf G), but their most spectacular manifestation comes in the form of wooden carvings. Shrines arrange tableaux containing as many as a dozen figures in a way that is calculated to insure that they command the visual attention of all who enter. Ensembles dedicated to male *edjo* typically depict the central spirit as a warrior surrounded by a legion of his brave followers or family members. Much like Ijo bush spirit images, males indicate their readiness to fight by displaying weapons and medicines. Songs and praise names allude to their military prowess. Female *edjo* tend to be more closely associated with water and concerned with procreation, and the figures that surround them allude to their fertility. Although *eshe* and *edjo* represent two different facets of Urhobo belief, both sculptural forms reinforce notions of masculine power and aggression—a recurrent theme in virtually all Delta cultures.

Part 2 : Environment and Cultural Confluence

Chapter 4
From River Horses to Dancing Sharks: Canoes and Fish in Ijo Art and Ritual

MARTHA G. ANDERSON

Paddle, paddle
Oh! Paddle
The carp was paddling
A canoe underwater
But the paddle
Broke in his hand
Paddle, paddle
Oh! Paddle
—Song sung by Ijo women while paddling to and from their farms

The extreme wateriness of the Niger Delta begs questions about the relationship between environment and culture. Though natural surroundings do not predetermine worldviews, art forms, or other cultural phenomena, they clearly limit the choices people make regarding such fundamental matters as modes of production and transportation. To a greater or lesser extent, they also define how people experience the world. Moreover, "most peoples do ascribe a sometimes capricious agency to their environment," according to Croll and Parkin, whose study of ecocosmologies explores a paradox: people create contrasting categories such as "village" and "bush" to explain their environments, then look for ways to build bridges between them (1992, 3).

Numerous studies indicate that work plays a critical role in the construction of social identity and cultural values (See Wallman 1979; Pahl 1988). Canoeing may not be a mode of production, but the canoe—called the "river horse" because of the role it plays in riverain cultures—often

4.1 Water spirit headdress. Ijo. Wood, brass, and ceramic. L: 71.8 cm. Krannert Art Museum and Kinkead Pavilion, University of Illinois, Urbana-Champaign; Faletti Family Collection. Carved in the clean geometric style of the Central and Western Ijo, this composite mask mixes skull-like human features with aquatic references. The element behind the head evokes either a fish tail or the stern of a canoe. The brass inlays on the forehead and the porcelain eyes suggest the bright, reflective surface of the water and the supernatural powers of the spirits who reside within it. Miniature masklike faces, such as adorn this headdress, typically represent the children or followers of the spirit.

4.2 Canoe headdress. Urhobo. Wood, pigment, and fiber. L: 60 cm. FMCH X86.2504; Anonymous Gift. Numerous Delta masquerade headdresses suggest canoe forms or incorporate scaled-down canoes, such as this Urhobo example. The neighboring Itsekiri make a version so large that it requires two maskers to support it. Headdresses representing modern conveyances—bicycles, helicopters, and airplanes—have also become popular, and some Kalabari Ijo headdresses depict ocean liners.

4.3   Paddle. Itsekiri. Wood. L: 124.5 cm.
FMCH X63.8; Gift of Mr. and Mrs. Peter Furst.

4.4   Paddle. Ijo or Itsekiri. Wood. L: 165.1 cm.
FMCH X65.4509; Gift of the Wellcome Trust.

4.5   Paddle. Ijo or Itsekiri. Wood. L: 139.7 cm.
FMCH X65.4522; Gift of the Wellcome Trust.

Paddles such as these, which are often labeled "Benin
River," seem to have been produced by the Itsekiri.
Local carvers probably made them as souvenirs for the
traders and colonial officials who visited the region
during the late nineteenth and early twentieth
centuries. Openwork designs render most of them
nonfunctional, and none shows signs of use. Many
combine intricate geometric patterning with figurative
motifs, including reptiles, aquatic creatures, and
occasionally human figures (Kathy Curnow, personal
communication, 2001).

functions as a tool in facilitating production (fig. 4.2). Paddling a canoe constitutes a form of work, because it involves the expenditure of energy and fulfills several other criteria of a "folk work" concept (Wallman 1979, 4; Wadel 1979, 370). Notions of work and play, however, vary from culture to culture and need not be well defined or mutually exclusive. As in Wallman's example of jogging (1979, 3), both canoeing and fishing—another activity appropriate to a riverain environment—may be work *or* recreation, or simultaneously work *and* recreation, depending on the mental attitude of the fisher or paddler. To complicate matters further, the actions of play can denote combat and other forms of "not play" (Bateson 1972, 177–93), and those of art and ritual often mimic or "play on" work.

The Ijo (or Izon) living near the center of the Delta place a high value on physical labor, particularly on work done outside the village (N. Leis 1964, 34, 79–80, 120). Adults communicate the idea that work is good in itself by encouraging children to practice paddling canoes and fishing, just as they reward them for working on "play farms" (P. Leis 1962, 119, 125, 145, 171). Moreover, one of many Ijo canoe proverbs observes that, "When you are paddling toward good things, the way does not seem long" (*Ebi iye timiyo you alaghe*). This saying, which can refer to a variety of tasks, not only confirms that the Ijo regard canoeing as labor but also suggests that they perceive varying degrees of work, depending on the destinations or goals that they pursue (figs. 4.3–4.5).

In a cross-cultural analysis of work, Schwimmer uses the Orokaiva of New Guinea, who garden, as an example of the close identification that can occur between work and moral values, and between workers and the environment in which they labor (1979, 294–302). Although Ijo living in freshwater regions of the Delta farm and perform numerous other land-based tasks, they tend to identify more closely with the riverain environment, especially the dugout canoes that enable them to maneuver and the fish that provide a prized part of their diet. They do not have a canoe/fish mythology comparable to the garden mythology of the Orokaiva, nor do they consider canoeing or fishing to be "a religious act like a sacrament," but the many ways they transform both activities into art and ritual suggest that they closely identify with and define themselves through them. Thus canoes and fish prove to be particularly useful vehicles for exploring how the Ijo respond to their watery surroundings.

Canoeing

The canoe operates as a common denominator of Ijo village life. In regions of the Delta where roads are nonexistent and even footpaths limited to seasonal use, canoes still provide the primary, and sometimes the only, means of transportation and intervillage communication. Indeed, the Ijo often measure distance by the time it takes to paddle from one point to another. Canoes seem so fundamental to their riverain lifestyle that some assume the art of canoe making "came from heaven with them" (Alagoa 1970, 323). Nearly every traditional occupation practiced in the freshwater region—including fishing, farming, distilling gin, and trading—necessitates water travel. Canoes also serve other mundane functions that are harder to classify, satisfy social and recreational needs, and figure prominently in performances of various types. Canoe effigies even play a role in shrines and rituals, as will be discussed below.

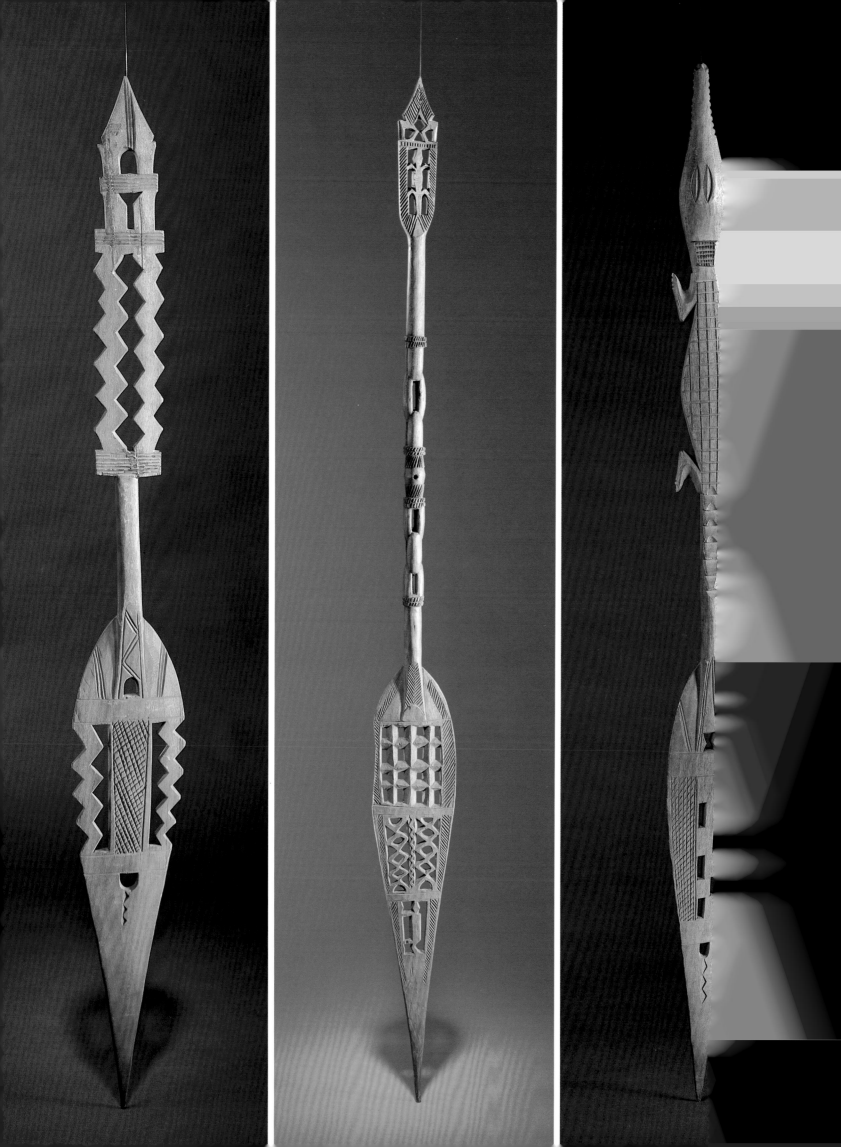

Learning to paddle seems to be largely a practical matter without religious or mythic significance, but the process plays a critical role in shaping the way people view the environment. As children, the Ijo begin to differentiate between two zones, the rivers and forests, and to associate different levels of danger with each. Though both present physical hazards, beliefs about their supernatural occupants clearly contribute to cultural attitudes expressed toward each realm. Parents teach children to fear not only the dangerous animals that live in the forests but the violent spirits who lurk about there, waiting to shoot people or club them to death. In contrast, despite concerns that adults express about water safety, youngsters learn to regard the rivers as a comparatively safe place to play. Although the Ijo occasionally blame evil spirits who reside in the rivers for killing people (see chapter 3 of this volume), stories about water spirits typically portray them as benevolent beings who live in fantastic underwater towns. Encounters with them, which often take place in canoes, tend to be magical, not fatal, affairs.

The Ijo first experience canoe travel at the age of about two or three months, when mothers begin taking their infants on almost daily trips to their riverside farms. As soon as they develop sufficient motor skills, children imitate adults by using sticks or small paddles—the only toys they own aside from dolls—to propel benches, planks, or verandah rails; they then hone their skills by pretending to help paddle real canoes. As all Ijo are expected to master the skills needed to maneuver a canoe, this type of play serves a practical purpose. Adults correct children who hold their paddles incorrectly or use them awkwardly, and praise those who match the rhythm and motions of adults. After youngsters learn to swim, at the age of about four or five,

4.6   Canoe headdress. Ogoni. Wood, iron, pigment, glass mirror, and incrustation. L: 69.5 cm. Indiana University Art Museum; Rita and John Grunwald Collection. Photograph by Michael Cavanagh and Kevin Montague © Indiana University Art Museum. This sculpture probably served as a masquerade headdress. The "house," which adds to the impression of domestic harmony, may have been included to shelter the canoe's occupants or cargo from the sun or rain on a long journey. The "wife" sits at the stern, like most Delta women, and acts as her husband's chauffeur.

parents allow them more freedom to practice on their own (P. Leis 1962, 99, 109). By the time they reach eight, they have usually developed sufficient dexterity to manage steering; one seven-year-old boy reported that he had already visited a neighboring town on his own, a trip that takes over an hour each way when traveling at average speed—about five kilometers an hour.

Given this emphasis on canoeing, one might expect the Ijo to have developed athletic contests based on ability, but the only competitions staged at present require contestants to paddle across a river while blindfolded, which results in comical meandering and does not test skills used in real life. Nevertheless, people who spend a good part of their lives in dugout canoes acquire excellent balancing skills, and boys and young men sometimes show off their agility by walking the length of a canoe along its edge.

As they grow older, children begin to use canoes for work as determined by gender: boys use them primarily to fish (fig. 4.7) and girls to assist their mothers in farming, fishing, and trading ventures. Although men continue to use canoes, their wives more frequently own them, because they bear primary responsibility for feeding their families. Women do the bulk of the fishing and need canoes on a regular basis to commute to their farms, which may be three or more hours away from the village. In fact, they spend so much time in canoes, they occasionally give birth in them; some families name babies who arrive in this fashion Arukubu, "Inside-bottom of canoe," or Arukeghezi, "Born in a canoe," to recall their origins. In addition, women typically serve as chauffeurs. If a husband and wife travel together, the man may offer to help paddle, but his wife typically takes the stern position and does at least the bulk of the work (fig. 4.6).

Women generally acquire their first canoe soon after they marry; others follow as needed at intervals of about seven years, depending on the type of wood used and the care taken in maintenance. Some men specialize in carving canoes, but a husband who lacks money to buy one for his wife may carve it himself, if sufficiently motivated and physically equipped to accomplish the arduous task (fig. 4.8). Demand nearly outstrips supply, for carvers often claim to sell canoes faster than they can produce them; however, most mix canoe carving with carpentry or other types of labor, because the work is so physically demanding.[1] A canoe of average size sold for about forty dollars in 1991, a substantial sum for people living in this region. Canoe thefts do occur. Remarkably, given the simplicity of the form, the Ijo can distinguish between canoes that look nearly identical to outsiders. Some even recall instances in which people visiting towns in other clans have spotted canoes stolen from friends back home.

A few men specialize in producing paddles, but traders also import them from other parts of the Delta. The decoratively carved paddles women once used can no longer be found in the Central Delta, and most now buy the simpler blank forms stocked by local tradesmen and take them to paddle painters for decoration. They generally choose to have their first names written on one side and their married names on the other, so paddle decoration becomes a statement about social identity as well as a means of marking personal property. Men use either the same type of paddle or a broader one, which requires more physical strength.

4.7　Boys fishing from canoes. Photograph by Martha G. Anderson Korokorosei, 1991.

4.8　Firing a dugout canoe so it can be bent into shape. Photograph by Martha G. Anderson, Korokorosei, 1991.

Canoes from Work and Play to Art and Ritual

The Ijo find innumerable uses for canoes. Besides transporting people, farm produce, fish, building materials, fuel, trade goods, corpses, unfinished canoes, and, until recently, the mail, they can serve as recreational vehicles. The Ijo even have an equivalent of a drive-in theater, for they sometimes watch masquerades from canoes (fig. 4.9). When moored at the waterside, canoes provide convenient places to play, eat, launder clothes, bathe, and eliminate wastes. A spirit medium drawn to the river when possessed by water spirits collapsed in one during a performance staged at a town in Apoi clan in 1991. On land, canoes can serve as bathtubs for invalids and as containers for separating palm oil.

Thrifty Ijo reuse worn-out canoes by turning them into everything from sacrificial vessels to duck houses. In former times, residents of at least one clan loaded the bodies of women who had died in childbirth into old canoes, then took them into the river and capsized them (Amangala 1939, 12). Taboos enforced by Owei, a war medicine shrine in Ondewari, suggest other, mostly outmoded forms of recycling: Owei forbids any Ondewari man to use fragments of a broken canoe as plates, firewood, or gutters designed to collect rainwater from roofs. According to his caretaker, he even kills people who eat food from anything used to bail canoes. On the other hand, the Nembe, who believe a particular type of wood brings luck to traders, patch new canoes with bits broken from damaged ones in hopes of transferring the older vessels' good fortune. Their inland neighbors, who provide them with canoes, may well share their beliefs about the magical and medicinal properties of various types of wood used to make them (Alagoa 1995, 126–31).

4.9 People watching a masquerade (Ungozu) from canoes on the river to avoid being injured by the masks. Photograph by Martha G. Anderson, Olugbobiri, 1992.

Canoes also perform a variety of esoteric functions. Even those ordinarily employed in domestic duties can become vehicles for communicating with the spirit world. Diviners occasionally work by interpreting the movements of their canoes as messages sent by water spirit contacts, and followers sometimes employ them to carry sacrifices to water spirits, who indicate where offerings should be deposited by causing vessels to falter. A special type of canoe known as *ikiyan aru* functions as a sacrifice to rid communities of pollution, avert disease, and keep evil forces at bay. The Ijo, who describe these scaled-down effigies as "spiritual war boats," sometimes man them with crudely carved warriors armed with guns and cutlasses. They load the vessels with offerings of food and drink, then mount them on forked sticks at the riverbank or set them in the water to float downstream (fig. 4.10). Larger examples can approach the size of real canoes, and bearers often parade them through town—escorted by drummers and supporters singing songs—before deploying them at the waterside.

Several types of canoes can participate in a single ritual. Rites performed to appease a powerful Korokorosei water spirit after it has been invoked to punish an enemy or a criminal include an ordinary canoe, two sacrificial canoes, and a conceptual canoe. When the rite's sponsors arrive at the waterside, shrine members push their canoe back three times before allowing them to land. Before the all-important masquerade can begin, the priest and several followers set off in a canoe to position the *ikiyan aru* above and below the town. These "war boats" supposedly prevent evil spirits and other forces from disturbing the performance. Finally, one of the masks executes a "canoe dance," as described below.

*4.10 A small sacrificial canoe (*ikiyan aru*) mounted along the riverbank to keep evil spirits and diseases from entering the town. Photograph by Martha G. Anderson, Korokorosei, 1992.*

4.11 Funeral party returning from the bush with firewood. The wood will be used in cooking food for visitors during the mourning period. Photograph by Martha G. Anderson, Korokorosei, 1979.

Though the Ijo do not ordinarily embellish canoes, they seem well aware of the aesthetic potential of aquatic expeditions, even when such excursions serve ostensibly practical functions, like collecting medicines for curing rituals or fetching firewood for funerals (fig. 4.11). They also take advantage of the river as a performance space by using canoes and other watercraft as moveable stages. Dancers perform on the river as their boats travel to and from funerals or festivals. Wrestling canoes announce their arrival by parading noisily along the waterside to the accompaniment of drums, songs, and vociferous boasting, and spectacular war canoes highlight festivals of various types, recalling the Ijos' warlike past. Manned by dozens of "warriors" sporting war paint, brandishing weapons, and chanting war songs, they assault the senses by incorporating sporadic gunfire and smoking medicines, along with conspicuous arrays of raffia fronds and other "bulletproofing" charms (fig. 4.12). Because water spirits, like people, navigate the waterways by boat, maskers—who represent them—can also exploit the intrinsic drama of aquatic travel by arriving from the water (fig. 4.13). When drums on shore hurl abuses at them, they threaten onlookers with their machetes. Some express their annoyance and eagerness to attack by cutting their paddlers for failing to move quickly enough.

The irony inherent in the idea of canoeing on dry land obviously appeals to the Ijo. In a dance introduced by bush spirits and copied by numerous villages in the region, young girls make paddling motions with appropriately shaped dance wands, then transform a bench into a canoe (fig. 4.14). They paddle it, dance on it, drag it around the arena, and eventually tumble onto

4.12 A war canoe appearing at a festival for Egbesu, the war god of Kolokuma clan. Photograph by Martha G. Anderson, Olobiri, 1978.

the ground when they "capsize" it. Masquerades often include similar parodies. Some reenact fishing expeditions, as discussed later in this chapter. A performance formerly staged at Korokorosei in Olodiama clan portrays the aftermath of a domestic quarrel. The wife prepares to leave for her father's house by loading her canoe one article at a time, while onlookers beg her to stay. At first their entreaties only make her more annoyed, but they finally persuade her to remain when she returns home to collect a forgotten machete. In another performance a mask named Eleke (who also figures later in this chapter) simply acts out the lyrics of a song, leading his followers in a dance that carries them forward and back, forward and back, to illustrate the way his canoe moves in the water.

References to canoeing also abound in songs and stories, especially those involving water spirits. Canoes, paddles, and fishing spears feature prominently in shrines, including those of certain bush and water spirits (fig. 4.15). In some cases, priests explain these articles as the gear their spirits use when traveling or fishing; in others they identify them as spirits or their emblems, noting that some turned up in the water and were subsequently "proved" by diviners to be water spirits.[2] In addition, residents of the area periodically report seeing spirit canoes, which mysteriously appear then vanish, in the rivers. Diviners in Korokorosei pour libations for Bolighe, or "Unfinished canoe," a bush spirit who owns and protects a sacred lake behind the town, "just like a father or guardian cares for his child." People say that another Bolighe—this one a water spirit—resides in an estuary west of Amassoma.

4.13 A masker representing Oki, or "Sawfish," traveling to the arena in his canoe. Photograph by Martha G. Anderson, Akedei, 1992.

4.14 A girl pretending to paddle a bench during a dance called Inamu, which was originated by bush spirits. Photograph by Martha G. Anderson, Korokorosei, 1991.

4.15 Shrine for a water spirit named Adumu. Photograph by Martha G. Anderson, Keme Mbiama, 1979.

4.16 Water spirit headdress. Eastern Ijo. Wood and iron nails. L: 39.3 cm. Charles and Kent Davis. The shape of this mask resembles Kalabari headpieces worn by a character called Igbo (see interleaf H), but its knoblike eyes and clean geometric lines may indicate an origin further to the west. It lacks references to reptiles, but, as in Igbo headpieces, its overall form clearly alludes to a canoe, a popular motif in both water spirit shrines and masquerades.

4.17 Water spirit headdress. Eastern Ijo. Wood. L: 35.5 cm. Charles and Kent Davis. Another variant of Igbo (cf. fig. 4.16), this highly abstracted headdress exaggerates the canoelike shape of the jaw and transforms the forehead into a rectangular block.

4.18 Barge loaded with dancers at the Ogori ba uge, or "Buffalo killing festival." Photograph by Martha G. Anderson, Odi, 1978.

Given the importance of canoes and canoeing to the Ijo, one might expect the canoe itself to have symbolic significance along the lines of the Akan stool, which is closely associated with the soul of its owner (Fraser 1972). A prohibition against sitting in the canoe of a woman whose husband has recently died seems to attest to a similar identification, but it may also refer to the symbolic role the canoe plays in the funerary context. The Ijo conceive of passage to the land of the dead as a trip across a river. Songs sung at burial rites sometimes allude to this journey, and mourners toss sacrificial coins onto the masquerade field to pay Saibo, the ferryman. One song likens death to a voyage and focuses on the reluctance of the living to part with the deceased: the dead person begs "Load the things in the canoe and let me paddle away," as family and friends try to persuade him or her to stay. Women may dramatize the lyrics by using a bench as a canoe.

The canoe obviously serves as a "vehicle for ideas" for the Ijo, as it does for the Fante of the Ghanaian coast (Coronel 1979) and the riverain Bamana of Mali (Ganay 1987), who similarly invest canoes with symbolic meanings or employ them in funerals, festivals, and other contexts divorced from the workaday world (figs. 4.16, 4.17). Nevertheless, the "concept of the canoe" does not appear to permeate "practically every aspect of social life" among the Ijo, as it does among the Fante, nor does it serve as a fundamental metaphor of and for Ijo social life, as it does for the distant Murik of New Guinea (Barlow and Lipset 1997). Though the Ijo have "canoe proverbs," canoe metaphors do not dominate or pervade either social or ritual contexts, nor do canoes play an important role in signifying rank and prestige.

By assigning emblematic meanings to canoes and exploiting their visual drama, the Ijo and other water-oriented people celebrate and reaffirm their aquatic lifestyle; moreover, as new modes of water transportation become available, new "traditions"—and meanings—emerge. An announcement that appeared in a Lagos newspaper in 1991 conjured up pleasant memories of a festival at Odi in Kolokuma clan, which the author attended in 1978. A barge, packed with colorfully garbed revelers and presided over by a "priest" and "priestess" dressed to resemble members of a popular Christian sect, moved up and down the river while a band played a local version of reggae (fig. 4.18). The advertisement endowed the 1991 event with a "Love Boat atmosphere," suggesting that the Ijo identification with water travel guides their taste in American television programs.

4.16

4.17

4.18

The word for canoe, *aru*, now designates a variety of vehicles. Drawings collected informally from Ijo children mix fantasy with reality by including: "engine" boats (*inzini aru*) and launches (*beke aru,* or "European canoes"), a common feature of Delta rivers these days; helicopters (*foin* or *fuin aru,* "air" or "flying canoes," also used for airplanes), which are seen carrying oil company employees in and out of the Delta from time to time; and cars (*biye you aru,* or "land canoes"), known to many only from trips to the mainland or videos, which have recently become available in even the most remote of Delta villages. Despite children's fascination with these more technologically advanced modes of travel, canoes and paddles feature prominently in almost every drawing—an indication of the central role they continue to play in village life.

Fishing

As might be expected, most residents of Central Delta villages not only fish but enthusiastically proclaim fish to be their favorite food. This dietary passion even extends to the ancestors and bush spirits, who often request fish as offerings. Indeed, area schoolteachers sometimes complain that they can only induce adults to attend educational programs by promising to teach them how to catch more fish. Women sometimes dance as they carry their fish into the village from the bush, rejoicing in their good fortune.

The Ijo obviously identify with fish on a deeper level, for references to fish and fishing turn up almost as frequently in verbal and visual arts as do those to canoes and canoeing. Fishing implements appear alongside canoes in shrines for water spirits, and wooden fish occasionally join paddles as props for dancing. Like other animals, fish can serve as metaphors for human beings; numerous proverbs hinge on either fish or fishing, including one that some masks have adopted as a praise name: I inimi indi siko kori indi baagho-unfe, or "You can't catch a fish by its fin." Moreover, as a form of hunting, fishing can stand for war, as it does in a war song sung for a bush spirit named Benaaghe, enshrined at Azama in Apoi clan. The lyrics employ the metaphor of a fishing expedition to chide him not to be lazy when called to battle:

> Benaaghe my father
> I've prepared my fishing basket
> And taken it to the lake
> Anyone who doesn't fish
> Is afraid of the lake

That fish should play such an important role in the lives of a riverain people is hardly surprising; more so are the results of a survey conducted in the late 1950s. In contrast with the saltwater region, where men and women fish nearly full-time, only one man and a few women living in the freshwater village of Korokorosei considered fishing to be their primary work (P. Leis 1962, 16; N. Leis 1964, 83–84). Indeed, Korokorosei men rarely fish while living at home, because, as already noted, their wives are charged with feeding their families. Nevertheless, numerous residents of this area have spent extended periods fishing along the coast, whether by joining fishing expeditions to the adjoining saltwater region or by traveling as far away as Calabar or Duala to reside in fishing camps for several months or years at a time (see Wilcox, forthcoming); thus, neighboring groups tend to think of the Ijo as fishermen.

Ijo men and women employ different methods of catching fish. Women fish using lines, traps, and baskets. The average woman manufactures between sixty and a hundred traps each season, adjusting the spacing of the struts to suit various prey, including prawns, lobsters, tilapias, and various types of swamp fish. The most ambitious may set over eighty traps at each of three locations, checking them daily, or at least every other day. In addition, women sometimes work together in groups, digging ponds to strand fish during the annual floods or driving them to one side of a shallow pond so they can be harvested more easily.

As soon as girls acquire sufficient dexterity, they assist their mothers by weaving traps and paddling their canoes. Young boys fish using the same methods as their mothers but gradually become more proficient at techniques employed by men, such as weaving and throwing nets, setting spring traps, and spearing fish at the waterside (see fig. 4.7). Like their sisters, they turn over any of the larger fish they catch to their mothers; thus, "fishing provides the principal means by which boys can contribute to household needs" (P. Leis 1962, 18, 142).

Women smoke fish for future use and occasionally for sale to traders, but their families' prodigious appetite for fish guarantees that they seldom have a surplus (P. Leis 1962, 18). In fact, many blame current shortages on modern technology. Older residents of the area agree that the Kainji Dam, located far up the Niger at Bussa Rapids, has significantly lowered flood levels in recent decades. Though reliable data is lacking, studies confirm that damming up the river has significantly lowered flood levels and nutrient inputs, and cut sedimentation rates by about 70 percent (Human Rights Watch 1999, 53, 97; Okonta and Douglas 2001). Exploitation of the Delta's rich oil reserves has proved to be far more devastating. Oil producers and government agencies made little attempt to monitor environmental changes before recent protests threatened to disrupt production. They now admit that hundreds of oil spills and ton after ton of industrial sludge dumped into the sensitive environment over nearly four decades have fouled both the coast and the Delta's inland waterways. Other activities involved in oil production— including dredging, operating large craft, constructing roads and canals, and flaring natural gas—have also damaged the environment (see Human Rights Watch 1999, 5, 56–97). One environmental watchdog group warns that constant flaring now causes acid rain to fall in the Delta one day in every ten, in addition to blanketing it with layer after layer of fine particles and reputedly cancer-causing soot (Environmental Research Foundation 1997). Overpopulation undoubtedly contributes to the diminishing returns reported by fishers; although reliable data are lacking, visual evidence alone suggests that area villages have expanded significantly over the past fifty years. In any case, shortages had become so severe by the 1970s that the Ijo began to supplement their diets with "ice fish," frozen cod imported from Northern Europe and purchased from mainland suppliers.

Fish and the Spirit World

In addition to observing taboos against eating specific types of fish as dictated by various shrines, the Ijo associate certain varieties with the spirit world. They freely kill and eat most catfish, which normally have brownish skin, but return rarer white ones (called *pere*) to the water, for they consider them to be manifestations of a water spirit known as Binipere, or "Rich man of the water."[3] They identify cichlids of the genus *Hemichromis* and characins of the genus *Alestes* as tricksters; instead of alerting water spirits that dry season is approaching, these cunning fish sometimes deceive them, causing them to become stranded on land when the floodwaters recede. A spirit medium who used to dive underwater to bring out a live fish while possessed still sings songs about various types of fish, including one that terms *Hemichromis,* "the trickiest man in the world." People also regard certain events involving fish as ominous; for example, if a small saltwater fish travels upriver and lands in a canoe as it leaps homeward, the occupant(s) will consult diviners or herbalists. This occurrence, which is unusual enough to be considered remarkable, may signal the onset of a minor illness.

The Ijo widely believe that anyone who excels at an endeavor has backing from the spirit world. Hunters, wrestlers, and warriors derive support from a variety of bush spirits, but rumor holds that successful fishers and traders have assistance from a prominent water spirit named Adumu, who is considered to be an aspect of the python (see fig. 4.15). A song sung for him conveys his whimsical nature—typical of water spirits in general—by relating a remarkable incident:

> As I was fishing, Adumu
> The owner of a small canoe
> Came straight to my canoe and took a fish
> Oh Adumu, what a wonderful story

A local school teacher invoked the old saw about carrying coals to Newcastle to explain why people would find the idea of the patron of fishing stealing fish to be so amazing. People can visit his shrines and those of other spirits to request help in fishing, or they can consult herbalists for charms to improve their luck.

Conversely, fishers repeatedly disappointed by the size of their catch might suspect sorcerers of burying charms to spoil their fishing. Some claim that witches (*foinyou* or *fuinyou,* lit. "the people who fly")—believed to have become active in the area around 1950—can also pose problems.[4] According to a tale that circulated in the 1970s, a Nembe man's *foin* mother got him a *foin* wife to help her claim him as one of her victims. One day he returned home from fishing to find his wife mortally wounded. She told him to gather people so she could tell them her secret before she died; once he had done so, she revealed that his mother had instructed her to turn herself into a shark, tear his net, then end his life by pulling him underwater. The plan backfired when the twine broke from his spear as he hurled it into her body. She showed him the wound she had suffered, then told him what to do to free himself from his mother's spell and regain the money he had lost due to her efforts. Like all good tales, this one alludes to eyewitnesses and provides enough details, including a reference to the wife's burial at the coast, to lend credibility.

Confronting large marine animals, such as sawfish and sharks, from canoes, as men do, would seem treacherous enough without the risks posed by witchcraft. Women fishing deep inside the forest swamps are also considered to be exposed to great danger, for bush spirits are notoriously hostile creatures, certain to inflict severe punishment on anyone who defiles their territory, transgresses their laws, or simply annoys them. Even if women assiduously avoid fishing at locations the spirits have claimed for themselves, they risk catching fish that have ventured outside; misfortunes can beset an entire family if someone kills a fish that incarnates a spirit.[5] On the other hand, women can take advantage of the bush spirits' vindictiveness by invoking them to punish people who steal fish from their traps.

In a recent twist on tradition, the Ijo have begun calling on Christian prophets to address problems with evil spirits blamed for spoiling their favorite fishing spots. An Olodiama woman disappointed by the size of her catch once asked a prophet to rid a place in the bush of "juju" but realized this plan had backfired when she and her sister no longer found any fish in traps set there. Fearing more serious repercussions from the spirit world, they turned to the priest of a bush spirit shrine, who determined that the holy oil the prophet dumped on the house of "a very great spirit" had landed directly on its head. After the priest propitiated the irate spirit and others in the vicinity, the women began catching fish again.

Many Ijo villages recognize spirits as the owners of lakes located in the surrounding forests (fig. 4.19). The presiding spirits usually permit access during festivals held at periodic intervals (often every seven years, the number considered to be most ritually auspicious). On these occasions, drums alert spirits to leave, so people can fish freely. The festival for the lake known as Dabiyeyinghi (lit., "Mother of kolas") commemorates a local legend about two hunters who witnessed a bush spirit funeral there and returned home to teach their townspeople how to perform the rites. Before fishing begins, Korokorosei residents anoint a cane coffin with chicken blood and set it on poles in the lake. In a festival for Danghanlughu, or "Tall palms," a lake behind the same town, people beg permission to fish from a shrine dedicated

4.19 People displaying a portion of their catch at the fishing festival for Lake Adigbe. Photograph by Martha G. Anderson, Ossiama, 1992.

4.20 Water spirit headdress. Ijo. Wood and pigment. L: 52.1 cm. FMCH X65.9041; Gift of the Wellcome Trust. This headdress would have been worn horizontally, with its skull-like face looking skyward. Like most composite types, it incorporates references to the aquatic world, including fins and a flaring form at the rear that could allude either to a fish tail or a canoe prow.

4.21 Water spirit mask, crocodile. Delta peoples. Wood. L: 145.1 cm. Iris and B. Gerald Cantor Center for Visual Arts at Stanford University; 1984.225 Gift of Victor and Paula Zurcher. The crocodile is a favorite at performances staged throughout the Delta. It appears alongside sawfish and sharks in Abua and Ekpeye masquerades, but the forms of crocodile masks collected from sites scattered around the Delta and the checkerboard patterns on their skins are quite similar. A generic "Delta" attribution therefore seems advisable for pieces that lack precise documentation or close resemblance to documented examples.

4.22 Multiheaded water spirit headdress. Ijo. Wood, pigment, and incrustation. H: 59.7 cm. Indiana University Art Museum: Gift of Toby and Barry Hecht, 89.24.3. Photograph by Michael Cavanagh and Kevin Montague © Indiana University Art Museum. Ijo headdresses represent hundreds of characters, many confined to single communities. This one probably represents Angala pele, or "Mangrove cutter," who appears in villages throughout the region. Most masks vigorously chase spectators, but Angala pele—whose name implies his ability to slice through even the toughest wood—is so hostile that he must be restrained by ropes or surrounded by attendants armed with sticks.

4.23 Janus water spirit headdress with feathers. Ijo. Wood and feathers. H: 54 cm. Peabody Essex Museum. Photograph by Jeffrey Dykes. Following a pattern seen among neighboring groups in Southern Nigeria, Central and Western Ijo headdresses that take the form of anthropomorphic heads and figures usually project vertically from the masker's head. This janus-headed example, with its strongly projecting mouths, is reminiscent of aggressive bush spirit figures. It's feather ruff may allude to status in the peri *warrior society.*

to that section of forest, erect two figures along the path to the lake, and leave offerings of fish for them when they return. In both cases, participants sing as many songs as possible and beat drums throughout the entire day.[6] In a third instance, residents of Amassoma in Ogboin clan say that crocodiles once prevented people from fishing in Lake Adigbe, so the community sent a slave inside the lake to deliver a sacrifice; after killing the slave, the crocodiles became calm and allowed people to fish. Nevertheless, each quarter of the town mounts a war canoe before fishing begins, suggesting that people must wage a symbolic battle against the lake's spirit owners over control of fish.

Water Spirits and Aquatic Masks

Most Ijo now consider themselves Christians, but the idea of a different world inside the Delta's rivers and creeks continues to captivate them. Some tell stories about encounters with aquatic spirits or describe marvelous, underwater towns they have visited in person or in dreams. Although these tales usually portray water spirits (*biniyou,* "water people," or *bini orumo,* "the water spirits") as more agreeable than their volatile counterparts in the forests, they live in a very different environment and resemble the Ijo less closely in both appearance and tastes. People often describe them as beautiful, light-skinned beings with long, flowing hair, but they can also materialize as animals, composite creatures, and objects that turn up in the water. In keeping with their image as wealthy "foreigners" with close ties to trade, many prefer offerings of corned beef and Sprite to local produce, such as plantains and palm wine, and designate manufactured goods—including dolls, cloth, and white saucers—to serve as their emblems. Of the major spirits, only Adumu, who is said to be dark-skinned and amphibious, calls for figurative images. Others, including Binipere, choose to remain in the water, and do not even have shrines.

The term *owu* (or *ou,* depending on the dialect in question), means mask, masquerader, and masquerade dance. All *owu* represent aquatic beings, although only a few are believed to incarnate them. Interestingly, however, masks neither conform to the stereotype of the beautiful, light-skinned mermaid nor capitalize on import symbolism, suggesting that they may represent an older conception, as well as a distinct category, of water spirits. Most maskers wear wooden headpieces (*ou tibi*) that depict water spirits in one of several ways: (1) as composite creatures that mix skeletal human features with aquatic motifs like crocodilian snouts and sharklike fins (much like "bush monster" masks found elsewhere in Africa combine the horns, tusks, and gaping jaws of land animals; fig. 4.20); (2) as bush cows, goats, and other land animals, as well as reptiles and aquatic animals (fig. 4.21); and (3) as human figures and heads (figs. 4.22, 4.23). Unlike anthropomorphic types, which stand upright, both composite and zoomorphic headpieces face skyward; the Ijo explain this unusual orientation by claiming that they look like spirits floating on the surface of the water. The majority of maskers alter their appearance further by mounting a structure known as a *siko,* or fin, over their buttocks (see fig. 4.32). By manipulating their costumes and assuming peculiar postures, they intensify the impression of beings from another world.

4.20

4.21

4.22

4.23

Western scholars have long considered the "Cubist" conception of composite headpieces to be quintessentially Ijo, but zoomorphic types may well precede them. The Nembe and Okrika Ijo originally named their dance societies after fish and other animals and made masks to represent them (Alagoa 1967, 145; Ibuluya 1982, 208); moreover, the unusual forms of guitar fish, skates, and other members of the ray family, could have suggested the oddly juxtaposed features of composite headpieces. Finally, although the Kalabari admit to borrowing specific masquerades, including Oki, or "Sawfish," from the Abua (Horton n. d., 65–66, caption no. 13, 103), it seems more likely that they and other coastal Ijo groups, who work as fishermen, originally introduced fish masks.

The contrasting styles of masquerade headpieces may seem antithetical, but abstraction and naturalism coexist in many Ijo villages (fig. 4.24). Masquerade ensembles not only mix composite and zoomorphic types but often include one anthropomorphic figure (fig. 4.25). The term "naturalism" should be qualified, however, for artists typically simplify forms and take great liberties with such details as the number and position of fins, so that the fiercest animals take on a whimsical or even cartoonlike appearance. The Ijo do not consider the relative naturalism of a mask to be an issue, given their belief that water spirits can materialize as anything from fish and mermaids to sticks of wood, iron pots, and sewing machines. When asked to account for differences in appearance, owners invariably explain that headpieces either resemble the spirits they represent or conform to instructions issued by the spirits themselves. Moreover, though maskers representing fish usually imitate their behavior, most depict predatory fish—sharks, barracuda, mackerel, and penfish—and chase spectators like composite and human types do.

4.24 Masks of different types appearing together at a festival for Kolokuma Egbesu, the clan war god. Photograph by Martha G. Anderson, Olobiri, 1978.

4.25 Water spirit headdress with janus figures. Delta peoples. Wood. H: 66 cm. FMCH X78.124; Anonymous Gift. This headpiece with its janus form—each figure baring its teeth—and its surmounting animal—apparently a monkey—resembles certain Ijo bush spirit images. On the other hand, the overall softness and delicacy of the features might indicate an origin among neighboring Edo or Igbo peoples on the northeastern fringes of the Delta.

4.26 Water spirit headdress, Pipligbo. Kalabari Ijo. Wood. H: 34.3 cm. Krannert Art Museum and Kinkead Pavilion, University of Illinois, Urbana-Champaign; Faletti Family Collection. This mask wears a British-style "crown" composed of a tortoise flanked by coiled snakes. The Kalabari believe that water spirits can materialize in the form of animals, and all reptiles are considered to have strong ties to water spirits. Ikaki the tortoise, a notorious trickster, features in stories told throughout the Delta (see chapter 8 of this volume). The small heads on the cheeks of the mask allude to the spirit's followers or children.

Masking

Masking provides the best opportunity for people raised on tales of water spirits to glimpse inside their fascinating underwater universe. Masquerades not only bring these wonderful beings to life but compound the central paradox of masking—masker as man/not man—by bringing them on land (4.26).

The Ijo, who credit water spirits with the invention of masking and particular masquerades, often tell of people who in the past watched water spirits dancing on distant sandbanks, stole or copied their masks, and returned home to stage the masquerades for their townspeople. Some accounts feature abductions by water spirits who teach their captives how to perform masquerades; others tell how spirits approach people as they travel by canoe, then return to them in dreams to offer instruction on songs and dance sequences. Diviners consulted about unusual phenomena can also communicate the instructions of spirits.

Residents of Ondewari tell a typical story about the man who introduced their Ofurumo, or "Shark," masquerade, some years before his death in 1936. A man known as Kperighada was fishing at Kongogbene in the Cameroons, when he vanished for seven days. When he reappeared, he told people that he'd been kidnapped by water spirits, who taught him how to dance a masquerade. He returned to [his hometown] Ondewari, where he called the elders together to inform them of the water spirits' ultimatum that he must perform the masquerade or he would die.

As in this instance, spirits often threaten their human sponsors with death if they do not agree to perform masquerades, but they also offer rewards; people often claim these performances avert evil spirits and disease and bring children and prosperity to their communities. When asked if masks demand sacrifices, an Ijo friend emphatically responded that masks *are* sacrifices. In addition to providing entertainment on secular occasions, they appear at funerals to accompany the dead into the afterworld; at purification ceremonies to sweep towns clean of pollution; and at performances held to call off enshrined spirits after they have been invoked to punish criminals or settle disputes.

Surprisingly, even though masquerades derive from the spirit world and involve a variety of sanctions and benefits, the spirits who introduce them may not be especially powerful or even particularly concerned about enforcing their edicts. For example, the custodians of a masquerade associated with a sacred lake arbitrarily changed one of the masks from a lake perch to a tilapia, a substitution that would be unthinkable in the rare instances in which masks are believed to be animated by deadly spirits, capable of killing performers for making the least mistake in carrying out their instructions.[7] Because most masks simply imitate, rather than embody spirits, Christians often feel free to wear them, as well as to participate in masquerades as musicians, supporters, and spectators. Masking societies like Ekine or Sekiapu, which control masking among the Eastern Ijo, do not exist west of the Nun. Individuals, families, friends, and shrines can own masks, and anyone who wishes to join in performances can generally do so.

The Ijo call masquerades "plays" and refer to masking as "playing," reflecting their belief that spirits initiate masquerades largely out of a desire to associate with their human friends.[8] Followers claim that even those exceptional masks that manifest deadly spirits delight in playing with their

followers. Performances typically begin with drum calls, libations, or songs inviting people and spirits to come play. Spirits—like people—seem to enjoy the artistic aspects of these occasions as well as the camaraderie they provide. An elderly horn blower reminisced that when he was a young virtuoso, the spirits expressed their appreciation for his exquisite music by "entertaining" him with gifts of food, so that fish filled the surface of the river whenever he played for one of the masquerades.

Fish Masquerades

The Ijo may consider water spirits to be more playful and less troublesome than the irritable spirits who roam the forests, but neither variety is bound by society's constraints. Although masks representing aquatic creatures rarely appear outside the Niger Delta region, they belong to a broader tradition that embraces both the fearsome "bush monsters" seen in other parts of Africa, including the Poro region of Liberia (Anderson and Kreamer 1989, 47–49), and the "wild beasts" that appear in other parts of the world, including Europe (Poppi 1994, 211). Like them, the aquatic creatures display threatening features, behave unpredictably, and aggressively attack people. Many enter the arena by slashing through palm frond fences (*fanu*) of the type that formerly shielded villages from evil spirits and other invaders. Armed with weapons, they spend much of their time chasing spectators.

Instead of taking the threatening demeanor of their aquatic monsters seriously, however, the Ijo tend to spoof it, finding humor in the way masks interact with other performers and members of the audience. The violence in Ijo masquerades tends to be of the cartoonish variety—exaggerated and mixed with liberal doses of slapstick. Though they can wound anyone who does not remain vigilant or run for cover when they approach, most maskers only play at being murderous. Nevertheless, the hostile, transgressive behavior they exhibit amounts to more than comic relief. Masquerades operate on the same principle as a type of ritual called *seimo* (to spoil), which attempts to beat back hostile spirits and neutralize their power. Indeed, maskers play much the same role as the spirit warriors who man *ikiyan aru,* the sacrificial canoes mentioned earlier.

4.27 Water spirit headdress. Ijo. Wood, basketry, nails, and pigment. L: 97.5 cm. Seattle Art Museum; Gift of Katherine White and the Boeing Company, 81.17.530. Photograph by Paul Macapia. All composite headdresses represent aggressive-looking monsters, but the toothsome, crocodilian snout of this example suggests that it represents a particularly voracious spirit. The Ijo generally explain the mix of features on headpieces of this type by saying that they look just like spirits do as they appear when floating on the surface of the water.

The risk of injury keeps performances lively. The audience judges the success of a masquerade not only by the maskers' skill at impersonating wild spirits and executing complicated dance steps but by their ability to "sweeten" the performance by exploiting the element of surprise. Both drummers (who instruct maskers to dance or chase spectators in drum language) and dance demonstrators (who show maskers which steps to perform by executing abbreviated versions of each sequence) control a masker's movements to a certain extent, but he can interrupt a dance sequence to dive at the drummers through the pole fence provided for their protection or dart around it to attack them. He might go crazy, slashing wildly at his own supporters until others join forces to restrain him, only to follow this by locking one of his human friends in an affectionate embrace. He relentlessly pursues spectators but periodically returns to the sidelines, where he patiently awaits his turn at dancing.

The Ijo often embellish these performances with stories, or *egberi,* which ostensibly portray events in the lives of water spirits but simultaneously mirror, mock, or pay tribute to some aspect of Ijo culture. The plots, often conveyed through songs that summarize the action, frequently assume the audience's familiarity with the situations being portrayed. They tend to be quite simple, for the Ijo believe that an elaborate plot might spoil the drama (Nzekwu 1960, 140–41). Maskers can also act out a series of vignettes or simply pantomime characteristic behaviors, like a sawfish that responds to a drummer's instructions to "chase mullets" by executing a sequence of mincing steps. Most performances, however, package social criticism and messages about proper behavior in the guise of entertainment (Alagoa 1967, 155). In any case, the audience finds the masks' antics hilarious.

The drama of the hunt—which can conclude with killing, or capturing, or taming a wild beast—makes it a crowd favorite. Elsewhere, it usually involves subduing bush spirits, as in the Bie masquerade performed by the Dan of Côte d'Ivoire (Fischer and Himmelheber 1984, 89–94), or stalking land animals, as in the bear hunt masquerades mounted by Alpine villages in Europe (Poppi 1994, 211). Though composite masks can play this role in the Niger Delta, the Ijo and others often add a paradoxical twist by bringing aquatic animals on land (fig. 4.27). Masks representing freshwater fish are fairly common in the Central and Western Delta, but the formidable size, intimidating appearance, and rapacious behavior of large, predatory sea animals—which, according to the Ijo, sometimes become water spirits—make them particularly popular as masquerade characters. Perched atop the maskers' heads, they manage to look both preposterous and menacing; the acquisition of human limbs allows them to wield machetes and give chase on land.

Although introduced by spirits, fish masquerades, like other Ijo performances, often draw inspiration from real-life situations: after braving the shark-infested waters off the coast in their canoes, generations of fishermen have undoubtedly returned home to tell spellbinding tales of their heroic exploits. By reenacting expeditions of this sort, performers transform the work of fishing into theater, but instead of glorifying it, they parody the dangers involved in capturing fearsome marine animals and mock tales about the big fish that almost got away. Instead of contrasting idealized humans with monstrous animals, as masquerades sometimes do (Poppi 1994, 196), these performances typically expose human follies.

4.28 A caged Ofurumo, or "Shark," being hauled upriver while a fisherman and his wife circle his raft in their canoe. Photograph by Martha G. Anderson, Ondewari, 1992.

The Ofurumo masquerade Kperighada introduced to Ondewari (see above) irreverently models itself on a shark hunt. The young men who recently revived Ofurumo credit it with driving evil spirits from the village. It begins when Izeghe, a masker wearing a mullet headpiece, runs through town to the accompaniment of a song warning, "Sharks are coming so little fishes should run and hide." Excitement builds as spectators anticipate his arrival; they rush to the riverbank to watch a canoe tow him upriver on a raft, as crew members and assorted supporters sing and drum his praises (fig. 4.28). As he and his retinue move slowly toward town, Ofurumo alternately dances and uses his machete to slash at the raffia-covered cage that contains him. Meanwhile, a fisherman and his wife repeatedly circle the raft in their canoe, as if stalking their prey. Each time the man throws his spear, the canoe capsizes, and the pair ends up in the water, acting out the lyrics of another song: "Anyone who spears this fish will upset his canoe."

After many dunkings, the performers come ashore, where Ofurumo's son and wife join him in dancing and chasing spectators. Their drum titles—Poupou-fi pou-fi, "Force someone to give food," and Fulo-opitei-ke-yei-piri-fi, "To remove all the fish and give fishless soup to one's husband"—suggest their antisocial dispositions and mischievous behavior, traits that typify nature spirits. The masquerade concludes with a pantomime in which the fishing couple reappears, dragging their canoe around the arena in pursuit of their prey (see pp. 2, 3). Even on dry land, they periodically capsize. Finally, after many misses, the man spears Ofurumo and hauls him into the canoe; remaining in character, he hawks his catch to members of the audience.

In the Central Delta, masks representing sawfish, dolphins, and sharks often only hint at the size larger marine animals can attain, partly because life-size headdresses would impede maskers when chasing spectators through crowded villages, as anyone who has ever attempted to maneuver a step ladder through a house can easily imagine. Ofurumo's supporters claim that he always wears a huge, cane-supported headdress on the raft but ordinarily exchanges it for a smaller, wooden one when he comes ashore. In the performance described above, Ofurumo and his son wore the larger versions on land because the wooden headpieces had deteriorated.[9] Because of their increased width, the maskers kept getting trapped in rafters, narrow passageways, and the fence that protects the drummers. One suspects that the enormous masks found to the east of the Nun among the Abua, Ekpeye, and their closest Ijo neighbors perform somewhat less athletically than the smaller versions commonly used further to the west (fig. 4.29).

4.29 Shark masquerade headdress. Delta peoples. Wood and pigment. L: 155.9 cm. Indianapolis Museum of Art; Gift of Mr. and Mrs. Harrison Eiteljorg, 1989.893a–g. Delta residents consider sharks to be terrifying and awesome. Headdresses can depict generic sharks or specific varieties, including hammerheads, barracudas, and tiger sharks. Many masquerades reenact shark hunts, which simultaneously capitalize on peoples' fear of these mammoth marine creatures and celebrate the courage and skill required in capturing or "taming" them.

Another colossal marine animal, Oki, or "Sawfish," stars in masquerades performed throughout the Delta (see fig. 4.13). Named for its distinctive rostrum—a long, rigid blade with fourteen to thirty-four pairs of enlarged toothlike scales mounted along its edges—this sharklike creature is classed as a ray within the order that includes both types of elasmobranchs. Though sawfish have not been well studied, scientists recognize six species: some prefer the shallow, brackish water of lagoons, mud flats, and estuaries, and rarely ascend rivers to visit freshwater areas; others frequent freshwater systems and only occasionally visit the coast (Bigelow and Schroeder 1953, 15-42). Two species—one primarily saltwater (*Pristis pectinata*) and the other primarily freshwater (*Pristis perotteti*)—inhabit Delta waters, but artists take such liberties in portraying Oki that it is impossible to determine which variety a particular mask represents.

Though full-grown sawfish range from ten to twenty feet in length—a size that makes them menacing enough to coastal fishermen—their wicked-looking snouts account for the extensive mythology that surrounds them in cultures scattered all over the globe, as well as for the tremendous popularity Oki enjoys in the Niger Delta. Despite rumors to the contrary, sawfish do not attack large animals and are incapable of "sawing" chunks out of their prey. Nevertheless, people have long associated them with warfare: several Oceanic groups once fashioned their "saws" into weapons, and a number of German and American vessels sported sawfish as insignia during World War II (McDavitt 1996).

Numerous Africans, including the Bidjogo, Akan, and Yoruba, revere sawfish or assign them supernatural powers. The Kalabari Ijo display their rostra in shrines as trophies, alongside crocodile and bush pig skulls (Matthew McDavitt, personal communication, 1998; Tasie 1977, pl. 3). Ijo living to the west of the Nun River regard Oki as a great spirit but are nonetheless eager to catch sawfish.[10] When struggling to capture one caught on their line, fishermen sometimes bring canoes loaded with supporters, including women possessed by Oki, and attempt to lure the reluctant fish out of the water by pouring libations, beating his praises on drums, beckoning him with horns, and calling, "Oki, come up. Let's play. The tide has already ebbed." When he cooperates, they kill him.

As in the previous instance, the masquerade performed at the Western Ijo town of Akedei in Oiyakiri clan capitalizes on the comic aspects of the situation by transferring the action to dry land. Oki appears in a canoe, which parades along the waterfront while songs and drums repeat the fishermen's invitation to come out and play on the sandbanks. He taxes the audience's ability to suspend disbelief even further when he comes ashore (fig. 4.30). There he chases after spectators with his cutlass and takes turns dancing with another mask that comes out to play with him.

The performance climaxes with a segment that reenacts the struggle described above: assistants help a fisherman drag his canoe into the arena, where he chases Oki around with his net. After many clumsy misses and mishaps, he nets the sawfish after the masker's headpiece becomes entangled in a fishing line. Assistants help haul the captured fish into the canoe, where the fisherman pretends to slit his throat (fig. 4.31). They carry Oki off, but he makes a dramatic comeback, triumphantly returning to the arena to play his part in the next segment. The mood now shifts from the humorous nonsense of the hunt to the serious business of preventive medicine: Oki grabs a baby, who awaits him in the center of the arena, then chops at it with his machete until someone comes to its rescue. A succession of mothers brings their babies to him, believing the ordeal will ward off illness and other dangers that account for a high rate of infant mortality in the region. The sequence confirms that the hunters, as inept as they may be, have succeeded in harnessing Oki's power for the good of the community. Spectators who participate in other masquerades might derive similar benefits, though most simply consider dodging the masks' blows to be an exhilarating form of play.

A masquerade associated with a sacred lake near Ossiama, another Oiyakiri town, represents one of the most sought after game fish in the world, the African tiger fish. These swift, rapacious, salmon-shaped characins—whose knifelike teeth show even when their mouths are closed—have earned a reputation as the freshwater counterparts of the great white shark (McEwan 1997). Though not nearly as large as the aptly named "goliath," which can exceed four feet and a hundred-and-fifty pounds, *Hydrocynus vittatus,* the species found in the Niger Delta, can measure more than two feet and attack prey nearly the same size. Tiger fish sometimes hunt in packs, much like their South American cousin, the piranha.

This masquerade differs from Oki and Ofurumo in several respects. According to legend, a tiger fish and a crocodile took up residence in Lake Adigbe, which was formed by an earthquake, and frustrated the ancestors by devouring most of the fish. When local fishermen eventually caught Kabi, the voracious tiger fish, townspeople decided they should harness his exceptional hostility by carving him as a mask. They added headpieces representing Uku, or "Golden perch," and Apedeu, or "Lake perch"—which descendants later replaced with Tabala, or "Tilapia"—to complete a set of three, the number the Ijo regard as the most auspicious after the number seven.

Unlike the previous examples, the Adigbe masquerade does not tell a story; the secondary masks come out first to warm up the crowd, then Kabi, the vicious carnivore, enters the arena in a portable cage. After slashing through it with his machete, he takes turns dancing in the arena and vigorously chasing spectators (fig. 4.32). The other masks also behave in typical *owu* fashion, abruptly switching from carefully controlled dance steps to wild rampages (fig. 4.33).

Christians now predominate in Ossiama, and the festival lacks the type of public fanfare formerly associated with events of this type, but some rites may still be performed privately at the shrine for Lake Adigbe. Though

4.30

4.31

4.32

4.33

4.30 Oki, or "Sawfish," appearing in a masquerade sponsored by the author. Photograph by Martha G. Anderson, Akedei, 1992.

4.31 Having netted Oki, a fisherman cuts his throat. Photograph by Martha G. Anderson, Akedei, 1992.

4.32 Kabi, or "Tiger fish," during a performance of his masquerade sponsored by the author. Photograph by Martha G. Anderson, Ossiama, 1992.

4.33 Apedeu, or "Lake perch," during a performance of the Kabi masquerade. Photograph by Martha G. Anderson, Ossiama, 1992.

people still consider the spirit owner of the lake to be very powerful, the masks' ties with the shrine appear to be rather loose. Their caretakers simply store them in the rafters of their houses. They pour libations before dancing the masks but claim to do so only to make the performance interesting. The masquerade probably had more significance in the past; townspeople say, "We dance it New Year's Day," or "when the water is down [the floods recede], we set a date for the Adigbe fishing festival and dance it then. When we dance we say, 'You are a very hostile fish, drive away all evils from the town.'" This explanation confirms masquerade's role as sacrifice and establishes its ties to the ritual calendar, which coincides with the rise and fall of the Niger's branches. The new year begins a lunar month after the floodwaters crest. Elsewhere in Africa, masking and ritual mark critical stages in the agricultural cycle; people living in the freshwater regions of the Delta farm, as well as fish, and rites must be staged to clear away pollution left behind by the floods before planting can begin. Sacrifices, including masquerades, may be necessary at other points in the dry season as well, because this is when villages are most vulnerable to epidemics.

If even comical performances like Oki and Ofurumo can avert misfortune and bestow other benefits, those at the other end of the spectrum, which actually incarnate deadly spirits, draw on their perceived power to protect their followers and enforce the law. Masks of this type ordinarily remain hidden inside shrines that are off-limits to most local women, as well as to outsiders. When people invoke them to punish criminals, they respond by killing off relatives of the guilty party until the affected family agrees to make reparations and sponsor the costly performance required to nullify most invocations. The cowry-covered medicine bands (*egbe* or *gbinye*) that encircle the maskers' headpieces on these occasions not only empower them but visibly manifest their potency. Because possession and other ritual elements make their performances particularly compelling, other masquerades often mimic them by including "priests" and employing "medicines" to cool the masks' hearts when they become overheated from chasing spectators.

Eleke, the Korokorosei *owu* whose dance mimics canoe motions, has a reputation for being so lethal that people living in far-off clans speak of him with awe. His name refers to a type of dolphin that reportedly appears in every pod; the Ijo, who consider dolphins dangerous prey, regard the white-finned eleke as the most wicked. Unlike the masks discussed above, Eleke's headpiece not only represents a water-dwelling mammal, instead of a true fish, but belongs to the composite type; it superimposes human features on a body that resembles that of a dolphin (fig. 4.34). His son, Kunokoroghe-owei, has a similar headpiece, but his slave, Ikirikawei, who completes the set, takes the form of an upright human figure.

The Eleke masquerade spans a three-day period and incorporates two sets of cloth masks in addition to the wooden ones. The most dramatic segment reenacts *peri toi,* the play performed by titled warriors who have killed human beings or certain animals, for Eleke, the notorious crime fighter, earned the title by killing people when invoked to do so. His priest wears the red jacket and cap reserved for titleholders in Olodiama clan, and all three masks display eagle feathers to denote his *peri* status. Despite his lethal tendencies, supporters claim that Eleke not only protects the community but that he promotes its welfare by bringing children and prosperity.

The Ijo have abandoned most of their mask shrines. Many seem to have called on powerful fish like Oki. The neighboring community of Ikebiri performed a masquerade known as Uguberi, or "Hammerhead shark," before abandoning his shrine about fifty years ago. The ensemble included four masks: Uguberi, the father; Noi-noi-ere (untranslatable), his wife; and their two sons, the furtive Miye-miye-gudu, or "Whatever he does he keeps in his mind," and the voracious Aka-karaghe-karaghe-buru-fi, or "He eats yam without carving his teeth." Residents recall that the male headpieces looked exactly like the intimidating sharks but say that the wife's took the form of a beautiful woman with plaited hair, a slender body, and a "very nice figure." Uguberi—described as so murderous that he held the *peri* title from birth— reportedly cut his victims' stomachs, causing them to urinate or defecate blood. He is rumored to have killed numerous followers for abandoning his shrine, yet people say he formerly protected Ikebiri from harm. They maintain that his priest could avert epidemics when he became possessed, simply by moving through town as he waved his sword and shouted, "Sickness is coming and I am driving it away."

4.34 Eleke embracing his priest. Photograph by Martha G. Anderson, Korokorosei, 1991.

Masking as Serious Play and Playful Work

Like masquerades everywhere, Ijo performances function on many levels and yield multiple layers of meaning. In addition to their stated aims of ensuring prosperity, averting misfortune, and enforcing the law, they provide an opportunity for youths, including a few daring girls, to display their physical prowess and courage—qualities the Ijo have historically prized—by daring masks to attack, then narrowly dodging their blows. The most audacious spectators taunt even enshrined masks like Eleke, whose tendency to become possessed makes them so dangerous that more cautious observers watch their performances from canoes anchored a safe distance from shore. By turning combat into play, masquerades must have once provided a training ground for warriors; thus, performances like Oki and Ofurumo might feature the fishing methods men employ, not only because they are more dramatic but also because they provide a clearer metaphor for warfare.

On the other hand, Ijo masquerades mock the same behaviors they reinforce. Even the most lighthearted examples, like Ofurumo, illustrate the negative consequences of antisocial behavior and comment on society's need to control overly contentious individuals. Though the Ijo valorize physical bravado, they realize that combativeness can exceed socially acceptable limits and turn people into wild, uncontrollable "beasts," like the domineering bully whose townsmen killed him, then "tamed" his spirit by providing it with a figure carving (see chapter 3 of this volume). As Horton (1967, 236–39) observes in his analysis of a Kalabari Ijo masquerade, masking provides a similar means of concretizing the fears of sociopaths that can surface in any community, then symbolically addressing them.

If catching unruly fish and taming wild spirits metaphorically harnesses their powers for the good of society, playing with masks can also mitigate people's fears of the vicious spirits and ferocious beasts that inhabit the natural environment. It is important to note, however, that the Ijo express a profound respect for nature rather than a desire to dominate it. For example, they mount a rite called *bou gbee* (pay the bush) to compensate the forest whenever someone kills a bush spirit, just as they compensate the families of humans who die as a result of murder, war, or accident. As sacrifices performed at the behest of nature spirits, masquerades likewise provide a means of repaying the environment for its gifts, including fish and the raw materials used in manufacturing canoes.

Finally, Horton (1963) has described Kalabari Ijo masquerades as approaching art for art's sake because they have more to do with aesthetic display than ritual. Despite their ritual significance, most masquerades performed by Ijo groups living to the west of the Nun River could easily be mistaken for secular performances. This may well be appropriate, for water spirits stage their own masquerades, as two Ijo friends reminded me. One recalled that anyone who ventured into the water during Uguberi risked being cut by water spirits, who not only mounted their own version inside the river but periodically sent pieces of dead fish to the surface to show how they dealt with spectators. The other—a diviner, whose numerous contacts keep her abreast of events in the spirit world—confided one morning that water spirits would be dancing Oki inside the water that afternoon and that she would be going to see it. Apparently these creative but often wayward spirits feel no need to justify their own performances as anything more than a day's entertainment.

Conclusion

Canoes and fish have transcended their roles as transportation and food to become emblematic of Delta cultures. War canoes and fishing tableaux adorn festival T-shirts, like one produced to celebrate a secular festival in Bumo clan in 1992 (fig. 4.35). Indeed, a close identification with a riverain lifestyle has figured in the development of at least a tentative regional identity. Despite ongoing ethnic bickering among groups living at its fringes, Delta residents have exhibited a surprising degree of political solidarity based partly on their shared environment; feelings of difference from mainland peoples helped fuel the movement to create Rivers, then Delta States.[11] The paddle proudly displayed beneath the Nigerian coat-of-arms on a school notebook for Rivers State, circa 1978, signifies this identity, as does the dazzling, if anatomically incorrect, Ofurumo who appears in the first calendar issued by Bayelsa State (created out of Rivers State in 1997). Befringed, befeathered, and gleaming with metallic paint, he serves as the sole example of the region's "cultural displays."

The use of canoes and fish in shrines and rituals has dwindled as Christianity has come to dominate the region and as increasing poverty limits the number of masquerades villages can support. The Ijo frequently complain that the lack of roads in the Delta has hampered their progress. If wishful thinking could overcome the many obstacles involved in engineering and paying for roadways in a swampy region traversed by rivers, beset by floods, and deluged by intense rainstorms, their relationship to the environment would change radically. For the foreseeable future, however, water still rules the Delta, and canoes and fish continue to hold a secure place, not only in the economic lives of its inhabitants but in their hearts.

4.35 *Fishing motif on T-shirt designed for a civic festival. Photograph by Martha G. Anderson, Opuama, 1992.*

Interleaf F
Water Spirit Shrines

Martha G. Anderson

F.1 Mami Wata figure. Ibibio, Utu Etim Ekpo Village. Twentieth Century. By Akpan Chukwu. Wood, plant fiber, and pigment. H: 36 cm. Herbert and Shelley Cole. Beliefs in water spirits certainly predate the use of the pidgin term "Mami Wata" as well as the popular lithograph of an Asian snake charmer that inspired this and countless other carvings.

Niger Delta peoples, who generally express positive attitudes toward the water, tell wonderful tales about well-appointed towns that exist inside the rivers and creeks surrounding their villages. They share many beliefs about these spirits, including their ability to bestow wealth and children. If an Ijo man excels at fishing or trading, for example, his neighbors are certain to suspect that Adumu, the patron of these occupations, must be "moving with him" (Anderson 1997). Yet many express some ambivalence about water spirits, who tend to be capricious and fickle characters capable of upsetting canoes, ripping fish nets, stirring up storms, and turning on their human friends for no apparent reason. Delta dwellers also tell cautionary tales about individuals who become fantastically rich by forming alliances with water spirits, only to have great disasters befall them.

The water spirits of the Delta have much in common with the Edo deity Olokun (see interleaf G) and Mami Wata, a spirit who manifests herself (and sometimes himself) in numerous forms throughout much of Africa (figs. F.1, F.2). Although neighboring peoples sometimes point to the Delta as the original home of Mami Wata, the inhabitants favor a host of locally named spirits (Drewal, 1988a, 1988b; Gore and Nevadomsky 1997; Jell-Bahlsen 1995). They tend to use the term *mami wata* as a gloss for "water spirits"—particularly those that bestow wealth—and to display the popular lithograph of Mami Wata as a snake charmer for the other spirits who manifest themselves as pythons. They claim spirits can materialize as animals, human beings, and objects, especially things people find in the water. Masks often portray them as composite monsters. Nevertheless, people asked to describe water spirits usually speak of fair-skinned beings with long "hanging" hair. Their taste in offerings—corned beef, rice, gin, and particularly sweet things, like refined sugar, "biscuits," and soft drinks—suggests their ties to foreign trade.

Although participation in the overseas trade undoubtedly intensified beliefs in the foreignness and commercial value of the spirits, scholars who have worked in this part of Nigeria have shown that much of the "import" symbolism associated with them—including everything from talcum powder to Gilbey's gin—is rooted in ideas that predate European contact. Their remarkable ability to live inside the water appears to underlie their image as exotic foreigners with access to astonishing wealth (fig. F.3). The color white connotes clarity, visibility, and openness, as well as clean, clear water. Light skin can therefore indicate connections with the spirit world (fig. F.4).

F.2   Many items similar to those housed in this Igbo Mami Wata shrine appear in shrines for locally named deities throughout the Delta. Photograph by Henry John Drewal, 1978.

F.3   Numerous Delta priests and diviners, including the older woman shown here, claim to have spent time—often seven days or even seven years— living inside the water while being instructed by water spirits. Many others acknowledge personal relationships with spirits. The younger woman shown here is being treated for childlessness, a condition that has been blamed on her "water husband." Photograph by Martha G. Anderson, Korokorosei, Olodiama clan, Central Ijo region, 1992.

164

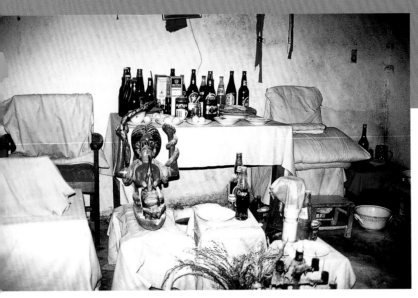

F 4.   *The Ogoni emphasize Mami Wata more than their Delta neighbors. Although this may be due to the influence of the nearby Ibibio, they claim that Mami Wata came from the Ijo region. Like many Delta shrines for water spirits, this one uses a white color scheme to evoke the bright, clear world the spirits inhabit. Photograph by Jill Salmons, Nyokwiri Boue, Babbe, 1992.*

F 5.   *Eri Anwan shrine in which found objects, including bronzes from the waters, are deposited. Photograph by Philip M. Peek, Ozoro, Isoko region, 1971.*

F.6   Teinma bronzes. Kalabari Ijo. Bronze. H (of knife): 52.1 cm. Collection of Toby and Barry Hecht. These bronzes served as the emblem of Temenaro, the head of the "heroes" of a small Kalabari village. Followers not only claimed that they were made by spirits but that they also kept themselves brightly burnished and mysteriously appeared and disappeared of their own accord. The two bracelets combined to form the most important part of the ensemble, a coil, which is said to have grown by one turn a year for seven years—a ritually auspicious number. With its reptilian head, the coil represents a python, an animal sacred to both heroes and water spirits. When photographed in situ, several small manillas were hung around its top, along with a small doubled cone representing the "diamond" each python carries on its head. The form that spirals around the handle of the knife may also allude to the python (Horton 1965b).

Shrines for water spirits contain everything from carvings to found objects and trade goods. Many shrine furnishings allude directly to the spirits' environment or to "watery" qualities such as brightness and shininess. Shiny objects recall the reflective surface of the water and suggest the spirits' wealth or ties to trade. The Lower Niger bronzes that turn up in water spirit shrines satisfy both criteria and may serve as precedents for European trade goods (figs. F.5, F.6). Some items—like miniature canoes, paddles, and fishing spears—have obvious associations with water; others—including plastic dolls, drinking glasses, spoons, white saucers, cloth, cowries, coral beads, and bronzes—allude to trade or water. Priests sometimes claim that the emblems of their spirits appeared to them magically, often while they were bathing in the river. Because of their supernatural origins, these may be hidden between white saucers or behind cloth curtains (fig. F.7).

When asked to explain why one seldom finds figure carvings in shrines for water spirits, an Ijo carver explained that water spirits live in the water and only pay brief visits to their shrines. Many spirits mentioned in songs, invocations, and stories do not even have shrines. As an aspect of the python, Adumu has both land and water characteristics, which may explain his exceptional preference for figure carvings, but other spirits associated with pythons do not have shrine images (fig. F.8).

F.7 This diviner (left) says the emblems in her shrine appeared magically, including the glass tumbler, which she discovered after hearing something fall during a storm. According to her, none of the objects here were made by human hands, including the wood carvings. This woman claims to be associated with one hundred and forty spirits. Photograph by Martha G. Anderson, Isuini, Oyakiri clan, Western Ijo, 1992.

F.8 Unlike most water spirits, Adumu is described as very dark skinned and is represented by figure carvings. Some of the carvings in his shrine are identified as the equipment he uses when he goes fishing, but spears, paddles, and other objects can also serve as spirit emblems. Photograph by Martha G. Anderson, Azuzama, Bassan clan, Central Ijo, 1979.

Chapter 5 The Isoko as a Delta People

PHILIP M. PEEK

Although of diverse origins, the seventeen Isoko clans[1] now inhabiting the northernmost portion of the Central Niger Delta definitely were not a "water people" originally. Anyone who has experienced the vast network of waterways and islands that constitute the Niger Delta will appreciate that this is an absolutely unique environment, one that surely places distinct demands on humans who settle in it. As the various ancestral groups of the Isoko migrated into this deltaic territory, how did their worldview and religious beliefs and practices alter to accommodate such a drastic relocation? And how did their masquerades and shrine arts reflect these changes?

Scholars have long argued that areas such as the Niger Delta were essentially uninhabitable; from such arguments what is known as the "refuge area thesis" arose. This theory assumes that any people who would settle in the Delta could not have done so freely but must have been in search of refuge from other, worse perils. Some Isoko clans do indeed have historical traditions that recount ancestors fleeing jealous or crazed rulers in Aka (as the Isoko call Benin City), but few specifics are given. In truth, it is more likely that the migrations of early settlers were not hasty but actually very deliberate. Nevertheless, the Delta surely posed some threats, and no one could feel comfortable moving through dense, unknown rain forest and risking possible encounters with more powerful forces. Only the most intrepid of great hunters would have been able to lead such expeditions. Even today most Isoko villages are but clearings in the rain forest (fig. 5.2). Such speculation still supports a land-based ancestry with the ancestors of the present-day Isoko fleeing a kingdom located far from any major body of water and taking a land route to their present home. We now know, however, that these journeys were not direct, that they involved a number of river encounters, and that they probably occurred over many centuries. Isoko

5.1 Left: Standing male figure with sword. Isoko. Wood. H: 120.5 cm. FMCH X81.1565; Gift of William Lloyd Davis and the Rogers Family Foundation. Right: Standing female figure with gourd. Isoko. Wood. H: 104.2 cm. FMCH X81.1566; Gift of William Lloyd Davis and the Rogers Family Foundation.

5.2 Forest at the edge of the town of Enwe. Photograph by Philip M. Peek, 1970.

clan traditions record a time of settlement and establishment of ruling families as early as the fifteenth century, which means the migrations began long before.

After the passing of so many centuries, one would hardly expect to encounter lively, ongoing theological debate concerning the spiritual forces inhabiting the water versus those who dwell on the land, conflicting cosmologies, myths of origin, and so forth; but surely there would be vestiges of so radical an adjustment. Perhaps I anticipated this because some of the first information that the Isoko imparted to me about water suggested a negative attitude toward it. Why else would they say they never learned to swim? Why else would death by drowning be referred to as a "bad death"? In retrospect, I sometimes wonder if I simply projected on my informants the sense of unease that I experienced when I first entered their unique water-filled environment.

Nevertheless, surely there had to be some adjustment from land to water, and Isoko religion should carry evidence of this dramatic shift in worldview and environmental orientation. Given religion's frequently cited role of assuaging fears and clarifying uncertainty, one would expect some commentary in the record of Isoko religion. The evidence, however, while indicating an ambivalent attitude toward water, provides no extreme stance either pro or con. Below I will review the situation of the Isoko in the Delta from their arrival up to the present with a consideration of both the physical environment and their cultural behavior over time.

First, it is necessary to establish the credentials of the Isoko as at least a "waterside" people if not deltaic per se. Some areas of Isoko country receive up to 130 inches of rain a year, and the whole territory experiences two flood seasons, the flooding of the Niger (July to October) and the later rain floods (October to December). The eastern boundary of the Isoko peoples is the Niger River with many (younger) Isoko villages situated between the Niger and the Ase River, which parallels the Niger to the west. Southward is the Niger Delta proper with two large creeks, Ekregbesi and Erohwa forming the boundaries with the Western Ijo clan of Kabowei. North and west are the Western Igbo and Urhobo peoples, respectively, situated in low-lying plains. There are two large swamp systems (Bethel and Owe) running roughly southwest to northeast through Isoko country, and countless lakes, ponds, and streams scattered everywhere (figs. 5.3–5.6). In the past many major towns were simply inaccessible by land during the height of the rainy season, but paved roads (first built by the foreign oil companies) have changed that situation somewhat.

The oral traditions of the Edo of Benin City and Edo-related peoples in Southern Nigeria generally agree that over the centuries there were numerous periods of migration from Benin in all directions; we need to remember that we are talking about long periods of time and much movement of different ethnic groups. Migration routes into the Isoko area immediately tell us something about who the Isoko are (Peek 1976a). With the exception of later, smaller migratory groups and Olomoro clan, no Isoko clan was founded by people entering the area from the north or west, that is, directly from Benin City. Nevertheless, of the "original" parent clans, three claim exclusive origin from Aka, or Benin City (Iyede, Okpe, and Uzere), and three others claim to have been founded by migrants from Aka and Igbo

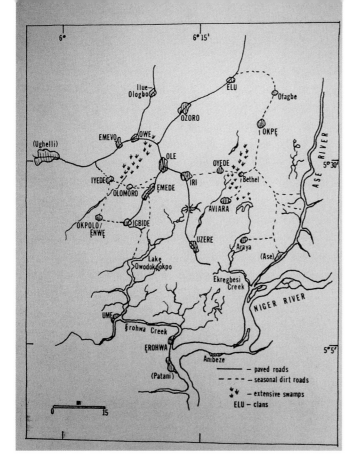

5.3 Map of major Isoko towns. Drawn by Philip M. Peek.

5.4 One of the myriad small lakes scattered throughout Isoko country. Photograph by Philip M. Peek, 1965.

5.5 A large canoe carrying raffia mats. Photograph by Philip M. Peek, Abraka, Ethiope River, 1971.

5.6 A bush path leads into the swamp as land and water merge. Photograph by Philip M. Peek, near Ofagbe, 1971.

migrants (Aviara, Igbide, and Okpolo/Enwe). Other Igbo roots are cited as well. One clan is exclusively Igbo (Ume), and another is a mix of Igbo and Delta Edo migrants (Emede). The two remaining "parent" clans are the Olomoro, founded from the Urhobo Olomu clan, and the ancient Erohwa clan, which claims to be autochthonous. Thus, a majority of Isoko clans recount migration routes eastward from Benin to the Niger and then southward; some went far into the Delta and settled in the Delta Edo areas around Degema, and some of these groups later moved across the Delta to settle in its north central area. It should be noted that the Delta Edo clans also have traditions of multiple origins of widely disparate peoples coming from as far north as Idah on the Niger, but they seem, ultimately, like the Isoko, to be primarily Igbo and Edo.

Other Isoko might have been part of the migrations led by Chima, the famous warrior (possibly a prince of the Benin court, more likely a Western Igbo leader), which resulted, by some accounts, in the settlements of Onitsha and Aboh. More likely, Isoko migrants arrived earlier because Aboh accepts that the Isoko had relations with the Akra (Akrai) who lived in Aboh before the Igbo arrived. Therefore, nearly all Isoko clans were founded by people entering the area from the south and east. It seems as if they went down the Niger until they encountered the head of the Delta and then turned either eastward as with the Delta Edo clans or westward with the Isoko. Ancestors of today's Isoko probably resided many years along the Niger as well as quite probably in the Degema area in the Eastern Delta.

Water and the Edo

Why the Isoko did not take a more direct route from Benin City is not clear. Although Urhobo clans now inhabit the territory between the Isoko and Benin City, all evidence indicates that they arrived after, not before, the Isoko. The Isoko, therefore, were not trying to avoid the Urhobo. The answer may lie in the traditions held by the Edo concerning water. There is evidence that the *oba* forbade his subjects to cross any bodies of water. According to Mockler-Ferryman, "They (Binis) were forbidden by juju either to leave their country or to cross water, and so it was hopeless for them to attempt trade, except through Jakri [Itsekiri] or other middlemen" (1892, 102). Bacon (1887) notes that the "Beni" were not even allowed to enter canoes. That the *oba* sought to insure control of trade is to be expected, but this extreme account remains a bit suspect.

There were other reasons for not migrating southward from Benin City. Due south are the creeks and lagoons of the Western Delta, the Bight of Benin, and the Atlantic Ocean. These were the realms of other peoples, including the Europeans. These were also the realms of death, of the spirits, and of Olokun, the Edo god of the sea. Olokun was especially associated with the Ethiope River, which was regarded as "the source of all the rivers and oceans of the world," and everyone accepted that the spirit world lay "across the waters" (P. Ben-Amos 1994, 120). Much safer then, with or without royal decrees, to go in a different direction. Nevadomsky makes a similar observation:

> The Bini are not a riverine people. They have played little part in the exploration of the delta rivers and have depended largely on the Urhobos, Ijaw, and Itsekiri for their fish. Indeed, the Bini tend to avoid close proximity to rivers. This may help to explain why, symbolically, rivers are regarded as almost insurmountable obstacles that only the most powerful individuals can overcome. [1984, 91, n.3]

Thus it would seem that prohibitions, if indeed there were any, were probably economic and related to trade restrictions rather than being spiritual in nature.[2] Whatever their origins, however, these accounts suggest that the Edo-related Isoko would have had negative reactions to rivers and the Niger Delta. The issue of cultural heritage is, however, not quite that simple.

When dealing with a divine king like the *oba* of Benin, it is virtually impossible to separate the realms of the sacred and the secular, and on further examination, we learn that water has many important meanings for the Edo. Indeed, for the Edo and others in Southern Nigeria, the earth itself is believed to have come from the water. For those on land, the *oba* controlled the products of the water. Just as he controlled ivory and bronze, he controlled ownership of kaolin (which is referred to as "chalk") and coral. Coral beads were significant prestige items that the *oba* distributed to lesser dignitaries. While chiefs and royalty thus honored could then wear these coral ornaments, they were usually returned to the *oba* when the recipient of the gift died. Although "chalk" remains a ubiquitous element in ritual life, its link with the *oba* of Benin was unique. Tradition held that the *oba* never ate food but did eat chalk. The association was so close that the initial public announcement of an *oba*'s death was the statement, "the chalk is broken," accompanied by the smashing of a huge piece of chalk. Further, the *oba* was incased in clay before he was buried (Nevadomsky 1984). In a discussion of Benin narratives, Dan Ben-Amos records the expression for the *oba*'s death as "the earth ate chalk" (1967, 55), which suggests the return of this sacred being to the earth.

These and other practices must be understood in relation to Olokun, the god of the sea, perhaps the most important deity for the Edo after the high god, Osanobua. In many ways, the *oba* and Olokun can be understood as parallel rulers, each controlling his respective realm, land and water (fig. 5.7 and compare fig. G.1). The relationship between the two leaders was always tense, and the *oba* never went to Olokun's major shrine in Urhonigbe. One praise name for Olokun translates as "The king of the sea is greater than the king of the land" (Rosen 1989, 44). While the *oba* controlled all wealth for those on land, much of that wealth came from the sea; in fact, according to one tradition, the *oba* originally stole cowries, brass, and coral from Olokun (P. Ben-Amos 1994, 120).

Although Olokun is not served by the Isoko, there are other correlations with Edo religious practice. The centrality of chalk is paramount in this case (although it is accepted that kaolin is used throughout Africa). The Isoko also value coral beads, a key feature of the royal regalia of the *oba*'s court, as well as cowrie shells. Many Isoko villages have special shrines for found objects, which are often ancient works in bronze hauled up from the creeks while

5.7 Oba *of Benin at the Igwe ceremonies.*
Photograph by Philip M. Peek, Benin City, 1966.

fishing and are thought to be from Eriwi (the spirit world; see also P. Ben-Amos 1994, 123–25). Of note, pots of liquid in Isoko shrines are yet another reminder of the ritual importance of water.

Interestingly the migration narratives of several Isoko clans, such as Okpe and Ozoro, relate that their ancestors were only able to cross rivers on the backs of crocodiles or manatees, which magically transformed themselves into logs. Perhaps, if there was indeed an edict by the divine *oba* prohibiting water travel, it could only be violated in such a supernatural fashion. These accounts parallel traditions still heard in the Igbo towns of Onitsha and Aboh on the Niger and may be evidence of common migrations.

In addition, it was said in the past in Onitsha that the king could not leave the palace and could not look at the Niger River (Isichei 1984, 237). Further evidence that the Igbo share some of the Isoko ambivalence toward water is Chukwuemeka Olisa's statement about the Riverain Igbo: "[M]ost Ibos are afraid of the River, while others were afraid of slave raiders. Even Benin people are non-swimmers and can only, out of desperation, seek refuge in an area near the River" (1990, 111). All of these accounts and traditions indicate that the ancient links of the Edo of Benin City with the Isoko, and perhaps the Igbo, may include highly charged associations with water. Clearly, although the Edo are land-based, they have highly elaborate beliefs relating to the sea, rivers, and lakes, which are portrayed as sources of great wealth and great danger (see figs. 1.5, 1.6).

The Isoko and Other Southern Nigerian Peoples

While the Isoko may be related to the Edo, they seldom comment on the relationship directly, and the two peoples share no physical borders. How then do the Isoko peoples identify themselves in relation to their neighbors in Southern Nigeria? And do they orient themselves toward waterside or land peoples? Thirteen of the seventeen officially recognized Isoko clans consider themselves to be totally or in part from Aka, but a couple of these came into the area from Elele and the area of the little-studied Delta Edo clans of the Eastern Delta.

The second largest grouping of clans in terms of origin would have to be considered Igbo, or better, Western Igbo. Even some of these groups, however, seem to have ties to Benin City; for example, the Isoko clan of Ume was founded from Onya, now an Igbo town along the Niger, which claims origin in Benin City via the Delta Edo clans. It appears that the Isoko were settled prior to the development of Aboh as the major force on the Niger River because, as noted earlier, even Aboh recognizes that the Isoko traded with the Akra (Akrai), whom the Aboh displaced. Although "Igabo" (literally, "those behind Aboh," one of the first European designations for the Isoko) is a term of insult today, it does demonstrate the eastward (rather than westward or Benin City) orientation of the Isoko clans. The Isoko continue to travel readily to Aboh and other Western Igbo (Ukwane [Ukwani] and Ndosimili [Ndusomili], i.e., land-bound and waterside Igbo groups) towns for trade, farming, and fishing. In discussing ancient trade networks along the Niger, Olisa writes, "long distance travel between Ossomala and Igala must have existed long before the slave trade began. For instance, Isoko fishermen were said to have developed trade in fish as early as the 11th Century" (1990, 56). Thus, in addition to historical contacts, there are ongoing associations between the two groups. Correspondences of terminology, cultural features, and artistic traditions seem to link the Isoko more to the Riverain Igbo than any other peoples. It is very difficult, for example, to distinguish Oguta and Isoko carvings, and one easily finds parallels in masking traditions (see Jones 1989b).

These contacts and affiliations are noteworthy in light of the absence of such identifications between the Isoko and others in the Delta area. Despite the references by some clans to origins in what is now an Ijo area, that is, the Delta Edo region, there are seldom references to the neighboring Ijo peoples. Some Ijo groups refer to the Isoko as Biotu, or "people of the interior" (i.e., further "inside" though not necessarily of land only). Reverend John W. Hubbard (1948) was much impressed by the extreme antagonisms that existed between Ijo and Isoko peoples. This might have resulted from the history of Ijo raiding of Isoko waterside villages. As noted in Martha Anderson's essay (see chapter 3 of this volume), there are still vivid recollections of Ijo raids, especially by "Bibi Cala" (Bibikeala). The Ijo drove the Erohwa from the site of today's major trading center of Patani, and there are scattered references linking Uzere clan with the Ijo. If there are Ijo cultural influences among the Isoko clans, they are barely recognized with the exception of the origins of *khikhi*, the lethal local "palm wine gin" said to have been first made by the Ijo. Despite their shared border (the Kabowei Ijo clan lies just south of the Isoko and the Erohwa), the Isoko seldom speak of traveling into the Delta for trade or fishing. Even the Isoko villages deep in the Delta, which are acknowledged as such by the Ijo, seem to have lost touch with their parent clans. There is some intermarriage between the Ijo and Isoko. As Kay Williamson has elaborated (see the appendix to this volume), the Isoko and Ijo languages come from different families. This difference is underscored by the shared vocabulary of the Isoko with the Edo and Igbo.[3]

In the face of all this evidence of difference, we should not forget that one of the most important ceremonial complexes among the Isoko, the Oworu celebrations, may derive in part from Ijo ceremonies. And, in turn, some Western Ijo communities acknowledge that they borrowed the *ivri* (see interleaf D and the preface to this volume, fig. A) from the Isoko (figs. 5.8, 5.9). Philip Leis has noted that the Western Ijo attribute their practice of *avuo* (sacred covenant of peace) to the Isoko (personal communication).

Turning in yet another direction, most Isoko seem very aware of the many similarities between themselves and the Urhobo clans. In fact, the mutual linguistic intelligibility between the two groups is often greater than among clans within either group. While the Isoko readily accept this general kinship with the Urhobo, they have simply had no contact with the Itsekiri. And, finally, as noted earlier, associations with the Edo are limited to ancient traditions. Some Isoko clans have very recent associations linking their *ivie* (priest-kings; sing. "*ovie*") and the *oba* and his court in Benin City; but these are suspect. There is never reference to Edo villages, except for the migration route of Uzere clan ancestors, who may have first gone north of Benin City.

Intraclan Orientation

Among themselves, the Isoko carefully distinguish land and waterside communities and those who migrate upriver to do seasonal fishing. Some clans, such as Igbide, embody these different orientations. The *ovie* ("priest-king")

5.8   *Figure holding an* ivri. *Isoko. Wood. H: 64 cm.*
John B. Ross.

5.9   *An old, damaged clan* ivri *with its new*
replacement. Photograph by Philip M. Peek, Ume, 1971.

of Igbide is not allowed to go near water, and he is associated with carvers and carpenters. These traditions are cited by the people to demonstrate the association of his quarter of town with Benin. The other quarters of the town are referred to as *uru-ame* (streets-water) and as Igbo. A noticeably bare "no-man's land" still separates the two sections of Igbide town, and until the late 1960s, a large wall served as an additional barrier. Intriguingly, given the apparent attempt to separate the *ovie* of Igbide from the water, his burial rites were explicitly linked to water. Elders told me that his skull was submerged in the swamp with the expectation that the flesh would be eaten away, and his body was buried in his compound in a canoe.

Okpolo/Enwe clan has an even more mixed heritage, one which is still marked today by intraclan antagonisms. There are two sections of the clan (as demonstrated by the split name); one Igbo and one Edo. Both Enwe and Igbide have associations with several other clans now considered Urhobo, which also came from Igbo country. Such examples not only demonstrate the diversity of origins of Isoko clans and the continued intragroup hostilities but, more importantly, that the Isoko continue to distinguish emphatically between land and water peoples even within their own communities. There are a number of Isoko villages on the Niger and between the Niger and Ase Rivers; but these are most often recent or Christian offshoots of major clan villages. Nevertheless, there are a few ancient Isoko villages on the Niger and deep in the Delta.

Most Isoko clans distinguish between the "owners of the land" (the eldest family, usually the clan/town founder) and the "rulers" (usually the family or families that control the *uvie,* or "kingship"). As well, most clans have both the Odio tradition of titled elders, which has Edo roots, and the

Igbu tradition of titled warriors, which has Igbo parallels. All of these social institutions are, if anything, land oriented.

Recognition of the Natural Environment

One means of dealing with the problem before us is simply to review cultural practices and land/water associations to see if some pattern emerges. We will first review land associations, continuing to assume an original land orientation no matter how ancient; we will then turn to water associations and, finally, general cultural complexes.

It is sometimes difficult to determine if the elaboration of cultural practices surrounding some life event or aspect of the environment is an indication of extreme attraction or repulsion—perhaps expressed through a dramatic sacred-versus-profane distinction or simply familiarity as opposed to ignorance about that dimension. For example, the Isoko seem to be far more exacting about ritual uses of fish than of land creatures. Welch (1936) found much evidence of this in the 1920s, as I did fifty years later. Fifteen different fish used in religious ceremonies are distinguished in Iyede clan, one of those furthest from the permanent water areas. This is not what one would expect from a "land people," so there is a question whether this results from an importance granted fish after long association with water or a fascination resulting from only recent contact.

Perhaps most significant is that the Isoko serve the Earth, Oto. The eldest male in the community (village or clan) serves the Earth at a special shrine. In some clans, this object of service is literally deified as a singular entity; but all clans and villages have services at their foundation sites to the Otewo (Earth of the town). Some clans distinguish separate shrines for the Earth and for the site where the founders first "civilized" the territory for human habition through specific rituals. The latter is usually marked by an *oyise* tree (*Newbouldia laevis* Seeman [family Bignoniaceae]), considered to be the oldest tree on earth. This is a custom shared with virtually all Southern Nigerian peoples. The Ijo also make this distinction of "settled earth" (civilized space) and Earth. While the Isoko do not venerate the Earth in anything near the elaborate fashion that the Owerri Igbo do with their *mbari* houses, there is absolutely no deification of water. No ritual recognition is made of water, which is never personified or sacralized as a general force in any way by the Isoko. There are no rituals for water alone as there are for the Earth, although there are numerous individual *edhame* ("deities [of] water"), some of whom are very important.

Additionally, we need note that the single most important object in any shrine is the *ovo* bundle, usually of seven twigs from the *Detarium senegalense* Gmelin tree, which symbolizes the ancestors who have served that shrine whether of a family, lineage, village, or clan (fig. 5.10). Again, this is land-based imagery relying on significant trees. Furthermore, all shrines are protected by palm frond barriers. As well, the major role played by the *iletu* (warriors) is always related to land-based conflicts and ceremonies.

In addition to shrines to Oto, every Isoko clan served the *edho* (deities) Eloho and Uloho to insure fertility in the community, primarily on the farms. Services by women for Eloho and by men for Uloho have diminished somewhat, but these *edho* are still acknowledged. The fact remains that the Isoko calendar is based on the farming cycle, although they are affected by

5.10 An ovo *bundle. Photograph by Philip M. Peek, Ume, 1971.*

periods of significant flooding. New Yam and other firstfruits or harvest festivals are celebrated, and these are always more significant than the relatively few fishing festivals.

Most Isoko communities are connected by land, except for those between the Ase and the Niger, those up the Niger River, or those located in the Delta. Of course, during the height of the floods, many towns and villages are cut off from each other and can be reached only by canoes. Even in the dry season, many Isoko travel by canoe or motor boat (fig. 5.11). In the past, although there is some dispute about this, it appears that most Isoko never learned to swim. Perk Foss (personal communication, 1998) reports the same for the Urhobo.

There is no question that Isoko territory is "watery," but how much do the Isoko know about water? Are they commercially involved with water through fishing, as they are with land and farming, or is their relationship with water of a more psychological or religious nature? As we have already seen, the Isoko definitely consider some of their members to live in waterside communities, and some Isoko believe there is discrimination by land-based communities against waterside Isoko (Adeline Apena, personal communication, 1998). It is recognized that a number of Isoko pursue fishing further south into the Delta as well as up the Niger even beyond Onitsha, and they have done so for centuries. This practice of *ukane*, or "traveling away for work," is engaged in by fisherfolk as well as those who rent oil palm trees from others.

As noted earlier, the number and types of fish that the Isoko categorize by ritual and in commercial contexts are another indication of the extent to which they might be considered a water people. They exhibit as well an extraordinarily sophisticated range of fishing techniques. These include a variety of baskets and hand-cast nets, poisons that stun the fish, and huge barricades, which they erect to create giant traps when the floods subside (figs. 5.12, 5.13).

Broadly speaking, the time of the rains is a "good" time (as opposed to the dry season with the Harmattan winds that bring sickness). The floods are thought to bring prosperity, and "water is taken to symbolize femininity, calmness, and peace" (Adeline Apena, personal communication, 1998). Indeed, the major women's ceremonies occur at the height of the floods. There are also other areas that demonstrate Isoko attitudes toward water.

5.11 *Ume town as seen from Erohwa Creek. Photograph by Philip M. Peek, 1971.*

5.12 *A fishing barricade approximately sixty feet high. Photograph by Philip M. Peek, Erohwa Creek near Ume, 1971.*

5.13 *Fishing nets along Erohwa Creek. Photograph by Philip M. Peek, 1971.*

Dreams and Verbal Arts

Reverend James Welch, an Anglican missionary who later completed a doctoral dissertation at Cambridge University based on his research among the Isoko, collected interpretations of over forty specific dreams with no contexts clarified (1936, 375–80). Reviewing these, however, provides no obvious pattern of positive or negative attitudes toward water or land. Welch was told, for example, that eating or receiving presents of dried fish portended the dreamer's sickness, but catching fresh fish meant good health. Equally unclear is the following: "If the dreamer is asked to fill a canoe and refuses to do so, he is safe; if he did not refuse, he will die" (1936, 375–77).

Perhaps more informative is the explanatory note that Welch added for another dream: "To dream of pulling [paddling] a canoe means a burial is near. (This is the interpretation put upon this dream by the inland villages; the people living by the water ignore this dream as it is so common.) This dream is commonest in October [the height of the flood season]" (Welch 1936, 376).

A review of the few collections available fails to reveal a clear concentration of proverbs or prose narratives dealing with water as opposed to land environments in either a negative or positive fashion. Both Welch and I collected a number of stories that involve the need for supernatural and/or animal aid to cross bodies of water. The accounts I recorded were termed *iku* (histories) and thus were considered truthful accounts of real events—I do not know what genre Welch collected. A few Isoko songs that I translated refer to the floods.

We might quickly note here that Isoko carvings include a boat-shaped container called an *oko* (fig. 5.14) that is used by carvers to hold tools and by ritual specialists for their sacred paraphernalia. But this may relate to a practice recorded in Benin City as opposed to one originating in the Delta. Nevadomsky reports that during the *oba*'s funeral rites, Ughoton villages dance with an *oko* sent from Benin: "This small canoe-shaped object is similar in meaning to the *okun* used in non-royal burial rites. Here it represents the wealth of the departed Oba that he carried with him to the other world" (1984, 49). This reminds us of the degree of "water orientation" that the Isoko ancestors from Benin may have brought with them. For the Edo, as noted previously, water was the source of much wealth.

5.14 Oko *carved by Eture Egbedi. This* oko *is similar to the one in which the carver carries his tools. Photograph by Philip M. Peek, 1970. This* oko *is presently in the collection of the Phoebe Hearst Museum of Anthropology, University of California, Berkeley, no. 2222 5-6317.*

Religious Beliefs and Practices

In respect to my initial questions concerning the movment of the Isoko into a watery environment, it seems reasonable to expect that some notice would have been taken of the radically changed environment. One might expect the people to have attributed some special quality, good or bad, to that which was new to them—the streams, swamps, and other bodies of water. But it is not readily evident that the Isoko made any special spiritual adjustment to their new Delta home. As we trace environmental associations among the Isoko clans in our attempt to determine if there is a distinct ethos associated with water, we find many examples that reflect a mixture of meanings, positive and negative, about the two basic elements of land and water.

To highlight the complexity of this issue, we might first note that the Isoko incorporate the world of water into their ritual lives literally from birth to death. Special trees are dedicated to newborn infants, and their umbilical cords are usually buried at the base of these. When challenged about origins, a person proudly points to his or her tree. If a man wishes his son to become a fisherman, however, he will throw his umbilical cord into a pond. When boys are circumcised, their foreskins are likened to *omorue*, a "slippery fish." Similarly, when women are "circumcised" (actually excised), the labia minora are thought to resemble the *obiova*, a reddish fish (Welch 1936, 118). It should be noted that these ceremonies for women occur from September to December, at the height of the floods. It would seem that this type of cultural symbolism could only develop among a people long accustomed to living near water.

Turning to the end of life in Akpo (this world), we learn that drowning is considered a bad death for the Isoko, but so is being killed by a falling branch or tree. Death under these circumstances requires that the body of the deceased be disposed of in *aho,* the "bad bush," without proper burial ceremonies. Plantain is used at the beginning and end of life in this world. A plantain stalk is laid across the doorway to mark the home of a newborn, and another is used to represent the deceased in the funeral, or "second burial," ceremonies. Many Isoko refer to the plantain as one of the oldest plants and one definitely associated with human habitation. It is clearly associated with the land. There are a few instances, such as in Igbide clan, when a canoe is used as a coffin. Overall, for the Isoko, however, the major ceremonies that bring one into this world and send one out are linked to the earth, not to water.

There are no complexes related to water that are comparable to these earthbound activities. As previously noted, water is not personified or honored in any specific manner. No religious complexes shared by all Isoko clans are oriented toward water in the same manner that we have noted for land, or better, the Earth. While fishing is a regulated activity and most lakes are controlled by clan deities, this is not the focal point of their services. Even those deities known as *edhame* were usually served for the general well-being and prosperity of the clan, not exclusively for water-related concerns.

Edho or *Edhame*?

Isoko elders distinguish an *edhame* as a type of *edho*; specifically an *edhame* is a deity who "moves between water and air," as opposed to a land deity who "moves between land and air." It is noteworthy that only occasionally was the term *edhovo* (*edho* meaning "deity" and *ovo* meaning "earth"*)* used

5.15 Uzere clan elders with the ovie *during annual celebrations at the lake belonging to Eni. Photograph by Philip M. Peek, 1965.*

5.16 Staffs belonging to elders line the shore of Lake Eni during celebrations. Photograph by Philip M. Peek, 1965.

to indicate an earth deity, which suggests that land-based deities are the norm. Nevertheless, of the approximately one hundred clan deities about whom I gathered information, the division between land and water was almost even when water or land links were identified. A pattern of sorts emerged in that land-based male *edho* tended to have water-based wives. The priest of the deity Oliho in Ole proudly describes his *edho* as having *edhame* wives. If such distinctions are made, it seems that male and land dominate over female and water; but this is not widespread or consistent.

Some clan deities were always based in water, such as Eni of Uzere; in fact, the migration of the founders of Uzere was supposedly determined by the movement of Eni from one body of water to another until he finally settled in a lake near Uzere. The *ovie* of Uzere, who is also chief priest of Eni, made an interesting declaration one day: "*Edho* show themselves. Eni can appear as a school of fish, or in the form of a crocodile, or you can only hear the voice" (October 15, 1971; figs. 5.15, 5.16). It must be added that Eni was the most powerful witch-finding oracle in the Delta—its prominence was rivaled only by the famous Aro Chukwu oracle in eastern Nigeria. Eni's power served to unify the Isoko clans in ways that had never before existed. Thus the most powerful clan *edho* among the Isoko was an *edhame*.

Other deities seem to have acquired an association with a body of water or local water deities some time after the clan had become established. But the addition of a "watery aspect" seems more an indication of the deity's expanding powers than a special adjustment to the environment. The "growth" of a deity in terms of powers and abilities was reckoned by an increase in followers and an inner "growth" of a family. In other words, the deity would "grow" (i.e., signify its greater powers) by acquiring a wife and then children. This is more a process of expansion (as opposed to addition), analogous to an inflatable object (a family, in this case), which expands from "the inside." A photograph of an Isoko shrine in the 1930s, perhaps taken by Reverend Hubbard, illustrates this dynamic (fig. 5.17). I believe a similar pattern might be in operation when it is revealed that a certain *edho* has powers in the water as well as land. Just as the deities' followings increase due to the continued success of their powers, their scope of operation broadens. Nevertheless, the direction or sequence of growth still gives prominence to land over water. An Ole elder offered the following description of the nature of the deity Oliho:

> Oliho looks and acts like a human male. He stays in water and on land. He lives in water because some of his wives are water deities; if only a land deity, he wouldn't marry water deities. Oliho moves like the breeze; he moves like thunder. His presence is signaled by the sound of ankle bells, by sudden darkness, or by sudden silence and stillness. When going to serve him, there is complete silence—this is a sign of his presence all around. [December 21, 1970]

This is certainly a dramatic description of the omnipresence of a deity. A complementary portrait of such clan *edho*, whose main duty is to "save" the people, was recorded during an interview with Oyede elders: "Be he a young man or old, [if] on water and there's trouble, call Ogwa-Oyede and he'll land him safely. If lost in the bush and [you] call, [he] will bring light" (March 27, 1971). Thus, Ogwa-Oyede protects his children on land or

5.17 *"Town juju to keep evil from town and to encourage the birth of many children." Photograph courtesy of the Church Mission Society, London. This photograph may have been taken by Reverend John. W. Hubbard in the 1930s.*

5.18 *A partially destroyed mud sculpture reveals its underlying wooden framework. Photograph by Philip M. Peek, Ebo-Iyede village, 1971.*

water. One of the clan deities of Okpe, Abrebo, is said to have aided the migration of the clan's ancestors into the area by turning crocodiles into logs, which provided a way for them to cross a river. This migration legend is found among many Riverain Igbo peoples.

Unfortunately, no tidy consistent pattern ever seems to have developed with the land "aspect" being senior to the water "aspect" as we might expect with a land people moving into a delta area; in fact, sometimes matters developed in the opposite direction. Okpe is one of the oldest and largest of Isoko clans, and its senior clan deity has two distinct aspects, one on the land and the other in the water. There was great debate during my interviews with Okpe clan elders, as they could not decide which of these aspects was senior.

Although I was not able to attend the celebration of Oro at Okpe, J. N. A. Odudu (1970, 10–12) has provided a good description of the activities. The merging of land and water references seems to permeate Oro's festival. "The Oro juju consists of two images representing a god and a goddess. The two images were made with the bodies of a native doctor and his wife." According to tradition, the couple had been invited from Kwale (Ukwane Igbo) to make a war god, and the Okpe people decided they could not leave so they killed them, pinned them to the ground, and later ants made mounds over them. The images were erected on these mounds. The "images represent god of land and goddess of water." On the last day of the festival, the chief priest carries a ram into Lake Oro, and while others hold him (because Oro really wants a human sacrifice), he throws the ram far into the lake. The chief priest's supporters then struggle to remove him from the water before he is drawn under by the deity. Interestingly, no clear distinction in the media used to represent water and land deities seems to have arisen. Where one might expect clay for water gods and wood for their land-based counterparts, the merging of the two media seemed more the issue: mud-sculpted figures were molded over wood framing, and wood carvings were covered with chalk (fig. 5.18; see also interleaf G).

Priests are chosen by the *edho*, but usually the chosen do not wish to assume these difficult responsibilities. Nevertheless, after a period of trouble and torment, they accept their calling. It is striking that part of the process

5.19a A two-story agure *with a large cared* ivri *on its center post. Photograph by Philip M. Peek, Enwe/Okpolo, 1971.*

5.19b The carved ivri *center post seen in the* agure *in figure 5.19a.*

of selection involves visiting the deity, but this only occurs with water deities. If a visitation is involved for conversion and training, then the priest goes down into a specified body of water to the deity's home. Here the prospective priest stays with the deity for seven days, surviving only on white chalk for food before returning to this world. This sacred diet recalls Edo traditions concerning the *oba*. Such accounts are never heard in relation to land-based deities. Several traditions of this sort were recorded in Uzere. Ogburu of Uzere invited Etemero, his first priest, into his lake for seven days (Aye-Ogburu, Ogburu's wife, is also said to "move in land and water spiritually"). A similar incident is described concerning Eni of Uzere.

It is tempting to see such traditions as derived from ancient associations with Olokun when the ancestors were still in Benin City. For the Edo water was associated with the wealth of Olokun and the Portuguese. Nevertheless, the Isoko traditions of visits with *edhame* are usually for spiritual training, although observations of vast wealth are occasionally made. Even in such cases, the acquisition of riches is never central to the narrative. Thus, while we might see these accounts as evidence of the retention of religious traditions, they also illustrate individual cultural adjustments.

Occasionally, Isoko clan deities associated with the water were referred to as "Mami Wata" or as being like her, although there is no service for Mami Wata per se. No attempt was made at the time of my research to correlate these references and, of course, comparative research had not yet revealed the cross-cultural associations of which we are now aware. But in regard to our basic issue of land versus water ethos, Mami Wata entities provide an apt image of dramatic ambivalence. These characters are vividly described as beautiful and generous but, at the same time, deadly and deceitful women. Perhaps the world of water holds such an ambivalent message for the Isoko in general.

Types of shrine offerings are another means by which we might be able to distinguish meaningful attitudes about land and water orientations. The *agure* ("men's meeting hall"; figs. 5.19a,b, 5.20) houses ancestral shrines where the skulls of great animals—such as leopards and bush cows—killed by men of the community are displayed (see interleaf G). To emphasize the (apparent) land orientation of such shrines, Welch (1936, 37) reports that large yams used to be hung as honorific offerings. Nevertheless, one can find the heads of the largest types of fish, such as *eba,* hung along with bush animal skulls at the *esemo* (ancestor) shrine in each compound's *ogwa* (meeting room). In Iyede approximately fifteen different fish were cited in commentaries concerning food prohibitions and shrine offerings for various clan *edho.* Given Iyede's distance from the larger lakes and streams, this seems an especially significant amount of attention being paid to water, as opposed to land, creatures. Of note is that Iyede's ancestors were originally settled much closer to water.

While different deities did require different offerings, data are limited as to correlations between land and water deities and land and water offerings. In Aviara clan, nearer to Ase River and larger permanent ponds, the *edhame* are served white cassava and no palm oil (i.e., their food is "white"), while the land deities are served "red" foods (red cassava and pounded yam with palm

5.20 Post. Isoko. Wood and pigment. H: 174 cm.
Collection of Toby and Barry Hecht.

5.21 Okao *masks such as these are performed only for* Oworu. *Photograph by Philip M. Peek, Iyede, 1971.*

5.22 *Mask for Erese festival. Igbo-Isoko. Wood, plant fiber, cowrie shells, and brass. H: 29.8 cm. Walt Disney-Tishman African Art Collection. Photograph by Jerry L. Thompson.*

oil). The symbolism of white for water, red for land may indeed be significant. Four of Aviara's nine clan *edho* are linked to lakes, including, in properly problematic fashion, Oto, the Earth. The *ovie* of Aviara always initiates the annual festival with gifts of fish to the clan *edho*. Eni of Uzere also had very explicit taboos concerning certain fish.

It seems that the most frequently encountered items in shrines are associated with water. Chalk is the most common offering, and cowrie shells played a far more important role in the past. Pots of water, often transformed into medicines, are usually found in shrines as well. Priests, as well as titled elders and *ivie,* often wear coral beads, perhaps in keeping with the court tradition of Benin.

Masquerades

Although some Isoko clans brought *edhame* with them as they migrated into the area, the best-known water-related deity, Oworu, was established after their settlement in this area. At one time, all clans celebrated Oworu. Given our focus on land and water, it is very tempting to find the etymology of Oworu to be key: *owu* is "water" and *oru* is "land" in most Ijo dialects. In fact, the Oworu complex seems to be very widespread in the Delta and contiguous areas (see interleaf I; Foss 1973; Cole and Aniakor 1984; see also Bentor, forthcoming). Additionally, aspects of it have possible sources throughout Southern Nigeria where a number of peoples have *owu* masks. For the Isoko, Oworu seems to have links to Igbo, Ijo, perhaps even Nupe traditions (Peek 1983). Even more striking similarities in mask forms exist between Isoko Oworu masks and those Jones photographed in Oguta (1989b; fig. 5.21). Although several of the masks are called Ugo (or "[vulturine fish] eagle"), Oworu is considered an *edhame* who is "danced to" yearly (rather than served regularly throughout the year). Oworu is invited to leave the water and join the people on land for the celebrations. On one day of the festival, rain is supposed to fall because it aids Oworu's movements in his canoe. The large Oni-Edho masquerade is not just the "mother" mask but is likened to a boat that must carry the other spirits away at the end of the celebrations. When the ceremonies end, Oworu is invited to leave and return to the waters. In fact, in Iyede clan the people insure his departure with the other spirits by staging a mock funeral and literally driving the masks out of the arena. A distinctive feature of the costumes of Oworu masqueraders is a projection from the buttocks. Although I never received a clear explanation of this from the Isoko, among the Ijo it is refered to as a fish's tail or fin (Martha Anderson, personal communication). Dance steps observed in Isoko Oworu masquerades and Ijo masquerades are virtually identical.

Another apparent reference to water can be seen in the intriguing shape of the *akwakwa,* the unique slit gong played only for Oworu (fig. 5.23). Perk Foss has informed me that some Urhobo communities actually use this for divination, submerging it in a swamp and then interpreting the contents that accumulate after some time (personal communication, 1999). Although no one told me it was "boat-shaped" or had special aquatic associations, the confirmed associations are enough to add it to our "water-oriented" items. It is also interesting that the Ijo do have water pot "drums," although the Isoko do not use such instruments.

Many Isoko carved decorative "dance paddles," which look like regular canoe paddles but are nicely painted and decorated with mirrors and fancy carving. Furthermore, when *iletu* (warriors) perform their special *idu* dance, they are described as making paddling motions with their cutlasses. Some Oworu traditions and many general dance complexes are said to originate from the observation of water spirits dancing on the shores of streams or lakes. The widespread traditions of either observing spirits at the water's edge or finding sacred paraphernalia left there by the spirits seems to echo Edo traditions (see P. Ben-Amos 1994); but they may also relate to similar accounts recorded among the Ijo.

In the past, the Oworu complex clearly served an integrative function for the Isoko as it drew upon a number of elements apparently from very different sources and was celebrated among all the clans. It should be noted that while these elements were assimilated, they could not be considered completely integrated. The Oworu festival complex thereby represents the composition process of the Isoko clans.

It is of note that Isoko masquerades rarely have literal depictions of fish, aquatic mammals, or boats. The majority are performed with representations of antelopes, other animals, or humans. One exception occurred at the opening of Iyede's town hall where some masqueraders wore large wooden crayfish on their heads with the rest of their costume the familiar Isoko "disguise," a wealth of brilliantly colored silk scarves. A few instances of fish masks have also been encountered but only in those communities situated on large creeks. Ume, an Isoko clan founded from the Niger River Igbo town of Onya, used to perform a variety of masks, many of which had aquatic images (fig. 5.24). Although I never witnessed it, I recorded several detailed descriptions of an extraordinary masquerade in Erohwa that involved hanging real fish on the masker. My disbelief had no impact on my informants so I must accept this account.

Ase, a large Ndosimili (Riverain) Igbo town on Ase Creek with extensive Isoko connections, has a festival (Erese) with elaborate carved masquerades. One of these is an extraordinary model of a river steamer. The mask is formally called "Ogbo-Oyibo" (ship-White man) and the carving has "Ase-Palm" (presumably the name of an old river steamer) written on the bow (fig. 5.25). I never encountered such masks among the Isoko, even the waterside communities.

Another masquerade might be mentioned simply because it is one of the few instances of possible borrowing from the Ijo. At the first stage of Eni's yearly celebrations in Uzere clan, the Emusuo dance is performed and the Ogri drum is beaten. One of the masks appears to be similar to the horizontal masks we associate with the Ijo, but in this case, it is worn on the back. There is no apparent confusion here for the elders who clearly assert, "The whole dance is done in a squatting position with masks tied on the dancer's backs, and they are covered with cloth; nothing special about the position, just the agreed method due to the music and rhythm." It was never clarified if this reference likened the dance to movements in water, perhaps as observed from shore.

Eni is said to have come with Uze, the founder of Uzere clan, from Benin City. There is another account, related by the Erohwa that Eni was one of their clan deities but left them for Uzere. All agree Eni is an *edhame*. The Erohwa, who are accepted by all as the first into this area, were displaced by the Kabowei Ijo who drove them from Patani. This might provide the link to the Ijo.

5.23 A spectacularly carved and painted akwakwa *in front of a men's meeting house. Photograph by Philip M. Peek, Enwe/Okpolo, 1971.*

Conclusion

Can we conclude from this survey that the Isoko are a land- or water-based people? Not really, but it does appear that, in the end, the Isoko are not afraid of the water. The Isoko are certainly not "water people" to the same degree that the Ijo are, though some waterside Isoko do consider themselves to be. Overall, the Isoko remain predominantly a land people. The calm with which the Isoko deal with water adds credibilty to reconstructed settlement dates of over five hundred years ago. This familiarity also recalls the number of Isoko clans with ties to the Delta Edo area and the Riverain Igbo adding further temporal and geographical evidence for a long-standing familiarity with the water.

But as well, I believe it demonstrates that the dichotomy I first drew is simply too extreme. Meaningful associations among the Isoko are not all land or all water. In terms of the questions initially posed, I saw no alterations of shrines that might reflect the changed environment. The fact that the Isoko have more mud sculptures in their shrines than the Urhobo (who have more wooden shrine sculptures) can not be correlated with the relatively more watery environment of the Isoko without much more research. The Isoko masquerades do reflect some use of "aquatic themes"

5.24 No longer performed, these masks testify to the extraordinary variety of Isoko masquerades. Photograph by Philip M. Peek, Ume, 1971.

5.25 In great detail, this "Ase-Palm" mask depicts one of the old trading ships on the Niger River. Photograph by Philip M. Peek, Ase, 1971.

but no more than many peoples who live even further from water. Perhaps the Edo and Igbo ancestors, though not "of the Delta," were simply not at odds with the watery environment of the Delta, as was originally thought. Therefore, their accommodation was without trauma, and as a consequence their beliefs and arts do not reflect any radical ideological or religious adjustments. Despite the centuries involved and the modifications that may have been lost, I believe some record of conflict would still be visible if indeed there had been a conflict.

At the risk of appearing to be an environmental determinist, I would suggest that the Isoko seem to represent a midpoint between land and water orientations of Southern Nigerian peoples. Despite their predominantly Edo origins, they lack the clear distinction between land and water that the Edo demonstrate. And they certainly do not reflect the almost exaggerated love-hate relationship with water, which is at once greatly feared and yet the source of great wealth. Nor, on the other hand, do the Isoko demonstrate the clear distinction between water and land spirits that the Ijo maintain. The Isoko will speak of deities inhabiting different locales and taking different offerings, and having different qualities; but their pantheons seem far more loosely structured. My original thesis that Isoko religion would clearly have demonstrated a reaction to the move into a more watery environment may indeed be upheld. The Isoko simply seem to have accommodated their new environment. Their old deities continued to serve them and new ones appeared.

In the end, the Isoko seem to have a rather well-balanced appreciation of both worlds. Their spectacular clay sculptures can perhaps stand as a metaphor for the combination of water and earth orientations that they have developed (Peek 1976b; see interleaf G). These are molded over wooden frames with special clays taken from the waterside and are then finished with a layer of chalk solution, "whitewashed" as it were. The ubiquitous chalk found in every shrine, though brought from the water, is treated as a sacred earth element by the Isoko. Thus, this appears to be another mediating element. Although the Isoko remain a land-oriented people, they have adjusted to the watery world of the Niger Delta, and apparently they did so long ago.

The Isoko seem to give almost equal ritual attention, positive and negative, to land and to water. They certainly value water more than they fear it. Although the Isoko only make passing references to Mami Wata, the famous seductress, one is always tempted to use this rich figure to represent an ambivalence held by humans about water beings. But a more appropriate example may be in the celebrations honoring Oworu. As with any beings of Eriwi (the spirit world), be they the ancestors or deities from land or water, it is wonderful for them to visit, but no one wants them to stay for very long.

Interleaf G
Molded Shrine Arts

Philip M. Peek

G.1 *Services at the main shrine for Olokun. Photograph by Philip M. Peek, Urhonigbe, 1965.*

G.2 *Egba, an important war deity (*edho*) has been served for several hundred years by members of Owe clan. Photograph by Philip M. Peek, Ilue-Ologbo, 1971.*

Surely among the most fascinating but least accessible arts of Africa are the large molded clay figures located in urban and rural shrines. Many communities in Southern Nigeria—especially those peoples living at the edges of the Niger Delta, such as the Isoko and Riverain Igbo—prize these spectacular sculpted images. Often larger than life-size, the immobile figures sometimes form part of complex groupings of interrelated individuals. Such shrine arts are an ancient tradition, and as the flamboyantly painted and elaborated molded Olokun shrines currently served in Benin City and Urhonigbe suggest, they show no signs of diminishing (fig. G.1; see Beier 1963; Galembo 1993). The extraordinary clay sculptures and molded figures of the *mbari* houses of the Owerri Igbo, so well studied by Herbert Cole (1982), are another widely recognized expression of this art form.

Among Delta peoples today, the Isoko seem to be the primary creators of large molded clay sculptures. The Urhobo do some work in this form, but their shrine arts tend to be large wooden sculptures. In the 1920s, P. A. Talbot recorded molded images in several Western Igbo communities (1932 [1967], figs. facing pp. 92, 142, 254); but tragically, nothing more has been learned about these sculptures. This Western Igbo tradition may well be critical because according to Isoko traditions, many molded figures were in the past prepared by Western Igbo herbalists and artists (Owode 1971; Peek 1976b).

Nevertheless, most mud sculptures in Isoko shrines were made and maintained by local artisans and priests. The majority were created to honor clan deities whose main duties related to warfare. Earlier Isoko mud sculptures might have been more abstract (see fig. 5.17), but now they are rather realistic although highly stylized. Usually they are single figures, portrayed in a formal upright seated posture with palms resting on the knees and legs widespread (figs. G.2, G.3). Sometimes a central male figure is "attended" by smaller female and male figures (figs. G.4, G.5).

Unlike wood carving, which is a subtractive process, these molded sculptures are additive. With our focus on the Delta environment and with the theme of "land people" moving in a "water world," one is tempted to see the molding of clay over wooden and metal superstructures as somehow symbolic of the merging of these two realms (see chapter 5 of this volume). While this may be the case, at least for the Isoko, these images did not necessarily represent water spirits because the Isoko usually waged their battles on land (figs. G.6, G.7). This model of the merging of land and water worlds finds resonance in the "dusting" of successful dancers with white talcum powder or kaolin chalk, much as wooden sculptures are whitened with kaolin chalk paint.

G.3 *"Miss M. B. Sheath with Village Juju." Photograph courtesy of the Church Mission Society, London. This photograph of the deity (edho) Egba (see fig. G.2) was taken circa 1930.*

G.4 *Evevewehe shrine. Photograph by Philip M. Peek, Emede, 1971.*

G.5 *Edho-Idodo shrine. Photograph by Philip M. Peek, Igbide, 1971.*

G.6 The war deity Eyere wears the striped skirt and feathered headdress of an iletu *(warrior)*. He also carries weapons appropriate to that role. The back wall of the shrine is covered with nsibidi *(an esoteric ideographic writing system that originated with the Ejagham of southeastern Nigeria and appears occasionally among peoples of the Delta)*. Photograph by Philip M. Peek, Aradhe town, 1971.

G.7 Egba, a war deity (edho). *Typically, molded and carved shrine images are partially covered. Behind this* edho *are offerings of coconuts and the skulls of sacrificial animals. Photograph by Philip M. Peek, Iri, 1971.*

Chapter 6

Celebrating Water Spirits: Influence, Confluence, and Difference in Ìjẹ̀bú-Yorùbá and Delta Masquerades

HENRY JOHN DREWAL

Children of the sea with shells on their heads
Ọmọlókun ògbólú

Rulers today, rulers tomorrow, rulers forever
Ọba loni, ọba lọ́la, ọba nígbà kugbà

Fire on the head that water quenches
Iná orí omi kúkú gbọ̀nà kú

—Praise for children of the sea, collected in Ìjẹ̀bú, 1982

Introduction

Much of art history is concerned with the question of "influence"—the presumed impact of one artistic or cultural form on another, diffusion versus independent invention, streams of traditions that sometimes converge, at other times diverge, or reconverge at some later time (see Vansina 1984, 185–95). What might at first appear to be a somewhat straightforward issue is in reality very complex. How does one determine the nature and direction(s) of influence? What kinds of evidence are needed? We begin with comparisons, where clusters of traits (the more arbitrary the more telling) reveal connections. For example, to say that because Ìjẹ̀bú masks are painted red like Ijo masks is not convincing evidence of "influence"—it could only be coincidence or convergence. There must be an array of distinctive and arbitrarily intentional features shared in both traditions to suggest historical/cultural connections between peoples and their arts. But multiple formal or stylistic similarities are not enough. Technological, iconological, and performative similarities would also strengthen the argument, as would sociocultural contexts and significances.

But then, the questions of history still remain. Who influenced whom? When? How? Why? The questions are many, the answers few. The following discussion illustrates the complexity of such art-historical issues while attempting to suggest an outline of a specific history of transcultural artistic inspiration over time and space. Here I consider comparatively Delta (Ijo and others) and Ìjẹ̀bú-Yorùbá visual, performance, historical, and cultural data in order to assess the sources and processes in the shaping of Ìjẹ̀bú-Yorùbá masquerades (Àgbó) in honor of water spirits. These data include: festival format; masquerade headdresses (style and iconography); costumes; and music and choreography. I begin with the assumption that the Ìjẹ̀bú-Yorùbá learned, adopted, and adapted water spirit masking arts from Delta

6.1   Headdress. Ìjẹ̀bú-Yorùbá. Wood, paint, mirrors, and fiber. L: 107 cm. Eric Robertson. This headdress echoes Ijo conventions but bears hallmarks of the Ìjẹ̀bú-Yorùbá type known as Òkẹ̀nẹ̀kẹ́nẹ́. Made of separate pieces of wood, it incorporates pointed ears and spiral forms possibly alluding to leaves, vines, or paddles. Birds perch on the fish-tail form sprouting from its head and on its long snout. Mirrors recall the reflective surface of the water and suggest access to the spirit world.

peoples (Ijo and possibly others as well), on the basis of unanimous testimonies from Ìjèbú respondents during my research of 1982 and 1986. I conclude with some reflections on transcultural processes in the creation of artistic and sociocultural realities.

The Setting

The coastal Delta of the Niger River is a vast network of channels, lagoons, creeks, and rivers spanning more than ten thousand square miles and connecting coastal waterways on both the east and west for a distance of almost eight hundred miles. This watery network has made possible the movement of people, goods, ideas, and arts over at least the last five hundred years, and probably much longer. As P. C. Lloyd (1963, 209) has remarked, "Today the creeks are thought of as inaccessible areas; but a fully manned canoe can travel as fast as a galloping horse, carrying a larger cargo or heavier arms. Movement here was, in the past, at least as easy as in the savannah and much easier than in the forests where one could travel only by foot."

Before the arrival of Europeans in this area in the late fifteenth century, Ijo peoples of the Niger Delta (and perhaps others) were carrying on an extensive commerce that traversed the entire region. Because of their water-oriented traditions and navigational skills, the Ijo became major agents for the exchange of ideas as well as goods. They also spread certain artistic traditions for they possess distinctive performance and sculptural styles that have been extremely influential over a wide area. One Ijo tradition, water spirit masquerades (known as Ekine among the Kalabari Ijo), has inspired related masking traditions among various peoples both within and beyond the Niger Delta. These include the Isoko, Urhobo, Iteskiri, Edo, Igbo, Abua, Ogoni, Duala, and possibly Grebo (see Rubin 1976, 22).

Ijo Water Spirit Masquerades

I begin with a general description and analysis of Ijo water spirit masking festivals, highlighting those features that also occur in Àgbó celebrations of the Ìjèbú-Yorùbá. In the interest of brevity, I have condensed or eliminated many aspects of Ijo festivals that do not appear among the Ìjèbú-Yorùbá. Some might criticize this, saying I have found only that for which I looked. Yet I believe the multiplicity of similarities, as well as the testimony of all my Ìjèbú teachers, confirm clear Ijo-Ìjèbú artistic interactions. The question is, precisely *which* Ijo groups? There are a series of hybrid Ijo/Yorùbá cultures living in the Western and Central Delta between the Ìjèbú and the Eastern Delta Ijo groups, including the Kalabari. Moving from west to east, these Ijo/Yorùbá communities include the Ìkálè, Ìlàjè, Àpọí, and Itsekiri—not to mention other cultures where Yorùbás reside that have been influenced by the Ijo—the Edo, Urhobo, and Isoko. In these complexly mixed cultural areas, numerous towns such as Òkìtìpupa, Ayétòrò, Máhìn, Igbobini, Sapele, Warri, Forcados, and so forth, may have been special trading partners and residences for transient Ìjèbú-Yorùbá communities. For example, Oyinadé Ògunbà (1967, 329) believes that Ìjèbú Àgbó masking may have originated among the Àpọí-Yorùbá in Igbobini. It then spread to the Ìjèbú coastal town of Ìwòpin and from there to other parts of Ìjèbúland. Ògunbà also told me (personal communication, 1982) that Robin Horton had taken some Ìjèbú Àgbó songs to Port Harcourt for Ijo to hear. The Ijo could not understand them, but they also knew they were not in Yorùbá. (See also Adétọ́lá Wẹ́wẹ̀ [1995] on Àpọí water spirit masquerades at Igbobini). I have not done research in these areas, but I suspect that many other hybrid water spirit masquerades exist in these places that would further complicate and enrich this history of transcultural inspirations. It may be that I have overemphasized Ìjẹ̀bú-Kalabari comparisons since examples of Kalabari masks are more fully documented in the literature.

Kalabari Ijo are renowned for elaborate masquerade performances (see interleaf H) in honor of the "water people," or *owu*. According to the Kalabari, performances to entertain and honor the water people were brought by the culture heroine Ekineba, who was abducted by the water spirits, taken to their home, witnessed their singing, dancing, and drumming, and later taught these arts to her people when she returned home. From this beginning, Ekineba became the patroness of the water spirit masquerades and the Kalabari Ijo established the Ekine, or Sekiapu (Dancing people), Society to organize the performances.[1] Among other Ijo groups, men as well as women learned masking from the spirits—sometimes in dreams, visions, or divination (Anderson 1997).

The "water people" control nature, in particular the watery environment that affects almost all aspects of Ijo life. Each spirit "owns" a portion of a creek, controlling its water level, currents, waves, the depth of its fish shoals, and so forth, and many of them are known for their unpredictable and occasionally troublesome behavior. While different from ancestral spirits, the water people share certain human traits along with their animal elements. They have their own distinct personalities and are often volatile and capricious, yet also playful and humorous. Their character is often portrayed in the masked performances as are specific episodes in their lives. Dramas, some of high tension and violence, alternate with comic interludes. Some enact the lechery of certain spirits, others their paranoia or self-pity (Horton 1960, 31). "This setting-off of successive climaxes of tension with a series of relaxed interludes is a favourite pattern in Kalabari ritual" (Horton 1960, 32). Kalabari view these performances at once as portrayals of the water spirits and as the plays once put on by the spirits themselves (Horton 1963, 105).

Ekine Festival Format

The festival begins with an invitation to the spirits, asking them to come in from the creeks to attend the performances in their honor. Traveling in a large canoe, the people approach the water people, offer them a gift of a goat, and beg them to come. As they return to the village, they sing Ekine songs believing that the *teme* (spirit) of the water spirits follows them home since they are calling their names by such actions. One or two days later, a dog is sacrificed to Ekineba and that night the *kikiro* drum is lowered onto its side in preparation for the start of the performances the next day (Horton 1960, 29).

The eve of the performances is devoted to important preparations. At the outset, an Ekine priest asks the spirit "to come and eat." Its mask is taken out of storage, the old paint washed off, and new colors applied. Refurbishment and libations of blood purify and prepare the mask so that it will work well. Prayers for purificaton, prosperity, and progeny follow, and then large numbers of people, mostly women, file past the mask, throwing coins and beseeching the water spirits to prevent illness and to protect the unborn. The men then share around the palm gin and, joined by other Ekine members, begin to sing the praises of the water spirits, sometimes through the night as the excitement about the arrival of the spirits mounts.

At the first light of dawn, the masqueraders are sewn into their costumes, a skintight white tunic that covers the hands but not the feet. A long narrow conical framework of palm midrib is tied at the back and extends horizontally to form the "tail" of the masker (Horton 1963, 99). In front a large stomach pad is strapped on to represent a protruding organ. Together these two costume elements create the body shape characteristic of the water spirits. Strands of locust bean pods encircle the dancers' ankles and serve as leg rattles. Cloths are tied onto the bottom of the headdress and over the body tunic.

The Ekineba shrine is at the foot of a tree where libations of gin are poured on the ground. Before going to the dancing arena, the masker receives the blessings given by the priest who then touches the moistened earth to the forehead and chest of the masker; this neutralizes any pollution and protects the performer. Thus prepared, the dancer steps strongly into the arena for his performance as the drummers call the name of the spirit.

In a trance state, the dancer performs with the mask. The spirit owner of the ensemble is thought to "lead" the dancer. As Horton explains (1960, 30), "Dancing an important masquerade is work for a man of strong *teme* (spirit) and dancing it successfully one of the most admired achievements in the community." Besides properly following the complex dance rhythms of the drums, the performer must also demonstrate his understanding of the drum language in pointing to twenty to thirty shrines as they are called by the drums. Each masquerade type has its own headdress, costume, drum rhythm, choreography, and songs. As Martha Anderson (1981, 150) explains: "An expert dancer impersonates the spirit 'owner,' inducing the spirit owner of the headdress to enter and control his movements."

Each *owu* is honored in turn in dances. In many Kalabari communities, these begin with three or four *owu* whose masquerades are the property of the Ekine Society as a whole. Those owned by lineages follow, and the final display is of the most powerful, communally owned *owu* (Horton 1960, 29). The gaps between these displays can be anywhere from four days to several months.

After each has been properly honored and entertained individually, the people perform the "filling of the canoe of the Water People"—a collective display in which each spirit is represented by one masquerader. They dance first at the central square and then move to a special beach known as "the resting place of the Water People." There, just before the ebb of the tide, the performers disrobe in secret and dip themselves in the water in order to speed the spirits back to their homes in the creeks. That night the great drum is lowered into the village well to conclude the festival for another year (Horton 1960, 29).

In contrast to the structured nature of Ekine performances among the Kalabari, the Central and Western Ijo ones vary a great deal—from highly secular entertainments to serious outings of deadly spirits like Eleke, who has important judicial functions (Anderson 1997). Masks are owned by individuals, families, wards, and communities, and groups of them may come out for several days or participate in both traditional festivals and modern civic celebrations. In many Central and Western Ijo performances, themes of aggression—warfare and head-hunting—seem to dominate, more so than among the Eastern Ijo (Anderson 1997).

Ìjẹ̀bú-Yorùbá Àgbó Festival Format

Ìjẹ̀bú-Yorùbáland occupies the coastal plain between the interior Yorùbá
kingdoms of Ifẹ̀, Ìjẹ̀shà, Ẹ̀gbá, Ibàdàn, and Ọ̀yọ́ and the coastal waterways
(the lagoons, creeks, and rivers). With their strategic position on the coast,
their navigable rivers and lagoons, their bountiful source of fish, their wealth
from trade with other Africans and later with Europeans, the Ìjẹ̀bú, like the
Ijo, concern themselves with the forces who control the arteries that make
such prosperity possible—the water spirits.

The Ìjẹ̀bú (and several other coastal Yorùbá and mixed Yorùbá and
Delta groups such as the Ìlàjẹ, Ìkálẹ̀, Àpọí, and Itsekiri) recognize the
presence and power of spirits controlling Delta waters and acknowledge
that they adopted and adapted their Àgbó masquerades from Niger Delta
peoples (most often identified as Ijo). While testimonies were unanimous
in identifying Delta/Ijo peoples, the precise "origins" of specific masks,
songs, dances, and so forth, were much less certain. For the Ìjẹ̀bú, Àgbó
masking is often concerned with progeny, specifically *ọmọlókun*, "children
of the sea," born through the intercession of Olókun, the sea goddess. As the
diviner Kolawole Ọ̀shítọ́lá explained, "*ọmọlókun* brought Àgbó to people and
Ìwòrì Ogbè is the Odù Ifá [divination verse] for Molókun/Àgbó" (personal
communication, 1982). He told me this story: "Ọlọ́ta (a stone) was a sick
child of Olókun. Olókun consulted Ifá and performed the proper sacrifices
so Ọlọ́ta would not die. Thus we say *ọta kìtkú,* 'stone cannot die.' Water
comes out of that stone.... In ancient times, we believe that money comes
from Olókun." The connection between wealth and the sea is evidenced in
other ways as well. Yorùbá market women put a large seashell on top of their
goods to attract customers. The sound one hears when holding such a shell
to the ear is said to be the sound of an active market with many buyers
(Bolaji and Lolade Campbell, personal communication, 1999). Kolawole
Ọ̀shítọ́lá went on to explain that Olókun has countless children in the sea,
and if humans celebrated her and her children, they too would have many.
But progeny is not the only concern. Inland communities perform Àgbó to
alleviate severe drought, since the water spirits control rain as well.

In some Ìjẹ̀bú communities, the opening of the Àgbó festival takes a
form similar to that described by Horton for the Kalabari Ijo. At Akió, Àgbó
Society members go in a large boat (fig. 6.2) to the water spirit shrine some
distance up the river. In the prow a male priest dressed as a female sings and
dances, exhorting the water spirits to come and enjoy the performances in
their honor. After some time, they return joyfully singing and dancing
bringing with them in a second canoe three masqueraders—two beautiful
females known as *onúrí,* or royal wives, accompanied by their comical
husband, Ajẹyẹ, the "One who eats birds or chickens," standing in the prow
(fig. 6.3). Their landing is heralded with rites of purification and protection,
and joyful dances (fig. 6.4). Such rites include the sacrifice of a tortoise and
libations on the heads and toes of the maskers—acts very similar to those
performed among the Kalabari Ijo and at Nembe (Alagoa 1982, 270–72).

In other Ìjẹ̀bú towns, the opening is quite different from that in
Kalabari Ijo country. Toward the end of a New Year's purification festival
known as Ebi (Drewal 1986, 32–34) comes a masquerade to herald the
water spirit celebration. It is known as Òkoóró and comes in the form of an
elegant, elaborately coiffed woman (with multiple braids or a single tall one)

6.2 Àgbó Society members from Akió travel to the water spirit shrine some distance up the river. Photograph by Henry John Drewal and Margaret Thompson Drewal, Ìjẹ̀bú, 1982.

6.3 A second canoe with two beautiful females ("onúrí," or royal wives) seated in the middle. They are accompanied by their comical husband, Ajẹyẹ (One who eats birds or chickens), who stands in the prow. Photograph by Henry John Drewal and Margaret Thompson Drewal, Ìjẹ̀bú, 1982.

6.4 An onúrí, or "royal wife," dances on the shore. Photograph by Henry John Drewal and Margaret Thompson Drewal, Ìjẹ̀bú, 1982.

draped in finely woven mats (fig. 6.5). In its style and iconography, it is remarkably similar to Gẹ̀lẹ̀dẹ, the well-known masking tradition of the western Yorùbá (Drewal and Drewal 1983), with which it is often confused. However the distinctive trait that marks an Òkoóró is the use of finely woven mats draped over the shoulders, a medium associated with coastal reeds, fishing traps, and, therefore, water spirits. The etymology of Òkoóró is uncertain. One possibility is the Ijo word for mat (*okuru*). The mat is used as a ritual dress among the Ijo and is the distinguishing costume for Òkoóró among the Ìjẹ̀bú. In its presentation of an elegant woman draped in a finely woven and dyed mat, Òkoóró may also have some connections with Urhobo (and Delta) traditions celebrating the puberty rites of girls where distinctive mats called *ewhere opha* and *ere opha* are woven and displayed (S. Foss 1978, 60–62).[2]

Some Òkoóró headdresses (figs. 6.6a,b) are worn on top of the head of the performer, a pair of braids rising like horns above the head. This coiffure is specific to queens and priestesses in Ìjẹ̀búland and is known as *òkè méjì*, "two [sacred] mountains." These are sometimes surrounded by a headdress construction that descends in a series of separate strands that represent beads, like those worn by Ìjẹ̀bú priestesses. A very old headdress (probably Òkoóró), photographed in Ìjẹ̀bú in 1959 by William Fagg (The William B. Fagg

Photographic Archive, The Metropolitan Museum of Art), displays another version of these tall braids of hair. In this version, a circle of tall, slender braids crowns the head. Projections at the sides, just below this crown, probably served as frames for mirrors. Below these is a distinctive coiffure in which the hair has been shaved at the sides leaving long braids at the back and two at the front that frame the face. Most fascinating of all, strips of copper or brass cover portions of the face, one down the center of the forehead and bridge of the nose, others forming three slightly oblique bands under the eyes and down the cheeks to represent Ìjèbú scarifications. I shall return to this use of metal later.

It seems probable that these Òkoóró maskers (like the male priest in the prow of the boat dressed as a female) are references to the Kalabari Ijo patroness of water spirit masking, Ekineba. They may also be comparable to the Urhobo "mother of the water spirits," Ohworu. Like the Ìjèbú-Yorùbá, the Urhobo also acknowledge that they learned about masking for water spirits from the Ijo (Foss 1973, 20). But Òkoóró also has specific Ìjèbú connotations. Her finely plaited and elegant coiffure is a reference to the above-noted special children (omolókun) born through the intercession of the sea goddess Olókun. Their sign of specialness is "a crown from the otherworld" (adé òrun)—thick curly hair likened to a crown of seashells (Drewal 1986, fig. 1). Like these otherworldly crowns of hair, water spirit headdresses are called adé orí, "crowns for the head."

The procession moves through the town (fig. 6.7) and Òkoóró dances for the town's ruler (fig. 6.8). She is accompanied by the water spirit priest. He is dressed completely in white and wears a white headtie or cap with a tassel (see fig. 6.7), traditions of ritual attire that suggest Delta/Ijo modes. His chieftancy title is Elekine. After performing prayers and offerings at certain shrines, Òkoóró moves to the shore to invite the water spirits to come and visit their human hosts who are about to honor and entertain them with

6.5   In some Ìjèbú towns, the festival is heralded by a masquerader known as Òkoóró—an elaborately coiffed woman draped in finely woven mats and wearing a necklace of freshly cut palm fronds. Photograph by Henry John Drewal and Margaret Thompson Drewal, Ìjèbú, 1982.

6.6a Some Òkoóró headdresses are worn on top of the head of the performer, a pair of braids rising like horns above the head, and strands of beads cascading down the back. Photograph by Henry John Drewal and Margaret Thompson Drewal, Ìjèbú, 1982.

6.6b Back view of the Òkoóró headdress illustrated in figure 6.6a. Photograph by Henry John Drewal and Margaret Thompson Drewal, Ìjèbú, 1982.

6.7   Òkoóró parades through the town, greeting the ruler, chiefs, elders, and others. She is accompanied by the water spirit priest known as the Elekine, or "Head of the Masking Society," who is dressed completely in white and wears a white headtie or cap with a tassel, traditions of ritual attire that suggest Delta/Ijo modes. Photograph by Henry John Drewal and Margaret Thompson Drewal, Ìjèbú, 1982.

6.8   Òkoóró dances for the town ruler. Photograph by Henry John Drewal and Margaret Thompson Drewal, Ìjèbú, 1982.

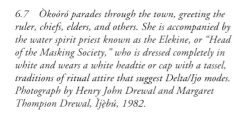

songs, dances, masks, and offerings. Following these opening rites by Òkoóró, a series of performances honoring specific spirits takes place over the next days, weeks, and even months, depending on the resources and commitment of the community. Some are serious, others playful—mirroring the festival format of the Ijo discussed above.

Many of the Àgbó masqueraders come out and perform in threes. While Ijo number symbolism may play some role here, this use of three is explained according to Yorùbá religious thought and practice. As Òshítólá (personal communication, 1982) explained, the water spirits are *imolè* (deities), and for them "we must do it in threes." He quoted the following Ifá saying: "*Ìgbà mèta làí kàn kùn tufè*" (It is three times we must knock on the door at Ifè [to begin a sacred rite]).

Thus there are some almost identical elements to the festival format in both Ijo and Ìjèbú communities but also some clear differences. The similarities include the carrying of spirits in a boat from the shrine to the village; welcoming or blessing rites; the initial female maskers representing Ekineba; the seriate and extended format of the festival; closing rites where the spirits are returned to their watery abode. The differences include the opening by Òkoóró and the meanings of certain icons and ritual elements.

Delta and Àgbó Masquerades Compared: Style, Iconography, Music, and Dance

The evocative qualities of a masking event are greater than the sum of the visual, kinetic, and temporal arts of masquerade ensemble, dance, and vocal and instrumental music. We need to develop nonhieratic ways of analyzing multimedia performances that are intended to be multivocal, multifocal, and multisensorial *simultaneously over time*, for that is their essence, their aesthetic power. The following discussion attempts to provide such an approach. The order in which elements of the masquerade are considered is, therefore, not meant to convey relative importance. Rather, I present the data following the comments of Delta and Ìjèbú-Yorùbá observers that the maskers "come floating on the surface of the water," that is from top to bottom as they metaphorically emerge from the water and dance on land.

Headdresses: Style and Imagery

Delta (espcially Western and Central) style may be characterized as angular, cubistic, bold, and generally stark (see fig. 4.1). One of the main sources for this angularity is, I believe, the representation of skeletal forms whether animal or human (see fig. 6.29). Despite the extensive literature on Delta and Ijo art, this aspect has not been given sufficient attention. Evidence in support of this observation comes from many sources. The very first European accounts of the Ijo stress the importance given to acquiring war trophies, described as "head-hunting," and the aggressive, warlike character of the Ijo (see chapter 3 of this volume). The Ijo were feared greatly by their enemies and neighbors as they became more and more involved in supplying captives for European "headhunters"—rapacious slavers who descended on the Niger Delta from different European ports.

Head-hunting for the Ijo was formerly an important road to prestige (Horton 1965, 1). The highest grade in the Ekine Society was formerly reserved for the bravest and most accomplished warriors, those who had taken heads. Barbot (in Hodgkin 1960, 154) describes Ijo sculpture and shrines at New Calabar in 1700 saying "many of them are dried heads of beasts" (thus skeletal forms and zoomorphic themes). There are also early descriptions of Ijo maskers wearing "dried heads." Actual animal skeletons appear in Ekine and Àgbó. Among the Ijo, the water spirit Duminea owns a basketwork tray that has a coiled relief of a python together with jawbones and skulls of horned animals (goats) attached around the rim (Horton 1960, 63–64). The shrine of Kal' Adumu, owner of the Santa Barbara River, displays the skulls of past animal offerings (Horton 1960, 25). In Ìjẹ̀bú, crocodile skulls are sometimes put on water spirit shrines.

A close analysis of form in Delta headdresses reveals this skeletal quality. The domed head consists of the frontal bone; left and right parietal bones; temporal bones at the sides; the maxilla, which includes the bones under the nasal orifice; the zygomatic, or cheekbones; and the mandible, or lower jawbone. Together these make up the skull—creating the "skull-like quality" of Ijo sculpture. The parietals and frontal and temporal bones are clearly shown in many Ijo pieces. And the presentation of the maxilla, cheekbones, and nasal orifice seems to be shown in the mask illustrated in figure 6.9. The eye sockets are tubular in shape. Tubular eye forms in Ijo masks are without flesh, without lids. They thus evoke eyeballs set in a skull. It should be remembered also that depictions of skulls, especially animal, are ancient in Southern Nigeria and the Niger Delta (see figs. 1.13, 1.22–1.24). There are numerous examples of metal skulls of animals (carnivores) found throughout the Lower Niger/Delta. One is now in the Berlin Museum (Fagg 1963, pl. 68). Two others were found in the Andoni Creeks east of the Delta. Some brasses were found in the Eastern Delta (Akpoma) depicting carnivore skulls (Horton 1965, 80–81, pls. 3a,b), and a leopard skull staff finial was recovered from the grave site at Igbo-Ukwu (Shaw 1970, 2: pls. 347–50).

Teeth, another important part of skeletal representations, are prominent in much Delta and Ijo art. For the Ijo, there are clear and important ideas associated with the depiction of teeth. Toothless babies must be kept away from certain places believed to be the haunts of spirits. They are also prevented from looking into mirrors (Anderson 1983, 94), presumably because babies are so close to the spirits that they could be taken away by them. Also, the

6.9   Headdress. Western Ijo. Wood and metal. L: 52 cm. Private Collection. The maxilla, cheekbones, and nasal orifice are shown in this mask.

6.10 In this Àgbó work the mouth is typically Yorùbá with two fleshy lips that conceal the teeth. Photograph by Henry John Drewal and Margaret Thompson Drewal, Ìjẹ̀bú, 1982.

6.11 In some Ìjẹ̀bú Àgbó headdresses, the teeth are emphasized by curved fanglike metallic cylinders. Ex. Pace Gallery, New York.

cutting of teeth is an important event in a child's development. It is equally important in the creation of a carving among the Central Ijo. The depiction or cutting of the teeth in a figure carving is regarded "as a critical stage in the production of a figure carving…it marks the time when the spirit for which it is intended enters the carving" (Anderson 1983, 96). We may assume the same is true for the carving of teeth in water spirit headdresses. Bared teeth are also a central motif in the *ivri* complex of the Delta (see interleaf D). Philip Peek suggests (1986, 46) that such an icon may refer to "verbal aggressiveness" as well as physical force, truculence or "adamance."

It is interesting to observe how the Yorùbá, who rarely depict teeth, because of their connotations of aggression, ferocity, and generally antisocial behavior, have handled this feature in Ìjẹ̀bú. In some Àgbó works (fig. 6.10), the mouth is typically Yorùbá—two fleshy lips that conceal the teeth. In others, the teeth appear between parted lips or are dramatically emphasized by curved fanglike metallic cylinders that seem to suggest the toothy Delta aesthetic (fig. 6.11).

The powerful impact of Ijo style is evident in Ìjẹ̀bú Àgbó masks called Ọ̀kẹ̀nẹ̀kẹ́nẹ́ (fig. 6.12) and Ìgòdò (figs. 6.13, 6.14). A bulging cubistic forehead is apparent on some examples along with thrusting tubular eyes, angular forms, the projecting paddle/prow form in front, and the long flat "ears" at the back. Python, progenitor of water spirits, coils its tail and slithers between the cylindrical eyes. A crocodile or sometimes birds decorate the end of the prow—all typical water-related motifs—while the brightly colored triangular patterning (common in many Delta headdresses and costumes) evokes the textured, shimmering quality of reptilian skin and thus watery realms. There may be some connection between this Ìjẹ̀bú Ìgòdò and an Edo mask, also called Ighodo (Igodo), from the Igbile cult for the water spirits at the Benin port of Ughoton (fig. 6.13). It has a long openwork superstructure with entwined snakes in high relief. These are also shown in low relief across the forehead. The mask's style is typically Ijo with tubular eyes, a high bridge of the nose, and a projecting mouth showing teeth.

As among the Ijo, the aggressive spirit, crocodile, appears in Àgbó (fig. 6.15). But notice how the angularity of Delta styling has been softened with more organic volumes in the Ìjẹ̀bú version. The distinctive checkerboard pattern of brightly contrasting colors and variegated surfaces persist. Certain antelopes, known as *agírá*, and regarded as aquatic creatures, also appear in Àgbó (fig. 6.16). This mask may refer to the African water chevrotain. It is a small animal that used to be plentiful in the Delta and has the remarkable ability to swim underwater for long distances (Rosalind Hackett, personal communication, 1986). Its rounded, organic volumes are painted in variegated colors as with so many of the masks. In performance *agírá* moves quickly and aggresively, striking its leg rattles to punctuate the rhythms of the drums.

The appearance of Àgbó masquerades may vary from an organic stylized naturalism to almost total abstraction. While most water spirit headdresses are carved of wood, cloth headdresses also occur (fig. 6.17). The maskers who wear these conical cloth headpieces are known as *ajó* or *igbilẹ̀*. Sewn over tall conical palm rib frameworks, these cloth headpieces have long tassels that hang down or fly outward as the performer dances. Society members bite this tassel to ensure protection and blessing during the dance. The buttocks are built up with basketry fish traps, and in some instances a stick wrapped in

6.12 Òkènèkéné headdress. Ìjèbú-Yorùbá. Wood and pigment. L: 34.3 cm. Seattle Art Museum; Gift of Katherine White and the Boeing Company, 81.17.531. Photograph by Paul Macapia.

6.13 Ighodo mask. Edo. Wood, incrustation, pigment, and fiber. L: 62.2 cm. Indiana University Art Museum; Raymond and Laura Wielgus Collection, 78.11.2. Photograph by Michael Cavanagh and Kevin Montague ©Indiana University Art Museum.

6.14 The powerful impact of Ijo style is evident in the Ìjèbú Àgbó mask called Ìgòdò. Note the domed forehead, tubular eyes, crocodile, bird, angular prow or paddle shape, and surface painted in brightly colored geometic shapes. Photograph by Henry John Drewal and Margaret Thompson Drewal, Ìjèbú, 1982.

6.15 *The Ìjèbú version of the aggressive spirit crocodile is less angular than that of the Ijo, but the distinctive checkerboard pattern, brightly contrasting colors, and variegated surface persist. Photograph by Henry John Drewal and Margaret Thompson Drewal, Ìjèbú, 1982.*

6.16 *The agírá mask in the Àgbó masquerade. Photograph by Henry John Drewal and Margaret Thompson Drewal, Ìjèbú, 1982.*

6.17 *Abstract cloth masks, known as ajó or igbilè, are sewn over tall conical palm rib frameworks. The long tassels that adorn them swing as the performer dances. Photograph by Henry John Drewal and Margaret Thompson Drewal, Ìjèbú, 1982.*

6.18 *Conical cloth constructions also appear during Àgbó festivals when young boys perform acrobatic feats as interludes. Photograph by Henry John Drewal and Margaret Thompson Drewal, Ìjèbú, 1982.*

cloth protrudes like a long, straight tail with a tassel. Almost identical constructions can be found among the Kalabari Ijo (Horton 1963, 99) and others (Anderson 1983). Conical cloth constructions like those of *ajó/igbilè* also appear during the Àgbó festival when young boys perform acrobatic feats as interludes (fig. 6.18).

One of the most embellished of Àgbó forms (fig. 6.19) plays on the themes of alluring beauty, fertility, plentiful progeny, wealth, and good fortune—the gifts bestowed by water spirits who have been honored properly in mask, dance, and song. Known as *ìdínlá*, literally "big butt," the maskers come dressed in layers of expensive cloth, bright paint, mirrors, and beads. The exaggerated buttocks are constructed with a woven fishtrap or basket. Their headdresses (one is a janus image) depict elaborate coiffures draped in cloth. The birds and small human figure perched at the back of one represent her progeny born through the benificence of the water spirits and evoke her praise name Òtùmò, àgbó gbómo gbó (Giver of children). The sensuous dance of "big butt" causes her jealous husband Ajèyè (One who eats birds or chickens) to chase men who approach in order to playfully caress her alluring attribute.

Such performance themes and costume constructions may be inspired by a particular Delta cultural institution—the fattening house—where sensual corpulence is a central part of female puberty rites. Like *ìdínlá* and *ajó/igbilè*, one Kalabari Ijo Ekine masquerader with large projecting buttocks (the wife of Agiri) performs the "slow waddling dance peculiar to young girls fresh from the fattening room" (Horton 1960, 38).

Composition/Orientation

Ijo headdresses are distinctive for each spirit. These carved wooden headpieces are regarded as the "seat" or the "name" of the masquerade's spirit owner (Horton 1963, 99). Most headdresses have three essential parts: (1) a forward projecting nose or snout, (2) a head, and (3) a tail or extension at the back. Many Ìjèbú headdresses also follow this tripartite composition.

Horizontality, dominant in water spirit headdresses, is a central theme in the myth and imagery of the water people (figs. 6.20). It occurs in the origin accounts where the spirits are first seen "floating" on the water as

6.19 Ìdínlá, *literally, "big butt," is one of the most embellished of Àgbó forms. Photograph by Henry John Drewal and Margaret Thompson Drewal, Ìjèbú, 1982.*

6.20 Headdresses. Ìjèbú-Yorùbá or Western Ijo. Wood and Pigment. H (left): 42.5 cm; (right): 38.7 cm. The Art Institute of Chicago; Gift of the Richard and Barbara Faletti Family Collection, 2000.321.1&2, 2000.321. These headdresses with their exuberant colors and exploding forms clearly belong to the water spirit complex even though they incorporate the tusks and horns of land animals. The Ìjèbú associate certain birds and animals with water spirits, and similarly Ijo headdresses sometimes depict land animals believed to inhabit the realm of these spirits.

described by Horton and others. Horton (1963, 100) illustrates one Otobo masker wearing the mask horizontally to evoke the way in which people often see hippos (fig. 6.21; see also fig. H.9). The persistent orientation of such headdresses is horizontal precisely because it evokes the position and movement of water spirits "floating on the surface of the waters"—as I was told by almost all Ìjèbú-Yorùbá persons—not because they are meant to be "hidden" from view. Ìjèbú maskers frequently bend sharply forward in the dance (fig. 6.22), tilting their heads backward to maintain a generally horizontal position for the headdress. In this dance posture, the masks are fully visible to onlookers as they "float" in the dance.

While the best-known and most widespread presentation of water spirit masks is horizontal, there is a significant corpus of examples that are vertical. They seem to be found mostly among the Central and Western Ijo and their neighbors. It seems likely that these Delta works influenced those found among the Edo at Ughoton where the water spirit society is known as Igbile (fig 6.24). One headdress in vertical format is a head in strongly Ijo style (tubular eyes, bared teeth), set on a tall, thick, conical neck with checkerboard motif (reptilian skin) to which is attached a wicker trim (Fagg 1963, fig. 107). This same kind of basketwork trim can be seen on Ekpeye Igbo water spirit

6.21 Hippopotami in the water. Photographer unknown.

6.22 In this Ìjèbú dance posture, the masks, which are fully visible to onlookers, are held horizontally to evoke swimming or "floating" movements. Photograph by Henry John Drewal and Margaret Thompson Drewal, Ìjèbú, 1982.

6.23 *A rare Kalabari headdress shows a janus head with pointed projections (one braided). Photograph from Talbot (1932, 47).*

6.24 *Headdress. Edo. Wood, pigment, and fiber. Photograph courtesy of Dimondstein Tribal Arts.*

headdresses at the Liverpool Museum (Fagg 1963, pls.120–21). Fagg said of these Igbile masks, "Although they were carved by Bini, the style is that of the western Ijo of the Delta, from whom the Ìlàjẹ Yorùbá adopted it; from them it was imported, together with Ìlàjẹ songs, by the Bini" (1963, pl. 106).

Imagery

A number of Central and Western Ijo headdresses have another recurrent iconic element, the janus image, either two heads back-to-back or a single head with two faces. An early illustration (fig. 6.23) of a rare Kalabari headdress—said by P. Amaury Talbot (1932, 47) to be "worn only at the conclusion of the long ceremony of Minji (water) Asaiya (the purifier) which lasts for seven years"—shows a janus head with several pointed projections, some braided. This Kalabari Ijo form seems to be closely related to a Western Ijo one (see fig. 4.23) and an Ìjẹ̀bú-Yorùbá one photographed by Fagg in 1959 (The William B. Fagg Photographic Archive, #1959/6–12). This Ìjẹ̀bú janus headdress, consisting of two flat disc faces mounted on a single central column and hemispherical base, has two distinctive horned forms rising from the top. In addition, two metal strips attached at the temples, provide other projections. At the center of the forehead, another brass sheet in the form of a large neck surmounted by a circular head with bulging eyes and mouth, echoes the bold features of the main face. There are several related Ìjẹ̀bú pieces in this corpus (see fig. 6.11).

Ijo, who conceive of the *owu* as half-human and half-animal, often combine both elements in mask iconography (see fig. 4.27). This fact is evident in many water spirit headdresses where the sleek streamlined forms of reptiles and aquatic creatures combine with the more angular depiction of a human head, a tray, or other items of culture such as medicine gourds, an abstracted prow, or paddle. Representing the "animals of the *oru*" (*oru nama*) or water spirits, headdresses show most commonly crocodiles, tortoises, bullfrogs, lizards, skinks, geckos, monitor lizards, and large poisonous snakes. All of these spirits are considered the children of the python.

Human interaction with the water is another important iconic theme. References to the prows of boats (see figs. 4.16, 4.17, 6.14, 6.22) are to be expected when one remembers that traditionally Ijo fish-buying families lived on their boats for nine months out of the year (Horton 1960, 10). Horton (1960, 15) also explains that the *teme* (invisible, spiritual sphere) controls the *oju* (visible, tangible realm) and that the water people control the behavior of the tangible realm. He goes on to say "and in this the Kalabari compare it with the helmsman of a boat." That is, the Ijo use a water-derived metaphor to describe a key concept in their worldview. In Ìjẹ̀bú Àgbó masks (fig. 6.25), the flowing forms of the prows of boats are evident in masks for the spirit Ìgòdò. This prow, the surface of which is flat and curves upward, synthesizes both prow and paddle shapes. In the Ìjẹ̀bú Ọ̀kẹ̀nẹ̀kẹ́nẹ́ mask (fig. 6.26), culture and nature are juxtaposed—the red dome of a human skull at the center is surrounded by vegetal tendrils and *woro* leaf from watery realms, long pointed ears, and a bird clutching its prey in its beak. Another headdress (fig. 6.27) depicts a house and clock to convey the richness of the abodes of the "water people" living in their sumptuous underwater towns.

Birds also appear frequently in water spirit headdresses (see fig. 6.26). For the Kalabari Ijo, these are probably references to *oru ogolo,* the talkative bulbul bird that is said to live in villages and to speak the language of the spirits. It communicates messages from the spirits to humans. Others may depict the fishing eagle, for eagle feathers are worn by important chiefs among the Ijo as well as being inserted into holes in the headdresses. Birds are thus messengers/mediators between humans and spirits. Birds also figure in culture hero (*oru*) myths where they become tired of living in the world and fly "off as birds into the sky" (Horton 1960, 17). In the Central Delta, three bird masks that perform on stilts at Korokorosei are seen as water spirits called Agula. They travel in the retinue of the hero Adumu (Anderson 1983, 202, and personal communication, May 1999). These bird-stilt masks may be related to the Ekeleke stilt dancers among the Igbo who are also seen as water spirits (Cole 1984, 186).

In Àgbó masks, birds ride on the backs of crocodiles and on the snouts of such masks as Ìgòdò and Ọ̀kẹ̀nẹ̀kẹ́nẹ́. In these latter instances, the bird is probably a fishing eagle. For the Ìjẹ̀bú, the bird is linked with water spirits, as it is in the Delta.

Media

The use of metal is widespread in Delta masks for the water spirits and to a lesser degree in Àgbó. According to Anderson (1983, 182), the rumor in Korokorosei is that the true emblem of the water spirit Eleke "is a brass mask kept secretly inside the cult house." Two other brasses, one a beautiful face and one an ugly one, are displayed at annual festivals at Lobia according to Anderson's assistant. One wonders if one of these might not be related to a metal mask with a bird on its forehead (fig. 1.1) thought to be Ijo. At Nembe, one masquerade has a bronze mask believed to have been made by the water spirits (Alagoa 1967, 51). Alagoa also reports brasses at the Western Ijo town of Oproza that are considered to be water spirit masks. They were reportedly seized from the water people who had used them as masquerade headpieces. The bell-shaped form of some of them suggests the Igbile headdresses of Ughoton (Fagg 1963, pl.107) discussed earlier and also Ìjẹ̀bú face bells (see fig. 1.8).

Bells and bell-shaped gongs (clapperless) seem to permeate the world of the water spirits. Bells are an important item of ritual regalia, worn by

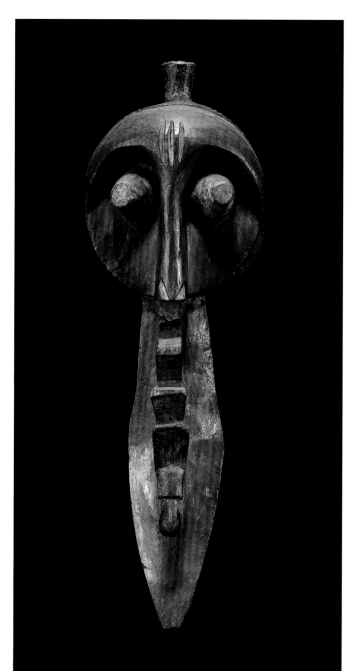

6.25 Mask, Ìjẹ̀bú-Yorùbá. Wood. H: 57.15 cm. FMCH X91.16; Anonymous Gift.

6.26 The imagery on an Òkènèkéné mask juxtaposes culture and nature. Photograph by Henry John Drewal and Margaret Thompson Drewal, Ìjẹ̀bú, 1982.

6.27 Water spirit headdress. Ìjẹ̀bú-Yorùbá. Wood, paint, iron, and mirror. L: 123.2 cm. This headdress depicts a house and clock to convey the abode of the "water people" living in their towns beneath the surface. The Fine Arts Museums of San Francisco, M. H. De Young Memorial Museum; Purchase by Exchange, acc. no. 76.12.1.

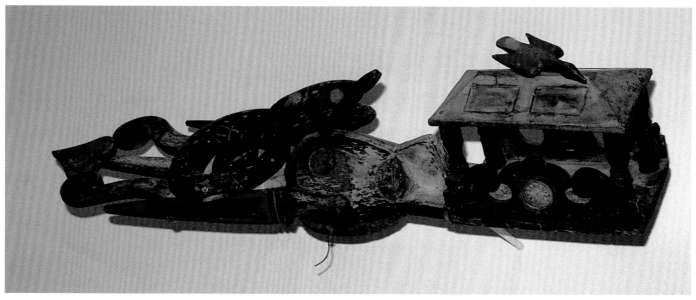

masqueraders and other mediums among the Ijo (Horton 1960, 39, 45) and others (Neaher 1976; Lorenz 1982, 52–60, figs. H6–12). Part of their significance lies in their medium, their source, and their function—metal traded from Europeans and their ships' bells (see Peek 1980, 64). Beyond the Delta, Ìjèbú chiefs wear figurated hip bells. In Benin, bells are worn by court officials and decorate royal altars that honor kings descended from Olókun, god of the sea. And a number of bronze bells have been documented among the Isoko (see chapter 1 of this volume; Peek 1980, figs. 4, 6, 9, 11, 12).

In addition to metal masks, metal occurs in carved wooden headdresses. A Western Delta headdress has eyes that are covered in metal—copper shotgun cartridges (The Metropolitan Museum of Art, 1978.412.559). Others appear to have had the same metal attachments as well (see figs. 6.1, 6.9). This treatment appears in headdresses of the Ìjèbú that I identify as Àgbó, where eyes (and/or face) are also metal covered. The significance of such incorporation of metal is at least partly due to its source, that is, Europeans. Imported items, such as cloth and other commercial goods are preferred by water spirits among the Central Ijo, as Martha Anderson informs me. I believe the reason lies in widespread African beliefs that view Euopeans as water beings associated with water spirits (see Drewal 1988). In this regard, it is important to remember that for a long time Europeans in the Delta traded from boats and later hulks anchored offshore. This would have certainly reinforced African perceptions of Europeans as "water creatures." Another telling incident adds further circumstantial evidence. In 1897, the Bini Igbile cult for the water spirits at Ughoton was said to have "paraded the masks…in the hope of repelling the [British Punitive] Expedition with supernatural aid" (Fagg 1963, pl. 107).

Costumes

Cloth has long been a major commodity in Delta trade and predates the arrival of the Europeans (Aronson 1992). In the water spirit complex, one particular type of cloth seems to have traveled in several directions and been picked up by different peoples at different times. Since at least the fifteenth century, the Ìjèbú-Yorùbá have been famous for cloth woven by women and men that was traded all through the Delta, the West African coast and, after the arrival of the Portuguese, Brazil—where it became known as *pano da costa*, "cloth from the coast [West Africa]." It is possible that Ìjèbú cloth was traded to the Kalabari Ijo primarily for the Ekine masquerade and as a prestige garment in the Delta. Dutch reports of the seventeenth century state that Ìjèbú cloth was traded in the lagoon to Ughoton and beyond (cf. Ryder 1969, 197–98, and Aronson 1992, 60). A cloth named Idoko *bide* (Idoko cloth) was used in water spirit festivals (Alagoa 1982, 283) and "by ladies of high status among the Egbema [Western Delta Ijo]. This is apparently a reference to the Ìjèbú country, since Idoko is said to have been one of a number of small kingdoms in the area incorporated by Ọbánta, founder of the current dynasty at Ìjèbú-Òde" (Alagoa 1970, 327).[3] The importance of "foreign" cloth used by the Ijo in their water spirit masquerades parallels the use of imported objects in the shrines of the spirits among the Central Ijo. They are precious commodities from across watery expanses, as well as being associated with those who come from "overseas"—Europeans.

It was the Ijo and others who traded this Ìjèbú cloth into the Delta. Seeing how popular this cloth was among their Delta neighbors, the Igbo

6.28 Tortoise-design cloth (ìkákí) is still woven on a small scale in Ìjèbú. Also known as aso ọlọnà, "artful cloth of many designs," it is being worn here by the Ọlọ́wá priest. Photograph by Henry John Drewal and Margaret Thompson Drewal, Ìjèbú, 1982.

weavers of Akwete copied it and soon replaced Ìjèbú as the source for the cloth. The Kalabari Ijo call it *ikaki,* "tortoise," for the main motif on the cloth (see chapter 8 of this volume). This same cloth design is still woven on a small scale in Ìjèbú and used as a ritual garment (fig. 6.28). Even though it was originally produced in Ìjèbú, it is now known in Ìjèbúland by its Ijo name—a wonderfully complicated history in the comings and goings of cultural products and ideas.

The Kalabari Ijo costume consists of a skintight tunic that covers the hands, arms, body, and legs of the dancer leaving only the feet uncovered. Tied onto this costume is a long conical construction of palm midribs that projects backward from the masker's buttocks to form a tail—or fin, according to Martha Anderson's Ijo teachers (personal communication, 1999). It thus recalls the tripartite composition of most headdresses and evokes, although not in any literal way, the shape of fish and other aquatic creatures. Some Ìjèbú-Yorùbá costumes re-create or approximate it (although the belly form did not carry over to Yorùbá), while others depart from this format. Those that are most Yorùbá-like have women's headties knotted around their waist/chest (see fig. 6.22) and some have a hip/buttocks construction very similar to Yorùbá Gèlèdé costumes to the west (see figs. 6.4, 6.17, 6.19; Drewal and Drewal 1983, 124).

As noted earlier, woven raffia mats are also a distinctive costume element. Seedpod leg rattles are another constant in the regalia of Ijo Ekine (Horton 1960, 22) and Yorùbá Àgbó maskers (see figs. 6.17, 6.19). According to Horton, these are locust bean pods. Ìjèbú, who call them *ude,* consider them rare and expensive and believe that they come from trees that grow by the waterside, close to the abode of the spirits, and are thus effective in attracting them. These same pods are used in other Ìjèbú ritual contexts as well.

All major water spirit costume elements—carved or cloth headdress, mats/cloth, tail construction, seedpod leg rattles, and handheld dance implements—are widely distributed among the Ìjèbú and their Delta neighbors near and far—the Ìlàjè, Itsekiri, Àpoí, Edo, Isoko, Urhobo, and Ijo—further evidence of extensive cultural and historical interactions.

Music and Movement

Horton (1963) identifies dance as the most important of the arts in Ekine. His critique of Western hieratic thinking about the so-called "fine" arts of sculpture and painting and the "lesser" arts of costume and dance is correct. However, in his effort to counter this tendency, he appears to simply replace one ranking system with another. I would suggest that we need the views of those from within the culture—artists, patrons, performers, audiences—as well as those from outside and that we need to recognize the "heterarchy" of differing perspectives. As the Igbo say "you cannot stand in one place to see [appreciate, understand] a masquerade." I also think we need to recognize African performances as not just multimedia events, but multisensorial ones (see Drewal 1994, 64–65). This broader perspective will, I believe, reveal other artistic dimensions heretofore ignored.

While he provides little dance description or analysis, Horton's illustrations tend to suggest some similarities with the choreography of Àgbó maskers. The solos, circled dances, and processions of maskers among the Ijo are paralleled among the Ìjèbú. The "graphic portrayals of character" described by Horton (1960, 31–32) appear among the Ìjèbú Àgbó maskers, but seem to be less varied and more muted, except for the comical bird-eating husband, Ajẹyẹ. The elaborate stories (*egberi*) that portray episodes in the lives of the water spirits among Ijo are also missing. And the games of risk between spirits and young men and the "drum-answering competitions" for maskers among the Ijo (Horton 1960, 32) are not very important in Ìjèbú.

What follows is a summary of some of the main choreographic motifs that I witnessed and filmed at several Ìjèbú Àgbó festivals (Akió, Òmù, Àgòrò, and Èpè) in 1982. The upper torsos of Ìgòdò maskers are inclined sharply forward (see fig. 6.22), arms extended to the sides and parallel with the ground. As among the Ijo, where they are known as *aku* (Worika 1982, 315), almost all Ìjèbú maskers hold sticks in their hands as dance implements. They raise their legs during the dance and strike their seedpod leg rattles with these sticks in order to punctuate and reinforce drum phrases. Anderson (1997, 133–34) describes exactly the same actions among the Central Ijo. They also lean on sticks during opening invocations in front of the drummers or before a shrine, and at certain moments of the dance, when the performers move on "all fours" in imitation of animals. One dancer used them to emphasize the drum rhythm, first stretching them out to the sides and then crossing them in front of his chest. Another, a crocodile masker, imitating a frail old creature, moved slowly and stiffly, using his sticks like canes. At other times, maskers would silently pray for people by rubbing their sticks three times in the extended palms of supplicants, who would then transfer this blessing by rubbing their heads and faces (Drewal, filmed performances, 1982).

Each of usually three maskers performs a solo, and then all three dance counterclockwise following a musician who strikes a hollow tortoise shell with a stick. The drum ensemble (usually three to four drummers) provides a rapid rhythm, accompanied by a chorus of women, men, and children singing and striking bamboo sticks and iron gongs in time with the drums. The masqueraders take short, rapid hopping steps, first forward, then backward, alternating with four hopping steps to each side. At other moments, they stand and then whirl with such velocity that attendants must sometimes catch them before they lose their balance and fall. Attendants keep close to the performers, fanning them constantly and offering words of encouragement, praise, correction, and sometimes critique.

Choreography embellishes costumes. Those maskers with extraordinary buttocks (see fig. 6.19) dance to emphasize this attribute—moving their hips and legs to make them wiggle and bounce provocatively. Those with tall conical headdresses and long tassels (see fig. 6.17) swing them and sometimes strike them on the ground in dramatic fashion, provoking ripples of excitement that run through the crowd until the water spirits retire to their shrine as the sun sets over sparkling waters.

Envoi—"Up a Creek *with* a Paddle"

In a recent article on archaeological work in Africa and using the Middle Niger floodplain as one example, McIntosh (1999, 57) stresses the antiquity of interactions of different cultures to create community networks of interlocking yet separate sites. These facilitated exchanges of expertise to benefit all—a pattern of "heterarchy" as opposed to "hierarchy." The Delta seems to have been another one of those sites. Yet how are we to fathom the complex, crosscurrents in the art histories of the Niger Delta (and adjacent Guinea Coast both east and west of the Delta), a massive area of watery networks? Myriad factors help explain the history, distribution, forms, and significances of arts in this area of enormous long-term, long-distance transcultural connections. One is linguistic. The Western Delta is inhabited by peoples whose languages fall within the Kwa group. This is evidence of physical proximity and interaction over a long time period, perhaps millennia—but such a *longue durée* tells us little of specific exchanges. At the same time linguistic evidence cannot explain other borrowings in the Delta. For example, there are clear Ijo influences in Abua masquerades near the Eastern Delta, yet the Abua are classified linguistically with Bantu peoples, the Ibibio, Ejagham, and others.

Political history is certainly another factor. There appear to have been a complex series of migrations, conquests, and intermarriages among various Delta groups (Alagoa 1972). Economic factors have been equally important. Long-term (pre-European) and long-distance trade in the area—north/south and east/west—is a dominant characteristic of the region. And remember that this was a trade in humans as well as produce. Waterways were the avenues of ideas, goods, and people, and the Ijo were their masters. Religious beliefs and practices about those who controlled these avenues—the *owu* or "water people"—developed and spread, which in turn helped spread water spirit masking traditions. And what spread was a masquerade performance tradition that varies from an almost total imitation of Ijo modes to radical transformations of them.

We sometimes assume that when artistic forms diffuse, they move with their associated ideas. Form and meaning, however, are independent variables. Icons and ideas are continually and imaginatively constructed by new audiences for new purposes. The transformation of Delta water spirit masking traditions into Ìjèbú-Yorùbá Àgbó has not been a simple, unidirectional process. Some forms have traveled with their meanings, others have not. Some have disappeared, others have been invented. Some Ìjèbú elements—like the *ikaki* cloth—became Akwete Igbo commodities, sold to Kalabari Ijo for Ekine, and its Ijo name (and identity) returned to Ìjèbú in a new form. The arts—expressive culture—are markers of people in time and space. The arts in honor of water spirits among the Ìjèbú-Yorùbá and Delta peoples are testaments to the creative imaginations of people open and willing to learn from others, to teach others, and to enrich themselves in the process.

6.29 Headdress. Ìlàjẹ-Yorùbá. Wood. L: 99.1 cm. Collection of Toby and Barry Hecht. This finely carved headdress closely resembles one purchased from an Ìlàjẹ (or Máhìn) Yorùbá ruler around 1950. Ijo groups living nearby have obviously influenced its style. At first glance, this headdress looks convincingly Ijo, but the flaring nostrils and the T-shaped conjunction of forehead and nose contrast with the skull- or helmet-like configuration seen on Ijo examples.

Interleaf H
The Dancing People:
Eastern Ijo Masking Traditions

Martha G. Anderson

H.1. *Members of the Ekine Society appearing at Owu aru sun (Canoe of the water people) in the Kalabari town of Buguma. Photograph by Joanne B. Eicher, 1991.*

H.2 *Mask appearing at Owu aru sun (Canoe of the water people) in the Kalabari town of Buguma. Photograph by Joanne B. Eicher, 1991.*

Throughout the Niger Delta, people perform masquerades known as *owu* (*ou*) that honor water spirits, creative but antisocial beings who are also called *owu*. The structure and the details of masking, however, differ widely. The Eastern Ijo perform masquerades within the context of societies called Sekiapu (Dancing people) or Ekine; the latter name is in deference to the legendary woman who taught men how to perform the plays (Horton 1963, 94; 1973). Some local differences persist. In Nembe, for example, all masks become the property of Sekiapu. In Kalabari, they belong to trading concerns called "canoe houses," which can acquire them from spirits, borrow them from other communities, or simply become expert in performing them (fig. H.1; Alagoa 1967, 150).

Each community has its own, independent masking society, but branches permit, and even expect, members of other chapters to join in any performances they attend. The primary function of these societies is the staging of an extensive cycle of masquerades. The Kalabari round climaxes in a grand finale called Owu aru sun, or "Canoe of the water people," in which dancers from all forty to fifty plays in the cycle appear (fig. H.2). The Nembe (fig. H.3) stage a similar festival called Owuaya aru, or "Canoe of the mother of masquerades." These events culminate one cycle and renew the spiritual element of the masks for the next (Horton 1963, 95; Alagoa in Nzewunwa 1982, 268–69). The entire repertoire might once have been staged in a single dry season but now takes many years to perform. A Kalabari sequence begun in 1946 ended in 1973 (Jenewari 1974, 3); the next one was completed in 1991.

Sekiapu masquerades provide a venue for renewing relationships with the spirit world (Horton 1960a; Tariah in Nzewunwa 1982, 308). In Okrika masquerades insured the "freedom to fish and trade" without being unduly harassed by the water people. "Traditionally…the well-being of the community depended on the success of the display" (Tamuno 1968, 70). Nevertheless, Sekiapu does not exist solely, or even essentially, for religious reasons. The spirits involved in Kalabari masquerades tend to be "marginal and even obnoxious," and members invoke them primarily to make the performance

H.3 *Performances often begin with songs and drum calls imploring water spirits to come out of the water to play. Maskers sometimes arrive by canoe or appear to exit into the water, and some Okrika masks actually perform in the water. Photograph by Barbara Sumberg, Nembe, 1993.*

H.4 *"Chiefs of Bonny: In the centre, a Chief in his Devil-Dress."* Gleaner Pictorial Album *1:25, fig. 5. Photograph Courtesy of the Church Mission Society, London. The "Devil-Dress" referred to in the caption from the* Gleaner Pictorial Album, *appears to be an Ekine headdress similar to the Nembe type seen in fig. H.5.*

H.5 *A heavily embellished mask. Photograph by Barbara Sumberg, Nembe, 1993.*

good. By placing religion at the service of art, the masquerades approach the Western notion of "art for art's sake" (Horton 1963; Alagba 1995).

Sekiapu also serves social and political functions. Even if it did not actually govern Eastern Ijo communities, community leaders were members (fig. H.4). In Nembe, it was charged with imbuing males with manly virtues and punishing them for offenses ranging from voyeurism (spying on the women's toilet) to more serious crimes such as rape and theft (Alagoa 1967, 147–49). There, as elsewhere, the society promotes cultural knowledge by requiring expertise in drum language, a system that involves rhythmic equivalents for spoken words and shares similar tone patterns (see Alagba 1995). A number of masquerades test the performer's skill through a sequence known as "the pointing ordeal." He must respond to drum calls by indicating the town or shrine being named. Failure to do so brings disgrace; success proves him to be a cultured member of society. The Kalabari used the ordeal to socialize the outsiders they inducted to swell their ranks. (Alagoa 1967, 14–55; Horton 1966, 175–81; 1960; Alagba 1995).

Eastern Ijo communities take great pride in these performances. Masks representing various canoe houses participate in displays and contests. The successful showing of a spectacular mask bestows prestige on the family who sponsors it. Women participate by singing and dancing around the field. The heirloom trade cloths and coral beads they wear to advertise their families' wealth and prosperity also recall centuries of participation in the overseas trade.

Many costumes incorporate wooden headpieces (see preface, fig. F, introduction, fig. 11, and figs. H.7–H.10), and one Nembe masquerade features bronze examples believed to have been made by water spirits (Alagoa 1967, 51). These may be so heavily embellished with feathers, fringe, and shiny baubles that they are virtually hidden from view; some masks consist entirely of gaudy materials. The proliferation of ornament reflects the comparative wealth of the region (fig. H.5). The performers emphasize the stratified nature of Kalabari society by wearing prestigious trade cloths and carrying fans, tusks, and other attributes of status.

H.6 *Ngbula is described by Horton as an "ugly, deaf, and paranoiac water-doctor, who stares at people as if to read their lips, then rushes savagely at them because he thinks they must have been insulting him in his infirmity" (Horton 1960, 31). This masquerade took place in the Kalabari town of Buguma. Photograph by Joanne B. Eicher, 1991.*

H.7 *Monkey mask appearing at Owu aru sun (Canoe of the water people) in the Kalabari town of Buguma. Photograph by Joanne B. Eicher, 1991.*

H.8 *Water spirit headdress representing the character known as Igbo. Kalabari Ijo. Wood and pigment. L: 30.5 cm. Collection of Toby and Barry Hecht. The prominent forehead, pointed face, diamond-shaped eyes, and coiled snakes on this headpiece correspond to the features of Igbo, one of the characters who engages in a contest that tests both the masker's command of drum language and his knowledge of Kalabari culture.*

Maskers portray familiar human types—including aristocrats, native doctors (fig. H.6), headhunters, and rogues. A performer's behavior suggests the personality of the mask (figs. H.7, H.9, H.10). Elephant's lumbering movements, which magnify his size and power (Eicher 1994), contrast with the "mincing gait" that is befitting of Ikaki, or "Tortoise," a renowned trickster (Horton 1967, 228–29; see chapter 8 of this volume). Opongi, who aspires to the title bestowed on proven warriors, backs into the arena and dances with furtive steps to dramatize his stealth while headhunting (Jenewari 1980, 9). Igbo (fig. H.8), who exemplifies the aristocratic ideal, performs the demanding pointing ordeal while pretending nonchalance, earning himself the praise name: "The bending mangrove that seems about to fall

H.9 Water spirit headdress in the form of a hippopotamus (Otobo). Kalabari Ijo. Wood, pigment, metal, and incrustation. H: 47 cm. Indiana University Art Museum; Raymond and Laura Wielgus Collection, 96.49. Photograph by Michael Cavanagh and Kevin Montague © Indiana University Art Museum. The sheer size of a hippopotamus (otobo) endows it with a sense of authority. The Kalabari praise otobo as the "Beast who holds up the flowing tide." The combination of human and animal features on this headdress conveys the dual nature of the masquerade character Otobo, who is part man and part hippo. His blue and white coloring recalls the skin of the python, another creature that mediates between land and water.

H.10 Water spirit headdress in the form of a hippopotamus (Otobo). Nembe Ijo. Wood and pigment. L: 34.3 cm. Collection of Toby and Barry Hecht. Unlike the brilliant abstractions that characterize Kalabari Ijo Otobo masks, Nembe artists suggest the head of a hippo as seen partially submerged in the water. The neighboring Abua and Ekpeye made increasingly abstract hippo headdresses.

but never does" (Horton 1966, 175–76, 179–82).

Performers typically act out simple plots. Even the breathtaking Odum, or "Python," masks of Okrika—which measure several hundred yards and perform in the water—engage in a form of storytelling by accomplishing a series of tasks. They sink miniature ships, coil around palm trees, and play with small fish before approaching land, where they "swallow" gifts of gin and fowl before gliding majestically back into the water (Tamuno 1968, 76; Rivers State Ministry of Information 197?). The more elaborate plot of a comic Kalabari masquerade starring Ikaki conveys a moral lesson by showing that even the best laid schemes of a consummate con artist are doomed to fail (Horton 1967, 236–39). Masks can even work a bit of narrative into the pointing ordeal by turning it into

a contest in which the drummer tries to confuse the dancer (Horton 1966, 175–76). Alagba portrays a woman who becomes distracted when spectators sing songs to remind her that she has forgotten something (see interleaf L). Instead of responding to the drum's instructions at once, she repeatedly interrupts her graceful dance to check for missing parts of her costume, then gets back to the business of pointing (Alagba 1995).

A number of other groups living in and around the Delta admit to imitating Ijo performances; however, shared beliefs in water spirits, which help account for the readiness of Delta groups to adopt masquerades from each other, complicate the issue of who copied what from whom. Reported borrowings sometimes fit neatly into local traditions or have no clear source.

Part 3 : Arts and Identity

Chapter 7

Everyone to His Quarter:
Ethnic Interaction,
Emulation, and Change in
Itsekiri Visual Culture

KATHY CURNOW

When interethnic conflicts are rife, as they are in the Niger Delta, two factors that illuminate political and historic relationships are the conscious projection of culture and the denial or acknowledgment of neighboring influences. Both are clearly visible amongst the Itsekiri (Jekri, Iwere) of the Warri Kingdom. A small ethnic group,[1] they once dominated the region. Significantly outnumbered by their immediate neighbors, the Urhobo and Ijo, their former position as overlords has been challenged repeatedly in this century. Today they fight for visibility within Nigeria's Delta State, using art and other forms of cultural expression to affirm their presence and attempt to reestablish paramountcy.

For over four centuries, the Itsekiri were regional masters of commerce, first supplying the Portuguese and other Europeans with slaves, cloths, and other goods, then, in the 1800s, shifting their emphasis to palm oil. Their population was heavily dependent on slaves, who came from a variety of inland ethnic groups. In particular, the Urhobo acted as their cassava and oil palm farmers, as well as their paddlers. The local Ijo, on the other hand, were trade partners, tenants, and, according to the Itsekiri, sometimes pirates. The colonial British government inverted Itsekiri ethnic supremacy in the Warri region. Within the past century, the abolition of slavery robbed them of both population and labor force. Furthermore, the early Western education of former subject peoples aggravated matters, as the Itsekiri began to be outmaneuvered in the newly established colonial civil service. Despite these shifts, old resentments continued. In 1952, the Urhobo rioted during an organized welcome for Itsekiri Chief Arthur Prest, a minister in the federal government, because he was perceived as "the chief organiser of Itsekiri claims to superiority" (Lloyd 1956, 79). After independence, the Nigerian government perpetuated the imported legal system, as well as certain British policies vis-à-vis traditional rulers, further undermining Itsekiri authority. Interethnic relationships shifted drastically. The Itsekiri ruler, the *olu*, can no longer appoint Ijo district titleholders as he once did; the Itsekiri have lost a number of land claims to the Ijo and especially to the Urhobo (Ayomike 1988; Moore 1936 [1970]; Obiomah n.d.); and even expected state entitlements have at times required court battles.

Particularly chafing to the Itsekiri were some perceived and sanctioned abuses of kingship, which occurred in 1991 when Bendel State was split into Edo and Delta States. Each Nigerian state has a council of traditional rulers who remain influential, though they have no active political role. Under the British, these rulers were graded ("First Class," "Second Class," "Third Class") according to their historical importance and spheres of influence. The postindependence Nigerian government continued this practice, also

7.1 Ogiame Atuwatse II, Olu of Warri, on the occasion of his installation as chancellor of the University of Nigeria. Olu Atuwatse II wears an academic gown over his wrapper and sashed chasuble; an academic cap was rejected in favor of one of the formal Portuguese crowns. Photograph by Kathy Curnow, Nsukka, 1994.

maintaining each monarch's graded government stipend. Under the former Bendel State, the Itsekiri *olu* (a "First Class" traditional ruler) was the permanent vice-chairman of the state's traditional council (the *oba* of Benin being its permanent chairman). The Itsekiri assumed this recognized position would place their *olu* as the head of the traditional council of the new Delta State, just as the *oba* would chair Edo State. To their dismay, Delta decided its own council would have a rotational head, and its first choice of chairman was the Urhobo ruler of Okpe. The Itsekiri viewed this decision as insulting in the extreme. They observed that, under the British, local Urhobo priest-leaders had been "upgraded" into traditional rulers for ease of indirect rule. They also pointed out that the Urhobo had always been decentralized and, as such, were undeserving of the council's initial recognition. In protest, the *olu* refused to attend council meetings.

Rancor has produced more than objections. In the last decade, area violence has grown steadily. The Urhobo have burnt the homes of prominent Itsekiri, tried to destroy an important Itsekiri tree shrine, and attempted to disrupt Itsekiri public festivities. In order to ensure peace and political neutrality, the Itsekiri petitioned the federal government to declare Warri town a "Federal Territory" in the mid-1990s, but without success. By late 1998, the Ogbe Ijo likewise burnt numerous Itsekiri homes and even staged a night marine attack on the island of Ode-Itsekiri, targeting the *olu*'s traditional palace (not his present residence, but an important ceremonial landmark). Retaliations have occurred, with many accompanying deaths and injuries.

Several issues are at stake. Urhobo resentment centers on land ownership, the concept of Itsekiri suzerainty, and perceived Itsekiri insults—the Itsekiri continued to refer to the Urhobo as their slaves well into this century (Lloyd 1956, 82). For decades the Urhobo, who make up the majority of Warri town's inhabitants, have sued unsuccessfully to change the *olu*'s legal title to "*olu* of Itsekiri," rather than "*olu* of Warri." Ijo hostility, on the other hand, was sparked in 1997 by a successful Itsekiri bid to shift a local government headquarters from an Ogbe Ijo to an Itsekiri enclave. By 1999, the Ogbe Ijo were still protesting the loss, petitioning the government to create a new local government for their use, and violence escalated during this year. Since the early 1900s, Itsekiri bitterness has centered on the Urhobo; the Ijo have only recently been viewed as active antagonists. These conflicts have had a significant impact on families. The Itsekiri treat intermarriage as a rule, rather than an exception. By the 1950s, Lloyd estimated 22 percent of the Itsekiri had Urhobo mothers (1956, 83), and the number seems to have increased since then. In the late 1980s, Olu Erejuwa II ruled that very distant relatives could marry, but most Itsekiri still consider any degree of relationship, no matter how remote, as unacceptable incest (*eguere*; Omoneukanrin 1942, 46–48). During crisis periods, Urhobo or Ijo mothers and wives (children are generally considered to have their father's ethnicity) are considered antagonists and told to "go to their own quarter." Currently many interethnic weddings have been canceled or postponed because of the crisis. Although numerous investigatory panels intended to stem ethnic violence and ill will have been formulated, no permanent settlement has yet resulted.

These reversals have threatened the Itsekiri, making them increasingly active and vocal promoters of their kingdom and its culture. Their struggle for visibility and both local and national recognition have incorporated numerous aspects of visual and performance art, from commercial and fashion statements to regalia and sacred forms. Art has become both territorial marker and border expander, while claims to origination of forms are viewed with legalistic zeal or blasé acceptance (depending on the appropriator). Visual distinction has become a key element in the one-upmanship that is a daily aspect of ethnic rivalry.

The question of identity and its projection is a complex one, for the Itsekiri are themselves an amalgam. As an ethnic entity, they conjoined in the late fifteenth century, uniting peoples of diverse origins. Most appear to have migrated into the Delta from a variety of Yoruba polities, particularly from the Ijebu region. Some linguists go so far as to refer to the Itsekiri language as a Yoruba dialect with numerous loan words. Other immigrants are said to have been Benin Edo, Igala, or Ijo (Moore 1936 [1970], 13; Sagay n.d. [1981], 2; Omoneukanrin 1942, 17). As a group, they coalesced under external leadership in the late fifteenth century when the exiled Benin crown prince Ginuwa canoed south into the Delta, accompanied by the heirs of Benin chiefs. After traveling to the coast and spending some time there among the Ijo, the party voyaged back into the creeks, finally settling on the island of Ode-Itsekiri (also known as Big Warri). Incorporating those people of mixed origins already occupying the area, they expanded, creating additional communities along the mangrove creeks. Their nation has had only one traditional ruler, the *olu*, who administered his state through his chiefs. Rival or breakaway chiefs often fled the capital, setting up communities some distance away; this expanded the kingdom's boundaries.

Foreign trade further affected Itsekiri culture. By about 1500, the Portuguese had already reached the area (Pereira 1937, 129),[2] and contact intensified within the next century. The court was Christianized, beginning a tradition of Catholic monarchs that was nearly unbroken until the nineteenth century. This coincided with an economy that was extremely externally oriented; many Itsekiri words for luxury imports (such as *seda* for "silk") come directly from the Portuguese. By the seventeenth century, the Dutch began to make trade inroads, followed by the French and the British. In the nineteenth century, the latter dominated the palm oil trade, which became the area mainstay after British stoppage of the slave trade.

In 1848, civil insurrection and an eighty-eight year interregnum followed the *olu*'s death and that of two of his heirs. Effective control was in the hands of a series of "governors" (*gofines*), who continued to operate even after the 1884 British-Itsekiri "protection" treaties and the 1891 integration of the Warri Kingdom into the Niger Coast Protectorate of Southern Nigeria. It was the British who built up what has become Warri town (once known as New Warri); their initial establishment quickly grew to incorporate Itsekiri, Urhobo, and Ijo lands. In 1936, the royal throne was reestablished, and by mid-century the *olu* had built a new palace in Warri town, an architectural statement that staked a claim on the mainland, leaving the ancient island palace as a ceremonial center for coronations, funerals, and festivals.

Questions of Itsekiri identity revolve around five groups: two parent cultures, the Edo of the Benin Kingdom and the Yoruba; their external allies the Portuguese; and two sources of contention, the Urhobo and Ijo. Ambivalence marks relations with the parent cultures. Benin is valued as the source of the monarchy, as well as for its undeniable historic presence. It is the origin of royal traditions such as a coral crown, netted coral garments, coral *odigbe* collar, ceremonial swords (*uda* and *eberen*), semicircular royal ancestral altars, many chiefly titles, and numerous elements of regalia. Independence from Benin authority and cultural innovations are, however, even more esteemed. Though the reports of some early travelers suggest that Warri may have been subject to Benin (Ryder 1959, 296, 301),[3] no ceremonial or other evidence supports this: the *oba* of Benin did not confirm new *olu*s (as he did the rulers of other subject peoples), nor were *olu*s buried at Benin (as some of the northern Urhobo leaders were). This type of origin reinforcement was common; even Benin itself continued to send certain remains of deceased *oba*s for interment at Ife, their dynastic home, until the late nineteenth century. In contrast, Itsekiri royal burials take place at Ijala, a settlement founded by the first *olu*, Ginuwa, who died and was buried there. His sons went on to found their capital at nearby Ode-Itsekiri.

Many more travelers asserted Warri's autonomy; if tribute was ever paid, it seems to have been sporadic and related to trade privileges, rather than political dominance. Benin and Itsekiri policies toward foreigners and neighbors differed, and numerous conflicts with Benin were noted from the sixteenth through nineteenth centuries (Ryder 1969, 75, 113, 226, 230, 274). The blood ties between Edo and Itsekiri royals, however, have never been disputed. Indeed, in the sixteenth century, two *olu*s were named for the recently deceased Oba Ozolua (Ojoluwa) and Oba Esigie; although the meaning of this gesture is unclear, the implications relating to royal reincarnation are intriguing. More often, however, the family relationship has been marked by filial rivalry. Throughout history, numerous Itsekiri chiefs have fled the *olu*'s wrath to take refuge with the *oba* of Benin (Ryder 1969,112, 230–31; Lloyd 1957,180). In a 1984 survey of interethnic preferences, Joseph Nevadomsky discovered Itsekiri participants ranked the Edo last in a list of nine groups, suggesting this might have resulted from "Itsekiri attempts to throw off what is left of Bini political hegemony" (Nevadomsky 1989, 639). Distaste for perceived cultural hegemony is also likely, for the Itsekiri are well aware that Benin has overshadowed their own place in world history.

With the exception of language, the Yoruba stamp on Itsekiri culture is minimal. The Itsekiri do practice Ifa divination (called Ife), but without a regularized priesthood, and the Yoruba pantheon is, for the most part, unrepresented. Only the war/iron god Ogun and the sea deity Umalokun (both of whom may have moved indirectly to Warri from Benin, where they are also worshiped as Ogun and Olokun) are found among the Itsekiri. Most styles of dancing and drumming are dissimilar, as are textile traditions, masquerades, architecture, and sculpture; the Itsekiri are instead key participants in general Niger Delta cultural patterns. There have, however, been some Yoruba associations. In 1820, John King described the *olu*'s crown as beaded, "with two birds' heads" (1822, 318), a form that clearly followed a Yoruba prototype for beaded crowns. This was not the official state crown, and may have been worn for fashion's sake; it may also, however, have had political implications, as similar choices did in this century. Olu Erejuwa II (r. 1951–1987) owned a collection of contemporary beaded crowns for less formal wear, modeled on the "everyday" crowns Yoruba rulers began to wear by mid-century. All Itsekiri informal crowns include a short, pierced projection for the (optional) insertion of a white egret feather, the same feather that appears on Yoruba state crowns; both peoples consider it a sign of authority. Olu Erejuwa II's political alliances may have influenced his choices: in the 1950s and early 1960s, he was aligned with the Yoruba-led Action Group, and his dressing showed an allegiance that disassociated him from Benin's Oba Akenzua II, a supporter of the rival NCNC party. Under Erejuwa II, official Itsekiri identification with the Yoruba was at its height; the Action Group even stated that the Itsekiri were part of the Yoruba (Sagay n.d. [1981], 187). This comment prompted another prominent Itsekiri, Chief Festus Okotie-Eboh, the *olu*'s political enemy, to accuse the monarch of having "sacrificed the greatness and identity of the Itsekiris and soiled our great history by saying Itsekiris are Yorubas" (Sagay n.d. [1981], 189). Under the present *olu*, Atuwatse II, considerable cultural distancing has taken place. Links with the Yoruba are not stressed, and popular exchanges in local magazines and newspapers protest that Itsekiri is not a Yoruba dialect. This is no indicator of conflict, but rather a continuous attempt to stress the differentiation of the Itsekiri as a cultural entity.[4]

Long association with the Portuguese helped make the Itsekiri unique in Southern Nigeria, and their contributions are consciously recalled and celebrated. Although the Ijo, Urhobo, Ijebu-Yoruba, and Edo also encountered the Portuguese long ago, their relationships with the foreigners were less sustained and close. Portuguese impact, though discernible among the Ijebu and Edo, is not immediately evident. Under the surface, the effects of Portuguese contact on the Warri Kingdom can still be felt. They derive from the European studies of an early Itsekiri prince, sustained missionization, repeated exchange of official letters, and favorable trade. The power Portuguese support (and weapons) gave the Itsekiri over their neighbors no longer exists, but its legacy is sustained through pride in the grandiosity and privilege of the past.

7.2 *European porcelain statue (probably Portuguese) belonging to an Itsekiri family and likely dating from the late eighteenth or early nineteenth century. This work was one of many antiques exhibited during a coronation anniversary activity. Photograph by Kathy Curnow, Warri, 1994.*

Many of the supposed Portuguese influences on the Itsekiri are superficial, but they have the advantage of being highly visible, as they involve dress, accessories and royal regalia. Itsekiri absorption of these kinds of Portuguese elements was a matter of choice. What is immediately apparent in present Itsekiri culture is a mystique of exaltedness, expressed through visual reminders of the glorious, outward-looking past (fig. 7.2 and see interleaf C). These reminders include both objects and attire. In the 1940s, a colonial observer mentioned that in a typical chief's house "Gold garters, swords, armour breast plate, and a melee of articles of the Victorian era greet your eyes, and if the chief was agreeable and took you within the sanctum of his home you would find he probably sleeps on a fifteenth century Portuguese four-poster" (Allen 1949, 757). P. C. Lloyd noted that the Itsekiri happily attribute "many heirlooms" to the Portuguese, even when their origin was elsewhere in Europe (Moore 1936 [1970], viii).

Many aspects of everyday dress originated through Portuguese trade: the ubiquitous use of Indian madras cottons and their more elaborate cousins (*george*; fig. 7.3), the women's traditional small knotted headtie made from handkerchiefs, imported silver and gold filigree jewelry (fig. 7.4). Other items, such as English derbies, straw boaters, top hats and fedoras, or shirts with pleated bibs, derive from later trading partners. In this decade, several chiefs and nobles use cowboy hats with their formal wear, an appropriation apparently resulting from contact with the Texans and other denizens of

7.3 *Itsekiri men in traditional* george *wrappers and European-derived shirts. Photograph by Kathy Curnow, Warri, 1994.*

7.4 *Chief Rita Lori, the* igba *of Warri, wearing hairpins of imported coral. Olu Erejuwa II was the first to create female chieftaincies. Photograph by Kathy Curnow, Warri, 1994.*

7.5 *The late* eson *of Warri wearing an imported top hat at an occasion celebrating his position as a Christian church elder. He sits beside several other Itsekiri chiefs, one of whom wears a cowboy hat. Photograph by Kathy Curnow, Warri, 1994.*

the American South who manage some of the Delta's many offshore oil rigs (fig. 7.5).

In most cases, it was aristocratic dress that was adopted and adapted, and a very strong sense of historicity persists. Not only is the average person familiar with which dress items are Portuguese-inspired (and familiar too with which costume names are Portuguese-derived), but there is also an interest in preserving specific dress and display items for reasons of family history and pride (fig. 7.6). Several recent coronation anniversary celebrations under Olu Atuwatse II have included antique contests for both objects and dress as part of the festivities. In 1994, a participant won with a family relic, a gold-braided French bicorne from the Napoleonic period. While this type of preservation might not be surprising in Europe or America, it is a conceptualization of dress that is uncommon in Africa, where newness, vitality, wealth, and power are intertwined clothing messages.

References to dress frequently allow the Itsekiri to articulate their disdain for the Urhobo, as for centuries their control of area trade meant they were the sole possessors of imported cloths, foreign hats, Mediterranean coral, and other jewelry in the Warri area. Elegance, rare textiles, and color coordination became their hallmarks (figs. 7.7, 7.8). That today others can not only afford such materials but also actively reproduce Itsekiri clothing traditions is considered irritating in the extreme. Photographs from the first

7.6 *Display of imported Indian* george *cloths from previous decades at a coronation anniversary exhibition. Many Itsekiri keep old cloths and value them for their age, even though they are highly critical of those not wearing the latest* georges *at public occasions. Photograph by Kathy Curnow, Warri, 1994.*

7.7 *Members of an Itsekiri club presenting gifts to the* olu *on his coronation anniversary. Photograph by D. Anthony Mahone, Ode-Itsekiri, 1994.*

7.8 *Fashionable Itsekiri woman wearing coordinated accessories and an imported* george *embroidered with the* olu's *picture for a coronation anniversary event. The Itsekiri originated the stiffened silk headties now worn throughout Southern Nigeria. Photograph by Kathy Curnow, Warri, 1994.*

half of this century show Itsekiri chiefs wearing long caped garments derived from the clothing of Catholic priests, a style that more recently surfaced as chiefly dress in Benin. Itsekiri chiefs currently, however, wear long-sleeved white shirts, white wrappers, and scarlet sashes (fig. 7.9), a switch they attribute to Urhobo adaptation of their previous style. Urhobo chiefs are also using the distinctive chokers (*oronwu*) worn by their Itsekiri counterparts: two large round corals flanking a central bead whose core is covered with contrasting geometrically patterned seed beads (fig. 7.10). This necklace is associated with priestly authority; although any Itsekiri can wear it to worship his ancestors, only chiefs were meant to wear it in public (Uwangue of Warri, personal communication, 1994). Known from even the earliest available nineteenth-century photographs, it is worn with dark red stone circlets of Benin origin (*oron okun*) and one large coral suspended on a long, plaited seed-bead strand (fig. 7.11). Urhobo use of such objects is viewed neither as assimilation nor homage, but as a proprietary challenge. The Itsekiri recalled the "good old days" when the Urhobo never ventured into competition through the saying: "The Whiteman is God to the Itsekiri; the Itsekiri is God to the Sobo [an abusive term for the Urhobo]" (Lloyd 1956, 82). A jealous, defensive posture toward heritage has developed. The Itsekiri broadcaster Egert Omoneukanrin caustically described Urhobo habits of appropriation in 1994:

> They imitate everything we have. You know, the Urhobos...most of the things they do today are not original to them. If you look at their dance now, you find that they've copied the Itsekiri dance...our type of graceful dance, they now dance it. It has never been part of their dance. It's straightforward imitation. They want to copy all the culture that we have and turn it into their own. And then the outside world will look at it and say it is the Urhobo man's culture. If not that some people already know the history of *george* [Indian madras], people will say that the Urhobos started wearing *george* before us! Do you know that even the waistcoat we wear today, they've started wearing it! Yes! It was never part of their own dressing. I called one of them one day. He was putting on the waistcoat at one of their ceremonies. I called him and said, "Do you people wear this, too?" He said yes. "What is the name?" He said, "It's waistcoat, now." I said, "Don't you have a name for it in your language?" He said, "No, it's waistcoat." I said, "You people copied this thing from the Itsekiri. The Itsekiri dress like this." He said, "No, it's our dressing from time." I said, "Shut up. It's not your dressing from time. If it's your dressing from time, why is it you don't have a name for it [in Urhobo]?" He said, "Do you people have a name for it?" I said, "Of course." He asked me to tell him the name. I wouldn't. I said, "If you know it is part of your dressing, go and ask your elders, let them tell you the name." They have no name for it.

The Itsekiri word for waistcoat, *culete*, is adapted from the Portuguese *colete*.

The *olu's* formal attire is based on Portuguese church dress. Olu Ginuwa II, installed in 1936, was photographed wearing a caped coronation robe (fig. 7.12). Olu Atuwatse II likewise wore a gold brocade cape with a train for his installation in 1987 and frequently wears sashed chasubles of luxurious fabrics for formal wear (fig. 7.1). It is in the sacred royal regalia, however, that the Portuguese connection is most exploited and given full cultural sanction. On state occasions, the *olu* wears several sets of rosary beads as

7.9 Three Itsekiri chiefs in contemporary formal attire, including sashes made of ododo, an imported scarlet cloth associated with leadership. They are bareheaded because they will appear in the presence of the olu. Photograph by Kathy Curnow, Nsukka, 1994.

7.10 Itsekiri chief wearing his chieftaincy necklaces. Only the circlets derive from Benin. Blue-beaded circlets are associated with women and are worn by chiefs who have notable females in their family line. Photograph by Kathy Curnow, Nsukka, 1994.

7.11 Itsekiri nobleman and his family. This late nineteenth-century image includes children dressed in European clothing. Reproduced with the permission of Unilever PLC (from an original in the Unilever Archives), box 25, folder 2, no. 2.

7.12 Ogiame Ginuwa II, Olu of Warri, at his installation in 1936. His cape, crown, and rosaries serve as reminders of past Catholic monarchs, while his high coral odigbe mouth cover and circlet beads point to the royal family's Benin origins. Photographer unknown.

7.13 Detail of Olu Atuwatse II's royal regalia, which includes several seventeenth-century rosaries, lantana bead circlets, various coral necklaces, and the branch coral beads worn only by the monarch. Photographer unknown, Warri, 1992.

necklaces, mixed among heavy strands of hanging coral and stone bead circlets (fig. 7.13). They are an indispensable aspect of kingship. A centuries-old emblem, they perform no Catholic function (Olu Atuwatse II is a Pentecostal Christian), although they retain a generally protective aspect. They, like the European crowns worn by the *olu*, are sacred links to an exotic history that gives the Itsekiri primacy in numerous ways.

The Itsekiri affirm that their original crown was of a coral-beaded Benin type (Iyatsere of Warri, personal communication, 1994; Bowen 1955, 62–63), but this has not been the official crown since the early seventeenth century. Instead, two European metal crowns are used for coronations and formal occasions. The "Diamond Crown," is made of open-worked gilt silver inset with colored stones and is topped with a curving cross; the other, made of bronze or brass, is also open-worked, and ends in a straight cross. Both were originally open at the top, but they are now inset with *ododo*, an imported scarlet cloth associated with leadership. This adaptation protects the ruler's head from public view, which aligns the pieces with other Southern Nigerian crowns. According to tradition, Dom Domingos, an Itsekiri prince who studied in Portugal for ten years, brought them back for himself and his Portuguese-born wife (Lloyd and Ryder 1957, 27–39). While style and documented knowledge of the prince make his commission of the works likely, neither piece has been worn by a royal wife, at least in recorded memory. Both are used officially, but the heavier "Diamond Crown" is now worn for coronations and some formal photographs, while the other is commonly used at major state occasions.

The elevation of this symbol above the Benin-style crown is clearly political, rather than religious, in impulse. In past centuries most Itsekiri adhered to traditional worship practices, not Christianity; many of the twelve baptized *olu*s were dual religionists, and at least three others were not Christians at all but continued to wear the state crowns. The crown reminded both *olu* and subjects of certain factors that differentiated them from their neighbors: a foreign deity, trade, education, and alliances—a package that made them unique.

Rosaries and crowns topped with crosses, long intrinsic parts of the regalia, are reminders to all Itsekiri that they can lay claim to the first Christian monarch in all of Nigeria, Olu Sebastião, as well as his son Dom Domingos, the first monarch to receive an overseas education and the first to marry a European. The crown is an instantly recognizable symbol of the *olu*, who makes the Itsekiri unique among Delta peoples. No other Delta ethnic group has a history of union under one ruler; this additional singularity ties the Itsekiri to other prominent centralized states and empires with whom they share a complex court structure and rich cultural heritage. This sense of their own history and position is the major factor in ethnic pride and nostalgia (figs. 7.14, 7.15). As the late Justice R. A. I. Ogbobine, an Itsekiri, put it, "The one strong criticism about them [the Itsekiri] is that they look with disdain and contempt on those whose background and history are not as rich as their own" (1995, 11–12).

The Itsekiri coat-of-arms distills the dual emblematic factors that make the society unique: the crossed *uda* and *eberen* ceremonial swords link the state with its powerful Edo progenitor, as they are a symbol of the Benin Kingdom, while the Portuguese crown surmounting the swords marks the

7.14 *Detail of Nigerian commemorative wax print created for the* olu's *coronation anniversary. The image shows Olu Atuwatse II in royal accoutrements and stresses love for the monarch through the heart and crown motifs on his gown. Photograph by Kathy Curnow, Warri, 1994.*

7.15 *Detail of Indian* george *cloth created for the* olu's *coronation anniversary. The machine-embroidered motif emphasizes the crown and the Benin-derived* odigbe *mouth cover, symbols of the unique past of the Itsekiri. Photograph by Kathy Curnow, Warri, 1994.*

7.16 *A motorized float in the form of a "regatta boat" complete with paddlers and prow dancers, sponsored by the United States oil company Texaco and emblazoned with its logos. Photograph by Kathy Curnow, Warri, 1994.*

divergent past of the Itsekiri, outward-looking qualities and a sense of apartness. Manipulation of these arms for political effect is frequent. The crest minus the *uda* sword is featured on the Warri town water-rate sticker, which is displayed in public places as proof of payment. Its posting is a constant irritant to the Urhobo inhabitants of Warri, as it figuratively expands the territory of the *olu* to those who are not his subjects.

Similarly, territory and alliances have been visually proclaimed in another venue. Olu Atuwatse II created an innovation in the annual coronation anniversary; while the major festivities take place at the Ode-Itsekiri homeland, some side attractions take place in Warri town itself. One such was his institution of the Coronation Carnival, a Rose Bowl-inspired parade with motorized floats in the form of regatta canoes. The parade is led by the *olu*'s scarlet-draped float, with a large foil-wrapped coat-of-arms at the front. His wife, the *olori*, has her own float, as do numerous chiefs, clubs, and prominent businesses, amongst which are foreign oil companies (fig. 7.16). The parade route leads throughout the town, passing

7.17 Bronze bust of the grandmother of Olu Atuwatse II as a young woman, made before 1992. The olu has supported the training of Itsekiri bronze casters and has commissioned numerous busts and figures of royal personages in a realistic style to decorate his palace and to give as royal gifts. Photograph by Kathy Curnow.

7.18 The royal boatmen standing before the doors to the royal ancestral shrine. These carved doors include images of past monarchs inspired by photographs. They were hung in the late 1980s. Photograph by D. Anthony Mahone, Ode-Itsekiri, 1994.

the review stand on a major road and finally ending in a field across from the *olu*'s palace. While colorful and festive, the parade has more than a celebratory function. The effect of circling the town with the royal symbol becomes a proprietary claim, a demarcation of royal territory, as even non-Itsekiri lands are enclosed. The participation of oil company floats also proclaims an intimate relationship between the Itsekiri and the major source of wealth in the area. Rival groups do not consider the intent of these gestures a matter of doubt; several carnivals have been interrupted by extremely violent clashes between the Itsekiri and the Urhobo, who interpret the exercise as political aggression. The state government has banned the display for the past several years.

Olu Atuwatse II, a London-educated lawyer, has also introduced and encouraged several other new art forms. Sponsorship of academically trained artists has led to the creation of realistic cast-bronze busts and figures representing the *olu*'s grandmother (fig. 7.17) and other royals for use as royal gifts. Figurative wooden doors now decorate various palace structures (fig. 7.18), as do sculpted metal gates (fig. 7.19). Works such as these parallel contemporary Benin gates and doors as well as historical bronze work; their introduction consciously challenges Benin's rich artistic history. Since Itsekiri palace art has no similar history, it concentrates on contemporary object types. Natural proportion and realism (often based on photographs) are favored, object placement is conspicuous, and no references to traditional religion occur.

Despite their strong views on "cultural copyrights," the Itsekiri themselves emulate others, although they do give them credit. Like many other Niger Delta peoples, they perform water spirit masquerades that frequently exhibit Ijo stylistic traits, and many seem to have an Ijo origin as well. The Itsekiri acknowledge this debt freely, while pointing out they also have masquerades that are "pure Itsekiri." When the two groups coexisted peacefully, mask origin was never an issue. As the Itsekiri consolidate themselves, feeling under siege, their changing relationship with the Ijo does affect issues of cultural emulation and sovereignty. The contexts in which credit is given to others and claims of cultural originality are made have shifted.

7.19 The gate to the olu's *temporary palace includes references to the monarch, his chiefs, and the royal arms. Photograph by Kathy Curnow, Warri, 1994.*

While some Western Ijo live amidst the Itsekiri, most live in areas closer to the coast and along the Forcados River. Itsekiri-Ijo interaction began in the fifteenth century, when the first Itsekiri *olu*, the Benin prince Ginuwa, married Derumo, an Ijo woman (Moore 1936 [1970], 18–19; Omoneukanrin 1942, 15; Ayomike 1988).[5] Itsekiri still remember subsequent dynastic marriages between royal Itsekiri women and Eastern Ijo rulers at Nembe and Bonny. Relations through the centuries have been, in the main, equitable and cooperative, although occasionally strained by piracy and attempts to limit Western Ijo participation in European trade (Ikime 1969). Exactly when and why the Ijo affected Itsekiri masquerading is unclear, but the connection is visible. Many Itsekiri water spirit masquerades, known as *umale*, strongly resemble their Ijo counterparts. The *umale* represent pre-Itsekiri residents of the area, who are said to have fled into the waters when Ginuwa arrived. There they transformed into spirits who now control the creeks. *Umale* have priests and shrines in creek villages; they are quite localized, and those honored and represented in one community are not usually worshiped in another.

Like Ijo masquerades, the *umale* wear multiple cloths, with either a finlike section (referred to as the tail) projecting from the rear or rounded, padded "buttocks." Arms and legs are covered. Performers tie locust-bean rattles at their ankles and dust their feet with camwood (fig. 7.20). Their headpieces are often wooden and horizontal with many carved in the hard-edged, geometric Western Ijo style. Many *umale* have Ijo names, are accompanied by Ijo lyrics, and share certain dance steps with Ijo performers. Itsekiri village masquerades, however, are not considered examples of "art for art's sake," as Robin Horton interprets Kalabari Ijo performances (1965a). Furthermore, they do not act out vignettes or plays. *Umale* dancing is more structured than that of the Ijo, and its singing and drumming styles are substantially different.[6]

The age and the circumstances of the introduction of most of these masks are uncertain, although the *umale* of Olugbo town suggests an early and intriguing relationship with the Ijo. This *umale* claims to be the Itsekiri monarch's equal, because it says it predates the arrival of his ancestors in the area. Only the *olu*'s appearance and personally conducted sacrifice will make it emerge from its grove. Its name, Otuekine, is Ijo; the Eastern Ijo consider Ekine or Ekineba to be the deified woman who introduced masking (Horton 1963, 94), and Ilaje- and Ijebu-Yoruba use the same name for their Ijo-style masking society. Otuekine's name and its claim to primacy at Olugbo suggest the Itsekiri may have pushed the Ijo out of the Warri area. Although the Itsekiri never actually identify any of the *umale* as Ijo, instead referring to the autochthons as subhuman (Omoneukanrin 1942, 17; Moore 1936 [1970], 14), their adoption of Ijo spirits and masking may have been intended to placate the displaced original creek owners.

Whatever their initial role, today villages use masks to invoke the *umale* for spiritual and material benefits. While these masked performances may reinforce village unity, they have no real impact on most Itsekiri or any non-Itsekiri, for they are unpublicized and perform solely for a small internal audience. The urban areas, on the other hand, provide an opportunity for the Itsekiri to solidify group identification and project aesthetic superiority by presenting masks in a highly visible arena. This new context also allows for a further examination of Itsekiri thoughts about cultural debts and

7.20 Itsekiri umale *masquerader from the Omo Ologbara Cultural Society. The masquerader represents a hammerhead shark. Photograph by D. Anthony Mahone, Warri, 1994.*

cultural originality, for city masks are chosen, rather than inherited as they are in the villages.

Social clubs perform urban masquerades. Their members come from all over the Warri Kingdom, and they feature mask types drawn from the traditions of many different communities, as well as new inventions. The clubs, also known as *umale* societies, operate primarily in the multiethnic cities of Warri and Sapele, as well as Lagos and Benin. Their festivals are widely promoted in advance on television and radio as well as through banners and invitations (fig. 7.21). Performances are held outdoors at highly visible venues, drawing large crowds of both Itsekiri and non-Itsekiri; television broadcasts increase their viewership. Knowing they are on display, nonmasked club dancers dress in expensive *george* wrappers and lace, sometimes changing up to three times daily (fig. 7.22). Because of their very public face, these urban performances allow the projection of a conscious "Itsekiri-ness," which is both unnecessary and nonexistent in the village masquerade context, but highly appropriate in the arena of urban ethnic rivalry.

Over twenty such clubs or cultural societies exist; many were founded in the 1950s. Membership is based on the ethnic affiliation of either parent and includes both men and women. Festivals are held once annually on Christian holidays—Christmas, New Year's, or Easter, depending on the club. A three-day spectacle is rigidly and consistently presented: the arena consists of a public square bounded at its far end by the drummers and canopied seating for dignitaries, fencing holds back spectators at each side, and the fourth side

7.21 Club banner proclaiming the annual masquerade display. These performances take place in public arenas abutting main roads in Warri. Photograph by Kathy Curnow, Warri, 1994.

7.22 Dancer with the Omo Ologbara Cultural Society. Both male and female members perform in the intervals between masquerade appearances. Photograph by Kathy Curnow, Warri, 1994.

is open to the street and passing cars. Usually three sets of *umale,* represented by three or four masks each, come out daily with club dancers entertaining during the intervals.

Like their village counterparts, these urban masquerades honor the *umale.* Their masks, costumes, dances, and drumming follow a village-established pattern. Motivation, however, is quite different. Urban visibility, aesthetic recognition, and innovation replace divine intervention as goals. The Itsekiri themselves quickly distinguish village and urban masquerades. Village participants refer to city performances as "elite festivals, what they use for enjoyment." Club members concede their own masquerades have no shrines or priest and thus no real spiritual power. They conduct no preliminary cleansing rites, nor do they "serve" the masks with sacrifices. *Umale* club members, however, do not actually behave as if their masks are powerless. Permission to use exclusive village mask types is secured from the appropriate *umale* priest, dancers still reinforce themselves with medicine and have to be restrained when overcome by spiritual forces (fig. 7.23). No female members are admitted to discussions of masks, and club women can neither look directly at masqueraders nor approach them in performance. Likewise, very strict Christians avoid membership altogether, despite its social status, and will not attend the societies' festivals because they do not regard them as purely entertainment in purpose. Still, club *umale*—unlike village masks—can be freely photographed and videotaped (although by men only) and draw substantial audiences.

7.23 *An attendant restrains an* umale *masquerader from the Omo Ologbara Cultural Society at an annual social performance. Photograph by D. Anthony Mahone, Warri, 1994.*

7.24 *Oki masqueraders of the Omo Ologbara Cultural Society, cutting through fresh raffia fences, just as they do in traditional village performances. Photograph by D. Anthony Mahone, Warri, 1994.*

Since club members select the masks they feature, they could certainly exclude Ijo-like examples but do not choose to do so. Their adoption, after all, occurred at a community level some time ago, and the popularity of these masks begs for their inclusion. The foreign origin of such *umale* is freely acknowledged—club members and spectators do not hesitate to say, "We borrowed this mask from the Ijo." Sometimes club members with Ijo fathers act as agents of introduction. The prototype often changes in appearance or performance details, however. The headpiece of the Ijo swordfish masquerade, Oki, is magnified by the Itsekiri (fig. 7.24) and shifts its behavior to an emphasis on capers: pivoting on its snout, inverting its headpiece to touch the earth, and climbing any available trees or poles.[7] Osibiri and Eyerobu, also attributed to the Ijo, are fierce dramatic masks (fig. 7.25). They have to be fenced in by plantain fronds, herded by attendants, and cooled by libations. Their violence has special crowd appeal.

Some club masks have an Ijo appearance but are described as "pure Itsekiri." Their names, rather than the headpiece and costume style, are considered the vital indicators of "Ijo-ness." Oki, for instance, is recognized as Ijo because of its name; the Itsekiri word for swordfish is *ejolude*. Oligbolara, in contrast, bears an Itsekiri name—"the proud one"—and is considered solely Itsekiri despite the very Ijo-like style of its geometric, horizontal headpiece. Sometimes the verses accompanying a mask are considered evidence of its creators but not always. As an *umale* society member noted:

7.25 Eyerobu masquerade of the Omatiton Cultural Society. Although a social performance, this Ijo-style headpiece is "served" by libations and attended by a youth dressed like a traditional priest. Photograph by D. Anthony Mahone, Ode-Itsekiri, 1994.

Even those masks that we did not borrow from Ijo, some of their songs
will still have some relation to Ijo songs. Our people…maybe because of
their interaction with the Ijos, they tend to compose more in the other
language. In most cases, [the composers] do that for those people who
are not initiates, to look at it as something strange…[the] Ijo language
[gets] those who are not initiates confused about the whole thing.

Although Ijo influence on club masks is apparent, recognized, and cited,
umale societies are increasingly valuing innovation, giving greatest prominence
to masks perceived as quintessentially Itsekiri.

Societies introduce new *umale* or variations on old ones. One popular
masquerade, the antelope-headed Igodo, traditionally included a dance passage
where performers briefly reclined on the earth. One club altered the sequence
so that an attendant rapidly inserted a pillow under the performers' heads, just
before they hit the ground. This deviation has since spread to all the societies.
One observer stated, "The pillow aspect is just to beautify the thing. As the club
members themselves don't sleep on ordinary ground, the masquerade doesn't
have to sleep on ordinary ground either." Some masks reflect everyday sights.
Plane, for example, represents the helicopters and airplanes of the oil fields.
Olitijuro, despite its orange color and lobsterlike extensions, represents
household scissors. Others fuel speculation. Jaba-Jaba, a mask that combines
human heads with fish bodies, does not represent Mami Wata or other merfolk,
despite its appearance. Instead, it represents imported stockfish (dried cod).
Since the fish is always sold headless in the market, people suspect there is
something odd about its head—that, in fact, the head is humanlike. Other
masks are abstract in concept, or just meant to be dazzling. Ebobo (which means
"wonderful") spotlights two or three performers who support one mask
together while dancing and turning independently (see fig. 14 in the introduction
to this volume). Such innovations can make a club's name. A member of
one's society commented on originality and its role in mystifying observers:

> Maybe a club patron has a certain carving in his house; maybe he brought
> it from somewhere, it may not even be connected with our own culture….
> To honor this our patron [we decide to] carve this thing. [We tell him],
> "We know you love it, that's why you kept it in your house." When
> outsiders see it, they may not know what is happening. What does this
> mean? What type of structure is this? People will be thinking. Fine!
> Continue to think!

An abstract mask, Ogienuranran, combines invention and non-Ijo stylistic
traits while emphasizing Itsekiri pride (fig. 7.26). This popular club-invented
umale behaves violently, repeatedly hurling sticks at spectators. Ogienuranran
may be translated as "The king has prominence"—a reference to the monarchy,
the Itsekiri rallying point. A club initiate describes Ogienuranran:

> It's an honor to the throne; usually they perform it last on any given
> day. Normally, all *olu*s are supposed to be feared by their subjects. All
> *olu*s—when they get annoyed, they're always very explosive, they can do
> anything at any time. Even though you find the mask becoming very
> aggressive, people will still troop to it. The royalty of the kingdom is not
> what anybody can toy with. It has its own pride, dignity, and prestige.

Prestige and aesthetic value contribute to a mask's position within a club's program. Those masks considered most spectacular end the day's performance; Ijo-like masks are played down, and, in contrast, are usually "openers."

Urban performance includes a strong sense of competition, both with other Itsekiri clubs and, especially, with rival ethnic groups. The Itsekiri affirm their own reputation for taste, elegance, even dandyism. All club masquerade cloths are chosen with an eye to color coordination and are often expensive textiles. Those masquerades considered most characteristically Itsekiri stress aesthetic beauty, in contrast to the Kalabari Ijo whose masks, according to Horton, are not "intended to convey beauty" (1965a, 14). Asamarigho, for instance, is the fashionable *umale*, described as "gorgeously-dressed with walking stick in hand," while Olesughu represents the attractiveness of coral beads.

Highly valued masks, such as Ogienuranran, wear distinctive scarlet *ododo*, the expensive cloth associated with the *olu* and his chiefs. Such performers often hold tusks, flywhisks, or ceremonial *eberen* swords, rather than the more customary paddles or cutlasses. As very distinguished *umale*, their stately, swaying dance is often performed seated, a position that befits their high status. The most magnificent of these *umale* is Olekun (fig. 7.27), considered the "mother of the masquerades," "the chief mermaid."[8] Usually a Janus mask, its two faces refer to its ability to see in all directions. The name Olekun means "door owner," for it stands at the entrance between the spirit and human worlds. Club members say Olekun "supports looks

7.26 The Ogienuranran masquerade represents certain monarchical qualities, and wears regal ododo *cloth. One of its royal traits is a hot temper, and it is shown here chasing around the arena throwing sticks at spectators who run for cover. Photograph by D. Anthony Mahone, Warri, 1994.*

and wealth"; it is the only masquerade all societies include and it is always their finale piece, their paean to wealth, beauty and originality (fig. 7.28).

Superstructures of plumes, paper flowers, mirrors, and yarn—sometimes even attached parasols or twinkling battery-operated Christmas lights—enhance Olekun's light-skinned features. The most consequential Olekun have exquisitely dressed female visitor masks called Ejoji to add to their impressive impact. Olekun and other "pure Itsekiri" masks are certainly the most enthusiastically received *umale*. Although their interest in distancing themselves from their neighbors has not led them to abandon their long-standing, Ijo-influenced masquerades completely, urban club performance has promoted a sort of masquerade revisionism that argues the superiority of Itsekiri taste.

Recognition and promotion of elegance, wealth, prestige, and aristocratic authority are vital aspects of club masquerades and speak directly to group self-image. Precolonial and colonial foreign observers often remarked on Itsekiri sophistication: "One is immediately impressed by their fine breeding and bearing" (Allen 1949, 757; see also de Negri 1968; Ekwensi 1964, 164–72). The Itsekiri themselves wax philosophical about it, "A really good life needs, besides…things of the flesh, things of beauty, nobility and great-mindedness. It is these things that are the stuff of which the Itsekiri are made"(Ogbobine 1995,10).

Contemporary political tensions have caused the Itsekiri to become increasingly anxious boosters of cultural distinction, stressing those manifestations that emphasize refinement, invention, and aristocratic heritage. As the Itsekiri "go to their own quarter" to build a sense of nationalism, their ambivalent changing views concerning cultural emulation and identity can be tracked clearly through numerous visual weapons. Though they maintain a protective cultural posture in respect to lost dominance and glory, the challenge of defending their identity (conceptually intertwined with status) is pushing the Itsekiri to increased creativity and resourcefulness. If the battle for political dominance is lost, as their small voting numbers would suggest, symbolic manipulation, public emphasis on "cultural property," and new developments and directions may yet lead to a cultural rout.

7.27 An Olekun masquerader, representing the "mother of the masquerades" who closes all club performances on the final day. Photograph by D. Anthony Mahone, Ode-Itsekiri, 1994.

7.28 Olekun masquerades from the Omo Ologbara club carrying eberen *swords and wearing scarlet* ododo *costume elements—features that emphasize their stateliness and status. Photograph by D. Anthony Mahone, Warri, 1994.*

Interleaf I
The Owu/Oworu Masquerade Complex

Philip M. Peek

Among the peoples of the Niger Delta—from the Riverain Igbo in the northeast corner to the Ijebu-Yoruba at the far western edge, from the Isoko and Urhobo in the north and northwest to the Kalabari Ijo and Obolo in the southeast—we find water spirit masquerade complexes that exhibit striking similarities. Even the names used by the various groups to identify these events—Owu, Owu aru sun, Owuaya aru, Oworu, Ohworu—resonate with each other. Although traditions linking these masquerades to the Ijo (in particular the Kalabari) are somewhat tenuous, there are so many correspondences that the association cannot be denied (see interleaf H). Yet these similarities raise as many questions as they answer, and one is left to wonder how one masquerade can be so widespread among such diverse peoples.

With the exception of the Ijo, all of the Delta peoples mentioned above have other masquerades, some of which are far more important in terms of their local deities and clan commemorations. And some groups, such as the Isoko, include elements (in this case a period of sexual license and ribald behavior) that others do not. Intriguingly, all the Isoko and many Urhobo clans claim to have once danced Oworu, though few do so any longer, and for some, the masquerade is managed by a separate priesthood. This complex, as with so many other aspects of the cultures of Niger Delta peoples, can tell us much about their interaction over the centuries, but we are only beginning to grasp the scope of this masquerade's linkages. Any and all components of a cultural complex can be transmitted, rejected, or adapted by others who take it up. Recent work by Henry John Drewal (see chapter 6 of this volume) and Eli Bentor (forthcoming) demonstrates the value of detailed research concerning all aspects of a single phenomenon. In the case of the Owu/Oworu complex, one must consider masks and costumes; music and instruments; dance movements; and song texts; as well as where, when, and why the performance occurs and whether traditions of origin exist (figs. I.1–I.3).

I.1 Rattle. Isoko. Wood. H: 39.4 cm. The Museum of Fine Arts, Houston; The Dr. Gus K. Nicholson Collection, acc. no. 91.1529.

I.2   Rattle. Urhobo/Isoko. Wood. H: 39.4 cm. Collection of Toby and Barry Hecht.

I.3   Staff. Urhobo. Wood and pigment. H: 71.1 cm. Collection of Toby and Barry Hecht.

I.4   *Two Oworu masqueraders performing in front of an* akwakwa *slit gong.*
Photograph by Philip M. Peek, Iyede, 1971.

I.5   *Oworu masqueraders. Photograph by Philip M. Peek, Igbide, 1971.*

I.6   *Oworu masqueraders. The huge raffia masquerade is carried by at least ten men. Photographer unknown, Igbide, circa 1960.*

I.7   *Mask. Urhobo. Wood and Pigment. H: 50.8 cm. Private Collection.*

As close as the Urhobo and Isoko peoples are, there seem to be significant differences in Oworu (or "Ohworu" for some Urhobo communities) performances (see Foss 1973; Peek 1983). Still the Isoko and Urhobo clans that continue to celebrate Oworu share a number of traditions not recorded elsewhere, such as the elaborate slit gong *akwakwa* (fig. I.4 and see fig. 5.23) and masqueraders adorned only in ferns or raffia-covered frames (figs. I.5, I.6). Intriguingly, the Isoko and Urhobo do not use the common Ijo horizontal mask form but employ face masks (figs. I.7, I.8), which the Isoko call *okao* as distinct from their own "normal" masks, *igbigbi*. The unique features of these masks (a chin "handle" and arching horns or "crowns"; figs. I.9, I.10) suggest links to the Elo masquerades of the Nupe far up the Niger River (Stevens 1973) and the feathered decorations of the Ogonya masks in Ogume (fig. I.11; see Jones 1989b). There are still fundamental Ijo elements to consider. After viewing Martha Anderson's videos of Central Ijo *owu* (*ou*) celebrations, I realized that the dance steps were virtually identical to those I had observed among the Isoko in 1971.

Of course, the most consistent element in this complex as observed throughout the Delta is that the entities depicted are considered to be water spirits. Humans are often thought to have learned the dances by watching water spirits cavorting along the shore. Thus, we have humans—land dwellers who migrated into the Delta area—inviting water creatures into their communities. And while much joyous celebration takes place, all communities make sure that their spiritual companions return to their own world. In the Isoko clan of Iyede, they go so far as to have a mock burial and then drive the water spirits back home at the end of the day. Is the whole Owu/Oworu complex reflective of the larger adjustment humans made as they moved into this new and different world? And just as we might invite our neighbors into our homes when we first arrive in a new town, might not those migrants centuries ago have sought to befriend their new acquaintances. Today Delta people and water spirits continue to celebrate their common enterprise in this watery world.

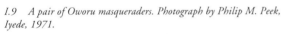

I.8   Mask. Urhobo. Wood. H: 42 cm. Collection of Mr. and Mrs. J. Thomas Lewis.

I.10   Urhobo Oworu masqueraders. Photograph by Jean Borgatti, Ohoro, near Ughelli, 1971.

I.9   A pair of Oworu masqueraders. Photograph by Philip M. Peek, Iyede, 1971.

I.11 Ogonya masqueraders. Photograph by G. I. Jones, Ogume, 1937.
© Cambridge University Museum of Archaeology and Anthropology,
acc. no. AA-8.

8.1   *King Jaja of Opobo dressed in* ikakibite, *Ibani royal and priestly attire. This photograph was taken just before Jaja was exiled by the British in 1887. Eliot Elisofon Photographic Archives, National Museum of African Art, Smithsonian Institution 1995-170061.*

8.2   *Amanyanabo Abbi Yesuku Amakiri, the current* amanyanabo *of Buguma, seen on the right posing with his brother on the left, Chief S. J. S. Amakiri, and his seated wife, who wears* abii ikakibite. *Photograph by Lisa Aronson, Buguma, 1978.*

Chapter 8 Tricks of the Trade: A Study of *Ikakibite* (Cloth of the Tortoise) among the Eastern Ijo

LISA ARONSON

A tortoise cannot stretch itself.
(*Ikaki negimaye bu sun.*)
Ikaki imitated Kugbo and exploded into pieces.
(*Ikaki kugbo digimate sani polo.*)
—Nimi Wariboko (personal communication, 1997)

During the early stages of British colonial rule in Nigeria, in the last decades of the nineteenth century, two Eastern Ijo kings, Jaja of Opobo and King Amakiri (Amachree) IV of Kalabari, chose to identify themselves with cloths bearing the name *ikakibite,* which may be translated as "cloth of the tortoise." Jaja, the founder of the Ibani Ijo city of Opobo, was known for clinging to traditional kingly attire and religious rituals in the face of British pressure to abandon them. This stance is reflected in a late nineteenth-century photograph taken of him wearing tortoise cloth imported from the Ijebu-Yoruba area (fig. 8.1). This cloth had become the official attire of the Ibani Ijo rulership by 1800, and nearly a century later, Jaja chose to wrap himself in it for his photograph, presumably to enhance his authority by upholding a hundred-year-old royal tradition.

King Abbi Amakiri IV of Kalabari identified himself with *ikakibite,* of a different variety and in a slightly different way, during his reign in the 1890s. A century before, his lineage founder, Amakiri I, had selected a plain white cloth, *ogborigbo,* as the official Amakiri dress (Nimi Wariboko, personal communication, 1997). Amakiri IV added to this royal repertoire a type of tortoise cloth possibly of Indian origin, traded by way of the British (fig. 8.2). Presented via a powerful masquerade known as Egbelegbe, *abii ikakibite*—the cloth's official name—became the exclusive ceremonial attire for all members of Amakiri's royal family.

While of different types, the cloths embraced by these late nineteenth-century rulers were both associated with the tortoise. Why the tortoise came to be woven into the political, and literal, fabric of Eastern Ijo life at this particular moment in history will be addressed below. Essential to this inquiry is an examination of the physical and behavioral features of the tortoise indigenous to the Eastern Ijo area, which will be followed by an analysis of the ways in which the Ijo have incorporated this creature into their worldview, as reflected in proverbs, stories, spiritual beliefs, and superstitions. The origins and the various trade channels by means of which the two types of tortoise cloth in question made their way to the Eastern Ijo area, as well as the basis upon which they came to be associated with the tortoise, will then be addressed. Finally, the various ritual contexts in which these Ijo tortoise cloths have come to function will be considered.

252   ARONSON
Tricks of the Trade:
A Study of Ikakibite *(Cloth of the Tortoise)*
among the Eastern Ijo

8.3   Kinixys belliana nogueyi *(Bell's hinge-back tortoise).*
Photograph courtesy of the British Chelonia Group.

Bell's Hinge-Back Tortoise

The tortoise is a reptile of the order *Chelonia* (also referred to as *Testudinata*), as is its close relative the turtle. As similar as turtles and tortoises may appear, they also have significant differences, the main one being that turtles are aquatic, whereas tortoises are terrestrial. This difference explains why turtles have streamlined shells and webbed feet for optimal movement below the water's surface while tortoises have large, mounded shells for protection and long nails for easier movement on land. Moreover, turtles have a fairly worldwide distribution, whereas tortoises are confined mainly to tropical and subtropical climates. Africa has more species of the tortoise than any other continent in the world, a fact that may account for the creature's widespread popularity throughout this vast continent.

The Eastern Ijo are familiar with turtles (*owoi*) and tortoises (*ikaki,* or *ikagi* in the Nembe dialect), both of which they rely on as a source of food. It is the tortoise alone, however, that they characterize prominently in their oral tradition and represent in their art. The species of tortoise most familiar to the Ijo is a type of hinge-back known as *Kinixys belliana,* or Bell's hinge-back (fig. 8.3).[1] A detailed description of this curious species will help us to understand the fascination the Eastern Ijo have with it.

Ranging anywhere from six to ten inches in length, the hinge-back is an exceedingly slow, awkward, and voiceless[2] creature who seems to thrive in his self-contained, earthbound world. Well-known for his voracious appetite, he prefers living in palm forests and areas near ponds where he can feed on dead frogs and tadpoles. He also eats palm fruits whenever he is fortunate enough to find them fallen from trees. The hinge-back is able to reach higher and to move more swiftly by raising himself on his large nails—as if walking on stilts.

The skin of the hinge-back has a dry, wrinkled, and scaly appearance that, combined with his slow lumbering gait, earns him the reputation for being a very old creature. His carapace, or shell, is unusual, and there are three features of it that the Ijo emphasize in particular. One of them is the striking surface design of rows of hexagons within hexagons etched in gray, brown, and black, creating a design that the Ijo call either *abili abili,* indicating a checkerboard, patchlike configuration, or *genigeni,* which may be translated as "variegated" or "multicolored." It is on the basis of this surface design that the Ijo equate the tortoise with spiritual beings, as will be discussed below. Second, the shell has a distinctive hump or mound. This feature serves to protect the tortoise from falling debris and from the feet of heavy creatures such as humans. But it also provides a refuge, allowing him to escape from the world. It is his tendency to retreat into his shell that contributes to his reputation for being shy, temperamental, and antisocial. Third, his shell has a hinge located about two-thirds of the way back that enables the tortoise to move the remaining portion downward (independent of the front) to close off its posterior. Protection is again the reason for this feature. Anyone who dared to put a finger between the lower shell and the back portion of the upper one as the two came together would risk getting it crushed. At the slightest whim, the tortoise may choose to contract his appendages and, with the use of his hinge, close down his shell to create an enclosed container in which he appears not only to hide himself from the world but to conceal all of his secrets as well.

Several authors have speculated as to why tortoises like the hinge-back are so provocative. Phil Peek argues that the notably silent nature of the tortoise implies wisdom and respect as well as secrecy and power (Peek 2000). Mary Douglas sees the tortoise as an anomaly within the larger animal world. Its shell distinguishes it from all other reptiles, and its egg-laying capability differentiates it from most other nonreptilian, four-legged creatures (Douglas 1975, 30). I would, in addition, propose that the tortoise is perceived as liminal between land and sea. He thrives in the bush but nevertheless hovers along the edge of shallow ponds, or what my informant Nimi Wariboko has aptly described as "watery land" (personal communication, 1997). His liminality is all the more accentuated by the fact that he is like but not like his aquatic cousin, the turtle. In divination rituals, the Ijo will float the tortoise on the top of water to see to which shore the tide will take him (Alagoa 1964, 35). Because of his many curious features, the Ijo regard the hinge-back as more than just a delectable addition to soups. They see in his provocative demeanor, his curious physical traits, and his liminal place within the world at large both a powerful spirit and a trickster par excellence.

The Tortoise as Trickster among the Kalabari Ijo

The beliefs of the Kalabari Ijo concerning the tortoise have been extensively documented and hence provide an excellent vantage point from which to examine his role among other Eastern Ijo groups. The Kalabari believe that Ikaki is a trickster spirit who once lived in a forest behind the ancient and now-defunct village of Oloma. In addition to being strong and tough like the shell that protects him, this bush creature is an old, wise, and even chiefly figure who has earned titles such as "old man of the forest" or "chief gray hair." Robin Horton aptly reflects Kalabari perceptions of Ikaki when he describes him as "full of wisdom and intelligence at the same time that he is impatient, full of lies, and even evil—simultaneously feared and awed" (1967, 230).

Ikaki is the subject of many proverbs and the protagonist in numerous Kalabari stories. One story featuring Ikaki and a delectable variety of fish called *kugbo* explains that the variegated pattern on the former's shell is the result of his own antics.

254 **ARONSON**
Tricks of the Trade:
A Study of Ikakibite *(Cloth of the Tortoise)*
among the Eastern Ijo

Kugbo is a very delicious saltwater fish, full of fats. Once upon a time Kugbo cooked and [he] invited Ikaki for dinner. Ikaki ate and found the food delicious, tastier than any he had ever eaten before. He asked Kugbo for the recipe to learn of the secret behind the taste. Kugbo explained that when the soup was about done he climbed onto the fire altar, and the heat of the fire melted his fat into the soup. The next day Ikaki attempted the trick, but the heat of the fire only made his shell explode. He picked up the pieces and went to a native doctor, who patched them together for him. [Nimi Wariboko, personal communication, 1997]

As with most African tales, this one communicates more than how the tortoise got his patterned shell. The story sends the message that individuals should stay within the limits of their abilities or risk destruction. The "patched" shell serves as a constant reminder of this truism.

Ikaki is similar to other African tricksters (e.g., Ananse the spider among Akan speakers or Ajapa the tortoise among the Yoruba) in that he is forever exhibiting paradoxical behavior. While he is a short stocky creature, and thus ill-equipped to prey on others, stories portray him tackling elephants, leopards, and other ferocious, powerful creatures—sometimes, but not always, with success. In addition, he attempts what would ordinarily be impossible for a tortoise by climbing trees to reach palm fruits or entering into cooking pots to enhance the flavor of stew, although again, as we have already seen, not always with success.

Like other African tricksters, Ikaki, in his own way offers guidelines for appropriate human behavior. Denise Paulme and others have argued that the animals portrayed in trickster tales are animals in name only (1975, 569). In reality their relationships are those of humans interacting with humans, or what Oyekan Owomoyela refers to as "human surrogates" (1990, 625).

The Kalabari regard the tortoise as more than just a trickster; he is divine in nature and belongs to an important category of spirit within their larger worldview. According to Robin Horton, the Kalabari divide their world into the realm of the living (*tomi kiri*, literally "the place of people") and that of the spirits (*teme*). The spirit realm is, in turn divided into three distinct domains or categories. The first is the *duen,* the spirits of all ancestors, the second, the *owu,* or "water people," and finally, the third, the *oru,* or "village heroes" (Horton 1962).

Oru is the category to which Ikaki primarily belongs.[3] Ikaki is one of a long list of largely reptilian *oru* referred to collectively as *oru nama*, which may be translated as "animals of the *oru.*" Also included among these reptilian *oru* are the python (*odum*) and other snakes (e.g., *agwaka* and *emein*), crocodiles (*seki*), bullfrogs (*ngu*), lizards (*ologboinboin*), skinks (*osomonimoni*), geckos (*waribulo*), and monitors (*awakiba*; Horton 1965a, 31–32). While each of these reptilian *oru nama* has its own personality, shape, and size, they all share in common intricate body surfaces—for example, the scaly skin of a crocodile or the variegated shell of the tortoise—the designs of which remind the Kalabari of the powers of the *oru*. Much of the decoration one sees on Kalabari sculpture as well as on textiles has its basis in *oru nama* skin surfaces, a point to which we will return later.

The Kalabari believe that the *oru* once lived together with humans in the physical world (*tomi kiri*) where they displayed superhuman powers.

Ultimately. however they departed for the spirit realm (*teme*). Robin Horton describes the *oru* as being "like people up to a point; but beyond that they are strangely different. The heroes, for instance, once lived among men. But they came to Kalabari villages mysteriously, displayed powers greater than those of ordinary men, and disappeared as strangely as they had come" (1965a, 32). Known for their generosity, the *oru* are credited with providing important gifts, such as the art of dancing or skills in warfare, for which they expect compensation in the form of sacrifice since they have departed from the world of humans. In a sense, the *oru* are a kind of mirror through which the living can see themselves and their foibles. Ikaki helps to sharpen that reflection. He presents humans with a set of guidelines for appropriate behavior by demonstrating the inappropriate through his buffoonery and his provocative and dangerous antics. A host of Kalabari proverbs and expressions also draw on the tortoise's physical idiosyncrasies as a way to define rules of social etiquette. The hinged shell, for example, is seen as a metaphor for someone who is sexually inaccessible or close minded. The proverb "You have tightened your anus (or vagina) like a tortoise" (*E ikaki okolo kpasi bara ke okolo kpasi wariari*) can either refer to a woman who is unwilling to make herself available for sex or to persons who shield themselves from the truth (Nimi Wariboko, personal communication,1987).

In the mythical past, the much revered Ikaki is reputed to have emerged occasionally from the forest to perform a rather frightening dance of death. While singing a song about his taste for human flesh, he lifted one leg, causing all the people in that direction to die.[4] He then repeated his song using the other leg, and producing the same deadly consequences. Since this mythical time, the Kalabari men's Ekine Society has created an entertaining masquerade in which Ikaki is the protagonist (fig. 8.4). Its aim, Horton argues, is to tame Ikaki's excessive and deadly powers (1967, 237). In it, Ikaki dances with leg movements that are considerably more restrained but similar enough to the deadly leg-lifting maneuvers of the myth to remind the Kalabari of the negative consequences of the latter. In general, Kalabari dance emphasizes the movement of the buttocks and hips more than the legs, suggesting that Ikaki has had some margin of success as a dance instructor.

The masquerade, like many stories, portrays Ikaki as a superman who defies nature by killing an elephant or climbing a palm tree to procure its fruit. While Ikaki devours fruits at the top of the tree, his moronic son Nimiaa Poku (which may be translated as "Know nothing") attempts to chop it down. In anger Ikaki throws his knife at Nimiaa Poku but instead kills his favorite son, Kalagidi.[5] It is not insignificant that Kalagidi is restored to life by the Ekine Society members performing this masquerade The message is presumably that well-behaved humans, rather than tricky and erratic tortoises, have the power to give life.

The shell is clearly a source of the tortoise's dangerous powers. The Kalabari's official drum name for the tortoise, Ploploma bio si (Ploploma bad inside), implies that the shell is a kind of container of secretive and potentially harmful things, if not a source of Ikaki's power, trickery, and deceit (Horton 1967, 230; Nimi Wariboko, personal communication, 1997).[6] It is worth noting that the Kalabari, and other Eastern Ijo groups, regard hunchbacks with a similar degree of fear and trepidation because of the mysterious mound on their backs and the perception that they exhibit an evil, sour temper.

8.4 *Ikaki masquerader in a performance created by the Kalabari men's Ekine Society. From Robin Horton, "The Gods as Guests: An Aspect of Kalabari Religious Life,"* Nigeria Magazine *(1960) 19: 23.*

256   ARONSON
*Tricks of the Trade:
A Study of* Ikakibite *(Cloth of the Tortoise)
among the Eastern Ijo*

Some other interesting Kalabari beliefs and superstitions about the tortoise also seem to confirm that its powers are deadly. For example, the Kalabari believe that people who hold onto a tortoise for a prolonged period risk being accused of witchcraft. To avoid this, customers are advised always to purchase a tortoise toward the end of their market visit and to slaughter it immediately after bringing it home. Kalabari women are also advised to avoid eating tortoise during pregnancy for fear that the baby will never develop beyond the stage of crawling close to the ground like a tortoise (Nimi Wariboko, personal communication, 1997). Interestingly, the tortoise appears at once infantile and aged.

The Tortoise and the Eastern Ijo

Discussion has thus far centered on tortoise beliefs and ritual practices among the Kalabari Ijo. There are substantial data, however, to suggest that the Ibani/Opobo, Nembe, and Okrika Ijo share some of these beliefs, as do the Central Ijo (fig. 8.5). The Ibani Ijo, for example, are among those who associate hunchbacks with the tortoise, their own word for hunchback being *ikaki obii* ("tortoise sickness"; Fombo 1975). This connection will have some bearing on our later discussion of the role *ikakibite* plays as royal attire among the Ibani/Opobo Ijo. The Kalabari are also not alone in having used the tortoise as a potent agent in spirit-related rituals. In his history of the Nembe, Alagoa claims that one of their original founders, the king of Oboloama, arranged for a local "juju" doctor to present a tortoise to his rival as an act of revenge.

8.5   *This tortoise masquerade was performed in 1979 in the Central Ijo town of Enewari (the Buwo clan). Dutch-wax cloth rests on a framework to resemble the shell of the tortoise ("yekoko," a Central Ijo word for tortoise seemingly related to the word "ikaki"). According to Anderson's informant, a bush spirit known as "the mad one" (Izekuru), seen here on stilts, recommended that the tortoise masquerade be performed to drive out illness. Photograph by Martha Anderson.*

> The doctor prepared a medicine with a live tortoise (*ikagi* in the Nembe dialect)—an animal sacred to the people of Olodiama. The king of Oboloama put this tortoise on the water at flood tide and the animal floated onto the shores of Olodiama. There was commotion in the town and people crowded to see the tortoise that had been miraculously brought in by the tide. At the ebb tide it floated back to Oboloama, but at Olodiama all the people who had come out to see the tortoise sickened and died. [Alagoa 1964, 35]

This image of the tortoise, a terrestrial creature, floating on the water's surface reminds us of his liminal place between land and sea.

It was not only in myth that the Ijo used tortoises as medicine, or "juju." In his early twentieth-century ethnographic writings, P. Amaury Talbot, noting the Ijos' fascination with the tortoise, cited numerous rituals, ceremonies, and oral traditions in which the tortoise featured prominently. For example, he observed an Okrika man secure a tortoise to the ground by driving a stake through its shell and body so as to make it visible to the Okrikas' own creator god, Fene ma so (1932, 86).

Ijo oral tradition suggests that these tortoise rituals and the underlying beliefs that motivate them have their origins among the Ibani Ijo, the easternmost group within the Eastern Ijo complex. The Nembe, who live at the westernmost end, claim that the very powerful tortoise credited with the death-causing song and dance came to them from the Kula forest area in the Kalabari region. In turn, the Kalabari claim that their Ikaki masquerade comes from Oloma, a village located east of the mouth of the San

Bartolomeo River in an area once incorporated under Ibani Ijo rule. This history, as will later be shown, has significant implications for Abbi Amakiri's appropriation of *ikakibite* as his lineage cloth.

As a result of the impact of Christianity, the Eastern Ijo have largely abandoned using the tortoise as a sacrifice. Yet the persistence of tortoise-related oral traditions, superstitions, and taboos indicates that the creature retains its potency in Ijo thought. In addition, cloths bearing tortoise symbolism continue to be prescribed ritual attire for women (*iriabo*) during their coming of age ceremony (*iria*), for Ijo priests (*pere*), and for kings (*amanyanabo*). But before discussing these various ritual and ceremonial contexts in which *ikakibite* appears, we need to understand the source of the imported cloths and the basis upon which they came to be associated with the tortoise.

Eastern Ijo and Trade

The Kalabari, and their Nembe, Okrika, and Ibani/Opobo counterparts, may be distinguished from their Central Ijo relatives not only on linguistic and cultural grounds but also on the basis of their long history of trade with other Africans around the Delta area and with Europeans (with the latter they traded slaves in the eighteenth century and palm oil in the nineteenth). It is safe to say that much of the social and political organization of these Eastern Ijo groups evolved from this prolonged period of transatlantic trading. Before the eighteenth century, each Ijo subgroup, or *ibe*, comprised a series of villages that were collectively headed by the eldest male, who also acted as community priest (*pere*). Political organization was thus based at the village level with age being the criterion for leadership. By the eighteenth century, Ijo leadership came to be based more on trading abilities, and Ijo political economies expanded to accommodate this increasing commercialism. The more centralized states that developed as a consequence were Nembe (Brass), and Kalabari (New Calabar), Okrika, and Ibani (Bonny)/Opobo, each with a series of canoe houses (*wari*), the heads of which owned and controlled the canoes used to transport goods.[7] These *wari* were collectively governed by a powerful ruler or king (*amanyanabo*), whose role is said to have evolved from that of the *pere*. The Ibani king Perekule (Pepple) and his son Fubara, as well as the Kalabari king Amakiri, were products of this change.

Cloths, including the two tortoise textiles introduced in the beginning of this essay, were among the many items traded to the Ijo through this expanded network. Many of the descendants of Eastern Ijo trading families have kept traded textiles stored in chests as valuable and cherished family heirlooms associated with the once prosperous trade. Such chests are typically used to contain the family's wealth and in addition to textiles might house coral and gold jewelry, crowns, and staffs. In their aggregate, these goods speak volumes about the varied networks of trade that once fed into the Eastern Ijo communities. The textiles, in particular, are now among our most valuable historical documents in that their oral histories allow us to reweave the various threads of the incoming trade and the complex social system that ennabled this commerce.

The Ijebu-Yoruba, Cloth, and Trade

The *ikakibite* that King Jaja is shown wearing in figure 8.1 originated in the Ijebu-Yoruba area. The Ijebu not only wove such cloth but traded it across

258 **ARONSON**
Tricks of the Trade:
A Study of Ikakibite *(Cloth of the Tortoise)*
among the Eastern Ijo

8.6 Ijebu-Yoruba chiefs and members of the Oshugbo (Ogboni) Society continue to use this type of "tortoise" cloth as their official attire (cf. fig. 8.1). This is a photograph of a chief and member of Oshugbo from Ijebu-Ife. Photograph by Lisa Aronson, 1978.

the Delta to the Eastern Ijo (Aronson 1980a; Aronson forthcoming). Because of its prime location in the southeasternmost corner of Yorubaland and on the western fringes of the Delta, the Ijebu-Yoruba region had long served as a gateway into the Delta for the trading of a variety of goods, textiles included. European sources inform us that the Ijebu were actively trading so-called "Jaboo" cloths as far west as the Volta River and over to the eastern side of the Niger Delta between the seventeenth and the nineteenth centuries (Law 1986; Bold 1823, 22). Descriptions inform us that the textiles the Ijebu were trading, included strip-woven cloth made by men on horizontal foot-treadle looms and wide cloths of blue and white stripes woven on upright frame looms by women (Bold 1823, 22). Both types are well represented in Eastern Ijo collections. The cloth King Jaja wears in figure 8.1 is an example of an Ijebu weft-float women's weave that is still produced for use in association with the Ijebu chieftaincy and their Oshugbo (Ogboni) Society (fig. 8.6; Aronson 1992).

It is important to note that the Ijebu do not associate any of their weft-float patterns with the tortoise. They refer to the entire cloth as *aso olona* (cloth with designs); the individual patterns on it are associated with a wide range of zoomorphic and other symbols. Thus the association with the tortoise was made by the Ijo after receipt of the cloth through trade. Curiously the trade of *aso olona* to the eastern side of the Delta was not mentioned by European merchants, but its presence in Ijo cloth collections and in nineteenth-century photographs confirms that it was exchanged (fig. 8.7).

We learn of the cloth's westward transport across the Delta from a Nembe Ijo masquerade performance in which it is used to purchase a mask. The Sekiapu (Ekine) members offer a piece of rare, handwoven cloth that is referred to in the ceremony as Iselema (Itsekiri) cloth. Liking the cloth very much, the priestess in charge of the masks accepts their offer and agrees to allow the masquerade to come out. The following is a translation of her comments about the cloth presented to her by the Sekiapu:

> The cloth is fine, very fine.
> Is this cloth not a unique cloth from Iselema (Warri) River
> The cloth is fine, very fine.
> This cloth that came from Iselema (Warri) River
> Is it not a special cloth? [Alagoa 1982, 281]

This transaction offers important information about the textile's perceived value, its origin, and the mechanics of its trade. The incantation of the Nembe priestess proceeds to estimate the cloth's worth at more than 1,001 manillas (a traditional form of currency in this area), or in excess of one million dollars. It also indicates that the textile has come from the direction of the Warri (Iselema) River, a waterway situated midway in the Delta between the Ijebu and the Ijo. The Warri River area is home to the Itsekiri, or the Iselema, as the Nembe call them, suggesting that the Itsekiri were the intermediaries in the cloth trade between the Ijebu-Yoruba to the west and the Eastern Ijo to the east.

European sources reveal that the Ijebu were actively trading cloth by the late eighteenth century. This was at the peak of the Ijebu Kingdom's power (1760–1780), an appropriate time to be trading the politically charged Ijebu cloths to ruling dignitaries in the Niger Delta (Ogunkoya 1956, 58). Furthermore, Ibani Ijo oral tradition informs us that King Fubara declared the tortoise cloth the official attire of his Perekule clan during his reign in the last decades of the eighteenth century. This indicates that the cloth had reached the Ibani Ijo region and been assigned its tortoise meaning by the time of Fubara's rule.

The British, Cloth, and Trade

The second type of *ikakibite* (fig. 8.8) reached the Niger Delta a good hundred years later, and this time through British rather than Ijebu-Yoruba hands. By the late nineteenth century, the British dominated cloth trade into the Eastern Ijo area. With European imperialist/colonialist interests in Africa on the rise, the British were actively competing with other European powers to expand their cloth markets.

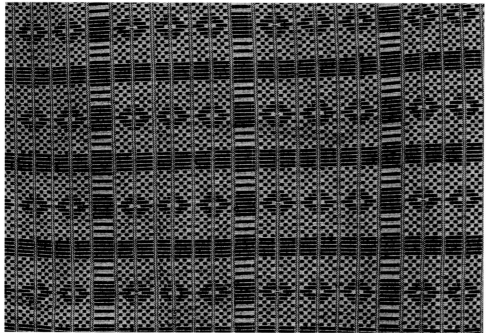

8.7 An example of ikakibite *traded from Ijebu-Ode documented in the cloth chest of Abonnema. Photograph by Lisa Aronson, 1978.*

8.8 Detail of abii ikakibite *cloth in a Kalabari cloth collection. Imported to southeastern Nigeria in the late nineteenth century through British hands. It is likely to have originated from a weaving center in India. Photograph by Lisa Aronson, 1978.*

260   **ARONSON**

Tricks of the Trade:
A Study of Ikakibite *(Cloth of the Tortoise)*
among the Eastern Ijo

In 1889 the British-appointed governor of Lagos, C. M. G. Moloney, acknowledged this initiative when he addressed members of the Manchester Geographical Society concerning cotton interests, both foreign and native, in West Africa. Lamenting the severe competition Manchester was experiencing with other European powers, he said, "[I]t would seem to be a duty specially incumbent on us…to consider, without loss of time, how, one [*sic*] and for all, we can best serve the interests of those countries on which we depend, not only to get rid of our surplus manufactures, but also for the raw material for such" (Moloney 1889, 255). Acknowledging Moloney's concerns, Manchester cotton magnates actively sought out raw cotton materials from Africa while simultaneously peddling large quantities of cotton fabric to many parts of the continent. The latter included machine-printed "calicos"; woven imitations of Indian cloths; and authentic Indian-manufactured cloths. The cloth type received by King Amakiri may well have come from India and most certainly was traded by British cloth merchants.

The British went to great lengths to manufacture cloths imitating African types or incorporating colors and patterns aimed to appeal to an African audience. Yet, while they were attuned to *what* was attractive to the Ijo, neither the Manchester cloth merchants, nor the Ijebu-Yoruba for that matter, were keenly aware of the underlying basis of the attraction of certain cloths.

"Cultural Authentication"

Joanne Eicher and Tonye Erekosima describe the complex process by which the Kalabari Ijo have taken in, renamed, and transformed traded artifacts to make them their own as "cultural authentication" (1981). The two traded cloths under consideration help to illustrate this authentication process if not to demonstrate its relevance to the Eastern Ijo at large. As noted earlier, the Kalabari are particularly drawn to the skins or other surface coverings of reptiles—the textured, variegated patterns and colors of which remind them of the potency and generosity of *oru* spirits. Kalabari sculptors would often add relief patterns resembling the skins of *oru nama* to the surface of their works to empower them (fig. 8.9).

In certain imported textiles the Eastern Ijo saw images whose patterns and colors they associated with the *oru* spirits, including the trickster Ikaki. Ijebu-originated cloth from an Abonemma woman's collection (see fig. 8.7) reveals a set of patterns that are not unlike a tortoise. The diamond shape appears to be the back of a tortoise whose legs are splayed out, reminding the Ijo of the creature when seen from a bird's-eye view. They also say that its diamond shapes recall the radiating hexagons one sees on the hinge-back's shell. They identify the other pattern on the cloth, a triangular "half-tortoise" shape, as Ikaki standing up, as he is envisioned when dancing, when climbing into cooking pots, or even when pursuing his female counterpart.

The English-traded cloth detailed in figure 8.8 lacks zoomorphic or other representational imagery. Madame Rosanna Dick Tom Big Harry, a Kalabari woman, informed me in 1978, however, that its geometric, woven designs— radiating hexagons in alternating blue and white—resemble the pattern of the tortoise's shell. Color contrast articulated through geometric design does appear to be essential in making the association with the tortoise. Nimi Wariboko argues, in fact, that it is not representational patterns that elicit *oru* spirits as much as it is alternating blue and white used in a checkerboard

8.9   Kalabari sculpture representing one of the village heros (oru) *with* oru *designs painted on the outer border. Photograph from Horton 1965a, fig. 15.*

8.10 This ikakibite *cloth from an Abonnema collection is from the Sudanic region of West Africa. The thinness of the weave, the dimensions of the cloth, and the scale of its checkerboard design suggest a Hausa origin. It is on the basis of the checkerboard design and color contrast that the Abonnema woman identified it as a tortoise cloth. Photograph by Lisa Aronson, 1978.*

pattern or other repeated design. I verified this in my surveys of tortoise cloths in Eastern Ijo collections, conducted in 1978 and again in 1990. In those surveys, I noted that several types of traded cloths—not just the two discussed in this essay—were associated with the ever-powerful trickster Ikaki. Of them, only the Ijebu-traded examples featured patterns suggesting the outline of the tortoise's body. All the others, including the English-traded variety, were strictly geometric with a checkerboard or herringbone-like pattern articulated in blue and white (fig. 8.10). Again, it was presumably the patterned surface of the tortoise shell that this abstract design and color system evoked.

Through its association with traded textiles, the tortoise spirit remains an active agent in a wide range of Ijo rituals. Not surprisingly, the Ijebu-traded variety with its long-standing history has the greatest and most widespread appeal within this region. There are several ritual contexts in which *ikakibite* must appear. Three important examples are: (1) as the prescribed attire in women's coming of age rituals (*iria*); (2) for use by priests as attire and as paraphernalia in their ritual practices; (3) and as the official dress of Ijo kings (*amanyanabo*) and members of the royal lineage.[8]

Women's Coming of Age (*iria*)

Ikakibite has an important place in the women's coming of age rituals (*iria*) that are practiced among certain Eastern Ijo groups (Ibani/Opobo, Kalabari, and Okrika Ijo). Detailed studies of *iria* can be found elsewhere (Daly 1984; Jewett 1988; Gleason and Mereghetti 1990; Gleason and Ibubuya 1991). For our purposes, it is sufficient to describe some of the ritual's general characteristics so as to determine the role that *ikakibite* plays.

Iria is an elaborate and multifaceted ritual through which young girls are transformed into women with all of the attendant privileges, such as marriage, the bearing of children, and the right to wear certain types of cloth in public. While *iria* vary from one Eastern Ijo group to another, they all require that the woman enter into ritual seclusion for a designated period of time. Traditionally, this would last up to a year or more, but today the seclusion is considerably shorter. During her isolation, the girl is educated

262   **ARONSON**
*Tricks of the Trade:
A Study of* Ikakibite *(Cloth of the Tortoise)
among the Eastern Ijo*

8.11   *This photograph of Chief Brown's daughter posing during the* opu-egennebite *phase of her* iria *ceremony was taken in 1897 in the Ibani town of Bonny, Niger Coast Protectorate. She wears and is surrounded by the Ijebu-traded version of* ikakibite *to mark this significant event in her life. Eliot Elisofon Photographic Archives, National Museum of African Art, Smithsonian Institution, 1995-240050.*

8.12   *Young woman from Finima at the completion of the* opu-egennebite *phase of her* iria. *Because the Ijebu-traded version of* ikakibite *is no longer available, she wears an Akwete version. Akwete weavers have been producing* ikakibite *and many other types of traded cloths for Ijo patrons since the early part of this century. Photograph by Lisa Aronson, 1990.*

to prepare for her eventual roles as wife and mother. To enhance her body and to accentuate her reproductive abilities, she is fed rich foods to fatten her and her skin is rubbed with oils to make it glisten. Ibani/Opobo and Okrika women undergoing *iria* are also painted with designs (*buruma*) to further enhance their beauty.

Cloths are among the essential aesthetic markers of the various stages of *iria* that follow the period of seclusion. The woman either poses while sitting, walks around the village, or dances wearing cloths of specified types at designated stages in the event. Exactly when *ikakibite* is worn seems crucial. In Ibani Ijo *iria,* for example, *ikakibite* marks the official exit from the ritual seclusion, an important stage known as *opu-egennebite* or "big tying of cloth" (figs. 8.11, 8.12). It is also worn when she goes to church for "Thanksgiving" after *opu-egennebite.* The Kalabari use *ikakibite* in the fourth of the sequence of five stages typical of their *iria,* so that it appears near the high-point, or finale, of the ceremony (Nimi Wariboko, personal communication,1997). Although no one has yet systematically studied the sequence of cloths appearing in the Okrika version of *iria,* Judith Gleason and Elisa Mereghetti's videotape of the event shows that it does have an important place within the ritual (1990).

Kalabari women who undergo *iria* appear to be mimicking "village hero" spirits (*oru*; Daly 1984, 142–43), and Ibani and Okrika women are said to symbolically marry male water spirits (*owu*; Gleason and Ibubuya 1991, 137). This spiritual component seems key in explaining why *ikakibite* appears in the *iria.* We have learned that the tortoise is the great enhancer of spiritual things, which explains why the tortoise and other *oru* imagery are applied to *owu* sculpture. In the context of *iria,* it is the woman, the *iriabo,* who is bedecked with the *ikaki* designs. A photograph taken in 1897 of an *iriabo* wearing *ikakibite* (see fig. 8.11) is particularly interesting in this regard. The cloth wrapped around the *iriabo* and used as a backdrop appears to enclose or encompass her as the shell does for the tortoise, suggesting that the *ikakibite* provides spiritual protection and confers power.

Wearing *ikakibite* in the context of *iria* may also be a means of emulating priests and kings, the two highest-ranking individuals in Eastern Ijo cultures, whose own status is marked by the donning of *ikakibite.* It is also not uncommon for Kalabari women to wear the bowler-type hats associated with male chieftaincy during certain stages of *iria.* These two examples suggest that women have appropriated male status symbols for use in their own status-achieving rituals.

Priests (*pere*)

The use of *ikakibite* by Ijo priests is well documented in oral tradition and ethnographic writings. Talbot—among the first to acknowledge its use—documented a ritual in which a Kalabari priest laid a cloth identified as "*ekaki egennibite*" on the floor so that its patterns faced upward to make them visible to spirits. The use of *ikakibite* reflects the way in which the Okrika priest cited earlier used an actual tortoise. As the Kalabari priest laid out the tortoise cloth, he uttered the words "If I wish, I can prevent you from going to my house" (Talbot 1932, 118), the implication being that the *ikakibite* had a certain *oru*-invoking potency that could impede human action.

Through his actions, the priest may have been emulating Owamekaso, head of the heroes among the Kalabari, who also made use of cloth bearing the images of the *oru* to accomplish magical feats (Horton 1965a, 31–32). As a Kalabari priest praised the *oru nama*, he sang the following song:

The fearfulness of the watersnake in your cloth,
Is in your cloth, big woman.
Our great mother, the persistent one,
Tied this cloth.
The fearfulness of the skink in your cloth,
Is in your cloth, big woman.
Our great mother, the persistent one,
Tied this cloth.
The fearfulness of the tortoise in your cloth,
Is in your cloth, big woman.
Our great mother, the persistent one,
Tied this cloth.
…and so on with a verse for each reptile. [Horton 1965a, 32]

Even today, Nembe Ijo priests typically wear shoulder cloths woven with tortoise-like imagery when tending their spirit shrines (fig. 8.13). These cloths are called *ikagibara* (similar to the tortoise). Presumably, the Nembe priest wears the cloth to enhance and empower him and the contents of the shrine he oversees, just as *oru*-inspired imagery enhances Kalabari spirit sculpture (see fig. 8.9).

Kings (*Amanyanabo*)

As noted earlier priests (*pere*) were once the leaders in Eastern Ijo societies, and their position provided a model for Eastern Ijo kingship as it took shape in the eighteenth century. It would then stand to reason that the Ijo king (*amanyanabo*) would also wear *ikakibite*, and, indeed, the cloth has long been an important bodily enhancement for Ijo kings.

In addition to the link to priesthood, there are other, equally compelling explanations of the association that exists between kings and the tortoise. Like a king, the tortoise is a wise and powerful elder but one whose power is forever needing to be controlled. The Ijo proverb "Ikaki knows everything" (*Kiri ikaki*) is intended to convey the message that there is a delicate balance between wisdom and diplomacy (the proverb can also refer to a know-it-all). One might say that *ikaki* imagery in Eastern Ijo culture functions like the egg-in-the-hand image in Asante culture or the mudfish-in-the-hand representation in Benin, each of which suggests the delicacy with which power must be exercised.[9] In addition, his liminal place between the land and the sea gives the tortoise a powerful position within the Eastern Ijo cosmology.

King Jaja of Opobo

As noted previously, the Ijebu-traded *ikakibite* cloth first came to be associated with Ibani kingship in the eighteenth century when the institution of kingship was gaining greater legitimacy. The late eighteenth-century king Fubara was responsible for making the Perekule lineage preeminent over the

8.13 *Nembe chief priest Owolo Ayebanumomoipri James Yousuo wearing* ikagibara *over his shoulder while sitting in front of his shrine. As chief priest, he is the guardian of the shrine devoted to Nembe's supreme deity Nyana Oru Korowei and oversees spirit possession. Photograph by Lisa Aronson, 1990.*

264   **ARONSON**

Tricks of the Trade:
A Study of Ikakibite *(Cloth of the Tortoise)*
among the Eastern Ijo

8.14 Photo of King Jaja dressed in Western attire and seated on a British-type royal throne. Private collection, Opobo, Nigeria.

8.15 Egbelegbe masquerade performed at the Buguma Centenary, 1984. Curiously, the outer cloth the masquerader wears is an Akwete version of the Ijebu-traded ikakibite. *The* abii ikakibite *may be underneath other cloths and, therefore, not visible (Joanne Eicher, personal communication, 1998). Photograph by Joanne B. Eicher.*

whole of the geographical area known as Bonny (Hargreaves 1987, 178), and he did so by giving paramount importance to the spirit shrine and by elaborating on existing ritual ceremony. Ibani Ijo oral tradition credits him as the one responsible for selecting cloth bearing the *ikaki* motif as the official attire of the Perekule lineage. It also informs us that Fubara was a hunchback. Whether true or not, such an assertion links him to the powerful but temperamental qualities the Ijo equate with the tortoise. To this day, Ibani chiefs wear *ikakibite* (*fubara alali,* or "Fubara celebration attire") for the ceremony commemorating Fubara.

One hundred years later, King Jaja of Opobo felt it important to be photographed wearing this same cloth. Jaja was an Igbo famous for having risen from slavery to become an enterprising Ibani Ijo palm oil trader. Faced with heightened economic competition— from within the Delta and from British traders—in the latter half of the nineteenth century Jaja and his crew of faithful followers moved several miles to the east to form a competing trading state called Opobo. He ruled over Opobo from roughly 1870 until his exile in 1887, around the time the photograph (see fig. 8.1) was taken. His rule officially ended when Vice-Consul Harry Johnston lured him onto a gunboat with the false promise of protection, only to kidnap him and to deport him shortly thereafter (Isichei 1973, 98–99).

King Jaja ruled at a time when the Ibani were increasingly under pressure from the British to abandon ritual attire and traditional beliefs. His trading rival, Oruigbi I (George Pepple), had complied by refusing to pay homage to Fubara and by discouraging sacrificial ceremonies. King Jaja himself was not entirely averse to British influence in the way of dress as at least one photograph attests (fig. 8.14). At the same time, he adhered to tradition in ways that his political rival did not. In figure 8.1, he wraps himself in a cloth bearing the powerful image of the tortoise and thereby evokes the role of priest on which the *amanyanabo*'s own position is historically based; to further this connection he raises his arm in the act of pouring a libation (E. J. Alagoa, personal communication,1998). He thus affirms his traditional power and authority while allying himself with the great Ibani leader Fubara, who one hundred years before initiated the use of tortoise cloth as the official attire of his Perekule lineage.

King Abbi Amakiri IV of Kalabari

Jaja's contemporary, the Kalabari king Abbi Amakiri IV, also claimed *ikakibite* as his own lineage cloth. In this case the English-traded version was appropriated (see fig. 8.2). According to Kalabari oral tradition, the king presented the traded cloth as his lineage's official dress through his sponsorship of a masquerade known as Egbelegbe (fig. 8.15). Named for a particularly violent *owu,* Egbelegbe is allowed to be performed only at specified times, such as the designated moment within the twenty-five-year cycle of all of the Sekiapu Societies' *owu* displays and at special ceremonies such as important funerals or centenary celebrations (Nimi Wariboko, personal communication, 1997).

I would propose that Amakiri consciously appropriated his Ibani Ijo rival's one-hundred-year-old tradition of wearing *ikakibite* as royal attire. As previously noted, the Kalabari point to the Ibani Ijo area as the source of their Ikaki masquerade, if not the tortoise beliefs that precipitated it. The

Egbelegbe masquerade was also acquired from a region formerly occupied by the Ibani Ijo. The Kalabari claim specifically that they acquired the masquerade from the Tombia area where it had floated to shore after the people of Okrika, its original owners, deemed it too dangerous and threw it into the water. Through spiritual consultation, the people of Tombia were then given the right to perform the masquerade provided they made the proper sacrifice of a dog anytime they wished to perform it (Nimi Wariboko, personal communication, 1997). What is significant is the fact that Tombia had been under Ibani Ijo rulership until Amakiri lured its people to the Kalabari area (Alagoa 1972, 156). This suggests that Abbi Amakiri IV, in taking on Egbelegbe and the tortoise cloth with it, was appropriating an art form once owned by people with a well-established admiration for the tortoise if not a long-standing tradition of using tortoise cloth as official royal attire.

Amakiri, however, appropriated the tortoise cloth associated with Egbelegbe in his own unique way by selecting the new European-traded variety of *ikakibite*. In addition, he preempted it according to the rules of Kalabari cloth protocol by designating it the official attire of a house. In this case, it is all members of the Abbi house of Buguma who have the right to wear *ikakibite* (the *abbi ikakibite* variety) to perform the Egbelegbe *owu* masquerade with which it is historically associated.[10] At important celebrations, such as the Buguma Centenary celebration in 1984, the commemorative statue honoring Abbi Amakiri is totally enshrouded with *abbi ikakibite* (fig. 8.16).

It is no coincidence that Amakiri IV was effectively politicizing a new form of *ikakibite* at precisely the time when the British were discouraging African dress as well as the very political systems with which it was associated. Perhaps Amakiri's effort to emulate an Ibani royal tradition was more than just an act of empowerment directed against his Ijo rival. It may also have been a subtle form of resistance against European influences. Whatever the motives, the historical context cannot be ignored. In each case, Ijo kings were identifying (or re-identifying) themselves with the image of the tortoise when British imperialist activity was increasingly causing rivalry both internally and between the Ijo and the British.

Ikakibite and Akwete Weaving

By the end of the nineteenth century, the Ijo had ceased to import the Ijebu version of *ikakibite* into their area of the Delta. Yet, its legacy as a cloth type and its role as the carrier of ideas about the tortoise were able to continue well beyond that time in two ways: (1) through the ritual use of Ijebu-traded cloths preserved in Ijo collections and (2) through the enterprising efforts of Igbo weavers from the village of Akwete who had begun weaving the *ikaki* design by the late nineteenth century (fig. 8.17).

Akwete was among the vital intermediary markets in the nineteenth-century palm oil trade. Most of the oil was manufactured in the Igbo hinterlands from whence it was traded southward through a stepping-stone system of markets before reaching the coast. Located just fifty miles to the north of the Ibani Ijo area and on the fringes of the Niger Delta, the village of Akwete served as one of the last major markets through which the oil was traded to the Ijo. Thus Akwete had always maintained cloth, commercial, and social ties with its Ijo neighbors to the south.

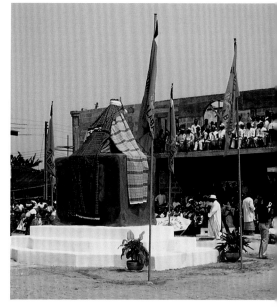

8.16 *Statue of Abbi Amakiri adorned with* abii ikakibite *during the opening ceremony of Buguma's Centenary in 1984. Photograph by Joanne B. Eicher.*

8.17 *Akwete Igbo woman weaving* ikaki *cloth commissioned by an Ijo patron. Even though the language spoken in Akwete is Igbo, the weavers there call this cloth design by the Ijo name for tortoise,* ikaki, *rather than the Igbo one,* mbe. *Photograph by Lisa Aronson, 1977.*

266   ARONSON
Tricks of the Trade:
A Study of Ikakibite *(Cloth of the Tortoise)*
among the Eastern Ijo

It was through these ties that Akwete Igbo weavers became aware of the Ijo passion for certain types of imported cloths, including the two tortoise cloths under consideration. This familiarity with the Ijo cloth aesthetic proved advantageous to Akwete weavers as they began competing with the British cloth manufacturers and traders for Ijo cloth patronage in the last decades of the nineteenth century. Competition prompted them to draw on a host of imported textile designs, including the *ikaki* cloth traded from the Ìjèbú-Yorùbá area (fig. 8.18). From that time until the present, Akwete weavers have been weaving versions of *ikakibite* for Ijo patrons (fig. 8.19). When Opuada Secundus Perekule was proclaimed king of the Ibani in 1979, it was an Akwete version of *ikakibite* that he wore as his official attire (fig. 8.20). Perekule represents just one of many Ijo patrons for whom Akwete weavers are now the chief, if not sole, suppliers of *ikakibite*.

8.18   *Detail of a cloth bearing the* ikaki *motif woven in the Akwete area in the late nineteenth century. Photograph courtesy of the British Museum, Beving 1934 3-7 115.*

8.19   *Akwete cloth covered with* ikaki *designs. Cotton. L: 78.8 cm. FMCH X84-3; Museum Purchase with Manus Fund. This cloth was collected by G. I. Jones in the 1930s.*

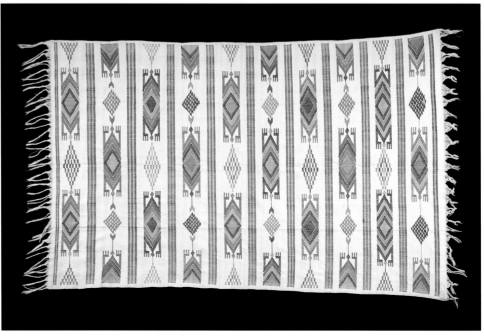

This weaver/patron relationship that began by the end of the nineteenth century marks an important point in a complex and dynamic historical process. Precipitating this process was Bell's hinge-back tortoise, whose perceived spiritual powers greatly influenced Eastern Ijo thought and, in turn, their receptivity to traded textiles. By being assigned meaning associated with this enigmatic creature, these two tortoise cloths remain to this day important politicizing and historicizing vehicles for Ijo kings, as their status evolves and changes over time.

8.20 Opuada Secundus Perekule being proclaimed amanyanabo *of the Ibani in 1979. The* ikakibite *he is wearing identifies him as a descendent of the royal Perekule lineage. This particular cloth was commissioned from Akwete Igbo weavers. Photograph by Lisa Aronson, 1978.*

Interleaf J
Maidens, Mothers, Mediums, and Matriarchs: Women of the Niger Delta

Martha G. Anderson

Delta women did not ordinarily wield political power, but they influenced political decisions and some held positions of authority. In the sixteenth century Queen Kambasa of Bonny reigned as an "effective ruler whose orders were obeyed by all." She increased overseas trade, introduced rank among priests and nobles, organized a royal bodyguard, and established a national masking society (Alagoa and Fombo 1972, 8–9). An early twentieth-century source describes members of the Okrika Ijo "wedding society" as "the big women of the town" who served as "women historians" and used to be "very powerful" (figs. J.1, J.2). A male informant credited them with stirring up the men "to prevent the coming of [colonial] Government" (Talbot 1932, 304). Numerous other Delta women have gained economic power through trading or exercised ritual authority by serving as priestesses and diviners. Nevertheless, Delta cultures accord primary importance to the ability of a woman to bear children (fig. J.3).

Photographs taken by J. A. Green, a native of Bonny, provide insights into the roles women played in Eastern Ijo societies around the turn of the last century. A survey of over a hundred photographs taken by Green revealed only a handful that feature women, and few of these women appear without men at their sides. Family portraits and scenes of local life may include mature women (fig. J.4), but more often they show young girls dressed for the ceremonies that marked their coming of age (fig. J.5). Sponsoring a girl through these rites brought prestige to both her father and her fiancé. The latter typically bore the expenses for the rites at a time when most participants married immediately after completing them (or completing a particular stage of the process, which often consisted of several phases and sometimes culminated with the birth of a first child).

J.1   "Wedding" society, Bonny, 1902. Reproduced with the permission of Unilever PLC (from an original in the Unilever Archives), box 25, folder 2, no. 33. This photograph by the Bonny photographer J. A. Green undoubtedly shows members of the local Egbelereme Society. Its members—women who have reached menopause—run the iria ceremonies and instruct the girls. The status of the two "brides" at the center is unclear, as is the presence of young girls. The latter are too young to be iriabo. The former appear to be too old, but at least today, some women may complete the second stage of the Bonny rites at forty, or even older.

J.2   Members of the Egbelereme Society, which guides initiates through iria. They are shown playing music on pots while an iriabo dances. Photograph by Lisa Aronson, Finima, Bonny region, 1990.

Many communities in the Lower Niger and Cross Rivers regions of Nigeria stage elaborate ceremonies to mark a young woman's coming of age. By preparing carefree girls for the heavy responsibilities of marriage and motherhood, these rites of passage play an instrumental role in constructing gender identity. Some observers have also noted the part the process plays in regulating morality, citing such practices as the certifying of chastity. Although many girls now forego initiation, refusing to participate can invite accusations of moral laxity. Conversely, completing the process brings pride to the young women and their families (fig. J.6).

J.3 Figure of a mother and child. Ijo. Wood and pigment. H: 109.2 cm. Indiana University Art Museum, no. 66.39. Photograph by Michael Cavanagh and Kevin Montague © Indiana University Art Museum. This figure represents a nature spirit. Delta men and women must marry and bear children to achieve adult status, and spirits must follow suit in order to be taken seriously. The Ijo believe that the ability to produce descendants is governed by the prenatal agreement each person makes with "Our Mother," the creator. They reason that the creator must be female because it is women who beget children.

J.4 Basket Makers, Bonny, 1897. Reproduced with the permission of Unilever PLC (from an original in the Unilever Archives), box 25, folder 2, no. 73. Though intended to record a typical occupation, the group shown here appears to be carefully posed. The idea of photographing scenes of this type suggests that J. A. Green, a Bonny native, had some knowledge of ethnographic photography by this date. He also documented women weaving and processing palm nuts, as well as a blacksmith at work.

J.5 Akenta Bob in "wedding" dress, Abonnema, Kalabari Ijo, 1898. Photograph by J. A. Green. Howie album. Courtesy of the Borad of Trustees of the National Museums and Galleries on Merseyside (Merseyside Maritime Museum), Liverpool, ref. no. N2001.2414. This photograph commemorates a young Kalabari Ijo girl's transformation into womanhood. Her ensemble identifies her as an iriabo.

The rites vary markedly, but typically include elements of confinement, pampering, and instruction, as well as public display and feting (figs. J.7, J.8). Some also involve excision. Western colonialists, fascinated by the idea of feeding the young girls to round out their bodies, termed this practice "the fatting house." The narrator of a film on the Okrika ceremony objects that girls are not "fattened for marriage like turkeys for Christmas [but made to] feel valued and attractive… honoring their path to womanhood" (Onwurah 1993). In addition to enhancing their appearance, "fattening" then ensures their health and fertility. Lavish clothing, accessories, and cosmetic embellishments (fig. J.9) draw attention to their special status and help them conform to cultural ideals.

J.6　In the Kalabari region, iria *formerly celebrated periods of transition in the female life cycle from late childhood to childbirth. Only two stages of* iria *now survive,* bite sara *and* iriabo. *Photograph by Joanne B. Eicher, Buguma, 1988.*

J.7　*An* iriabo *dressed for the final and most public* iria *event. Photograph by Lisa Aronson, Finima, Bonny region, 1990.*

J.8   Women's hats (angara sun). Kalabari Ijo. Cloth, beads, plastic, ribbon, and braid trim. Twentieth century. Collection of Joanne B. Eicher. Kalabari iria *rites celebrate the transitions girls make as they move from childhood through motherhood. Each stage requires certain forms of dress, including hats made of various materials. Elliptical or crown-shaped hats may incorporate coral beads or imported brocades, materials highly valued by the Kalabari.*

J.9   *A female initiate in the Bonny region is shown having designs painted on her body over a base of camwood paste. A pattern identified as* ikoli, *or crab, is among the motifs employed. Photograph by Lisa Aronson, Finima, Bonny region, 1990.*

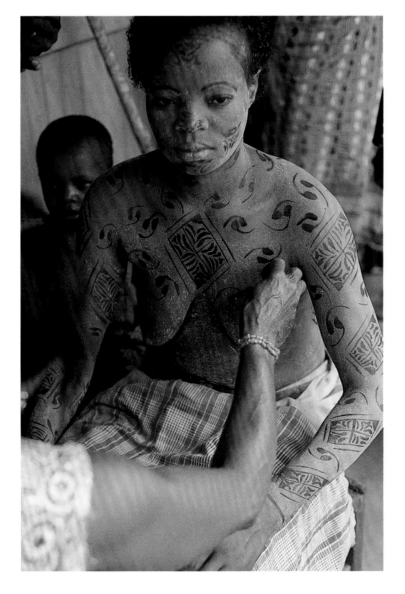

J.10 Among the Isoko, ceremonies for women mark adulthood, not availability. Initiates are married women and often have several children. Their husbands pay for the ceremony. Photograph by Philip M. Peek, Emevo town, 1971.

J.11 An Urhobo initiate wearing the elaborate costume that betokens her special status. Her skin glistens with a mixture of camwood and palm oil. Its reddish-orange color signifies that the powers she possesses could be dangerous if ignored and reminds people to accord her the same respect that they give to kings and spirits. She sits in state on a stool covered with "bridal" mats (ewhere opha), like the one seen in figure J.12. An intricately woven weaver's mat (ere opha) is placed in front of her. Photograph by Jean Borgatti, Orhuwhorun, 1972.

A local schoolmaster described an important phase of the rites in 1916: "On this occasion the Iria girls wear the most costly cloths of all, carry looking-glasses and wear coral beads and anklets.... They dance in time to the drum, a hundred and twenty or more together—wearing their cloths in a roll round the waist. Above this nothing was worn, so as to show the painting upon their bodies, as also that the girls are fat and well-looking.... As soon as the third day is over, the girl is free.... To yield to any wooer before the Iria ceremony has been performed is a shame and reproach that can never be quite wiped out" (Talbot 1932, 174–75).

In the Urhobo and Isoko regions (figs. J.10–J.13), girls once enjoyed nine months of leisure following excision, but the period has been shortened to accommodate the school calendar. Attended by younger girls, the *opha (ova),* or initiate, consumes rich food, parades in fine clothing, and receives guests bearing gifts. The Urhobo refer to her as "She who sits as king," acknowledging that the powers and privileges they grant her are usually reserved for kings.

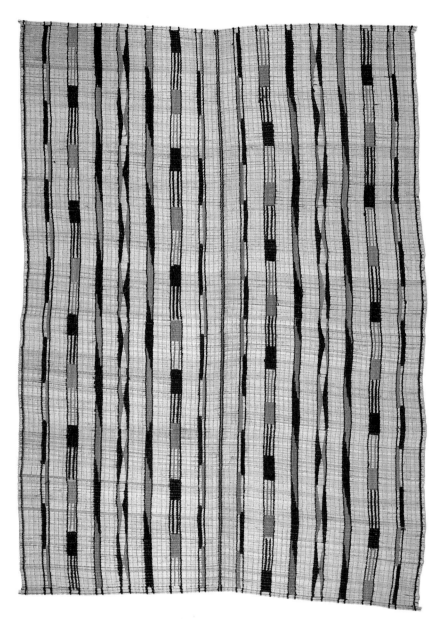

J.12 Mat (ewhere opha). Urhobo. Dyed, woven, and stitched straw. L: 154 cm. FMCH X76.1698; Gift of Mrs. W. Thomas Davis, in memory of W. Thomas Davis. Urhobo women transform simple materials into elaborate tapestries to honor girls as they become young women. Special mats like this one (ewhere opha) drape the "throne" where the opha, *or initiate, sits in state and receives visitors bearing gifts of money. The patterns woven into the mat may protect her. After being displayed when she receives visitors—and is exposed to jealous rivals—the mat hangs next to her bed and may help keep witches and evil at bay (S. Foss 1978).*

J.13 Figure representing a young woman who "Sits as a king." Urhobo, Agbarho or Agbon village groups. H: 104.2 cm. Walt Disney-Tishman African Art Collection. Photograph by Jerry L. Thompson. This figure's attire, which includes a conical beaded hairstyle, coral beads, and reddish camwood paste, indicates that she is an opha, *an Urhobo girl who has recently completed coming-of-age rites. The sculpture probably represented the daughter or bride in a group of shrine figures commemorating a forest or water spirit (P. Foss, 1981).*

Chapter 9 The Arts of the Ogoni

SONPIE KPONE-TONWE and

JILL SALMONS

The Ogoni inhabit an alluvial plain bounded on the north by the Imo River and their Igbo neighbors, on the south by the littoral flats inhabited by the Obolo (Andoni), on the east by the Opobo River and the Ibibio, and on the west by the Ikwere (Ikwerre), the large city of Port Harcourt, and, across the creeks, the so-called city-states of the Niger Delta. They currently number about five hundred thousand (Kpone-Tonwe 1990, 19; Saro-Wiwa 1992, 9). Tradition states that during a civil war the ancestors of the Ogoni migrated from ancient Ghana under the leadership of a great woman named Gbenekwaanwaa. After fighting and wandering in the hinterland for years, the group, carrying iron-tipped weapons called *ega*, finally arrived at the Atlantic Coast. From there they traveled along the coast in canoes until they came to the area now known as Ogoniland and settled at a place called Nama. Linguistic and archaeological evidence indicate that the Ogoni are the oldest settlers in the Eastern Niger Delta, and among the oldest in the entire Delta region (Kpone-Tonwe 1990, 66–67).

According to Nick Ashton-Jones (1995, 31), until the end of the nineteenth century the Ogoni probably lived in the more accessible areas of the densely forested Ogoni plain, engaging in farming, fishing, and hunting. The area was long known as "the breadbasket of the Delta," and it is likely that for several centuries the Ogoni provided many of the provisions taken on board slave ships for the notorious Atlantic passage. However, early in the twentieth century, with increased population growth and demand for farm produce from other parts of the Delta, large areas of forest were cleared to provide farmland. "Accelerated population growth...began to push the human population beyond ecological viability by about 1960" (Ashton-Jones 1995, 31). Today the pressure for farmland is so great that even the wetter areas are being cultivated for quick cassava crops in the dry season, threatening valuable water sources and impoverishing soils. The ubiquitous oil and raffia palm trees, which have grown in place of forest trees, do, however, provide a valuable source of income from their multitudinous products. Farms of yam, plantain, three-leaf yam, cassava, peppers, and maize flourish near settlements, benefiting from household manure. The current ecological problems of the Ogoni have been exacerbated over the past thirty years by the rapid growth of the mineral oil industry, including a large refinery at Alesa Eleme (see fig. 11.1). The oil industry infrastructure sequestered scarce agricultural land, blocked footpaths with pipelines, and contaminated water and land with oil spills. Until 1993 gas flares caused acid rain damage to tin roofs, crops, and people's health (Saro-Wiwa 1992).

9.1   Mask of a man with a "house." Ogoni. Wood, fiber, cord, and pigment. H: 27.9 cm. FMCH X76.1841; Gift of Mrs. W. Thomas Davis, in memory of W. Thomas Davis. The structure atop this typically Ogoni face—a small house or perhaps a shrine with chevron designs on three sides—was probably intended to indicate membership in Amanikpo or Nkoo Societies, both of which had special meeting houses (see fig. 9.28).

Most Ogoni villages have at their heart a large clearing, overshadowed by at least one huge tree, said to have been planted at the time the village was founded but possibly a remnant of the original rain forest. Such trees are said to be endowed with sacred properties, and there are numerous laws concerning their well-being. Generally there are shrines dedicated to the founding ancestors of the village within the tree's huge buttresses. On one side of the clearing many villages have an Amanikpo (Amarikpo) hall, a relatively inconspicuous cement building with a corrugated iron roof and verandah. This is the meeting house for one of the most important secret societies of the area, and no noninitiate may cross its threshold. Every three or four days the village will hold a market in the clearing where locally grown produce is sold beside goods brought from Bori, the only sizeable town in the Ogoni area, or from Port Harcourt. All villages have their own primary school; some have secondary schools, but all are sadly lacking in equipment and staff. The majority of villages do not have electricity, piped water, or tarred roads. Individual compounds nestle in groves of plantain and banana, the houses having earth walls and palm-mat roofs. Many of these are now being replaced by concrete block single-story houses with corrugated iron roofs.

According to the Ogoni worldview, the supreme goddess, creator of the sky, the earth, and all things, was named Bari, or Kawa Bari (Mother of God). From her home in the sky she observes all human doings. Formal worship, however, is not directed to her but to the ancestral spirits of the Ogoni, the Gbene (Kpone-Tonwe 1990, 26). Among this original founding group were warriors and spirit mediums, and since that time reverence for the ancestors with their warrior ethos and for the power of the spirit mediums has dominated Ogoni belief (Kpone-Tonwe 1990, 28). According to oral tradition, having cleared the forest, cultivated the land, and driven away the wild animals, the ancestors began to disperse and found their own settlements. When desirable land was already occupied wars often broke out.

Wherever they migrated, groups would always return to Nama, especially to perform the necessary rites to enable them to become founders of new towns, or holders of the Gbene title. To this day the most important ritual leaders are not recognized unless they have completed at least one pilgrimage to Nama. Gbene is the title given to all the members of the founding group, including women, who are cited by name. Descendants of Gbene hold privileged positions in villages as it is believed that a Gbene, at death, becomes a spirit with the power to return to the world in order to possess an adult descendant. In this state they are thought capable not only of revealing past events but also of skillfully influencing current community affairs. Most village heads and local politicians now aspire to perform the Gbene title rites, although traditionally this would have involved accomplishing superhuman feats of bravery, the breaking of certain taboos, and the provision of human sacrificial victims.

The seven ancient political divisions of Ogoni were known as Eraba Edo Khana, or the "Seven multitudes of Khana people." These comprised Boue, Gokana, Eleme, Tee, Luekun-Bangha, Baen, and Babbe (Kpone-Tonwe 1990, 99). Nowadays these have been grouped into Nyokana (Upper Khana), Babbe, Kekana (Lower Khana), Gokana, Tai, and Eleme. Over a considerable period of time the political framework of the individual villages evolved, varying slightly from clan to clan. In Babbe clan the control of the village was in the hands of the Pya Bee Bue, a group that consisted of the founders of the village, together with the Pya Te Ere Bue or Pya Mene Bue, the "Owners," or the "Wealthy of the town," since such leaders possessed most of the land and livestock. The leading Gbenemene (Clan head) was therefore the "Great wealthy one." As the village grew, more men would be co-opted into government, and they became known as Pya Kanee, or "Mature men," and Pya Zuguru, or "Lieutenants," who were younger men (Kpone-Tonwe 1990, 244–78)

The teaching of group history and traditions became of paramount importance to the village or whole clan, particularly aspects concerning war. Such traditions were collectively rehearsed annually in the form of festivals. According to oral history, cadres of young warriors, led by men such as the legendary Gbenesaako were "the embodiment of the war spirit" (Kpone-Tonwe 1990, 114). In the Babbe area they formed an institution called Yaa. "In ancient Ogoni, the Yaa tradition involved recruitment into the people's fighting force. Virtually every Yaa initiate was a warrior, and training was warlike" (Kpone-Tonwe 1990, 94). Furthermore, men who did not undergo Yaa initiation were said to be "spiritually deficient, spiritually inactive and spiritually unwise. They were therefore incapable of good leadership. Accordingly, they were not listed as soldiers in time of war, because it was believed that at such times a man's spiritual soundness as a warrior was crucial" (Kpone-Tonwe 1990, 251). The equivalent titles elsewhere were Be (Tai) and Dogo (Gokana). Without these titles men could not play an important political or religious role in the community.

In precolonial society, opportunities also existed for individuals to achieve higher social status through the accumulation of wealth, especially through yam cultivation. For example, in the Eleme area, titles in yam production became the chief means of social recognition and political ascendancy. Performance of an act of bravery, either in warfare or hunting, and association with certain religious organizations would, in the past, have achieved similar ends. Title-taking retains great importance in contemporary Ogoni society. A wealthy Kana man wishing to achieve social recognition publicly declares his intention to perform the Yaanwi, or "Sons of Yaa," tradition. Parents of sufficient means take their adolescent sons to him for initiation. He then conducts a series of rituals with the boys over a three-day period, culminating in the teaching of the use of the *kobege* (knife) as working tool and weapon of war. The boys then enter into an economic relationship with the sponsor, working on his farm, tapping his wine, harvesting his palm fruits, and, in times of war, fighting for him. Such youths are regarded as potential elders and treated with some respect. This tradition allows for the emergence of suitable leaders and warriors in each generation. In turn, the sponsor, after two or three years of training such youths, receives the title of Kabaari, and his house is classified as one of the tribute-collecting houses of the town (Kpone-Tonwe 1990, 241). While this is no longer an annual ceremony, many elders still encourage their sons to be initiated—the Be initiation witnessed by Salmons in Tai in 1992 involved no less than fifteen boys whose ages ranged from three years to the mid-twenties (fig. 9.2).

The coastal groups and particularly the ports of Okrika, Bonny, and Opobo established and maintained a trade monopoly with the Europeans

9.2   Be celebrants with Mbiudam (female members of the Society). Photograph by Jill Salmons, Kpite, Tai, 1992.

over hundreds of years and effectively blocked the Ogoni from direct contact with overseas traders. For this reason the Ogoni did not meet the British until 1901, when the latter established a base at Kono and proclaimed Ogoniland to be part of the Oil Rivers Protectorate. Hostile to the British, whom they attacked in 1905 and 1913, the Ogoni were finally subdued after the British destroyed the Gbenebeka shrine in 1914. The British then appointed new Ogoni rulers purely on the grounds of who had rendered assistance. It was also during this time that the first missionaries arrived, and schools and churches began to be established. Consequently, while the people of Bonny on the coast can boast of many generations of Christianity and Western education, the Ogoni feel they have been "left behind" in this respect. This has meant, however, that they have maintained far more of their precolonial culture than many other peoples of the area, and although their art has been subject to some iconoclasm, this has been slight compared to that experienced by groups such as the Eket or Kalabari.

The arts of the Ogoni are far more substantial than the nonrepresentative collections known in the West would suggest. While there are a number of underlying cultural similarities throughout Ogoniland, especially in connection with certain institutions such as Amanikpo, each region shows much individuality of expression. Despite its great variety, most Ogoni wood sculpture falls into one of the following categories:

1. Small, delicately carved face masks representing men and women, normally given the generic term *elu* (spirit) and used for a variety of masquerades. These generally do not cover the wearer's face completely. Pert, retroussé noses and childlike features are common. Many, though not all such masks are cut across the mouth and have a simple mechanism allowing the wearer to articulate the hinged jaw and open the mouth, revealing narrow teeth, usually made of cane. Such masks are often surmounted by representations of human heads, skulls, birds, or title regalia and are generally decorated in bright, light colors (figs. 9.3, 9.4).

2. Larger face masks of a more grotesque nature, often colored black or polychrome. Some have hinged jaws, and most are carved with exaggerated human features to represent unruly or restless spirits such as Ekpo and O-u-o-lu (fig. 9.5).

3. Small face masks depicting animals such as deer, antelope, goat, dog, and monkey, utilized particularly by the Karikpo Society but also used for other festivities (fig. 9.6).

4. Large face masks depicting fierce animals such as elephant, bush pig, leopard, bush cow, and crocodile. These are most often used in a regulatory role.

5. Human figures representing title holders or ancestors, worn on top of the head in the form of cap-masks or headdresses, e.g., Ka-elu (fig. 9.7).

6. Headdresses worn horizontally on top of the head or tilted forward, representing marine creatures of the pan-Delta *owu* type or anthropomorphic spirits (fig. 9.31).

7. Carved figures of title holders, ancestors, or depictions of Mami Wata, usually commissioned for shrines (fig. 9.17).

8. Puppets, generally carved with articulated jaws and moveable limbs, manipulated by wires and strings through the central body of the puppet. Used exclusively by the Amanikpo Society (figs. 9.8a,b).

Correspondingly, the masquerades performed in this relatively small region are extraordinarily varied. Most, if not all, Ogoni villages have their own festivals, some of long standing, others introduced within living memory. The festivals are held to commemorate the founding of the village, to pay allegiance to particular ancestral land or water spirits, to mark the planting and harvesting seasons, to recognize the taking of titles, to restore peace in a troubled community, to maintain cohesion within social groupings, and for general entertainment.

9.3 Mask of a woman with a local hairstyle. Ogoni. Wood. H: 19.69 cm. FMCH X78.382; Museum Purchase. This carved wooden mask has an articulated jaw that can be opened to reveal sticklike teeth. This mask probably represents a beautiful young maiden who has completed initiation and is ready for marriage. Her hair is elaborately coiffed in spiraling braids.

9.4   *Mask with human and birdlike features.*
Ogoni. Wood. H: 18.4 cm. Krannert Art Museum
and Kinkead Pavilion, University of Illinois,
Urbana-Champaign; Faletti Family Collection.

9.5   *Mask. Ogoni. Wood, pigment, cane, plant fiber,*
and feathers. H: 58.5 cm. FMCH X65.8234; Gift
of the Wellcome Trust. Many Ogoni masks convey
masculine strength and aggression. Large, grotesque
face masks with exaggerated human or animal features
are used by Ekpo and O-u-o-lu Societies or are
employed as regulatory masks by village elders.
Nowadays, they play a largely recreational role at
funerary and Christmas celebrations. Unlike O-u-o-lu
masks, which are polychromed and worn on top of the
head like water spirit types, Ekpo masks cover the face
and are blackened.

9.6   *Karikpo mask. Ogoni. Wood and pigment.*
H: 63.5 cm. FMCH X90.441; Gift of Peter Jay
Kuhn. The Karikpo Society was charged in the past
with insuring agricultural fertility. Karikpo masks
typically depict animals such as deer, antelope, goats,
and monkeys. The masqueraders perform acrobatic
feats requiring considerable agility. This is especially
true in the case of those wearing horned masks, such as
this one, where the masquerader must jump especially
high when performing the customary somersaults.

9.7   Headdress surmounted by a male and a female. Ogoni. Wood. H: 49.5 cm. Collection of Toby and Barry Hecht.

9.8a Female Puppet. Ogoni. Wood and pigment. H: 53.3 cm. FMCH X67.608; Gift of the Wellcome Trust. The Ogoni borrowed the art of puppetry from the Ibibio, adapting it to fit preexisting patterns of social criticism. This puppet depicts a young girl going through the initiation process. During this period adolescent females are pampered and fed rich foods to enhance their appearance and assure their health and fertility.

9.8b Side view of figure 9.8a.

In some cases the demise of a particular masquerade may be due to missionary impact, or it may simply be the result of disenchantment with repetitive performance. Similarly, while trade is a strong disseminator of new and varied styles, some areas prefer to continue with their old traditions, and others thirst for injections of new vitality. This is not a new nor a unique phenomenon. Kenneth Murray (unpublished notes), writing of the Ogoni in the 1930s, said that "it is not easy to get a clear picture of the purpose and organization of the many plays with masks and headdresses. Many plays are said to be defunct, and others probably have changed from their original religious intention to Xmas masquerades. Moreover, the names are confusing in different parts of Ogoni—the same play may have a different name and a different play may have the same name." To complicate matters further, masks carved for one society can sometimes be used for different masquerades in the absence of appropriate mask forms. For example, Salmons observed that many Karikpo masks were used by the Nu-alu Society for the New Yam celebrations in Tai in 1992 (figs. 9.10–9.12).

9.9 Karikpo Mask. Ogoni. Wood, pigment, and metal tacks in ornamental pattern. H: 64.8 cm. Iris and B. Gerald Cantor Center for Visual Arts at Stanford University; 1992.193 Museum purchase, with funds realized through the deaccession and sale of gifts from Mr. and Mrs. Kenneth Christensen, Dr. E. J. Howell, Mr. and Mrs. Edward Knowlton, Mrs. Charlotte Mack, Richard and Shirley Umhoefer, and in memory of Pamela Djerassi Class of 1971 by her parents.

9.10 Small face masks worn for Nu-alu masquerade, New Yam festival. Photograph by Jill Salmons, Tai, 1992.

9.11 Nu-alu masqueraders, New Yam festival. Photograph by Jill Salmons, between Ue-eken and Korokoro, Tai, 1992.

9.12 Nu-alu masquerader, New Yam festival.
Photograph by Jill Salmons, Tai, 1992.

The Ka-elu or Ka-eru masquerade found in Babbe, Tai, and Gokana, however, appears to be a truly indigenous play performed for fertility purposes prior to the New Yam festival (figs. 9.13, 9.14). Although some villages abandoned the play long ago, others, such as E-eke, perform it biannually. At the Ka-elu performance at E-eke in July 1992, more than twenty masqueraders, representing the different families in the town, paraded and visited family compounds in order to bring blessings from the ancestors and dispel evil spirits. Every afternoon a public performance was held in the town square, where each masker was accompanied by a retinue of small boys. The costume consisted of a voluminous robe covering the body and head of the wearer, surmounted by a cap mask in the form of a seated or standing figure; some of these were decorated by radiating feather rods. Each figure represented a particular family, in varying forms such as a beautiful woman, a chief, or a fisherman. Under the cloth costume, tied round the buttocks, was a structure that when manipulated by agitated dancing gave the impression of a twitching tail. All performers carried a decorative paddle, which was used to accentuate the sweeping movements of the masqueraders' arms. Interspersed with these elegant, stately dancers were other masqueraders wearing face masks. These included Borgogara, representing a debtor being dragged along by his creditors, Gberegbere with large eyes and open mouth, said to dispel the unseen evil spirits mingling in the crowd and help check adultery, and Teebee, an aggressive character chasing and attacking noninitiates, hence keeping the younger generation in check. The large crowds evident at this festival confirmed the beliefs expressed to us by the title holders and elders that the performances are important not only in paying homage to the spirit of the wife of the founder of the town but also in ensuring the fertility of crops, livestock, and people. Chief J. Barile Subeesua Katah, Mene-bue of E-eke, said they also help maintain community harmony by periodically attracting the youth to return from their modern lifestyles in the cities and participate in the traditional beliefs and values of the home community.

*9.13 Ka-elu masquerade. Photograph by Jill Salmons,
E-eke, Babbe, 1992.*

9.14 Ka-elu masquerade. Photograph by Jill Salmons, E-eke, Babbe, 1992.

*9.15 Carver Samuel Mbakin Akpakpa of Ue-eken, Tai, with Karikpo masks.
Photograph by Jill Salmons, 1992.*

Another, relatively peaceful masquerade, utilizing a classic form of Ogoni hinged-jaw face mask, small and painted white, is called Koromum. One performance, at the village of Taabaa, witnessed by Sarah Travis Cobb in 1990, represented gentle-natured, high-status individuals of either sex. According to their spokesman, the dance was revealed to the villagers by spirits at the time of the transatlantic trade, and they have performed it ever since. The dancers wore rich, brightly colored textile costumes combined with a thick horseshoe-shaped belt of raffia, a raffia neckpiece, and a raffia headpiece culminating in a knot at the top of the mask with feathers inserted into the topknot. They carried items denoting wealth, including mirrors and fans, and danced with well-articulated steps. The lead masker carried a small skin box containing potions that allowed him to detect hostile medicines. He wore a small black hat to indicate that he was a native doctor and had face painting reminiscent of that worn by such specialists when consulting the spirits. The leaders of the play explained that "the society we try to present is the ideal in the sense that everybody in it is presented as either beautiful or handsome and very trendy and they love one another" (Cobb 1995, ch. 4, 116). The Koromum Society also performed in order to instruct women on correct public behavior and to reveal offenses perpetrated by particular women. Kpone-Tonwe was told that Koromum and Amanikpo maintain mutual respect for each other as they are both regulatory societies.

The mask style for which the Ogoni are probably most renowned is that known as Karikpo (Babbe), Kanikpo (Tai), or Zammo (Gokana). The Karikpo mask (fig. 9.15) represents a mammal and is worn on the front of the face. It is used for an acrobatic play performed nowadays for recreational purposes throughout the year, but originally it was employed in association with the planting and harvesting of crops in order to ensure fertility. A special drum, known as Kere Karikpo is utilized, and a "run" set up in an appropriate place to allow the masqueraders to perform feats of great agility and bravado—cartwheels, jumps, and backward and forward somersaults. Individual members wear masks representing specific bush animals, especially species of deer (fig. 9.16), but also domestic animals such as goats, dogs, and sheep. Some antelope masks have antlers up to three feet tall, which means that the wearer has to jump spectacularly high in order to execute somersaults. Each animal will act according to character, shaking its head, pawing the ground, perhaps unpredictably charging the crowd—thus creating lively entertainment. According to Court Fornaa, a master carver from Nyokwiri Boue (fig. 9.17), the *nam* (cow) appears last in the sequence of Karikpo characters, and the *nam* masquerader has to be a particularly accomplished acrobat in the Karikpo interpretation of a wild, uncontrollable bush cow, or buffalo (personal communication, 1992).

Annual holidays, in particular Christmas and the New Year, allow those working in Port Harcourt or further afield to travel home. A number of masquerade groups have been formed for such annual entertainment, and they too can be asked to perform for visiting dignitaries or at state festivals. One such group is Kanutete, created by the carver Nwinwin in Bodo Town and rehearsed in his compound. For this play he has carved a series of face masks representing various village types. Most of the masks are painted brown or black and have sad, often grotesque, faces. They wear ragtag costumes and dance alone, often engaging in aimless activities; they are meant to evoke the ill health or misfortune that can befall any person. Masks shown to

9.16 Karikpo mask. Ogoni. Wood. H: 61.5 cm. FMCH X75.912; Gift of Helen and Dr. Robert Kuhn.

9.17 Carver Court Fornaa, Nyokwiri Boue, Babbe, with carving of Mami Wata. Photograph by Jill Salmons, 1992. This carving is presently in the collection of the Horniman Museum, Forest Hill, London.

9.18 Possible Nwe-e mask of the Ekpo Society. Ogoni. Wood, pigment, kaolin, plant fiber, and cord. H: 40 cm. FMCH X73.381; Museum Purchase. In some areas, a bloodthirsty character known as Nwe-e, "The executioner," appears in Ekpo masquerades, which the Ogoni borrowed from their neighbors. Ekpo masks bring the dead to life, including the ghosts of those who have led disreputable lives. The executioner usually wears a small white face mask, slashes at plantain stands, and calls on the rest of the maskers to complete the destruction.

Kpone-Tonwe in 1998 included caricatures such as "Poke Nose," representing a nosy character, and "Policeman," suggesting the oppressive side of the law.

While the mask forms discussed above represent a relatively passive, calm side of Ogoni life, a large proportion of masquerades concern masculine strength and aggression (figs. 9.18, 9.19). In some villages certain masks are kept for specific regulatory purposes. For example, in Kala-Oko is found Nwiiyor Naabana, a masquerade group that is brought out by the elders to curse people who steal, commit adultery, or do not pay the correct bride price. In Kono Boue a masquerader called Awugbo was used until the 1950s to chase and punish womanizers. The mask has a hollow container on top of the head into which the guilty person would be required to place appeasement offerings. In 1990 Chief Matthew Tonwe, Mene-bue of Kono Boue, ordered that the mask be hung from the neck of a proven thief, who was then paraded naked, in great humiliation, around the village before being publicly flogged. Duu was a Tai masquerade used in the past when a person was accused of a serious crime, such as theft or killing. It would accompany the accused person to be tried by the village court. Similarly a mask representing a crocodile, Paa, was used in court cases.

The Ikpong masquerade, as reported by both Degbara Vencent Nwinunu and Cobb, is held during the first week of October in Kpaen village to honor the god Yogoro, patron of the village and of all fishing localities of the region. According to Nwinunu (1982, 10), the purpose of the masquerade is to keep the town "intact and stable." This entails a single masquerader visiting all the important compounds in Kpaen, where he will be offered drink and money. Thus the relationship between the important families of the town and Yogoro is reaffirmed. The masquerader is accompanied by young male spectators wearing makeshift costumes, including hats (preferably of military type), and brandishing machetes; these attendants most importantly respond to the masquerader's specific acts of aggression with gruesome facial gestures. Yogoro's violent nature, underlined by the incorporation of skulls into the mask headdress, is manifested in the underlying fear that the masquerader may run amok. The elders see the performance as a mock battle in which the young men prepare to become warriors.

It is not the intention of the carvers of Ikpong masks to evoke a specific animal, but, rather, the concept of "the beast." Such a creation may, however, possess the characteristics of, say, an elephant. Ikpong presents a sinister sight, even if one is unaware of the two human skulls hidden in the basketry headdress. The mask is approximately three feet high, while the canoe-shaped basketry headdress is more than seven feet wide. A large gaping, irregularly shaped hole signifies the mouth, and the nose is deformed. Suspended from the rear of Ikpong's costume hang three animal skins—two of antelope and one of a brindled carnivore (perhaps a civet cat). In stark contrast to the gruesome mask, the masquerader wears a sporty costume of clean white, loose-fitting short trousers, an ivory bracelet, and matching ivory bands around the upper calves. Ikpong behavior is similarly oppositional—its actions are in turn controlled and erratic, benign and dangerous (Nwinunu 1982).

The society known as Zim or Zimpie (Babbe) is called Zimko among the Tai and Gimko among the Gokana; and in each place it differs greatly in form, function, and social importance (fig. 9.20). According to village elders in Babbe, Zimpie has existed from the founding of the village. It is played once every five years to correspond with the cultivation of the piece of land that was first cultivated by the village founder, Gbene Baligboro. Before the masqueraders can perform in the public square, they practice for thirty-five days in the forest. On performance days, bamboo poles are placed at the entrances and exits of the town square to exclude noninitiates. Sacrifices are made at three main village shrines to ask for peace and order, many children, and successful harvests. The first masked figure to appear is Ikarakop, who represents a spirit of the dead. It acts as comic relief to inspire fear in the young but laughter in the adults. It is also said to counter the forces of death. The masquerader is dressed like a corpse, with the whole body encased in a straight, stiff mat. Ikarakop visits all compounds in the village and expects gifts of food and drink in return for blessings from the ancestors.

After this has been done a public performance takes place in the village square. The leader of the masquerade is called Zimsin. He wears a headdress that incorporates a male and a female human skull representing the first sacrificial victims of Gbene Kote, another founding father. From his costume are hung live chickens, together with fish and pepper; he carries a spear. Sarazim represents the oldest son of the spirits, while a gruesome mask called Ii-neezim, or "Corpse of the ancestor," represents people who have died of a swelling or otherwise disfiguring disease, and whose bodies have been thrown into the "bad bush." Such a mask is reddened with camwood and wears a red cap. Alokpo, or "The provost," is the masquerader who pursues any noninitiate who has violated the laws of the Society. He is greatly feared and a person so hounded is compelled to become an initiate.

A further mask represents the house of Gbene Kote called Kotekaranwaa. This character carries a traditional stool on his shoulder and drops it periodically to indicate that he is tired. At this public performance a member can indicate his wish to initiate his eldest son into the Society, but this only occurs if the child has already undergone the Yaa ceremony. The father will provide large quantities of palm wine, which will be poured into a ceremonial palm wine pot, Yere Moiikane, from which all members drink. As the masquerade concerns the well-being of the whole community, each compound is expected to provide a masquerader. If there is no suitable young person to wear the mask, someone from another family has to be found. If not, on the first day of the performance, Alokpo will go to their

9.19 Mask showing a face surmounted by a skull resting on a title stool. Ogoni. Wood, bamboo, and fiber. H: 31.1 cm. Seattle Art Museum 81.17.536; Gift of Katherine White and the Boeing Company. Photograph by Paul Macapia. This mask may indicate that the wearer is a warrior title holder who has performed feats of bravery to achieve his title stool.

compound and slash down branches of plantain pending spiritual consequences of their disobedience. Apart from this five-year cycle, once a year the spirit of Gbene Kote is approached in order to allow the leader of Zimpie to move around the village and make necessary sacrifices. This is the time when the land tenancy agreements are reinforced, and after this ceremony has been conducted, a person is not allowed to use rented land until more money has been pledged.

As a child, Kpone-Tonwe was fortunate enough to observe a unique masquerade known as Zimfere, or "Ancestral plates," in the Babbe area. This utilizes an elaborate costume displaying prized family plates and mirrors. According to oral tradition, this play dates back to the time when European trade goods first reached the town of Ko on the Imo River. It was decided to display the delicacy and prestige of such items through performance. The headdress is a flat, shieldlike framework that cleverly holds in place the prized objects. The masquerader, urged on by his various sponsors, has to prove his agility by gliding gracefully around the town square, the body carefully controlled but capable of giving appropriate turns at designated places to thrill the spectators. Accompanying masqueraders include Kotekaranwaa and Imiabeezim, or "Ancestor with a head of fire," who inspires fear while pursuing the crowd and keeping it in check.

Another expression of Ogoni male aggression is the masquerade O-u-o-lu, or "If you want to die, come!" This is still popular in a number of villages throughout the region. Each prominent family within the community is represented by a particular mask. The masks are very large, and many of them have superstructures consisting of stylized skulls. When the masquerade is being performed, there is always one masker who is more dangerous than any other—the one bearing a representation of a dog. This reflects the local perception that dogs are often wicked and dangerous. A group witnessed by Cobb at Bianu Bangha village, Nyokana, in 1990 had masks incorporating representations of hats, mammals, crocodiles, or snakes together with a series of numbers painted on them. An older mask, photographed in the village of

9.20 Zimpie masks. Photograph by Jill Salmons, Kono Boue, Babbe, 1992.

9.21 Ekpo masks. The small white mask represents Nwe-e, the executioner. Photograph by Jill Salmons, Kono Boue, Babbe, 1992.

E-eke had extremely prominent teeth and a protuberant brow and eyelids above hemispherical cheeks. The mask is reminiscent of Ogoni masks used in the early years of this century and published in Talbot (1923, fig. 37). As many as forty members can rampage through a community. The leader, called Adamsi, carries a large bag in which he secretes any fowl or dog having the misfortune to cross his path. The Society is considered to be almost as important as Amanikpo in some areas and comes out at night whenever there is a threat to a community, as well as for the funerals of its members.

Many areas have adopted the Ekpo masquerade from their Ibibio and Anaang neighbors (fig. 9.21), although it has been modified greatly and now fulfils a mostly recreational role at Christmas or at funerals. Most of the face masks are black and fearsome, often with hinged jaws. The masqueraders are led by one of their number called Bii-deesi. In some areas a bloodthirsty character known as Nwe-e, or "The executioner," wears a small white face mask. This masquerader will slash plantain stands and call the rest of the group to complete the destruction. The mother of Ekpo, Ka Ekpo, carries two masks—one worn in the normal manner at the front of the head, the other on the back. Fish, alligator pepper, and live chickens are attached to the costume. If a member of the group dies, the Nwe-e masquerader will come to the deceased's compound and call on all the members to destroy the man's property unless the family gives them appropriate food and drink. Like the Ibibio, Ogoni Ekpo masquerades utilize blackened raffia costumes and carry weapons. A combination of Kana and Ibibio language is used for their songs. Some villages have never played Ekpo, while others have abandoned it.

There are some similarities between O-u-o-lu masks and Ekpo masks, particularly their large size and portrayal of aggressive facial features. The main differences, however, are as follows: O-u-o-lu masks are worn on top of the head, rather than as face masks, they tend to be painted in polychrome, in contrast to black, and characteristically the costume is composed of lank natural plant fiber (to European eyes reminiscent of the coat of an Afghan hound), very unlike the dyed black raffia and cloth costume of most Ekpo masqueraders. The manner in which O-u-o-lu masks are worn deserves special comment here. Sometimes they are worn horizontally on top of the head, sometimes at an angle of around forty-five degrees with the weight apparently resting on the forehead. In speculative art historical terms, it is as though the O-u-o-lu masks of the Ogoni represent a transitional type between the forward-facing ancestor masks of land-based peoples such as the Anaang and the sky-facing water spirit masks of the Delta peoples such as the Ijo.

A further example of the Ogoni talent of adapting the art of other peoples for their own needs is that of Amanikpo, the Ogoni secret society, which represents the power and will of the ancestral spirits and utilizes puppets (figs. 9.22, 9.23). In the course of researching Ogoni oral history, Kpone-Tonwe found evidence for the existence of many traditional male associations, including Kpaankpaan, Teekara, and Koromum, in precolonial times. Some of these "secret societies" performed, among other things, the function of social criticism, drawing the attention to certain trends in the community or to innovations happening elsewhere. The members were keen observers of individuals, groups, and events and would employ the media of music and satirical song to convey criticism or praise. As a form of social control such societies effectively curbed outrageous or antisocial behavior and exposed potentially dangerous political skullduggery. Customarily, members were not liable to revenge, litigation, or punishment as it was believed that they were simply conduits of the ancestral spirits, *elu*, and were therefore not personally responsible. As further proof of their spirit nature, they disguised their voices, and their sayings were attributed to the Society, not to individuals.

In 1998, Kpone-Tonwe was told by Inatura Inayo, incumbent chief of Gbene Kote house, Kono Boue, that puppet art was introduced into Ogoniland by Akara Kote, a medicine man who was a frequent traveler to Ibibioland. There he witnessed a puppet performance, paid the necessary fees to become a member, and on learning the secret techniques of manipulating the puppets and the accompanying songs, returned home and taught his own people. Legend states that on a subsequent visit to Ibibioland he was murdered for having divulged the secrets of the club. However, in Tai in 1992, Salmons was told by Chief Mican Gbii of Kpaen, Tai, that his great-grandfather Kaala Legbanwaa had first brought Amanikpo from the Ibibio. Kaala, a trader in palm oil with Ukanafon (an Anaang village), was initiated into the Society, and on returning home and telling his people what a powerful society it was, he was sent back to collect further knowledge of it for them. His name is always called first in libations at the beginning of a performance. Augustus Karanwa of Kpaen insisted that "we changed it to playing in the night. What makes Amanikpo so powerful is its secrets—it is far more powerful than over there." He compared it to someone who has trained as a bicycle repairer and has the sense to go on and build a car: "Ibibio is the bicycle, Ogoni is the car!"

Confusingly, the name Amanikpo is a bastardization of the Ibibio term "*aman* Ekpo," which means to "play" or "perform" Ekpo, the ancestral spirits. Several informants claimed that Amanikpo "is called Ekpo over there" (i.e., in Ibibioland). However, while the Ibibio Ekpo ancestral society performs dramatic visual representations of the ancestors in the form of masqueraders, it does not employ puppets. The Anaang and Ibibio do, however, have the Ekong puppet play, which exposes moral transgressors to public ridicule.

9.22 Amanikpo Society puppets in performance at the funeral of a Kono Boue elder. Photograph by Sarah Travis Cobb, Kono Boue, 1987.

9.23 Female puppet with mortar and pestle. Probably Ibibio. Wood and pigment. H: 33 cm. FMCH X67.606; Gift of the Wellcome Trust. This appealing female puppet may represent a young wife or daughter. Visitors to Delta villages are likely to see women using mortars to prepare food. We can only guess how this activity might have figured into the plot of the performance in which this character appeared.

It is this aspect of Ibibio culture that the Ogoni grafted onto their existing institutions, and the name of the puppets, Amanikpo, has, over time, come to represent a virtually Ogoni-wide, all-encompassing, regulatory society.

The earliest known visual record of Ogoni puppets is a photograph taken by J. A. Green at Bonny in 1899 (Jones 1984, 174), which shows what appears to be a mixture of Ibibio and Ogoni carvings (fig. 9.24). The Glasgow Art Gallery and Museum has a pair of figures collected by Fleet Surgeon J. Neil Robertson, who in 1903/1904 had been a member of a punitive expedition in the Bonny River area, intended to "stamp out cannibalism." These "talking jujus," as they are described in the register, "were involved in cannibal ceremonies and confiscated." As Jacobs has written:

9.24 *Photograph of Ibibio and Ogoni carvings, taken by J. A. Green of Bonny, 1899. Private Collection.*

9.25 *Ogoni puppet collected by Brabazon Rees during a punitive raid into Ogoni territory conducted by the British Army in 1913. The Manchester Museum, The University of Manchester, 0.8306.*

[T]he figures are ingenious. The limbs are attached to the torso with nails, the head articulated at the neck, and the lower jaw articulated on the head, made to move by pushing up and down a stick fastened to the chin and passing down a hole burned through the torso to the base [figs. 9.26a,b]. The flaring, pronounced lips open to reveal carved teeth. The figure illustrated has copper studs for eyes and is painted yellow, with hat, features, and torso motifs in black and lips in red. The other one, also yellow, has a hat of a slightly European appearance. The figures are probably Ogoni. [Jacobs 1986, 37–38]

P. A. Talbot was a district officer in the Eket area of southeast Nigeria in the years immediately before the First World War. Tantalizingly, he (1923, ch. 6) gives a lengthy description of the Ekong play, which he calls "Akan," performed by the Ibibio, but he makes no mention of the Ogoni puppets or masks that he photographed at the same time. He also describes Utughu, the spider play, which includes the performance of two masked acrobats suspended from a network of cords. The photograph that he took (Talbot 1923, facing p. 80), however, not only shows the two masked Utughu figures suspended from ropes but also, below the ropes, a puppet booth of the type that the Ogoni and Ibibio still use to this day.

In 1913 Captain Brabazon Rees of the British army took part in a punitive raid into Ogoni territory (fig. 9.25). He described coming across a "juju house" and wrote the following:

9.26a Female puppet. Ibibio. Wood and pigment. H: 49.5 cm. FMCH X65.9036; Gift of the Wellcome Trust. Although her grimace gives her a more forbidding appearance than the character seen in figures 9.8a,b, this puppet also represents a young girl who has completed initiation rites and is ready for marriage.

9.26b Side view of figure 9.26a.

The door was decorated with human heads and the inside was a miniature theatre with a grass screen where we should have the curtain. Behind the screen was the part of the hut where the juju man worked. In the roof I found some dolls, 2 smallish jujus with movable jaws (which open and shut their mouths when a piece of wood or grass is pulled), rolled up in banana leaves and hidden in the roof behind the screen. One of the dolls was intended, apparently, to shoot poisoned darts. In the banana leaf with the doll was a little bow and some arrows, apparently poisoned, constructed from the rib of a palm branch. The masks were found in another hut. [Rees 1913]

These items are now on display in the Manchester University Museum. While it cannot be guaranteed that these are Amanikpo puppets or that the juju house (which was later burnt down) was an Amanikpo house, it does confirm that puppets were kept with care and secrecy in the most important building in the village. Kpone-Tonwe believes that during this period the puppets were used as a means of subtle communication and protest against the colonial authorities. The puppets accused the colonial administrators of arrogantly pretending to be like the ancestral gods, Zim or Jim, who would not speak except through an interpreter. The British district officers were depicted by a puppet with a long nose and neck, wearing a high-crowned pith helmet and bandolier, and they were nicknamed Jim—a name that over the years has also come to represent the Society (fig. 9.27).

9.27 Mask of a foreigner. Ogoni. Wood, pigment, and fiber. H: 23.5 cm. FMCH X86.1096; Gift in Memory of Barbara Jean Jacoby. Although long-nosed, pith-helmeted British District Officers appear in Ogoni puppet performances, masks depicting European characters are quite rare. Elsewhere in Africa, masks of this type often mock the peculiar behaviors of foreigners, and one suspects that this one did likewise.

In 1931 M. D. W. Jeffreys produced an "Intelligence Report on the Ogoni" in which he wrote the following:

> The Amarikpo club is the most important and seems to include several branches (in different towns). When the yams were planted the sacrifice was to the Amarikpo juju; and the head member sat in a glade at the entrance to the town and seized as victims the people who passed along the road. There appears to have been no limit to the number of sacrifices at that time. In nearly all the towns, especially in those mentioned above, human skulls quite fresh were found, especially at Biara which was burnt down. This town was one of the principal centres of the Amarikpo club. The idols consisted of dolls about 2–3 ft. high painted white and well carved. The lower jaw moves by means of a string passing through the centre of the figure. When the mouth is open it displays long teeth painted white, made of pieces of bamboo, the teeth about an inch long. These figures are placed in rows and work like a marionette from underneath a table or bench and were made to speak, eat, etc. at the will of the operator hidden from public view. The club is a very new acquisition of the Ogoni people and was imported from the Ibibio with whom they have intercourse. [Jeffreys 1931]

When Murray conducted his research in the thirties the Society was called Ewanikpo in Babbe, Amanikpo in Tai, and Gbogim in Gokana. He described it as an important ancient play whose members had to be wealthy and noted that the performance consisted of puppets, eighteen inches high, with hinged jaws manipulated from behind a seven-foot-high curtain. At Nonwa the curtain was seven yards long, and there were fifteen figures.

In the 1990s, although in some areas the Society was virtually defunct, in other areas it still held a strong position, both as a regulatory society and as an expression of traditional beliefs. The people of Eleme, however, claim that they never had Amanikpo. The Society often performs its regulatory role without a puppet performance. For example, if the elders want communal work to be done and a person refuses to participate, members of the Society will go to that person's house at night and seize his property until he conforms. At Biara it was said that Amanikpo justice is preferred to that of the government. Therefore, if a youth commits a crime and is a member of the Society, he will be dealt with by Amanikpo rather than by the police. In this village young men are still very keen to join, and most men still initiate their first-born son, even if they are Christian. Well-respected elderly women are also given token membership, though they are not allowed to know the secrets of the puppet mechanism. According to Chief J. S. Yaadag, Tesi Mene of Sii, Babbe, even though Amanikpo was introduced from the Ibibio, it became more powerful than the indigenous Kpaankpaan. In the case of a serious transgressor, Amanikpo members would order the Kpaankpaan to carry out his execution. To this day, in Kaa, Salmons was told by Chief Douglas Yorkirika that if a woman insults another woman, especially referring to her sexual organs, complaint can be lodged with the Society. Amanikpo will force the woman who is accused of delivering the insult to pay a fine of money and illicit gin, and if found guilty, she has to provide a goat sufficiently large to allow you to "put your fingers up its nose," together with twenty yams, a bunch of plantain, jar of palm wine, jar of *kaikai*, and one hundred *naira*, "so that you will never curse someone's private parts again."

9.28 Nkoo Society booth. Photograph by Jill Salmons, Barako, Gokana, 1992.

The use of a booth for the performance of singing, dancing, and satirical plays would appear to be widespread in the region, though not always under the aegis of Amanikpo or accompanied by puppets. In the 1930s Murray described a performance at Yeghe: "Anuwe is an Ogoni club. Here the younger members are singing behind a cloth stretched across the end of a compound. The host and his friends sit in front of the cloth and drink palmwine and talk" (unpublished notes). The photograph accompanying this description shows a row of hinged-jaw masks appearing above the screen. In 1992, at Barako, Gokana, villagers constructed an Nkoo house (fig. 9.28), very similar in appearance to an Amanikpo booth, made of cloth with a superstructure on which there was a carved angel. In the case of theft or transgression of certain taboos within the community, some Nkoo members would sing about it from within the house, while others would dance in front; puppets or masks were not utilized. While they had not performed Amanikpo in this village for nearly twenty years, a young carver had been asked to produce a set of puppets with the intention of using them that autumn.

The puppet performance traditionally takes place at night, when between nine and sixteen puppet characters appear on top of a twelve-foot-high screen of cloth that hides both the puppeteers and the musicians. Sometimes the cloth constitutes a single piece of material, but normally it consists of individual cloths contributed by the members who have possession of the puppets. In the Tai region Chief Philip Naah of Korokoro explained that the first puppet to come out is called Kasi and that it has a treble voice. The alto is called Tuagere, the tenor Akee, and the bass Kadume. The "voices" of the puppets are created by using a small piece of bamboo covered with a thin membrane of bat's wing, which when blown sounds like a kazoo or paper-and-comb. In Kono Boue, Babbe, the most important puppet is called Awolo, the "royal" masquerader. It resembles a skull with large white teeth, black mouth and ears, and feathers radiating from the top of the head. Awolo's wife carries a mirror in one hand and a knife in the other. Other puppets represent an elderly person, a python, a young girl undergoing prenuptial fattening (figs. 9.29a,b), a palm-wine tapper, and other recognizable types. The puppets are manipulated by a

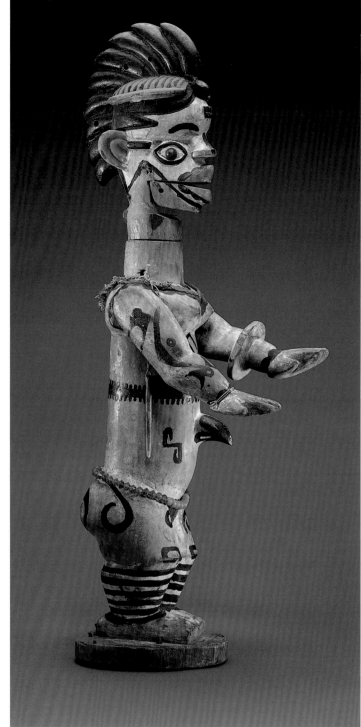

9.29a Female puppet. Ibibio. Wood, pigment, and beads. H: 66 cm. FMCH X67.607a,b; Gift of the Wellcome Trust. The elaborate coiffure, ornaments, and body painting seen on this puppet indicate that it is intended to represent another young female initiate poised at the threshold of marriage and motherhood (cf. figs. 9.8a.b and 9.26a,b).

9.29b Side view of figure 9.29a.

stick through which strings are passed to allow the articulation of the lower jaws and limbs so that they can be made to dance, shoot guns, cut off heads, copulate, and perform various amusing feats. Many of the heads of the puppets are surmounted by black-and-white feather rods to enhance the dramatic effect.

The overall format and style of the play does not appear to have changed a great deal since the time when Jeffreys and Murray witnessed it. Formerly the performance could not take place unless a human being had been sacrificed, and to this day the cost of the various animals and drink demanded by its members makes performances infrequent. Nowadays it is most often performed at funeral celebrations for an important personage. In 1992, in Tai, a young boy had just been initiated by his father who contributed a goat, a chicken, *kaikai*, three yams, a bunch of plantain, and three thousand *naira*.

The three main occasions when those Amanikpo groups still maintaining puppets bring them out are: to celebrate the success of an important member, when one of their number dies, and at the time of the second burial celebrations.

In Kono Boue, however, Amanikpo is played every June, for it is believed that if it is not performed, the village will suffer. Recognizing the entertainment aspect of the performance, the Amanikpo puppet play is performed for visiting dignitaries, both political and religious. The encouragement of local and national festivals of the arts has led to some Amanikpo puppet plays being toured to other parts of the country, for example, Amanikpo from Kpite, Tai, had performed in Kaduna, Northern Nigeria, and a photograph of the performance appears in a primary school textbook. In such cases, however, absolute secrecy concerning the methods of working the puppets is still maintained.

People in the community are alerted as to when there will be a performance by the sounding of a wooden gong, though recently announcements have also been made on local radio. At Kpite they play three metal gongs and a special horn that is made to resound within a pot. Everyone will converge on the village field next to the Amanikpo house where the puppet booth is erected. Music and singing can be performed inside the booth without the puppets coming out, but when they do, they represent all walks of human life as well as animals. Although both women and men are represented, the puppets do not represent specific persons but are, rather, stereotypes. Gbene or other title holders, however, are never depicted. Members take turns manipulating puppets to represent different characters, and sometimes the play can last several hours. Members dance outside the booth and nonmembers also dance, though they are not allowed to go into the booth or the clubhouse. New songs are invented every year.

Several large villages have more than one Amanikpo house. The Gokana clan head comes from the founding family of Amanikpo in that area, and any village seeking to set up a new Amanikpo house has to seek permission directly from him. If a child is born while Amanikpo is playing, the child is taken to a shrine and various rituals are performed to ascertain whether the child is disturbed by Amanikpo spirits. If it is determined to be, the child will then be called Amanikpo. Amanikpo is thought to be particularly powerful in cases of witchcraft and sorcery. Any villager using a charm against another would be exposed by the Society who would also destroy his compound. This close connection with sorcery has made the Society a particular target of various Christian churches. Whereas Christians are allowed to belong to a number of indigenous societies, the Roman Catholic church, for example, excommunicates its members if they are found to be Amanikpo adherents. Sometimes it would appear that although theoretically they are under the control of the elders, young Amanikpo members can get out of hand. Chief O. B. Nalelo, J. P., Menebua bokpo of Biare, Gokana, said in 1992:

> I am often in disagreement with them [Amanikpo members]. They always try to force youths to become members. When we saw they were too powerful, the chiefs came together and made a rule and took it to the government for support. When they started their singing, we would give them time to start and stop but even then they broke the rules. There is not much the government can do since they are not there to check them—the chiefs have to do that instead—then they can be punished through the civil courts not the village ones.

However, another instance proves how powerful Amanikpo can still be. A local secondary school had experienced serious fighting between pupils,

9.30 *Mami Wata figure, sculpted in clay by Christopher Miige. Photograph by Jill Salmons, 1992.*

and even the principal had been physically assaulted. The principal appealed to the chief, and twelve boys were taken in handcuffs to the civil courts. But the parents who belonged to the Amanikpo Society went to the chief and demanded a goat, yams, and cocks for interfering. He was forced to agree, and the boys were freed, amongst much controversy (personal communication, Gbenetee James Booburah, Kono Boue, 1992). The ultimate fine for a transgression against Amanikpo is a goat, although it is said that in the past an offender might lose his or her life.

Although the majority of Ogoni rituals concern recognition of the ancestors, the growing of crops, and rearing of animals, there are numerous examples of the significance of water to the Ogoni (fig. 9.30). As might be expected from long-term trading with Bonny, Opobo, and Okrika, many masquerades have been introduced from the coastal region. True water spirit masquerades are prevalent among coastal Ogoni villages and under the generic term *owu*, though villages often have specific names for such plays. For example masquerades incorporating large masks—mostly worn horizontally on top of the masker's head and representing various types of marine creatures—are popular in the waterside towns of Bodo and Kono (fig. 9.31). At Kono an annual play called Legbo incorporates the usual horizontal masks but also involves the participants paddling to a place believed to be the home of the water spirit and making sacrifices at the shrine of "Down Below," a site at the mouth of the Imo River. A white chicken is sacrificed, and generally a Mami Wata priestess accompanies the participants to placate the spirits as they emerge from the water. Kono used to perform Anungu, which was introduced from Abonnema or Ahoada and incorporated representations of airplanes, fish, and canoes, together with Mami Wata. They also play Paragad, which employs stilts.

In Kaa, a waterside community destroyed in the Ogoni troubles of 1993, horizontal masks represented fish, crab, tilapia, crocodile, and python. One called Otobo, the hippopotamus, acted in a particularly violent way, being the owner of the sea. They had two shrines for the *owu* spirits, one on land and another, called Gbenegara, at sea, which used to contain carved

9.31 *Girl's troupe with shark masquerade. Photograph by Jill Salmons, Bodo Town, 1992.*

figures. Elders confirmed that they had learned such masquerades from Bonny. In Eleme the most important cultural play is called Nkpaa Egoni; it utilizes horizontal masks portraying fish, mammals, and birds. Several coastal villages play variations of Nwaatam, thought to have originated among the Ndokki and performed annually in Opobo Town. The leading masquerader, dressed in black and wearing a cap mask in the form of a stylized human head, jumps on rooftops and performs in a generally unruly manner. At Kpaen, Nwaatam is celebrated every Christmas and New Year's Day. Before the performance members go to the forest where they sacrifice a goat and play at night before coming to the edge of the village where food and wine is left to ward off evil spirits. The carver at Kpaen, Dormu Kiko, claimed that whenever he carves a Nwaatam mask, he is disturbed by spirits.

Some of the older carvers still maintained shrines to carving spirits, and they made sacrifices to these spirits before commencing work; but the younger generation of carvers followed no such rituals, though they were all careful to maintain complete secrecy when carving. Although most of the carvers also pursue farming or trading activities as well as carving, several artists make a good living not only by supplying a local clientele but also by working for weeks and sometimes months in the villages of Igbo or Ijo patrons. Nowadays there is a demand for "fantastic" masks and sculptures incorporating representations of subjects as diverse as Mami Wata, the Pope, international football players, and movie stars.

There is ample evidence of Ogoni artists influencing neighboring groups. For example, the young carvers Lenu Naagbiwa of Uegwere (fig. 9.33) and

9.32 *Mask with manilla. Ogoni. Wood, stick, fiber, and pigment. H: 20.6 cm. FMCH X79.81; Gift of Mr. and Mrs. Jon Herman. This mask displays a manilla, a type of metal currency that once circulated in the region, on its headdress. The motif still suggests prosperity, and it may have identified a trader or well-to-do person.*

9.33 *Carver Lenu Naagbiwa of Uegwere Boue, Babbe, with a masquerade headdress composed of two joined figures. This mask was used in* MOSOP *demonstratons as a symbol of Ogoni national identity and strength. Photograph by Jill Salmons, Birabii. 1992.*

Kponanyie Tornyie Deekor of Barako (fig. 9.34) spend several months each year carving for Igbo groups including Etche and Ndokki. In addition, Naaregbene of Zaakpon has carved in both Bonny and Ikwere districts. Bodo has strong links with the town of Tiko in western Cameroon, and a number of Ogoni carvers spoke of having carved for different ethnic communities living there, including Yoruba and Igbo from Nigeria, as well as various Cameroonian groups. Our view that long-standing stylistic links have existed between the sculpture of the Ogoni and that of coastal Cameroon is corroborated by certain findings in Ros Wilcox's fieldwork in western Cameroon (see Wilcox, forthcoming).

In spite of ecological problems facing the Ogoni during the period that fieldwork was undertaken by Cobb and Salmons—during the late 1980s and early 1990s respectively—mass participation in and enjoyment of myriad masquerade forms was palpable. At this time, understandably, the Ogoni had developed great bitterness toward the oil industry in general and Shell International in particular, as well as the federal government, because little of the wealth gained by oil exploitation over more than three decades was perceived to have been redistributed to Ogoniland. Discontent that had been steadily rising throughout the 1980s expressed itself finally in a popular movement led by Ken Saro-Wiwa, the Movement for the Survival of the Ogoni People (MOSOP). Saro-Wiwa was a well-known writer, recognized particularly for his biting satirical television soap opera, *Basi & Co.,* a modern version, if ever, of Amanikpo puppetry!

According to Kpone-Tonwe, in the late 1980s Saro-Wiwa was influenced by Kpone-Tonwe's studies of Ogoni history, particularly as

9.34 "Beast" mask carved by Kponanyie Tornyie Deekor of Barako, Gokana. Photograph by Jill Salmons, 1992.

focused on traditional youth organizations. When Saro-Wiwa drew up his blueprint for the National Youth Council of the Ogoni People (NYCOP), he successfully applied the principles and methods used by Ogoni secret societies, particularly Amanikpo, to mobilize his people, whom he referred to as the "Shell-shocked" Ogoni, against the company of that name. Just as the Ogoni, through the mouths of Amanikpo puppets, had once opposed colonial officials, so NYCOP, which had in effect become the activist arm of MOSOP, exposed Shell, the Nigerian Government, and those Ogoni chiefs who had collaborated to strong criticism.

Tragically, in 1993–1995 this led to reprisals by government forces, including the widespread destruction of villages and imprisonment and subsequent infamous hanging of nine MOSOP leaders, including Saro-Wiwa. As Ashton-Jones, the last westerner allowed to conduct research in the area before the atrocities, noted, MOSOP "is the prime focus of hope in people's lives and the one positive thing in a modern society that is careless of them: the people are proud to belong to the movement and the Ogoni anthem is often sung" (Ashton-Jones 1995, 34). Video recordings made by Saro-Wiwa before his imprisonment have been used in a number of documentary programs broadcast worldwide in recent years. These show masquerades accompanying jubilant crowds attending MOSOP rallies, reinforcing Ogoni identity and demonstrating the continuing pride that the people justly have in their rich cultural heritage. It is to be hoped that this brave nation will soon be allowed to resume a life free from persecution and gross exploitation.

Interleaf K
Obolo Arts

Keith Nicklin

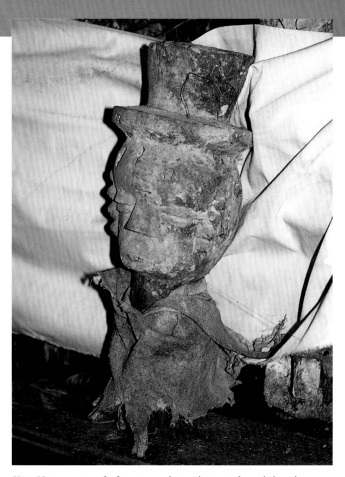

K.1 A libation being poured at the ancestral shrine, Isi Ebikan, of Chief Smith O. E. Arong, Okaan-Obolo of Andoni. A whale skull, and the tusk and tooth of an elephant are situated at the forefront of the altar. This shrine also contains spiral manillas and a large penannular manilla; at the funeral of a prominent person, the former would be worn by women, and the latter would be worn around the neck of a man. Photograph by Keith Nicklin, Ngo-Andoni, 1992.

K.2 Upper portion of a figurative sculpture that must formerly have been about 70 cm high and once formed part of the Isi Ebikan Ogboyok Edeh shrine. Vertical rows of scarification appear on the center of the forehead and at either temple, and the figure wears a Victorian-style top hat. Photograph by Keith Nicklin, 1992.

K.3 Isi Ebikan Okpangwung Edeh displayed on the verandah of a house. It consists of four skull frames commemorating deceased male elders and a line of wooden sticks in honor of deceased women. Decoration with white pigment and white cloth is conducted in the course of annual rites. Placed on the ground in front of the sacred objects is a large penannular manilla. Photograph by Keith Nicklin, 1992.

With the notable exception of N. C. Ejituwu's book (1991) on the history of his own people, very little indeed has been published about the Obolo, who have long been called the Andoni by Europeans. Together with their neighbors the Ibino, the Obolo were classified as Delta Ibibio by G. I. Jones (1988, 467ff) and described as "an ancient Ibibio cultural division which has today largely disappeared." They occupy the foreshore, mangrove swamp, and forest between the Andoni and Qua Ibo Rivers, south of Ogoniland. The Imo River divides their territory into two, the western portion lying in Rivers State, the eastern in Akwa Ibom. I visited the area in 1992.

Throughout the segmentary lineages comprising village communities in Obolo today, Isi Ebikan, the household shrine of the ancestors, is of central importance (fig. K.1). This shrine usually comprises the skulls of animals sacrificed in honor of the deceased; these skulls are preserved in a canework frame and decorated with white pigment (fig. K.3). Goat, sheep, and cow skulls predominate, and wild species including crocodile and antelope occur as well. I also found fragments of wooden carvings representing women at several Obolo ancestral shrines.

This evidence, combined with statements made by informants, suggests that Obolo female elders were commemorated by sculptures comparable to the Oron Ekpu figures made in honor of deceased male elders (fig. K.2). According to M. D. W. Jeffreys (1930, 100–12), as the Obolo practice matrilineal descent, in contrast to most of their neighbors—including the Oron—who are patrilineal, "it follows that quite a number of the [canework] frames [constituting their Isi Ebikan] are dedicated to women." Significantly, the major diagnostic feature of the Ekpu genre—the depiction of an elongated narrow beard—was absent in respect of the Obolo carvings (Nicklin 1999, 77–92). My own data indicate that racks of animal skulls commemorate Obolo male ancestors, while carved wooden figures or sticks of wood honor female ancestors.

K.4   Carved wooden staffs decorated with camwood and face masks used by the Oka-Uji, "Palm kernel," masquerade. This is performed every January or on the occasion of an elder's death. Photograph by Keith Nicklin, Agwut Obolo, 1992.

K.5   Ikot Ikem, "Mother of crayfish" (i.e., lobster), headdress with representations of fish traps (uket), tilapia (ikop), fishing canoe (uji), periwinkle (ntutut), and crab (uka). Real cockle shells (ikpok urung) are also attached. This headdress, used in an owu masquerade called Ifit Yok, was made by Obolo artist Longjohn Boari and used the previous December. Photograph by Keith Nicklin, Ataba town, 1992.

K.6   Pair of Eriembuu masks representing a bull with horns pointing upward and a cow with drooping horns. Photograph by Keith Nicklin, Ataba town, 1992.

K.7   Ekuku, a face mask representing death that is used in festivals in December and April. Photograph by Keith Nicklin, Ataba town, 1992.

K.8   Butterfly and moth headdresses, Ikpok Ukwa, used in festivals in December and April. Carved by Obolo artist Robert Sunday. Photograph by Keith Nicklin, Ataba town, 1992.

K.9 *Okpan-gun, "First son," face mask by Robert Sunday. Photograph by Keith Nicklin, Ataba town, 1992.*

K.10 *Akamute puppet ensemble at New Agana. The characters, from left to right, are: a male puppet called Ebirien with both hands extended to grasp a bottle and drinking cup, a wobbly head, and an articulated penis; male puppet Okoutokwaa, the "Singer," with a moveable arm so that the slit drum held in the other hand may be beaten; Ada, the first daughter, with orange-colored face and body painting; Ujagoun, "Fine boy," with "been-to" hair parting; a policeman in uniform with peaked cap; Piti, the second daughter with a protuberant decorated navel; Ngagoun, the mother, carrying a market basket on her head. Photograph by Keith Nicklin, 1992.*

The Obolo hold water spirit, or *owu*, masquerades twice annually. Carved headdresses represent mermaid (*egbelegbe*), sawfish (*oki*), crayfish (*ikot*), and other species that fall within the range of Ijo *owu* characters, as well as butterfly (*ikpok ukwa*). Some of these are obtained from the Ogoni, others made by the Obolo (fig. K.8).

The Obolo have a satirical puppet play called Akamute, which is performed in a "house" (*akpatan*), a mobile structure festooned with fine cloth that serves to hide the puppeteers (fig. K.10). The group that I encountered at New Agana had performed recently at funerals in Ngo and Unyengala under the leadership of Chief Okparagun Edeh. A few local artists, including Iwo Ekpukunon, who died in the mid-1980s, made puppets, but otherwise they are commissioned directly from the Ogoni. Of the ensemble seen at New Agana, five were Ogoni in style (though lacking the forward-directed rendition of the legs typical of older Ogoni puppets) and two Anaang. As in the case of Ogoni, Anaang, and Ibibio puppets, those of the Obolo represent stock characters and possess articulated lower jaws and arms. One of Chief Edeh's puppets, known as Ebirien, was said to urinate and fornicate on stage.

Chapter 10 Fitting Farewells: The Fine Art of Kalabari Funerals

JOANNE B. EICHER and

TONYE V. EREKOSIMA

> Among most Southern Nigerian tribes the proper carrying out of the burial ceremonies is the most important duty in life…especially the case in those parts where worship of ancestors is most strongly developed.… Families often impoverish themselves for years in order to give a fitting farewell to an important member.
>
> —Talbot 1926, 469

Among the Delta peoples of Nigeria, the Kalabari Ijo are known for lavish funerals that mark the end of the lives of elders and chiefs with a flourish. This ending honors deceased elders by sending them off to join Kalabari ancestors with the expectation that they will look back with satisfaction and benevolence on their earthly relatives. The Kalabari worldview indicates that there are four categories of the self (Ereks 1973): vital body or flesh (*oju*); the personality or soul (*teme*); spirit or fate and fortune (*so*); and the corpse (*duein*). The physical act of dying is only a transition into a state of being where the self exists as a disembodied energy in the realm of the soul and spirits. The corpse (*buruduein*, or "decaying self") of an elder becomes the medium permitting a transition to membership among the ancestors (*oruduein*, or "potent self") and must therefore be honored appropriately and placated. When a person dies and becomes a corpse, he or she leaves the body behind, merely shifting from one realm to another, and essentially remaining the same in spirit and soul.

"Fitting farewells" among the Kalabari fall into several categories that relate to this belief. In general, anyone who survives into adulthood in Kalabari society is honored with a funeral at which the corpse lies in state on a funeral bed. However, there are certain exceptions; some categories of individuals are believed to have had such a "bitter, bitter death"[1] that it is not fitting for them to lie in state nor to have their lives celebrated. Their deaths are mourned but not marked with public acknowledgment through ritual or ceremony. These cases include children (usually defined as those under fifteen), women who die in childbirth, adults who drown, or anyone who has been identified as a witch (Eicher and Erekosima 1987; Erekosima et al. 1991; Da-Wariboko 1991).[2] The appropriate acknowledgment of death for adults ages fifteen to fifty or sixty[3] years of age, with the above exceptions, is for the corpse to be laid upon a bed of state before burial with no further ado after interment (fig. 10.2). For the death of distinguished chiefs and the king, distinctly different kinds of farewell funerals are observed; these have captured the attention of several writers, including P. Amaury Talbot, who as a British colonial officer assigned to oversee the southern Niger Delta area chronicled the early 1900s. Tonye V. Erekosima et al. (1991) and R. M. C. Da-Wariboko (1991) focus on the special cases of these preeminent citizens who are placed on a mat or on those who have a boat regatta mounted in

10.1 *The first of three rooms prepared for a Kalabari funeral is shown here adorned with the preferred choice of fabrics for the walls and bed: madras plaids from India in burgundy, red, indigo, and white. Photograph by Joanne B. Eicher, Buguma, 1983.*

10.2 *A corpse lying in state on an* ede *(bed) before burial. Photograph by Joanne B. Eicher, Buguma, 1983.*

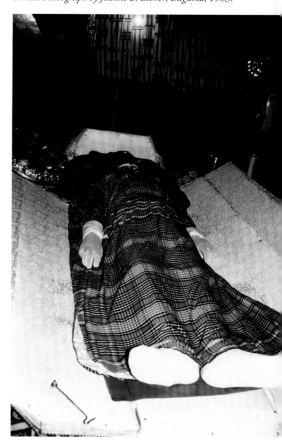

their honor as part of the funeral celebration. In the contemporary world of the Kalabari, however, lavish funerals exist for all esteemed elders, both men and women, and are found almost every weekend on the Kalabari islands.

Background

Funerals for honored elders are glorious festivals celebrating a successful life within the framework of Kalabari beliefs and cultural values. They affirm the bonds of kinship and reintegrate the kin left behind. Each event features dancing, praise singing, drumming, and eating in an ordered sequence over an eight-day period along with the display of family wealth and prestige through the dress, textiles, and jewelry important in Kalabari life. Da-Wariboko, a Kalabari woman writing on funerals, states:

> According to the Kalabari adage, a person once born must live long; sixty years upwards seems the most conceptual ripe age in Kalabari to taste of death. This category is a highly respected and appreciable occasion. It is a merry-making epoch. They are accorded pre- and post-burial wake-keepings where children and relatives exhibit their wealth of acquisition, songs, dances, etc.; coffins and lying-in-state beds (*ede*) are artistically dressed and the corpse finally buried naturally at the cemetery before many sympathizers. (1991, 152)

Who are the Kalabari Ijo who give such attention to the end of life? They are one of the Ijo groups who live on thirty-two islands in the Niger Delta and are known for their savoir faire and fastidiousness in personal dress (Daly, Eicher, and Erekosima 1986; Erekosima and Eicher 1994). The involvement of Kalabari men is key in historical and contemporary funeral celebrations, for they traded overland in Africa before the arrival of the Portuguese in the late 1400s as well as by sea with European merchants after that time. Their overland trade brought textiles and other goods from West African sources: cloth from Ewe weavers in the country now known as Ghana, Yoruba weavers in the western area of Nigeria, and Igbo weavers of the Nigerian town of Akwete, only a few miles north of the Kalabari islands. Their trade by sea provided them access to material goods from faraway places well beyond island boundaries and mangrove swamps: Indian cotton madras plaids and velvets embroidered with silver or gold threads, English printed woolen flannels, fine woolen worsteds, top hats, derbies, canes, and walking sticks, Italian coral and glass beads, and a variety of European shirt styles.

The Kalabari chose, and still choose, many of these articles in regard to color, texture, and general appearance and combine them in unique fashions for dress and funeral customs. They take pride in pulling out old cloth, apparel, and jewelry from their treasure trunks, as well as purchasing new items when needed. They often continue use of a particular style long after it has fallen out of fashion elsewhere, both because they treasure old items as reminders of the long history of the family as traders and because they value an item as aesthetically appealing. To understand the arts involved in Kalabari funerals and their interrelationship with the Kalabari worldview, we must understand that the history of the Kalabari involves a world far beyond their homeland. In addition, the structure of Kalabari society rests on a hierarchical system that ranks age, gender, and prestige of families.

The hierarchy of men's power differs from that of women; the gendered hierarchy for both is still visible through ranked categories of dress that feature garments and accessories from their trade history. Valorous and enterprising males historically demonstrated their ability to defend Kalabari communities and, as a result of demonstrating these skills, became chiefs. Only men were traders (with one documented exception)[4] and headed the Kalabari House (*wari*) as chiefs. Age was, and is, an important sociopolitical factor as well.

Men's rankings begin with early adulthood, the bottom level being designated *asawo* (glossed as "the young men that matter"), followed by *opu asawo* (gentlemen), *alapu* (chiefs), and the *amanyanabo* (king). Types of dress for each category are named according to the top garment of the outfit. Thus, the "young men that matter" wear an *etibo,* which is an outfit consisting of a shirt and wrapper; the gentlemen wear a *woko,* a more formal top garment worn with wrapper or trousers; the chiefs, a *doni,* a long gown with wrapper underneath; and the king, an *ebu,* a gown of madras plaid with matching wrapper. A fifth ensemble, the *attigra,* is a ceremonial gown usually made of deep-colored velvet, embroidered with gold or silver threads, that is not connected to a specific rank but is reserved for display during special occasions (Erekosima 1989; Michelman and Erekosima 1992; Erekosima and Eicher 1994).

Women's rankings are also associated with age, but they begin in childhood, connecting to socially defined stages of biological development and the assumption of child-rearing responsibilities instead of sociopolitical position.[5] Dress prescribed for each position provides the name for each stage and is based on the garment that covers the lower half of the woman's body: *ikuta de* (bead stage) for the youngest girl; *bite pakri iwain* (a bit of cloth) for the pre-nubile girl; *konju fina* (half a wrapper) for the nubile adolescent; and *bite sara* (full wrapper) for the mature woman, assumed to be married (Iyalla 1968; Daly 1984; Erekosima et al. 1991; Michelman and Erekosima 1992). A woman who has had a child and experienced the final socialization process called *iria*[6] is known as an *iriabo* and wears appropriate ensembles that characterize her status. She is fed and cosseted in seclusion after childbirth while someone else cares for her baby, and she is treated to her choice of foods. Eventually, she presents herself to the community in a prescribed series of knee-length wrappers to show off her legs and feet when she dances and show off a range of wealth in fabrics, appropriate jewelry, and other accessories.

As we illustrate below, the *iria* ensembles, combining textiles, garments, jewelry, and other accessories, become prominent in the funeral celebrations; appropriate ensembles are expected to be worn for different stages of the funeral by the chief mourners and other family members. In addition, valuable textiles and garments from the wardrobes of deceased family members are brought out to decorate the funeral beds.

Dress for funerals extends to outfitting not only the mourners but also rooms and beds that honor the departed, highly respected elders (Eicher and Erekosima 1987; 1989; 1996).[7] These Kalabari funerals deviate from many other African mortuary rituals in that the corpse is not immediately interred to be followed by a later celebration of a "second burial." Instead, the corpse is embalmed or frozen until the family members make decisions about and prepare for both the burial and the elaborate funeral celebration. Immediate members of the family from nearby and far away are quickly notified and expected to be available to participate in the last rites. Because the extended family members collaborate in making arrangements and making decisions about the date and event, a lapse of several months often occurs between the actual date of death and the funeral.

This lapse accommodates the time commitments of various family members whether at home or away and enables them to raise sufficient funds to support the elaborate and expensive event, an event that reinforces the prestige of the extended family in the war canoe house system (known as "*wari*").[8] To accomplish this financial goal, adult men and women of the extended family hold a series of meetings to determine priorities for funeral expenses and to be sure family members commit time and money. Projected expenses include the purchase of a casket (often highly expensive or "classy") along with requisite quantities of beer, soft drinks, spirits, and food, even whole cows, for entertaining the community of mourners. Sometimes, even rebuilding a substantial part of the family home for the body to lie in state is deemed necessary. In some extreme cases time is even allowed for constructing an entirely new modern building so that visiting guests can be comfortably received in air-conditioned living rooms and served cool drinks from electric refrigerators while listening to electronically delivered music.

10.3   Female mourners wear pelete bite *wrappers, red madras headties, and sometimes T-shirts with the deceased's portrait as they escort the casket from the mortuary to the house in the first stages of a Kalabari funeral celebration. Photograph by Joanne B. Eicher, Buguma, 1983.*

Chronology of a Kalabari Funeral

The sequence of events in preparation for the funeral of an elder begins with taking the corpse to a mortuary after death and notifying family members "abroad"[9] about the plans for the specific timing and event. Planning the details can consume as much as two or three months. Elaborate funerals are planned to fall over two weekends, beginning on a Friday and ending a week from Saturday night (or on Sunday if a religious "Thanksgiving" service is planned); this is done for the convenience of family members who are employed, as well as for those coming from abroad. On the first Friday morning, close adult relatives escort the body in a casket by truck from the mortuary in Port Harcourt to the wharf, where it will be taken by boat to the home island. The portrait of the deceased is held over the cab of the truck by a male mourner standing in the truck bed in front of the casket. Other males help lift the casket on and off the truck, stand in the truck bed surrounding the casket, and also escort it on the boat. Upon reaching the island, the men, accompanied by the female mourners, carry the casket to the family home, which has been readied for the funeral celebration. To escort the corpse, the women wear indigo wrapper sets that are an ethnic marker of Kalabari heritage along with a white blouse and a red Indian madras plaid headtie. The textiles used for these wrapper sets are called *pelete bite* (cut-thread cloth) and are worn by both Kalabari men and women for special occasions, including the first stages of a funeral celebration (fig. 10.3). *Pelete bite* comes from a tradition of women cutting and removing the white or bright threads from checked or plaid handloomed Indian textiles (Erekosima and Eicher 1981; Eicher and Erekosima with Thieme 1982; Renne 2001), which leaves a new, lacy-patterned cloth, one that is exclusive to the Kalabari as a group demarcator. Sometimes a T-shirt with the desceased's portrait is worn by the mourners (see fig. 10.3).

Relatives prepare the house by clearing three rooms[10] of all furniture before positioning a bed in the center of each room where the corpse is placed. These three rooms are the innermost bedroom (*kalabio*), the family room (*biokiri*), and the parlor (*warikubu*). In each room, the bed and walls are painstakingly covered with specific combinations of textiles that are intertwined with the long trade history of the Kalabari. Several women of the family cooperate under the leadership of one of them (fig. 10.4) who takes responsibility for selecting the vivid colors and vibrating patterns of the cloth considered appropriate for each type of room. The women (*ededapu*) who dress the beds pick and arrange cloths from an array that extended family members of the *wari* lend from their "cloth boxes" and "strong rooms" where treasured textiles inherited from past family members are stored for such use. For the first room, the innermost bedroom, the preferred choice is madras plaid of burgundy, red, indigo and white (fig. 10.1). An alternative can be Indian madras combined with heavily textured *akwete* cloths handwoven in the Igbo town north of the Kalabari islands. For the second room, the family room, heavier cloth is used, either alone or in combination. Possible selections are bright-colored *akwete* (fig. 10.5); striped cloth called *gom,* which is handwoven in India; or *blangidi,* a printed woolen flannel manufactured in England. For the walls and bed of the third room, the parlor, the preferred textiles are either silver or gold-embroidered Indian velvets of deep indigo, black, or brown or striped silks of indigo, violet, and pink hues, also from India (fig. 10.6). When the deceased's Christian background is paramount,

10.4   One woman, the "ededabo," takes primary responsibility for selecting appropriate cloths from family cloth boxes and storage rooms. Photograph by Joanne B. Eicher, Buguma, 1980.

10.5 Two favored cloth alternatives for the second room, handwoven akwete *and handwoven* gom *are found on this bed. The center textiles are arranged to resemble a hat or headtie. Photograph by Joanne B. Eicher, Buguma, 1983.*

10.6 The walls and bed of the third room (warikubu) are covered with panne and gold-embroidered velvets from India. This woman's bed is further embellished with red coral jewelry and three iriabo *hats. The two red hats are made from red coral beads and branch coral. Photograph by Joanne B. Eicher, Buguma, 1983.*

however, the third room may have white fabrics draping the walls and covering the bed (fig. 10.7). For an affluent family, a fourth room will be added in order to feature the Christian aspect of the deceased's life.

In preparing the bed for the corpse to lie in state, the *ededapu* fold the cloths (women's wrappers about three yards long) to form narrow strips that they lay flat on the bed (fig. 10.8). The coffin containing the corpse or the corpse itself is placed directly on the bed (fig. 10.9). When a four-poster bed is used, a canopy of velvet or plush completes the decor. Each room, except for a white one, pulses with color and pattern as several examples show (figs. 10.10, 10.11). A white room often has added touches of silver tinsel or pastel-colored bows pinned to the edges of the canopy or trimming the headboard and pillow and is sometimes decorated with Christmas tree lights. The extravagant massing of cloth indicates family wealth and prestige. New cloth alone is not a symbol of pride, for old and tattered wrapper pieces of madras or tarnished metallic embroidered threads indicate a family that has a long history in the trade system. Another measure of prestige and renewal of interlineage ties is the decoration of more than three rooms. This occurs when the family as a corporate group or a distinguished chief mourner (the eldest son or daughter) goes on to display or even flaunt the prominence of the family heritage through the display of cloth in other kin compounds to which the deceased traces lineage. This may include a room in the compound of the deceased's father or mother or even in both compounds.

Family mourners move the corpse from bed to bed through the night of wake-keeping in the home of the deceased as mourners file through the rooms to pay their respects, both to the deceased and the mourning family. At times, the clothing of the corpse is changed before the corpse is moved to the next room so that the dress of the corpse is coordinated with the room's fabrics. To identify the deceased as Christian, the corpse may be dressed in white to be placed on the "Christian bed" (see fig. 10.9).

In preparation to receive visitors for the first wake-keeping and following week's events, tarpaulins are pitched and chairs placed at the edge of an open space outside the funeral rooms. Drummers are engaged or stereo music played. Praise singing by club members belonging to social organizations with which the chief mourners are or the deceased was associated occurs along with dancing throughout the night. Christian families arrange a time for hymn singing during the night wake-keeping, usually ending by midnight when the ceremonies of the traditional watch take over. Dancing, drumming, and stereo music continue under the tarpaulins. Near the bedside of the corpse inside the house, female relatives sing dirges commemorating the highlights of the deceased's life or honoring the reputation of the family.

10.7   Sheer white fabrics called "lace" drape the walls and bed decorated to honor a deceased person who was a Christian. Photograph by Joanne B. Eicher, Buguma, 1983.

10.8   The madras cloth on the funeral bed is neatly folded in flat narrow strips to receive the corpse. In this case, the corpse has just been removed from the bed, hence its somewhat rumpled appearance. Photograph by Joanne B. Eicher, Buguma, 1983.

10.9 The corpse itself, or alternatively the casket that holds the corpse, is placed directly on the bed. In this Christian room, the corpse is also dressed in white and adorned with the precious gold and coral jewelry worn in life. Photograph by Joanne B. Eicher, Buguma, 1980.

10.10 The red coiled fabric at the bottom of the photograph and the beige coil of fabric on the pillow are called "sinuous python" (odum ikelekele). Photograph by Joanne B. Eicher, Buguma, 1983.

10.11 A different arrangement of the bed seen in figure 10.10. An example of a funeral room called warikubu. *The velvet fabrics on the bed are folded in the style called* alapa, *or "jellyfish," motif. A portrait of the deceased sits at the head of the bed. This woman's bed is further embellished with red coral jewelry, and two* iriabo *hats made from red coral beads. A headtie adorns the pillow. Photograph by Joanne B. Eicher, Buguma, 1983.*

10.12 *Family members of the deceased are shown on the morning of the burial. Coral jewelry and the expensive fabrics serve to honor the dead by displaying the family's wealth. The turban-type headwear on the men is an expected style for them as chief mourners on the burial day. Photograph by Joanne B. Eicher, Buguma, 1987.*

On the next day, the corpse must be buried before noon, and the family's chief mourners dress for the occasion. Men and boys have their heads wrapped turban style with cloth and wear a sash around their waist. Women and girls dress with expensive headties, blouses, wrappers, and jewelry (fig. 10.12). The body is carried directly to the cemetery, or, in the case of a Christian, first to a church for a religious funeral service and then to the burial place (now often to another island designated as a cemetery, which must be reached by boat). A Christian service includes a sermon, a printed program with an obituary and a list of descendants, and a choir that follows the casket to the cemetery with the mourners. A non-Christian observance involves carrying the casket directly from the household resting place to the burial spot. Whether Christian or not, family members, since the early 1980s, have arranged to have a video made of the funeral event, often from the point of taking the body from the mortuary through to the final activities of the following week.

If the deceased was a "young adult," as discussed earlier, or from an impoverished family, the funeral observances end with the burial. When the deceased is a distinguished elder whose family can afford the expenses involved, another week of events takes place. On Monday, the extended family organizes the final events for the weekend to come. The female family members begin to practice their dancing for the Friday night wake-keeping, under the tutelage of an older woman who knows the steps and associated protocol. The chief female mourner is normally an *ede iriabo*, that is, a woman who artfully dresses for the funeral ceremonies in the ensemble of an *iriabo* and goes through a secluded pampering process. This parallels the *iria* events for a mother as she prepares to participate as a star in the final outing event (Daly 1987).

Other family members prepare in other ways. Ordinarily, men take charge of the financial arrangements involved for the refreshments needed for the Friday and Saturday evening activities and for the family members who are home for the funeral events. Both friends and relatives bring gifts of food and money to the family for support of the occasion; these gifts are

10.13   *Textiles and accessories such as jewelry, taken from the extended family's storage boxes, are fastidiously arranged on funeral beds by the* ededabo. *This Christian bed has a white velvet wrapper folded over the headboard and a woman's ceremonial hat displayed on the pillow. Photograph by Joanne B. Eicher, Buguma, 1983.*

10.14   *A funeral bed decorated with a woven arrangement of folded madras wrappers and the special motif called "fan" (*efenge*). Photograph by Joanne B. Eicher, Buguma, 1983.*

10.15   *Many varieties of fabric folded and arranged in the style called "jellyfish" (*alapa*) in a post-burial bed. Photograph by Joanne B. Eicher, Buguma, 1983.*

10.16   *This bed shows off the family's large inventory of* pelete bite *or cut-thread, cloth wrappers. Photograph by Joanne B. Eicher, Buguma, 1983.*

carefully recorded at the time of their visit. Women prepare for the cooking that takes place during the week and especially for the last weekend. Consultations take place among family members about what everyone will wear for the last wake-keeping on the final Friday night, the parade around the town on Saturday morning, and the last dance on Saturday night. And after the corpse has been buried, the *ededapu* are expected to refold the textiles each day in fanciful shapes,[11] placing precious jewelry, hats, and other expensive accessories on the bed in the position where the corpse has lain (Eicher and Erekosima 1989).

Although men occasionally take part in the decoration of the beds, it is primarily women who execute the arrangement of the textiles and accessory items on each funeral bed, under the direction of one woman who, as has been previously noted, is known for her taste and expertise (fig. 10.13). If the extended family does not have such an expert, the chief mourner or mourners (the eldest descendant of the bloodline, preferably the male or female offspring, or failing that, the closest sibling in age) will engage the services of a woman in the community who is a connoisseur. The textile arrangements are imaginative fabric sculptures, perhaps most easily described as resembling giant fabric origami. They often have named motifs such as "fan" (*efenge*; fig. 10.14) or "sinuous python" (*odum ikelekele*), two different examples of which may be seen in figure 10.10. Figures 10.11 and 10.15 show the motif called "jellyfish" (*alapa*). Still another popular motif is that of women's headties as in figure 10.5. When the elder is a woman and the extended family has a large inventory of cut-thread cloth wrappers, one bed may be adorned with these fabrics (fig. 10.16). Not all bed decorations have named motifs, however, as in the example of figure 10.17 where the women in charge said they merely focused on designing a pattern and not on giving it a name. One Kalabari man admiringly referred to this work by women, saying, "Our women are very fanciful."

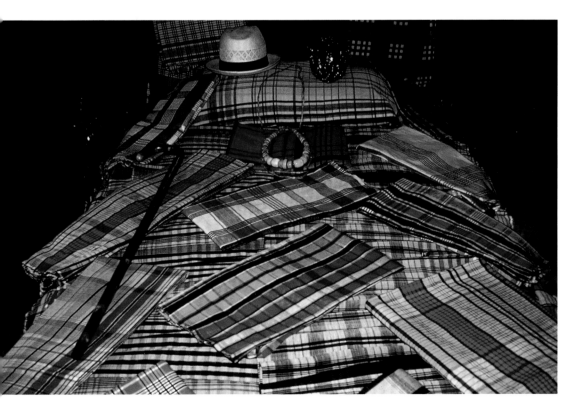

10.17 A "fanciful" arrangement of plaid wrappers on a woman's funeral bed. Accessories from the deceased's iriabo ensembles are also displayed, such as a walking stick, straw hat, coral beads, and gold ceremonial hat. Photograph by Joanne B. Eicher, Buguma, 1983.

In addition to the display of textiles, hats, jewelry, and handheld accessories are positioned on the beds as though the corpse were still there: hats on the pillow, necklaces below or at the bottom of it, and bracelets, watches, walking sticks, canes, fans, or elephant tusks about midway down the length of the bed (see figs. 10.6, 10.10, 10.11, 10.17). Portraits of the deceased, sometimes alone and sometimes with family members, lean against the foot of the bed on the floor or at the sides of the pillow propped against the headboard (see figs. 10.10, 10.11). These funeral rooms and cherished possessions display family standing and corporate wealth and are admired by members of the community who stroll leisurely through the rooms during the week to pay their respects to the family. The symbols of family history and wealth do not go unnoticed as mourners admire the women's handiwork in arranging them.[12]

On the final Friday evening, the female family members dress in Indian madras *iriabo* ensembles of knee-length wrappers that are gathered full around the waist (fig. 10.18). Town members again gather at the family compound for dancing, refreshments, and to watch the *iriapu*[13] dance. On Saturday morning, the family members assemble to dress for the parade called *amabro* (walk around the town), and the immediate family of the deceased may choose to distribute commemorative souvenirs, such as the tray seen in figure 10.19. The male mourners, both men and boys, display themselves in *doni* and *ebu* gowns ordinarily worn by chiefs and the king or in the special robe (*attigra*) saved for ceremonial events (figs. 10.20, 10.21). Women and girls again dress as *iriabo* in Indian madras ensembles as another sign of prestige. When a family has the ability to dress a large number of women and girls in this way, a common occurrence is for community members to count and comment on how many are passing by (fig. 10.22). All family mourners form a line behind an elderly woman who takes the lead, usually carrying a portrait of the deceased. First to follow her are the male relatives, then the female relatives, and finally townswomen who engage in hand clapping and praise singing. The line weaves through the town, proceeding from one family compound to another with the mourners ending up at the family compound of the deceased, where they began.

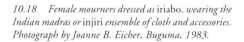

10.18   Female mourners dressed as iriabo, *wearing the Indian madras or* injiri *ensemble of cloth and accessories. Photograph by Joanne B. Eicher, Buguma, 1983.*

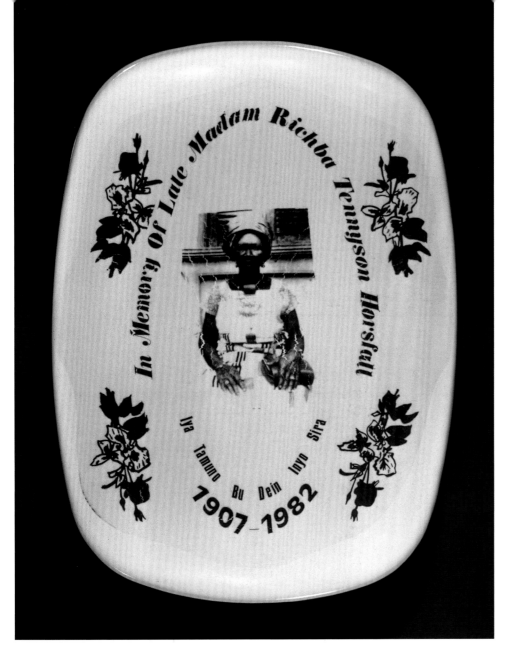

In Memory Of Late Madam Richba Tennyson Horsfall

Iya Tamuno Bu Dein Inyo Sira
1907-1982

10.19   *A commemorative white plastic tray given as a funeral souvenir. Collection of Joanne B. Eicher. Photograph by Otto C. Thieme, 1983.*

10.20   *Male relatives of the deceased wearing various examples of chief's dress as they wait for the* amabro, *or "funeral parade," to begin. Photograph by Joanne B. Eicher, Buguma, 1983.*

On Saturday night, the final round-up event known as *din krama ti* takes the form of a dance. To prepare for it, the women mourners change into the most opulent of *iriabo* ensembles, wearing either striped Indian silk wrappers called *loko* or Indian velvets embroidered with metallic threads of gold or silver (fig. 10.23). Men wear the velvet and silk gowns of the afternoon or where possible, a different ensemble, to demonstrate the family treasure trove of special garments (fig. 10.24). Chairs ring a central arena, and the chief male and female mourners sit across from each other with a table in front of them decked with bottles of spirits and soft drinks. The chief mourners enter the open arena to dance, beginning with men dancing alone and then the women dancing alone. Admirers and well wishers frequently give money (called "dash") to those who dance well. Toward the end of the special dance repertoires, women suddenly cross the arena and ask men to dance with them, not the usual practice. Then, almost as suddenly, the chief mourners, both male and female, form a single line and go off into the darkness, their last gesture of farewell to the departed. To show the finality of their farewell, they are expected to sleep away from their own houses that night. The living relatives may not occupy the space that they had shared as a corporate unit with the deceased. The dawn brings in a different, if not renewed, formation of the corporate family and community, reconstituted to carry on the business of living. The next morning, Christian families, in special garb, often attend Sunday church for what they call a "Thanksgiving" service (fig. 10.25).

10.21   Cliscent Horsfall, the chief mourner of the deceased, dressed in the special ceremonial robe known as attigra. *Photograph by Joanne B. Eicher, Buguma, 1983.*

10.22   A portion of the Saturday morning funeral parade with female relatives dressed as iriapu. *Their abundant number and elegant appearance reflect the prestige of the deceased's family. Photograph by Joanne B. Eicher, Buguma, 1988.*

10.23   *Women relatives at* din krama ti *wearing the opulent ensembles of the* iriabo. *Photograph by Joanne B. Eicher, Buguma, 1983.*

10.24   *Cliscent Horsfall, the chief mourner, dances at* din krama ti *wearing a gold-embroidered red velvet* attigra *gown. He carries a matching fan in one hand and an elephant tusk in the other. Photograph by Joanne B. Eicher, Buguma, 1983.*

10.25   *A Christian family walking to the Sunday "Thanksgiving" services at church. The woman in front, as chief mourner, wears a velvet india wrapper. Photograph by Joanne B. Eicher, Buguma, 1988.*

Historical Comparison

What part do material artifacts play in the funerals in giving homage to the distinguished departed who will become one of the esteemed ancestors? Talbot's description of funerals primarily concerned those of eminent chiefs, such as the king and ritual leaders:

> The body is enclosed in mats, and the blood of sacrificed fowls and goats sprinkled over the feet, after which more mats are wrapped round it and it is then interred amid salvos of cannon under the Bio-kiri room. Coral beads, gold and silver ornaments, yard upon yard of silk and the finest of cloths are laid in the grave, together with tobacco, snuff, a plate, knife, and bottle of gin. [Talbot 1926, 488]

This is distinguishable, however, from the traditionally prescribed format of fixed times and number of shots that occur throughout the week of a chief's burial. Some of these practices seem to have been appropriated for the funerals of any well-regarded elder. The shooting of a cannon has become a fairly common act at the time of burial. Although no longer buried with the corpse, the textiles and jewelry displayed on the funeral beds are similar to those on Talbot's list. Members of one family explained that sons of a wealthy chief in the early twentieth century rebelled against burying their family wealth with their father's corpse, insisting that family goods should be handed on from generation to generation, thus the practice was discontinued. One man in his mid-fifties in 1988—proud of his interest in Kalabari history—said that before the migration from Elem Ama to Buguma, the corpse was dressed in so much cloth that you couldn't see it. He also declared:

> The last time all things were buried with the chief was about eighty years ago. The chief was Ikpoye Ikiriko (from Harry compound). When he died the family decided to put everything—*kalali* [coral], all the cloth he had into the coffin and his first son, Chief Benibo Ikiriko, protested that some of these things should be kept for the younger ones to use, so he forced his way to the coffin and brought some of these things out. So the family said, "Oh, you must have wanted your father to die so you could inherit these," and they invaded him. So he ran to King Abbi [Amachree] and took refuge. Then after some time, King Abbi gave him some land to settle [at the other end of town] as he could not come back to his former compound. That was how the whole thing ended. [Eicher fieldnotes 1988]

Although burying of precious items has stopped, burning some precious items owned by the deceased by the waterside at full tide during the days following the burial does occur. Some women family members assemble and burn the cloth and other material directly touched by the corpse. They also identify to be burnt at the same time any objects to which the deceased was particularly attached or which represented very personal mementos. These may be an item of dress, a favorite chair, a briefcase that the person always carried, or a cherished watch. Although claimed to be personal objects that the deceased person will use in the netherworld, they serve as a ritualized acknowledgment of the personal identity of the deceased.

Other items that the individual privately owned or used, such as clothing, slippers, perfumes, shoes, hats, albums, or other forms of self-identifying property, are also collected from the deceased's immediate family members. A day is fixed for all members of the extended lineage to gather. Each person will pick one item of his or her choice from the collection, even if it is an oversized coat or only one of a pair of slippers. Through this process, each person who believes he or she has a claim on the deceased has the opportunity to assert it. Any intruders are challenged.

Although we assumed (along with Robin Horton)[14] that the practice of decorating the bed and walls with cloth was an old tradition, field interviews conducted in 1988 revealed that it probably began around the turn of the twentieth century. The same man who discussed the cessation of burying items with the corpse, above, offered an account of how dressing the walls began:

> This thing of dressing the wall started not more than sixty years ago in Buguma, or so, maybe fifty years ago. It was not so in Old Shipping. Chief Brown-West, when he died, his uncle, Chief Kio Young Jack of Abonnema came for the burial. When he came for the burial, it was a stick building, not a real building, but old, almost falling down, a dirty building. It didn't look like where somebody can paint it. Before now, when a chief dies, what they do, they put down the bed, then exhibit his wealth by hanging *doni* on the wall, not with hanger, but knock some nail. Now this man said, if we hang these on the wall, expensive *india* and so on, they'll be dirty because the house is so dirty, so why don't we use some cloth to seal the whole room before hanging the expensive cloth. So they asked women to bring less-expensive cloth—*accraa* cloth and so on. So Chief Young Jack introduced it to the Kalabari. [Eicher fieldnotes 1988]

The above account implies a date of 1930 because it parallels that of an elderly woman who said that the Chief Fubara Brown-West main house erupted in a fire that raged for ten days, destroying not only the property but also its owner. She stated that subsequently an unnamed man brought his own personal property to dress the bed for the chief's funeral: "Instead of looking at the corpse, they looked at walls and beds, and this showed the family was still wealthy" (Eicher fieldnotes 1988). This woman remembered that at the time of this fire, her son, born in 1928, was crawling, making the date approximately 1929/1930.

Talbot's only comments about funeral customs for women are that "The bodies of free-born women are borne back to their father's house, while the aged ones receive burial like chiefs" (1926, 490). He reports on the funeral practices for Kalabari males that involve the preparation of the corpse by immediate relatives and the expected behavior of the "lawful" and "secondary" wives. He says the procedure for preparation of the deceased was carried out by "full brothers, sisters and adult sons" who wash the corpse in the backyard after the lawful and secondary wives leave. He also declares that after the body is painted with red camwood and black dyes, it is wrapped with a raffia cloth (called *okuru*) that is "passed round the loins by his sister." Only after this do the lawful wives return and wrap a fathom of cloth (of unnamed type) around the corpse "while some of the dead man's most valuable cloths are laid over all" (1926, 487). His comments illustrate the significance of the funeral in two ways: they indicate how cognatic lineage reintegration is generated and how Kalabari cultural values concerning kinship are emphasized.

We can analyze Talbot's description with the acknowledgment that rubbing the corpse with the red camwood (*awu*) and other dyes (*buruma*) serves the aesthetic function of making the skin glisten and also may have had preservative effects. These procedures, in the days before Western embalming techniques, were quite elaborate, but this step also gave the deceased the dignity of being claimed by kin. As the sister of the deceased covered his private parts with fabric, she participated in a prescribed ritual. This assertive act, symbolically carried out within the bonds of kinship, countermanded the vulnerability of death. Although females who represented fecundity were found in close proximity to a naked male, this ritual was not about reproduction or sexuality; wives were not, and still are not included. Instead, only women relatives with whom intercourse is taboo were and are admitted.[15]

Since the time of Talbot's account, we have observed a change regarding the closest female and male relatives who dress the deceased's body. At the end of the twentieth century, a sister rarely undertakes the act of tying the cloth over a man's loins (*amana*). Instead, the first son assumes responsibility in the case of men and the eldest daughter for women. The critical factor is that only those who will not divulge family secrets (such as whether any blemishes were apparent on the corpse) share in this most intimate moment of exposure when kinship is paramount. This act seals kin solidarity as the corpse is readied to enter the spirit realm.

The spirit realm, for the Kalabari, is not strictly mundane. It does not refer to causative or quantitative phenomena; it is not related to the embodied or the time-bound. Nevertheless, the spirits can be motivated to yield good or render damage; they can be placated, assuaged, deflected, or directed.[16] Thus, the kin who are left behind indicate their goodwill toward those spirits who have become ancestors. They do so by launching them into the ancestor world with a spectacular sendoff.

The four categories of the self—the corpse, vital body, the soul, and one's spirit destiny (which refers to fate and fortune beyond one's control)—also relate to three Kalabari classes of free spirits within the spirit realm. These three exclude the first category of the corpse and are the good dead or ancestors (*duein*), the societal forces (*oru*), and the water people (*owuame*) of the rivers and creeks of the Kalabari environment. The ancestors keep direct oversight on lineage well-being as a biological unit, involving such matters as fertility and health and the labors of a member's family. The societal forces (*oru*) are often referred to as community heroes. Among them are the goddess of artistic performance and general aesthetic sensibilities (Ekineba) and the tutelary deity who is responsible for prosperity and wealth (Owamekaso). Ekineba advances areas such as communal peace and prosperity, and mediates between the ancestral dead and the water people. Owamekaso controls the forces of nature and confers personal success. Only through the goodwill and control of the water people can the wealth and position of any individual be determined.

However, the spirit realm does not address the sacred realm, that of the divine and ultimate power or the supernatural. This sacred realm is set off from the reverential realm of the spirits, deities, and gods, and is specifically delineated only by the dual and complementary forces of Tamuno and So. These two matrices, Tamuno, the invisible creative one, and So, the directive one, conjointly explain the entire ordered universe of the Kalabari. Tamuno, the creative force is seen as having the superabundant fecundity of femaleness, and So is viewed as having an organizing modality of maleness. They join to embody the Kalabari worldview. This view reflects and sustains the clearly marked yet complementary roles that are found in the funeral rituals. The heightened focus of attention that funerals bring to the occasion of death underscores fundamental values of the Kalabari belief system. The poignant concern with death and continuity that is found in the rituals of Niger Delta funeral rites led Talbot to observe that "the proper carrying out of the burial ceremonies is the most important duty in life…especially in those parts where worship of ancestors is most developed" (1926, 469).

Conclusion

Before the 1980s, the arts of dressing the bodies of the mourners and the beds for the deceased had gone undocumented except for the brief passages mentioned by Talbot (1926). By the 1980s, however, the practice appeared so well established that lavish funerals were referred to as "traditional" practices and led many observers to think that these rituals had always been carried out in the same way. No doubt a century ago impressive funerals were carried out to honor chiefs, the king, and some elderly women. What is the purpose served by the flamboyance of contemporary funerals in comparison to practices of the past? Obviously, the early practice began with honoring the life of chiefs who had established themselves in their Kalabari communities by providing a material base and moral structure that sustained their extended families. The fruits of their trading success, as shown by the imported artifacts they had accumulated for themselves and their loved ones, were displayed to emphasize and underscore their importance and prestige. At some time after the possessions themselves were no longer buried with the deceased, the fanciful art of dressing the beds and walls developed. This was primarily practiced by women who used the same items that had been used in the past to denote success. This visible display continues to announce the success of the deceased to the community and the high regard in which he or she is held by family members.

The intersection of Tamuno and So, female and male, becomes highlighted in Kalabari life during the funeral event as the display of the success of the men through family artifacts that are lovingly arranged by the women of the family. In addition, the intersection of the living with the spirits, the ancestral dead, and the one who goes on to join them is of paramount concern. The display of wealth at the funeral provides an elaborate and gorgeous array of material artifacts belonging to the lineage, along with the personal belongings of the deceased. Such a display acknowledges how a particular family accumulated prestige, power, and wealth, and simultaneously symbolizes the contribution of the water people (*owuame*) to the fame and fortune of the person and his or her family.

During the twentieth century significant shifts have occurred in carrying out a fitting farewell. Many Kalabari people are now Christian, and the Christian communities within each island town are vigorously healthy with large Sunday service attendance. However, an overlay of what is termed the "traditional" Kalabari belief system with the four categories of the self has continued to influence funeral practices. How people are treated upon death takes on major importance as they enter the world of the ancestors. If an individual was mean spirited or industrious and solicitous in life upon earth, he or she will continue to be so in the world of the ancestors (*duein*). These ancestors must feel appreciated and well-regarded by the family who honors their death: "They are seen as taking care of their living descendants even as they did before they died. They demand respect from their heirs" (Erekosima et al. 1991, 94).

Through the pervasive embrace of Christian beliefs and practices, many ritual elements have been dropped or diluted. Their significance is largely forgotten if not deliberately denied. The ceremonial component has become more prominent and underlines a shift of new economic and power alignments in the public sphere. The earlier emphasis on moral order and cultural reaffirmations recedes under the influence of a globally advancing secularization and greater focus on material well-being and display.

The influence of trade continues to be key in funeral celebrations and is important to our understanding of the Kalabari funeral customs and the fitting farewell for the deceased. This is shown by the textiles and personal accessories, such as jewelry, hats, and canes, from global sources. The family mourners, particularly the chief mourners, display an art of dress by wearing a specified array of fine textiles throughout the week in appropriate ensembles through a specified sequence: escorting the body to the family compound, the burial, the parade of kin through the town, and the final dance. The funeral rooms with decorated beds—where first the corpse is displayed and later the well-wishers pass—exhibit an ephemeral art that allows the community to pay its respects to the family of the deceased while admiring the family's wealth. The imported textiles, gorgeous baubles of coral, silver, and gold, along with impressive hats, canes, and other accessories add to the fanciful arts that the women create to honor the deceased and family.

A Commentary on Talbot's Description of Most Eminent Funerals for the Kalabari—*Tonye V. Erekosima*

In contrast to the fitting farewells for esteemed elders that have just been described, Talbot's report of the Kalabari funeral practices known as *emine* held for the most eminent Kalabari deserves some mention. These funerals are held for the king and national ritual leaders, such as the chief priest of the national tutelary goddess or the master drummer of the Ekine Men's Dancing Society—membership in which spans the entire society—as well as other personages such as paramount chiefs. The analysis that follows is based on the author's knowledge of Kalabari custom and information concerning two *emine* funerals, that of his uncle, Amanyanabo Cotton Amachree, who reigned from the late 1960s to the early 1970s, and that of Chief Wokoma Horsfall.

Many aspects of Talbot's description of how the body is dressed for lying-in-state contrast with the regular practice described earlier in this essay. In recent memory, only the funerals of dyed-in-the-wool traditionalists (those who never embraced church membership, for instance), the king, priests to the deities, and the three paramount chieftaincies of George, Omekwe Horsfall, and John Bull have retained the basic form Talbot reported: "For those who had visited the Aro Chukwu oracle or were members of the Peri Club, chalk is rubbed up the right arm and a manilla placed round the right wrist, on which feathers and blood from sacrificial fowls are smeared, while an eagle's feather is fixed in the hair" (Talbot 1926, 488).

Although Talbot does not add that the corpse must be laid out on a mat on the floor during the time sacrifices are made and a particular masquerade dance (*ekplenaba*) is presented, he portrays the most revered form of Kalabari burial, known as *emine*. This form is more prestigious than the funerals of regular chiefs. The latter are highlighted by a colorful canoe regatta and prescribed cannon volley salutes. A brief analysis of *emine* follows, describing the elements of the traditional funeral for Kalabari's foremost sons, which differs markedly from the contemporary practices we have just described. Although rarely practiced, the *emine* funeral was enacted for the late King Cotton Charlie Kieni Amachree[17] and the late Chief Wokoma Horsfall.[18] Of note, King Cotton Charlie Kieni Amachree was succeeded by King Obaye Abiyesuku, who died in 1998 and had not yet been buried as of June 1999.

Some practices or elements of the *emine* continue and have been elaborated. The most important shift, however, has been from the earlier focus on virtuosity to an emphasis on the material achievements of the elder and his family. The latter, which has become prominent at the end of the twentieth century, stresses accomplishments in this lifetime. The former stressed the moral dimension: living by values that qualify one to become an ancestor and making a successful transition into the realm of the soul and the spirits. Horton discusses the importance of this transitional ritual for handling of the corpse with regard to regular ancestor canonization in *Ikpataka Dogi: A Kalabari Funeral Rite* (1968). This is the state-level observance.

Applying the white chalk (*toru*) described by Talbot to the body at once elevates the corpse to a representation of the body's surviving effluence. It demarcates the existence of the self from the physical and material realm, and signifies issues of the soul or qualitative living. The chalk mark made up the right arm and the manilla armlet on the right wrist indicate the exemplary character and material accomplishments derived from living as a mature man. These acts cross-reference the self as a physical entity with the essence of a person, or one's quantitative entity with the qualitative identity. The white chalk, or kaolin, is symbolic and ritualizes or validates one's existence through the dimensions of object and spirit, visible and invisible being. Of note, chalk is applied around the eyes of a priestess who is reputed to be able to see beyond what is normal and to look into the movement and activities of the denizens of the spirit world. The manilla as the former trade currency portrays the strength involved in bringing prosperity to the family through entrepreneurial leadership. It meant sustenance as well as protection of one's own.

Talbot's references to visiting the Aro Chukwu oracle or joining the "Peri Club" relate to demonstrations of moral uprightness and valor in the spheres of community engagement and service. A "Peri Club" member produced an enemy skull as a war trophy that testified to his ably rising to the defense of the community. To have survived the verdict of an Aro Chukwu oracle was to assume a mantle of innocence and rectitude in public matters. The Aro oracle emerged during the era of slave export in an Igbo enclave; it was one among hundreds of local eastern Nigerian deities who arbitrated an endless variety of criminal allegations in the various societies.[19] The Aro were able to elevate their oracle to imperial rank through the authority it exercised over scores of surrounding ethnic groups and communities. This oracle helped to contain internal conflicts and mediate the external relations of these diverse clans and cultures. European merchant adventurers often instigated intertribal warfare with their gifts of guns and alcohol to neighboring community leaders, and the oracle also served to mitigate the complete social chaos that could have resulted from the inexorable demand for slaves by these merchants. Other mechanisms of cohesion among the coastal Delta communities included the mythology of an underwater goddess (Oruyingi) who was mother to the respective guardian gods and goddesses of city-states such as Nembe, Kalabari, Bonny, and Okrika, which were prone to much conflict.[20]

The Aro deity's verdicts were generally final and not open to further appeal. In practice, this was a means by which people were taken from the diverse Nigerian societies, smuggled out, and handed to the Europeans seeking healthy able-bodied adults as slaves. The accused was either cleared of wrongdoing and returned to society as an innocent and decent person or was deemed a wizard who, the community assumed, had deservedly lost his life for his crime and consequently missed the honor of receiving a fit burial.[21] When a Kalabari elder died, therefore, without being trapped in an Aro oracle's verdict, it meant he had passed muster in terms of his integrity.

The eagle feather that was stuck to the hair of the deceased or in the region of the head marked the ultimate of excellence, the best of human aspirations. The deceased accomplished the full ideal of positive human activism. The rarity of eagles and the lofty heights at which they soared, along with the rarefied symbol of a white eagle feather, converged to communicate this message. The blood of innocent animals (like that of the slaughtered fowl or sheep) smeared on the corpse, stood for a different level of intervention or memorializing. Briefly, it forged the link to the sacred realm of the Creator Spirit, the Ultimate Creative/Directive Center of human destiny where vitality and its nemesis abut. Asking for mediation from these animals, which lack the human motivation toward negativity and malevolence (they never attack or maul even their assailants), aligns the energy or spirit of the departed with the same course and cause of the Creator or life-giving Spirit. With such sacrifice, the spirit of the departed—having traveled destiny's route toward fortune and not blight—negotiates a linkage with the soul, and within the scope of its positive potential, it makes the soul accessible to continue on the same distinguished trajectory of providing succor to the living. Hence the Kalabari were little concerned with the verdict from a divine perspective. Everything was measured by its impact on the living and how the departed's vital-energy was itself oriented or disposed.

The machinations engaged in to provide these spirits with sufficient displays of attention to prevent their wanting to return among the living or to exert any negative sanctions (especially since disembodied life-energy is always more potent) explain a good part of the additional funeral rites that follow. After ritual preparation of the corpse, Talbot generally states that a cannon goes off and the sons and brothers lift the body and carry it into the *Wari Kubu* hall to lie in state on a bed. The lawful wives stand behind the head of the bed with lawful daughters and sisters in two rows on each side, "fanning the body with a heavily scented handkerchief" (1926, 488). This generally supported the embalming of the body, where traditional techniques were used with such steps as emptying the corpse of all fluid and filling it with prescribed special spices to insure several days of effective preservation. There is always a lingering odor of decay, however, that this activity fails to camouflage. The women wail through the night as the town's chiefs come to "take farewell of the dead man and bring gifts." If the deceased was a member of the Sekiapu club, "the members come and sing a farewell song, and in the case of a rich free-born woman, give an Owu play." Soon after dawn the body is buried, first enclosed in mats, sprinkled with the blood of sacrificial fowls and goats, then wrapped with more mats and interred under the innermost bedroom amid the sounds of cannon shots. Talbot specifically mentions precious trade goods that were buried with the deceased: coral, gold and silver, yards of silk and other cloths "together with tobacco, snuff, a plate, knife and bottle of gin" (1926, 488). These were symbols of wishing the departed to continue in the opulence that he had experienced on earth.

Talbot indicates that these practices were not undertaken for "those who are not members of the great societies" (1926, 489). Instead, only the sound of a cannon goes off to announce the death of such others, a practice that continues morning and evening for the next six days to proclaim the progression of the funeral. Other details that Talbot provides relate to the expectations concerning the widows during and after a funeral, a series of practices that involved isolation along with deprivation. These practices relate to daily cycles of eating and toileting to show the widows' bereavement and loyalty. For instance, the hardship of sleeping only on plank or some pieces of wood might have been intended to punish and inflict pain on the wives or to implicate them in the crime of causing their husband's death. These explanations, however, are unlikely because this was prescribed conduct for all deaths of a male spouse. Clearly death was generally expected. In contrast, this society placed a premium on the psychological aspect of living. Hence they focused on expunging or draining the widows' grief through parallel exertion. The pain of physically sharp discomfort would, by its distraction, neutralize and displace the ache of fond memories. Many non-Western societies include such acts and some of the others noted above as a critical essence of mourning rituals. Today the West retains selective remnants of these acts only in church services.

Interleaf L
Making Waves: The Art of Bruce Onobrakpeya and Sokari Douglas Camp

Martha G. Anderson

Bruce Onobrakpeya

Born in the Urhobo region, Bruce Onobrakpeya has played a prominent role in Nigeria as an artist and a teacher, and is widely considered to be the foremost printmaker in Africa (figs. L.1, L.3). He first came to international attention in 1965, when the Duke of Edinburgh acquired two of his prints. After garnering many awards in the following decades, he was chosen to represent Nigeria at the Venice Biennale in 1990. Reporting on the African exhibition there, David Joselit noted how he "deftly combined folkloric or mythic content with contemporary formal strategies" (1990, 161).

Onobrakpeya would certainly be pleased with Joselit's assessment. In the late 1950s, he and several other Nigerian art students—the so-called Zaria Rebels—advocated a synthesis of academic styles and techniques with African subjects and sources so that their work would be more meaningful to their own people. The trend they initiated, sometimes called "nativism" (Oguibe 1997, 136), profoundly affected the course of contemporary Nigerian art.

Onobrakpeya's work often refers to the Urhobo folktales he heard during his childhood, but he draws on a wide variety of other sources, ranging from Tuareg jewelry and Yoruba beadwork to Hausa robes and Benin bronze reliefs (fig. L.2). In addition, he has always intended his work to express his strong sense of social responsibility. According to Onobrakpeya, "producing art works

backed by ideas and philosophies which are calculated to help upgrade and lift the life of the people [provides a] way to give our people self identity" (Ezra 1990, 79).

In his Sahelian Masquerades series of the 1980s, Onobrakpeya addressed environmental issues. Though the series was named for the arid regions to the north, Onobrakpeya extended his concern to Southern Nigeria, where he deplored "the abuse of the environment through over-cropping of trees, bush burning, indiscriminate mineral exploitation leading to oils spills particularly in the Niger Delta" (Onobrakpeya 1988, xi). His poem, "Nigeria" (which is written in English and Urhobo), reflects his concerns for the impoverished people of the region:

> Where drums of oil
> Gush forth from the ground
> Where material resources were lavished
> By her sons and daughters
> The spirit has now moved
> From Uloho the god of plenty
> To the useless uweruwe
> Here is a lesson
> Children of Nigeria.
> [Onobrakpeya 1988, 27]

A technical innovator as well as a visionary, Onobrakpeya developed a deep etching technique in 1967 that involves the use of epoxy on linoleum to produce "plastographs." He later began to recycle prints taken from plaster casts of the original works into reliefs, and eventually into three-dimensional forms, sometimes covered with metal foil. An avid collector, he displays his wide-ranging collections of African art at his Ovuomaroro Studio and Gallery in Lagos.

L.1 Bruce Onobrakpeya. Emedjo, 1974. Plastograph print. 53.5 x 79 cm. Collection of the Artist.

L.2   Bruce Onobrakpeya. Akporode. *Photographs, paper, plastic, metal, ivory, steel, bronze, leather, and found materials. This installation was exhibited in London in 1995 and in Malmö, Sweden, in 1996. In the exhibition process, it has gone through structural changes, and some artworks have been added. Onobrakpeya has said of this work:* "Akporode *represents a striving toward higher, richer, and bigger life. The word* akporode *is derived from two Urhobo words:* akpo *(life, world) and* orode *(big, great). It is an assemblage of artworks (both linear and sculptural) of different shapes, color, design, and materials, which together reflect the grandeur and beauty often associated with Nigerian traditional religions, shrines, and the architectural décor of palaces. The art pieces—created through experiments over a period of two decades—have themes based on the worldview of our people and their cultural values, wisdom, beliefs, mythology, and cosmology. Some crave ethnic and national unity, religious tolerance, as well as prayer for a better environment. The varied themes are repeated in different techniques and materials…in an attempt to discover the best visual representation of the ideals, local and foreign, which have been synthesized in response to change. The process results in a kind of metamorphosis, which is in tune with traditional shrines that diminish for lack of repairs or increase when new items are added to them. Finally, the predominantly vertical nature of the artworks, a concept derived from the Urhobo pillar symbol for Oghene, the supreme intelligence, has another meaning for the installation. It is a prayer for divine support and continued growth toward divine greatness."*

L.3   Bruce Onobrakpeya. Peak Regatta, *1985. Plastograph print. 79 x 107 cm. Collection of the Artist.*

Sokari Douglas Camp

Sokari Douglas Camp spent her early childhood in the Kalabari Ijo town of Buguma, before going abroad to continue her education. After a brief stint at an art school in California, she returned to Britain, where she earned a master's degree at the Royal College of Art in 1986. Sokari, as she is known, has settled in London, and her colorful sculptures have captivated audiences on both sides of the Atlantic. She is acutely aware of the unique position she occupies: an African woman who works with a traditionally "masculine" material—steel—and whose subjects sometimes venture into territory dominated by men, such as the masquerade society known as Ekine (fig. L.4; see interleaf H).

Living "the reality of being both Nigerian and British," while feeling outside both cultures (Aidin 2000), probably accounts for the incisive—and often bemused—stance that informs Sokari's work. She creates wry portraits of local characters, such as the ladies armed with shopping bags and youths shod in Adidas who inhabit her South London neighborhood. Fascinated by psychoanalysis, which she considers a "modern tonic…particular to Westerners/white people," she recently turned her outsider's eye on a Western icon, Sigmund Freud (Douglas Camp 2002). At the same time, she continues to produce work that draws from and comments upon her African roots, such as *Church Ede*, the funeral bed she made to mourn her father in 1984, and the more recent *Assessment,* a commentary on the ecological disasters that have resulted from oil production in the Niger Delta.

L.4 Sokari Douglas Camp. Sekibo, 1994. Steel, feathers, and wood. H: 222 cm. American Museum of Natural History, 90.2/9024. Sokari has said that "Sekibo (a person who dances)…represents the men that are part of the secret society that both dance with the masqueraders and dress up as masqueraders. He is a link between the audience and the spiritual world of the masquerade characters. I have always admired how Kalabari men can dress in a traditional outfit of tartan patterned skirts, Victorian night shirts with bowler hats and walking sticks. In this unusually stylish attire they jump and turn in the air following the masqueraders and keep the crowd back whilst sometimes also leading the masquerade procession itself" (Douglas Camp 2002).

L.5 Sokari Douglas Camp. Green Alagba, 1995. Steel, wood, and feathers. H: 52 cm. Private Collection. Photograph by Denis Finin. This is a maquette for a large-scale sculpture. Alagba, an important masquerade character, also appears as the central figure on a Kalabari ancestral screen illustrated in figure B.6.

As an African artist who works in a Western idiom, Sokari has had to reconcile Western aesthetics with African sensibilities. When asked what spiritual significance her work holds for her, she responded: "I never used to tell people at home that I actually made objects, because an object is a very powerful thing. It would be like someone making hundreds of crucifixes…. It's not something you talk about easily—I was tampering with something religious" (National Museum of African Art, Smithsonian Institution 1988, 15). She has also attempted to bridge the gap between Western museums, where masks hang on walls, and African festivals, where they form an integral part of spectacular, spiritually meaningful, and often educational performances. In her work, masks inhabit a place between "tradition" and modernity. To the delight of her largely Western audience, they belong to fully costumed figures, who sometimes actually "dance" (figs. L.5–L.7). Though based on particular characters, she invariably injects them with her own wit and whimsy. As Olu Oguibe (1999) puts it, "Douglas Camp's work symbolizes life, movement, elegance, inventiveness, and technical skill."

L.6   Sokari Douglas Camp. Big Masquerade with Boat and Household on His Head, *1995. Steel, wood, and feathers. H: 255 cm. Collection of the Artist. Photograph by Doran Ross. Boat masquerades acknowledge the importance of Kalabari participation in overseas trade from the era of tall ships to that of ocean liners. Robin Horton terms the Bekiniarusibi, or "White Man's Boat"—connected to a water spirit of the same name—a "light hearted masquerade" (1960, 46). Sokari reinterprets this character as both spiritually powerful, as indicated by the splashes of sacrificial blood, and physically intimidating, as conveyed by its size and weapons.*

L.7   Sokari Douglas Camp. Otobo (Hippo) Masquerade, *1995. Steel, wood, and palm stem brooms. H: 183 cm. Photograph by Doran Ross. This sculpture is presently in the collection of the British Museum, London. The hippopotamus figures prominently in Eastern Ijo masquerades. Examples of Otobo headdresses are illustrated in figures H.9 and H.10, as well as in the foreground of this photograph.*

11.1 Oil flare in Ogoniland. Photograph by Jill Salmons, 1992.

Conclusion: Reflections– Looking Back on Our Journey

MARTHA G. ANDERSON and

PHILIP M. PEEK

The mystic drum beat in my inside
and fishes danced in the rivers
and men and women danced on land
to the rhythm of my drum.
　　　　　　—Gabriel Okara[1]

The wailing is for the fields of men:
For the barren wedded ones;
for perishing children…
The wailing is for the Great River:
Her pot-bellied watchers
Despoil her.
　　　　　　—Christopher Okigbo

The Niger Delta has a way of providing its own metaphors for cultural interaction. The essays gathered here show the remarkable fluidity of art forms, styles, and traditions in a region marked by great ethnic and linguistic diversity. Its people share comparable—at times virtually identical—carvings, masks, dance steps, and scarification patterns, and they express similar attitudes toward certain materials, such as mud, chalk, coral, camwood, and bronze. They use a host of imported goods, including cloth, in similar ways. To put a new twist on a phrase that Rene Bravmann coined in describing similar phenomena on dry land: the "floodgates," not the "frontiers," have long been open. Yet the peoples of this region, woven together by rivers (figs. 11.2, 11.3), as well as by intermarriage and trade, have managed to maintain distinct identities and diverse cultural traditions.

The authors have found no single answer as to why cultures converge and diverge but have considered the roles language, history, ecology, and worldview play in the complex process of defining identity. The ambivalence the Ijo and others express concerning their respective self-images clearly indicates that identities can be layered, ambiguous, and even contradictory. In noting that traits have spread from one group to another and asking how and why they have done so, many authors suggest that the Delta's unique topography has been instrumental in promoting cultural similarities. Indeed, they have sometimes found it difficult to emphasize the importance of the ecological setting enough without verging on environmental determinism. Though a watery environment may not predetermine belief in water spirits, their essays argue that it can suggest the possibility that such spirits exist and ensure the popularity of performances in which they materialize on land.

11.2 Two women paddling a canoe. Photograph by
Martha Anderson, 1992.

11.3 Women transporting plantains in a canoe.
Photograph by Martha Anderson, 1991.

The environment has also figured into this equation by stimulating trade. Long before sailing vessels linked them with Manchester (figs. 11.4, 11.5) and Madras, canoes connected Delta groups with each other and with communities far along the coast. The extent of these networks surprised even the authors. As has already been noted, in the years before roads linked mainland communities, canoes could not only carry heavier loads but, with the judicious use of tides, travel much faster than a man on horseback (Lloyd 1967, 222).

If trading stimulated cultural congruence, it also engendered adaptive strategies, as exemplified by the development of city-states on both sides of the Delta. Ecological factors encouraged certain groups to engage more heavily in trade; the Eastern Ijo and Itsekiri became middlemen, while those in between, who were cut off from the new source of wealth, largely participated in the trade by committing acts of piracy. Consequently, Jaja and Amakiri (Amachree), the Eastern Ijo potentates described in chapter 8, have more in common with Nanna, the Itsekiri merchant prince (who appears in interleaf C), than they do with the Central Ijo pirate and Western Ijo warrior who figure in chapter 3, even though the latter are contemporaries who belong to the same language group.

If people are shaped by their environment, they inevitably also give their environment shape by developing a set of attitudes and beliefs. Why have certain forms and patterns spread, and not others? How have they been altered in the course of transmission? In many cases, the answer to the first question proves to be the most logical: the Ijo, for example, have adopted the *ivri* complex from the neighboring Urhobo and Isoko because it dovetails quite neatly with preexisting beliefs about forest spirits. Moreover, all three groups espouse a "warrior ethos," granting titles to men who have killed human beings or powerful animals. In other situations, the issue becomes more complicated. Aquatic masquerades appeal to land-based people, as well as those in riverain areas, and many now perform variations. To take Kay Williamson's suggestion a step further (see the appendix to this volume), masking may have helped spread belief in water spirits, as well as the terms used for certain fish. The promises of wealth and an easier, more luxurious life, which these spirits are thought to offer, also explain their allure.

11.4 Bonny Cathedral. Photograph by Lisa Aronson, 1978.

11.5 A "Thanksgiving" procession following an iria *ceremony. Photograph by Lisa Aronson, Opobo, 1978.*

Masking provides an obvious opportunity to address the second question as well, for Delta water spirit masquerades show nearly as many differences in form and function as they do similarities. For example, although the Ijebu-Yoruba admit to copying their Agbo masquerades from the Ijo, they find bared teeth to be antisocial, and their masks do not employ this feature. Likewise, their maskers perform in a less aggressive, "more Yoruba," fashion. Finally, there are striking differences in masking even within the Ijo region. The Kalabari Ijo, for example, whose performances may once have resembled the masquerades staged in the Central and Western Delta today, turned masking into a mechanism for inducting outsiders into their communities.

In addition to sharing masquerade traditions, groups throughout the area have transformed trade items ranging from top hats, playing cards, and shiny metallic baubles into ritual objects, status markers, and a host of other art forms. Imported goods recall valued, historic trading relationships while acquiring new meanings through the process of cultural authentication, as seen in the elaborate funeral beds the Kalabari decorate with European and Indian textiles (see chapter 10). Nevertheless, the Delta's love affair with foreign products does not reflect a desire to assimilate. As noted in several of the essays, Delta cultures welcomed trade but adamantly resisted colonialism.

Perhaps the Itsekiri and the Ogoni, two small groups sandwiched between other, larger groups, present the best example of how the arts can define and project corporate identity (fig. 11.6). Both groups have admittedly incorporated many art forms from their neighbors but have embraced these traditions as their own. In one case, a name suffices to transform an Ijo-looking mask into an Itsekiri one. Likewise, the Ogoni, who have links to the Cross Rivers area as well as to the Delta, express pride in their culture by maintaining a fascinating variety of traditions, some peculiar to themselves, others drawn from their neighbors.

Questions remain about the origins of widespread traditions and beliefs, for we lack sufficient knowledge of many areas of the Delta. Although most generally credit the Ijo with originating water spirit masquerades, it proves difficult to reconstruct the routes of transmission. No clear patterns have emerged, such as weaker or less populous groups borrowing from those

11.6 Carver Isaac Legbara of Uegwere Boue, Babbe.
Photograph by Jill Salmons, 1992.

that are stronger or more densely populated. Forms and meanings travel independently in a manner that is far from orderly and predictable, and borrowing can be denied, forgotten, or unconscious. For example, though the Isoko neither acknowledge nor deny Ijo influence, the two groups share many cultural features. Peek looks to Benin to explain the underwater sojourns Isoko diviners claim to have made, yet this tale is common among Ijo diviners, like Queen (who appears in chapter 3), and may well be repeated throughout the region. Further research may resolve issues of this sort but will undoubtedly reveal great complexity.

This volume undertook to investigate two themes found throughout the Delta, a "water-related ethos" and a "warrior ethos." Though the essays have shown that some groups in the area see themselves as "water people" and some do not, they all partake in a "water-related ethos" to the extent that they perform water spirit masquerades. Though fewer essays have touched on the "warrior ethos," it proves to have had a profound effect on virtually all the cultures treated here. Many of the figures in the exhibition visually manifest this ethos, as do the ceremonial canoes that appear in regattas throughout the Delta (see interleaf M), for they are the descendants of the "war canoes" that once carried troops into combat. The warrior societies found among Igbo and Cross Rivers groups, who have much in common with those in the Delta, offer promising possibilities for comparative research.

This ethos has resurfaced in two arenas. In the early 1990s, a new generation of warriors began protesting the environmental degradation caused by the exploitation of oil reserves in the region and the government's failure to share the wealth generated by oil with the people who "owned" it. By the end of the decade, wire services and Web sites blared headlines such as "Ten Die as Oil Production Threatens Itsekiri Community," "Youth Disrupt Liquefied Gas Production in Niger Delta," and "Community Vows to Resist Niger River Dredging" (see fig. 11.1). Unfortunately, local politics have also sparked a series of violent ethnic clashes in the Warri region. By highlighting similarities and differences among Niger Delta art forms, the authors wish to emphasize that we in no way intend to foster this sort of ethnic divisiveness. We propose that Delta people look for common ground, as they have in their artistic expressions, to resolve their political problems.

The impetus for coming together often involves a common enemy. Nigeria has proven to be fragile as a "nation-state." Years of corruption defeated nationalist sentiments that had prevailed during the colonial period and sparked a revival of regional and ethnic chauvinism. Ironically, flagrant abuses by both the government and multinational oil companies have provided a new rallying point. In February 1999 a number of protest groups from across the region gathered at the Niger Delta Ethnic Nationalities Conference and released a communiqué citing diversity as a positive factor. They enumerated their common complaints and issued demands for an end to gross injustices and violations of environmental and human rights. In this now radically altered deltaic environment, the importation of fish and the peoples' demonstrations for clean water acquire a special poignancy.

Many of the authors have voiced their concern about the unrest in the Delta. All share the world's outrage at the brutal deaths suffered by Ken Saro-Wiwa and other protestors at the hands of the Nigerian military and feel that the oil companies, whether or not they actively colluded in these

11.7 Village street. Photograph by Philip M. Peek Okpe, 1971.

reprehensible acts, must share the blame. Those who dismiss demands for compensation as being motivated by greed should read *The Price of Oil: Corporate Responsibility and Human Rights Violations in Nigeria's Oil Producing Communities* (1999). This thorough and well-documented study summarizes findings of Human Rights Watch on the consequences of environmental degradation and investigates the roles the Nigerian government and the petroleum industry have played in creating this deplorable situation. An even more recent inditement of the depredation caused in the region by the oil industry, written from a Nigerian perspective, may be found in Ike Okanta and Douglas Oronto's *Where Vultures Feast: Shell, Human Rights, and Oil in the Niger Delta* (2001).

The intimacy Niger Delta peoples share with their environment—evidenced by their extensive lore about animals and water spirits, as well as by their fondness for regattas and other aquatic displays—makes damage to the region's delicate ecosystems all the more deplorable. It often seems that the most economically depressed and politically ignored areas of Africa prove to be the richest in terms of artistic expression. The Delta has suffered neglect from the earliest times to the present. We hope the essays in this book and the wonderful array of art forms represented in the accompanying exhibition will convince others that these cultures must be treasured and their people protected from this most recent threat to their well-being. We salute the peoples of the Niger Delta, applaud their remarkable cultural heritage, and express our hopes for a glorious future.

Interleaf M
Regattas, Then and Now

Martha G. Anderson

According to *Webster's Dictionary,* the term *regatta,* which originally referred to gondola races held in Venice, has come to encompass any type of race or series of races where boats or yachts contend for prizes. West Africans use the term to cover a multitude of performances involving watercraft. All along the coast and on many inland waterways, people celebrate their aquatic lifestyles with spectacular nautical displays. In the Niger Delta such events are common, but never commonplace, for communities, ethnic groups, and states actively compete with each other to produce the most breathtaking decorations and the finest dancing. Participants have even been known to resort to novelties, such as the use of puppets, in their quest for distinction.

Though colonial officials seem to have encouraged this type of display (figs. M.1, M.2), modern Delta regattas have numerous indigenous precedents. These include war canoes (fig. M.3), which now appear in ceremonial form at a variety of festivals; wrestling canoes, which transport boastful competitors to intervillage meets; dance canoes, which carry performers to festivals and wakes; and masquerade canoes, which ferry maskers to performance venues. Even canoe sacrifices, which are still performed throughout the region, can be considered prototypes for secular displays.

In Warri the origin of the royal regatta can be traced to Ginuwa, the first Itsekiri monarch (*olu*), who ruled in the late fifteenth century (Kathy Curnow, personal communication, 2001). A convoy of boats is said to have accompanied the *olu* when he went out into the Atlantic to present offerings to the god of the sea, Umalokun, asking him to assure the well-being of the Itsekiri people

M.1 Group of canoes, Bonny, 1901. Reproduced with the permission of Unilever PLC (from an original in the Unilever Archives), box 25, folder 2, no. 30.

and to provide abundant fish (Ohangbon 1979). Because the current *olu* is a Pentecostal Christian, he no longer presents offerings, but he nonetheless keeps the tradition alive. During the annual festival held to mark the anniversary of the coronation, he and his chiefs stage a royal regatta to commemorate Ginuwa's pilgrimmage by traveling from the town of Warri on the mainland to the island of Ode-Itsekiri (figs. M.4, M.5). Inspired by California's Rose Bowl Parade, the *olu* has even introduced motorized "land regattas" in which floats bedecked with "paddlers" drive through the streets of Warri.

Nowadays, regattas are held on a wide variety of occasions and serve many different purposes, in addition to providing spectacular entertainment (fig. M.6). Rulers still celebrate their inaugurations or periodically inscribe the extent of their influence by touring their territories with flotillas of ceremonial canoes. Communities stage regattas to highlight festivals or honor visits by important dignitaries.

States mount them to celebrate special occasions, a notable example of which was the silver anniversary of Rivers State. The federal government sponsors them to entertain crowds of visitors, as it did during FESTAC (International Festival of Black Arts and Culture) in 1977. As one enthusiast has expressed it, the regatta serves social, religious, and political purposes. It unites people from all walks of life and brings them together from disparate places to pay tribute to the Delta's glorious cultural heritage (Ohangbon 1979).

M.2 Chief Kio Horsfal's canoe, Degema, 1904. Reproduced with the permission of Unilever PLC (from an original in the Unilever Archives), box 25, folder 2, no. 90.

M.3 Forty young men paddle a war canoe honoring the funeral of Chief Koki.
Three chiefs sit on a platform at the back, and a priest with palm leaves
covering his face stands at the bow. Stopping at each waterside compound,
the canoe was greeted with cannons, pushed off three times, and supplied
with bottles of gin. Photograph by Barbara Sumberg, 1993.

M.4 This Itsekiri regatta is held annually as part of the Coronation
Anniversary, the most important pan-Itsekiri festival. The boat draped with
ododo, an imported scarlet material associated with leadership, is the olu's.
His trumpet bearer (his junior brother) stands in the stern. Photograph by
D. Anthony Mahone, 1994.

M.5 *Regatta boats on the river between Warri town and Ode-Itsekiri. The olu's boat can be seen in the distance. Following it are other boats belonging to chiefs or important families. These often have dancers in the prow or at the stern. Photograph by D. Anthony Mahone, 1994.*

M.6 *A chieftaincy boat appears in a regatta held to celebrate the centenary of the Kalabari Ijo town of Buguma. Photograph by Joanne B. Eicher, 1985.*

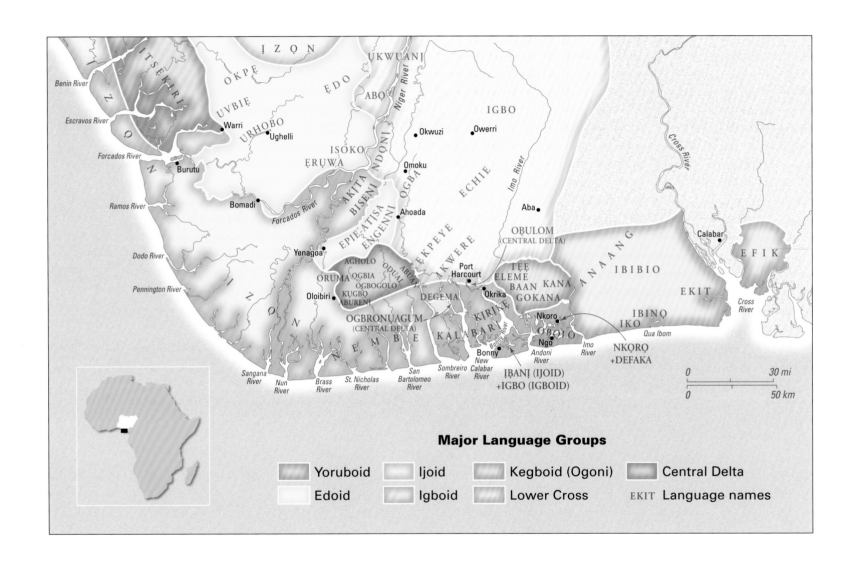

ITSEKIRI

IZON

OKPE

UKWUANI

Benin River

EDO

UVBIE

URHOBO

Warri

Ughelli

ISOKO

ERUWA

Niger River

ABO

IGBO

Okwuzi

Owerri

Omoku

Escravos River

Forcados River

Burutu

Bomadi

Forcados River

AKITA
BISENI
NDONI
OGBA

Ahoada

Imo River

ECHIE

Ramos River

EPIE-ATISA
ENGENNI

EKPEYE

Aba

Dodo River

Yenagoa

AGHOLO
ORUMA OGBIA
OGBOGOLO
KUGBO
ABURENI

ODUAL
ABUA

AKWERE

OBULOM
(CENTRAL DELTA)

Calabar

EFIK

Pennington River

Oloibiri

Port
Harcourt

TEE
ELEME
BAAN KANA
GOKANA

ANAANG

IBIBIO

EKIT

OGBRONUAGUM
(CENTRAL DELTA)

DEGEMA

Okrika

KIRIKE

Nkoro

IBINO
IKO

Cross River

IZON

NEMBE

KALABARI

OBOLO

NKORO
+DEFAKA

Ngo

Qua Ibom

Sangana
River

Nun
River

Brass
River

St. Nicholas
River

San
Bartolomeo
River

Sombreiro
River

New
Calabar
River

Bonny

Bonny River

Andoni
River

Imo
River

IBANI (IJOID)
+IGBO (IGBOID)

0   30 mi

0   50 km

Major Language Groups

Yoruboid   Ijoid   Kegboid (Ogoni)   Central Delta

Edoid   Igboid   Lower Cross   EKIT Language names

Appendix Crosscurrents and Confluences: Linguistic Clues to Cultural Development

KAY WILLIAMSON and

E. E. EFERE

Up to the mid-twentieth century the Niger Delta was largely inaccessible by road, and even now there are many areas that are reached only by the boats or helicopters of the oil companies or the canoes of local people. Many different linguistic communities have made this area their home over the millennia, and the language map has a diversity that is often not appreciated outside the area itself. This essay will consider how this diversity could have come about and what it suggests concerning the prehistory of the Delta.

In an area where written records are scanty before the nineteenth century, it is important to make use of other methods to write its history. These include archaeology, the collection and interpretation of oral traditions, and the use of linguistic evidence. The latter involves several steps: (1) knowing which languages are related to others and how closely; (2) studying the present geographical distribution of the languages; (3) taking into account the geographical features of the area and working out the most likely routes by which speakers of the various languages arrived in their present positions. Several assumptions underlie this process of linguistic investigation: (1) as languages spread over an area, they develop dialectal variations, which, if the speakers have little contact with one another, gradually develop into different languages; (2) the area in which the languages of the same group show the greatest variation is likely to be the original area of settlement from which other languages have spread out more recently; (3) attempts to quantify degrees of difference have not succeeded in developing a reliable dating system for the separation of languages from one another—as was once hoped with glottochronology—because of distorting factors introduced by language contact.[1]

Language contact is normal and distorts the regular patterns of dialect and later language divergence. When speakers of mutually unintelligible languages come into contact for trade or through intermarriage, for example, they either have to learn one another's languages or adopt a common language to facilitate communication. In the Niger Delta, a high degree of multilingualism is common; one often meets people who have a good command of four, five, or six languages, and at least one linguist who grew up in Warri claims that she cannot say what her "first language" is because as a child she learned four simultaneously! The other alternative, adopting a common language for common purposes, has led to the spread of Nigerian Pidgin English, or simply Pidgin, to the extent that it is learned as a first language by many people in the Warri-Sapele area and to a lesser extent around Port Harcourt, although it is not regarded as a "mother tongue" or language of ethnic identity (Donwa-Ifode 1983/84). Through various processes, such as forced or voluntary migration, learning the language of one's neighbors for daily interaction, or deliberate political integration, languages spread as they acquire more speakers or contract as they lose them, the extreme case being where a language dies out. These dynamic processes are well attested in the Niger Delta and must be considered in relation to oral traditions and other methods of historical inquiry; see, for example, the reconstruction of history in the Western Delta by Hubbard (1948).

The map shown here (fig. X.1) gives an idea of the variety of the linguistic groups in the Delta. All of them belong either to the Ịjọ or Benue-Congo branches of the Niger-Congo phylum. Ijoid taken as a whole is extremely different from its neighbors, both in basic vocabulary and in grammatical structure. In modern internal classifications of Niger-Congo it has been placed at a much higher level of the family tree than any of the neighboring groups, which are all included in (New) Benue-Congo. A simplified version of this classification is given in figure X.2 (based on Williamson and Blench, 2000).

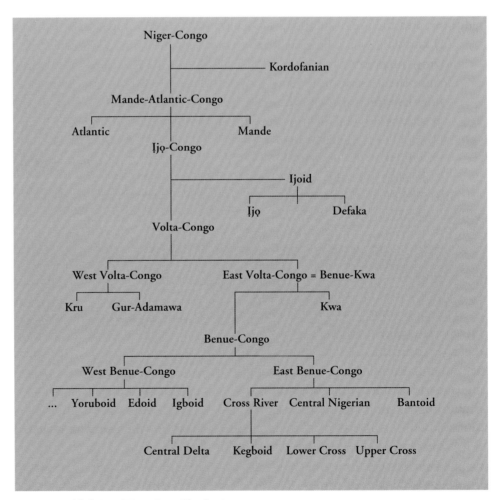

Fig. X.2 Simplified Tree of Niger-Congo Classification

The center of the Delta is occupied by an almost continuous block of Ịjǫ languages, which extends from the Atlantic Ocean inland, from the freshwater ocean fringe strip through mangrove swamps and a considerable area of freshwater forest. These languages are closely related among themselves to the point that they are often referred to as "dialects"; they are, however, more correctly described as a "language cluster," in which major groupings can be discerned with partial intelligibility extending over the boundaries. Related to Ịjǫ is the endangered Defaka language, spoken in one ward of a single town, Nkǫrǫ, whose speakers are bilingual in Nkǫrǫ. Defaka and Ịjǫ together are described as Ijoid. Figure X.3 shows the internal groupings of Ijoid.

No detailed convincing resemblances have been discovered between Ijoid and more remote language groups, although one cultural fact suggests a clue: in Ịjǫ the numeral "three" is regularly associated with men, "four" with women. This correlation has not been reported among the Benue-Congo neighbors of Ịjǫ, but it is common outside Benue-Congo in languages far to the north. This supports the non-Benue-Congo affiliation of Ijoid.

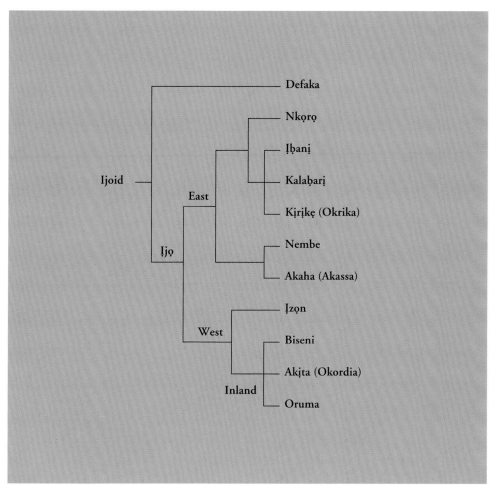

Fig. X.3 Classification of Ijoid Languages

The original settlement of Ijoid speakers is likely to have been in the east of the Niger Delta, because it is there that both Defaka and Ịjọ are found, suggesting that this is where the differentiation between the two took place. Looking at the modern distribution, it seems likely that Defaka was originally spoken to the east of Ịjọ; the tiny number of modern speakers combined with its linguistic distinctness suggests that it must once have been part of a larger continuum. Williamson (1997) has therefore suggested that Defaka-related languages once spread further east, perhaps as far as the mouth of the Cross River, and have been replaced by languages of other groups whose speakers later moved into the coastal areas.

It is therefore reasonable to conclude that Ijoid speakers separated from the other branches of Niger-Congo a very long time ago. Presumably they moved into the Niger Delta at an early date, and whatever links may have originally connected them to other language groups have been obliterated by subsequent movements or by language shift. There is no evidence either for or against the existence of an earlier non-Ijoid-speaking population in the Niger Delta.

Figure X.1 also shows a large area of the central part of the Niger Delta occupied by a language group appropriately named Central Delta. The languages of this group also form a language cluster; they include Abuan, Oḍual, the various groups collectively known as Ọgbia, and smaller outlying groups to the east of the main body, such as Oḅulom and Ogbronụagum. Their tentative relationships are summarized in figure X.4.

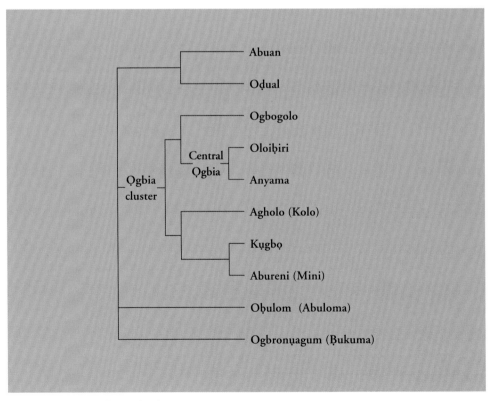

Fig. X.4 Classification of Central Delta

Speakers of Central Delta languages occupy some mangrove areas and more extensive freshwater forest areas like the Ijoid speakers. The map (see fig. X.1) shows the Central Delta languages nestled into surrounding Ịjọ languages. It appears that on their entry into the heart of the Delta they must have either taken over some of the territory that was earlier settled, even if sparsely, by Ịjọ speakers, or the Ịjọ speakers must have expanded around their large block established in the central area. We would expect in such circumstances to find evidence of much interaction between the two language groups, and this is in fact the case. Ịjọ influence in even basic vocabulary is found in some Central Delta languages; thus the typical Ịjọ word *ɓeri* for "ear" is borrowed into Abuan, Oḍual, and Kụgbọ as *aɓeri,* while Ọgbia retains the old Niger-Congo word for "ear" in the form *ato.* On the other hand, the small Ịjọ dialect Oruma, surrounded by Ọgbia speakers, has *síe* for "dog," borrowed from Ọgbia *isía,* while all the rest of Ịjọ has *obiri* or *ebiri.* Further evidence of interaction is the extensive bilingualism between Ịjọ and Central Delta forms of speech in the southern part of the area.

Unlike Ijoid speakers, speakers of Central Delta languages have related language groups inside the Niger Delta; these are the Kegboid (or Ogoni) languages on the eastern edge of the Delta and the Lower Cross speakers stretching from Obolo (or Andoni) in the Niger Delta to the lower reaches of the Cross River and extending into Cameroon. Together with the Upper Cross group, who are found further inland along the Cross River, these groups of languages, together with Central Delta, are known as the Delta-Cross sub-branch of the Cross River branch of Benue-Congo. Since these related groups are all to the east of the Central Delta languages, it appears that the Central Delta speakers must have entered the Delta from the east. The map shows two of the other groups of Cross River languages, Kegboid and Lower Cross. The Kegboid languages (usually known as Ogoni, although this name is not acceptable to speakers of all the languages grouped under it) are spoken immediately to the east of Ijoid. The Lower Cross languages are spoken to the east of Kegboid. North of Lower Cross is the Upper Cross group. It would seem that the speakers of Delta-Cross moved south along the Cross River, and on reaching the coastal creeks spread out and adopted a fishing mode of life, while those who settled farther north adopted farming. Figure X.5 shows the internal relationships of Kegboid, and figure X.6 shows the internal relationships of Lower Cross (Connell 1991).

Just as it is obvious that the Delta-Cross groups must have entered the Delta from the east, so it is clear that others entered from the west. Figure X.1 shows the Delta Edoid languages (Epie-Atịsa, Engenni, and Degema) embedded deeply within the Delta, while the South-West Edoid languages (Ẹrụwa, Isoko, Urhobo, Uvbiẹ, and Okpẹ) lie to the north and west of Ịjọ; the Edoid group also continues north of there. This suggests that Edoid speakers entered the Delta from the north and west. The deeper penetration of the Delta Edoid indicates that they entered first, followed by the South-West Edoid. This is partly supported by the fact that although the Ẹrụwa

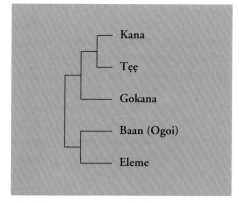

Fig. X.5 Classification of Kegboid (Ogoni)

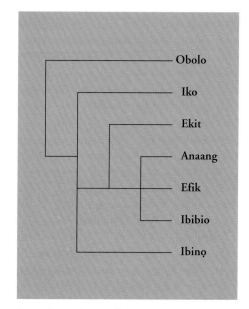

Fig. X.6 Classification of Lower Cross

claim autochthony in the area (Hubbard 1948, 96–101), the other South-West Edoid groups claim to have come from Benin or other places; the Delta Edoid also did not claim to have come from Benin when first questioned. Edoid language groups, however, are more closely related than Delta-Cross ones; this indicates that Edoid speakers entered the Delta at a later date than Delta-Cross speakers. Figure X.7 shows the relationship of the South-West and Delta Edoid languages.

The extreme Western Delta contains speakers of Yoruboid langugages, the Itsẹkiri, and further to the west some Yorùbá groups, such as the Ilajẹ. The location of the Yoruboid languages, beyond the Edoid languages, shows a coastal movement into the Delta from the west. Itsẹkiri is closely related to Yorùbá, which suggests a relatively short period since they separated. Figure X.8 shows the relationship of the Yoruboid languages.

North and east of the Delta Edoid live the speakers of the Igboid languages. Igbo with its vast dialectal complexity is one of the three largest Nigerian languages. Around its periphery lie a number of communities that are more different from one another than are the acknowledged dialects of Igbo, and whose members think of themselves as speaking languages distinct from Igbo although closely related to it. The most distinct of these languages from Igbo is Ẹkpeye; others in the Delta are the Abọ (Aboh)-Ụkwụanị-Ndọnị cluster, Ọgba, and Ikwere (Ikwerre). Figure X.9 shows their relationship schematically. As already indicated, the relationship of the Igboid languages is very close, suggesting that their entry into the Delta has been relatively recent and from a northern direction.

Williamson (1997) proposed that the Kegboid and Lower Cross groups (and perhaps also Central Delta) occupy, at least in part, areas that were earlier settled by speakers of Ijoid, probably of Defaka-related languages. The Ijoid languages have left their traces in these languages, as can be seen in words like "mangrove." Mangroves are found growing in salt or brackish water; they form a belt of differing thickness just behind the beach ridge soils that fringe the coast. Thus mangroves would probably not have been known to Delta-Cross speakers when they lived up the Cross River, but would have been encountered as these groups approached the coast. Interestingly, forms of a single word for "mangrove" are found in most of the Delta, as shown in Figure X.10. Most of these words resemble one another closely. It is therefore likely that they have been borrowed from one language to another, starting from the language group that was first in the area. Judging from the distribution of the languages, this is likely to have been Ijoid, as has already been suggested.

The mangrove environment has a distinctive fauna, which includes mudskippers, oysters, and manatees. In many groups, these creatures have similar names, suggesting long ages of contact. For example, the mudskipper (family *Periopthalmidae*) is called *íchìlá* in Kịrịkẹ, *àtịlà* in Ịzọn, *íshịlá* in Abuan, and *tîán* in Gokana. The oyster that grows on mangrove roots (*Crassostrea gasar osteaceae*) is called *ḿgbè* in East Ịjọ, *ímgbè* in Ịzọn, *ígbè*

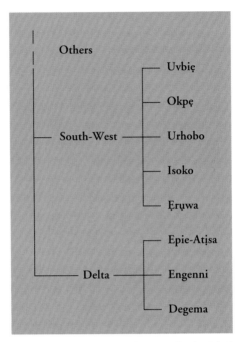

Fig. X.7 Classification of South-West and Delta Edoid

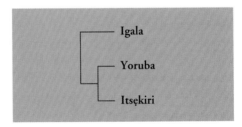

Fig. X.8 Classification of Yoruboid

in Abuan, and *ḿgbà* in Ikwere. The manatee (*Trichechus senegalensis*) is called *òmèín* in East Ịjọ, *èmêîn* in Ịzọn, *èmâny* in Abuan, and *emenyi* in Ọgba.

A similar pattern may be observed in the names for various kinds of fish. For example, the shark (*Carcharhinidae* spp.) is called *ófịrịmá* in East Ịjọ; *ọfúrúmá* in Ịzọn, Abuan, and Ọgbia; *ọfúrúmọ́* in Epie and Degema; *ófúrúmá* in Obolo; *fínímáá* in Tẹẹ. (In the case of Tẹẹ, this is the only word in the language with an "f," so it is obviously borrowed.) Similarly, the sawfish (*Pristis* spp.) is known as *òkí* throughout the Ịjọ area and also in the Central Delta area. Many of these large dramatic fishes feature as masks in masquerade dances, and it is quite likely that some of the linguistic similarities noted are due to the borrowing of the masquerade, rather than the knowledge of the actual fish.

Many features of culture are also borrowed. The word for "masquerade," or at least for the type regarded as derived from the dances of the water spirits, is *ówú* (or a variant) throughout Ịjọ, in Ikwere, in Ẹkpeye, and in Oḍual; the central position of Ịjọ here indicates that this is where the word originated. The word for "castnet" is *ìgbọ́* throughout Ịjọ, in Ikwere, Ọgba, Ẹkpeye, Epie, and Engenni. Words for "money" are usually derived from an old form of currency; those based on an old word for "manilla" are found throughout the Eastern Delta: Kalaḅarị *ìgbìkì*, Nembe *ìgbògí*, Ịzọn *ìgbègí*, Obolo *ìkpòkò*, Central Delta *ìkpòki*, Kana *kpùgì*, Gokana *kpègè*, and Eleme *èkpìì*. Such widespread words, common to many of the different language groups in the Niger Delta, show us that people have for centuries, perhaps millennia, interacted with their neighbors and mutually enriched their cultures and their languages.

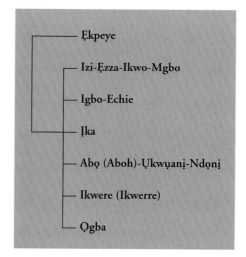

Fig. X.9 Classification of Igboid

Group	Language	Word for mangrove
Ịjọ	Kalaḅarị-Kịrịkẹ-Nkọrọ; Ịbanị	ángálá; ngálá
Ịjọ	Ịzọn	àngálá; àgàlà
Ịjọ	Oruma, Akịta; Biseni	ágálá; ángílẹ́
Central Delta	Abuan, Ọgbia; Oḍual, Kụgbọ	àgálá; àgàlá
Kegboid	Kana, Tẹẹ; Eleme	gárá; ńgálá
Lower Cross	Obolo, Iko; Ibinọ	ńgálá; ńkáná
Delta Edoid	Epie	àgálá, plural ìgálá
Delta Edoid	Degema	ùngála, plural ìngála
Igboid	Ikwere: Akpọ	àgálá

Fig. X.10 Words for "Mangrove" in the Niger Delta

Notes to the Text

Preface (Leis)

1. Among the Isoko, "carved *ivri* figures commemorate ancient warriors, validate office holders, and celebrate the ethos of tenacity and aggression" (Peek 1986, 43).

2. Although we use the terms "cultural identity" and "ethnic identity" interchangeably in this preface, the emphasis on the former is intended to convey the contemporary understanding of "cultures" as being discrete social groupings within larger social units, as in the examples of a "university's culture" or the conflicting "cultures" of two business organizations in the process of merging—all of these existing within American culture and society. Ethnic groups and categories have assumed the meaning that cultures once had of referring to the broadest defined social groupings whose members presumably share beliefs and practices in common.

3. The estimates for the Ijo, Isoko/Urhobo, and Itsekiri are from Grimes (1996).

Chapter 1 (Peek and Nicklin)

1. The early dates determined in the area remind us of the interesting enclaves to be found in the Niger Delta, such as the group of "Delta Edo" clans near Degema.

2. Fieldwork conducted in the Eastern Niger Delta in 1992 was funded by the Horniman Public Museum and Public Park Trust, and research permission kindly granted by the Nigerian National Commission for Museums and Monuments. The project would not have been possible without the generous assistance of Dr. N. C. Ejituwu and all the Obolo leaders and others to whom he introduced me. Various facilities were provided by Professor E. J. Alagoa, University of Port Harcourt, and NCMM staff at Lagos, Port Harcourt, Calabar, Oron, and Uyo. I am particularly grateful for hospitality provided by Mrs. Violetta Ekpo, Dr. Joseph Eboreime, Mr. Aniefiok Akpan, Mrs. Emma Brown, and their families, as well as to my wife, Jill Salmons, for collaboration in the field and throughout the writing of this paper. I am also grateful to Dr. Nigel Barley, Museum of Mankind, for making available to me archival material concerning the Andoni bronzes, to Professor Frank Willett for providing me with his own Andoni photographs, and to him and Dr. Philip M. Peek for encouraging my Nigerian metalwork studies over many years.

3. According to Ejituwu (1991, xi), the Obolo "have always called themselves 'Ebi-Obolo' or, more succinctly, 'Obolo'…[which] is both a linguistic and ethnic term." These are the people that the Europeans have called "Andoni."

Chapter 3 (Anderson)

Field and archival research for this paper was conducted with the support of a Kress Doctoral Dissertation Fellowship for fourteen months in Great Britain and Nigeria in 1978–1979, an Alfred University summer grant for a month in Great Britain in 1986, and a Council for International Education Faculty Research Grant for twelve months in Nigeria in 1991–1992.

1. This was also the case among neighboring groups, including the Igbo (Basden 1921 [1966], 202; Thomas 1913–1914, 108; Isichei 1976, 78–79; Ijoma 1983, 14). I would like to thank Philip Peek and Philip Leis for commenting on earlier drafts of this chapter and Richard Freeman for providing proper orthography for Ijo terms.

2. Philip Peek (personal communication, 1998) notes that Isoko men gained higher status by killing other men, much as Native Americans did in coup counting. He adds that the manner by which men advanced through age groups accounts for the sporadic nature of Isoko warfare. He also contrasts the Urhobo, Isoko, and Ijo with the Yoruba, who emphasize hunters rather than warriors. His informants described Isoko covenants as elaborate affairs that involved sacrificing slaves, as may also have been the case among the Ijo.

3. They also intended to introduce a cash currency and establish a labor market to replace slaves. The British documents consulted at the Public Records Office in Kew Gardens include:

CO 520, vol. 13, 8798, Feb. 8, 1902, Despatch: "Piracy on the Lower Niger"

CO 520, vol. 13, 10513, Feb. 15, 1902: "State of Affairs in Lower Niger"

CO 520, vol. 13, 14480, March 16, 1902: "Operations on the Lower Niger"

CO 520, vol. 14, 16427, April 4, 1902: "Despatch from R. Moor"

CO 520, vol. 15, 18724, April 17, 1902: "Aro Expedition March 25 1902 Final Report"

CO 520, vol. 15, 18725, April 18, 1902: "Political Report"

CO 520, vol. 15, 41428, Aug. 22, 1902: "Opening Up of Certain Territories

CO 520, vol. 20, 38356, Sept. 20, 1903: "Operations against Bibi-Cala"

CO 520, vol. 20, 41602, Oct. 21, 1903: "Operations against Pirate Chief Bibi-Cala"

N 38356, received Oct. 19, 1903; S. Nigeria #41601 and #41801, received Nov. 16, 1903

4. According to Alagoa (1972, 26, n. 1) the Population Census of Nigeria, 1963, lists the population of Kolokuma clan, which is far larger than most other clans in the region, at 29,475. Even if the British reports refer to a broader area, the population was probably much lower in 1903, so some men must have had several guns.

5. A reconnaissance report of the area known as Wilberforce Island follows the announcement of the second campaign against the "pirate," together with notes on towns believed friendly and hostile to Bibikeala, and those he was known to frequent for purposes of trade. A map locates "Bibi-Cala's stronghold," a bush camp, consisting of about ten houses occupied by forty followers, on a small creek some distance from Igbedi. (See Public Records Office, Kew Gardens, CO 520, vol. 20, 38356, Sept. 20, 1903.)

6. The collection is in the County Museum. Museum records indicate accession numbers 4.2.04.16–49, but some pieces are reported as missing or do not appear on the current list. It seems likely that Whitehouse, who wrote articles on Igbo *mbari* houses and the Aro Chukwu oracle, collected at least basic information on the Ijo objects, but no documentation survives at either Liverpool or the Public Records Office.

7. Richard Freeman, who grew up in nearby Ikebiri, tells me that nearly every Ijo village once had a shrine for Odewei. He identifies him as a hunting god, but this function may have been emphasized after local warfare ceased.

8. Though raised as a Christian, she took over as priestess around 1990, while in her early teens, after learning that the spirits had killed her father for refusing to serve them. Her great-grandmother, a diviner, had previously served as priestess.

9. Levi Yeiyei of Ondewari claims that she had been divining for twenty-eight years by the time she came to Ondewari, but she brought her son with her, and I recall hearing that he was still a boy. Thus, she seems unlikely to have been more than sixty when she arrived and may well have been in her fifties. I have added some details from a version of the story told in Korokorosei, which conforms to Levi Yeiyei's in most respects but differs in others, including the order of events and the number of canoes. A written account compiled by Richard Freeman, my research assistant, refers repeatedly to Queen's activities as a "war" against evil spirits. It estimates the date of the ritual as 1974, but an earlier date seems more likely.

10. Okpotuwari, a settlement across the river from Ondewari, still performs an annual ceremony to recall the covenant with the bush, following instructions issued by a male diviner from Oporoma. Ondewari called on another man from neighboring Oporoma around 1956 to fend off the evil spirits from Okoroko bush blamed for disfiguring children.

11. Philip Peek (personal communication, 1998) notes that Isoko shrines experienced a renaissance during the war. This may also have happened in the Ijo area, for some Ijo priests, including Isobowei's, claim that returning soldiers came great distances to acknowledge their spirits' support in battle. However, the fervent evangelical Christians who looted and burned his shrine and a number of others when a wave of iconoclasm swept the region in the decade following the war might represent another manifestation of the same ethos.

12. See the Web site of the Urhobo Historical Society, "A Compendium of Graffiti Left Behind at Odi by Invading Nigerian Soldiers, Compiled on Christmas Day, 1999": http://www.waado.org/Environment/FedGovt NigerDelta/BayelsaInvasion/AssessmentOfInvasion/Graffiti.html. Also refer

to the Update on Human Rights Violations in the Niger (Human Rights Watch Backgrounder, New York, December 14, 2000): http://www.hrw.org/backgrounder/africa/nigeriabkg1214.htm; and finally to "Military Must Account for Abuses: Washington Should Press President Obasanjo (Human Rights Watch, Washington, May 11, 2001): http://www.hrw.org/press/2001/05/bush0511.htmNigeria.

Chapter 4 (Anderson)

Field and archival research for this paper was conducted with the support of a Kress Doctoral Dissertation Fellowship for fourteen months in England and Nigeria in 1978–1979; an Alfred University summer grant for a month in England in 1986; and a Council for International Education Faculty Research Grant for twelve months in Nigeria in 1991–1992. I would like to thank Philip Peek and Philip Leis for commenting on earlier drafts of this chapter and Richard Freeman for providing the proper spelling and orthography of Ijo words.

1. Most carvers report that they carved about one canoe a month and a dozen canoes per year while in their prime. The work also carries spiritual risks, although the carvers I interviewed in 1991 did not emphasize this aspect of the profession. Spirits sometimes live in trees, so anyone who cuts one down has to take precautions or risk their wrath. In 1979, rumors blamed one man's death and another's loss of eyesight on cutting down trees to carve canoes.
2. One diviner clarified this by saying that these objects are merely the emblems spirits have chosen as physical manifestations and that the spirits they represent, who reside in the rivers, are really very beautiful.
3. My first research assistant, Israel Kigibie, offered this explanation, but according to my second research assistant, Richard Freeman, the Ijo consider all whitish or purplish fish to be kings and queens within their categories and do not eat them.
4. The term *foinyou* can refer to either vampires, who fly about at night and suck blood from their victims, or witches, who kill family members to be shared at feasts with their friends. People blame the initial influx of *foinyou* on wives imported from the Isoko area.
5. People consider some of the fish living in the forest to be bush spirits but say water spirits can travel up creeks, settle there, and intermarry with bush spirits.
6. Most lakes call for bush spirit songs, but those sung for Dabiyeyinghi are funeral songs. As of 1979, the Dabiyeyinghi festival had not been held for many years due to a boundary dispute with a neighboring town. The festival for "Tall palms" was to be held in 1979 but was canceled due to a funeral. The figures had deteriorated, and the shrine was in the process of being rebuilt; but a party engaged in a bush spirit ritual paused to libate where they once stood. (See chapter 3 of this volume.)
7. Townspeople explain the substitution by saying they could not find an artist who knew how to carve the headpiece of the original fish.
8. Their word for play, *toi*, has roughly the same range of connotations as its English counterpart (Horton 1960, 69; Kay Williamson, personal communication, 1978).
9. Most Central Ijo headpieces measure less than three feet in length. The players used the money earned from this performance to commission a new set of smaller, wooden headpieces. Father and son wear similar headpieces; that of the wife takes the form of a female figure.
10. My informant, Richard Freeman, later explained that the sawfish is one of the hostile, gigantic fish that sometimes becomes a water spirit.
11. See Alagoa and Tamuno 1989, 143–52, where Ben Naanen and A. I. Pepple identify the foremost factor as minority opposition to majority domination in the Eastern region but also note cultural and historical differences with peoples on the mainland and "the peculiar development needs" of the region. They refer as well to a "mainland/riverine dichotomy" within Rivers State that fueled demands for the creation of a Port Harcourt State, comprising Ahoada, Ogoni, and Port Harcourt Divisions. This resulted in forming Bayelsa State from the western part of Rivers State in 1997.

Chapter 5 (Peek)

My deepest appreciation to Edward "Crooz" Ugboma—a true "man of words"—without whom my research on Isoko history and culture would never have occurred. I also thank Dr. Adeline Apena (and her whole family!) for many years of support and aid.

1. Technically, "clan" is not appropriate for the Isoko political units because none are composed exclusively of related peoples. Nevertheless, this is the term the Isoko use. The Isoko clan units do represent people who have chosen to live together and to be identified with each other as if they all shared a common ancestor.
2. Kathy Curnow reports that her Edo family was very concerned about her trips into the Delta and were especially distressed when she waded into the ocean at Bar Beach in Lagos!
3. Another form of communication comes to mind with this reference to the ubiquitous multilingualism of the Delta. Despite assurances of the uniqueness of the single forehead to nose-tip scar by Isoko elders, one can find this mark throughout the Delta on older men and women as well as carvings.

Chapter 6 (Drewal)

An earlier condensed version of this essay was presented at the Seventh Triennial Symposium on African Art at UCLA, April 5, 1986. I gratefully acknowledge the support of grants from the National Endowment for the Humanities awarded in 1981 (RO-20072-81-2184) and 1985 (RO-21030-85) for the fieldwork in Ìjẹ̀búland, Nigeria, and two Andrew W. Mellon Senior Fellowships at the Metropolitan Museum of Art in 1985 and 1986 for archival research and writing. I am also pleased to acknowledge the assistance of the University of Ifẹ̀ (now Ọbáfẹ́mi Awólọ́wọ̀ University), Nigeria, for research affiliations and the Nigerian Museum for permission to use its archives and collections. Thanks are especially due all my Yorùbá and American friends, colleagues, and teachers who gave freely of their time and wisdom to provide information and insights for this work. They include: Oyin Ògunbà; Rowland Abíódún; Bọ́lájí and Lọ́ládé Campbell; Àdisá Awókọ̀yà; Jimoh Bákàrè; Gabriel Omísanmí; Abíódún Kàsálí; Adépéré Ògúnsanmí; Adéníyì, the Àlùke of Òmu; Saliu Jókotadé, artist, Ìjẹ̀bú-Musin; Chief Ayọdèjì Bìsìríù, the Olówá of Ìjẹ̀bú-Òde; Oba Adéọyè, the Ọlọ́kọ̀ of Ìjẹ̀bú-Musin; Sálíyù Rájí, the Ajíróba of Òmu; Ọba Fẹ̀sọ̀gbadé II, the Ọlọ́jà of Èpẹ́; Chief Olúfowóbí, Èpẹ́; Ọba S. A. Sólé and his son Sunday, Òmu; Ọládélé Sánlọlá; Margaret Thompson Drewal; John Mason; Perkins Foss; Martha Anderson; and Philip Peek. Finally I pay my respects to those denizens of the deep—the water people, Ọsun, Yemoja, Ọbà, Ọya, Olókun, Ọlọ́sà, Mami Wata, et al.— as artists and the devout have done for centuries. This essay is dedicated to the memory of Ana Araiz, daughter of Osun.

1. This summary is based on Horton (1960, 1963) for the Eastern Ijo, specifically Kalabari, and Anderson (1997b) for the Central and Western Ijo. Among the Kalabari, membership in the Ekine/Sekiapu Society is regarded as one of a man's most important accomplishments in life and as such, is celebrated after his death. Ekine headdresses are represented in the memorial screens of the Kalabari Ijo where "a man's prowess with a particular *owu* is one of his most important attributes" (Horton 1960, 32). And one of the most important and deeply felt parts of a man's funeral commemoration is the performance of the mask that was so much a part of his identity during his life (Horton 1963, 108). Martha Anderson (1997b) notes that Western and Central Delta Ijo do not have an Ekine/Sekiapu Society, although they do masquerade for the *owu* (water people).
2. For a fascinating history of the probable re-creation of Òkoóró masking in association with Gẹlẹ̀dẹ́ and Olókun celebrations among the Bini and Yorùbá/Lucumi (Ìjẹ̀bú, Àwórì, and Ègbádò) in Cuba, see Mason (1996, 19–21).
3. From my own research in Ìjẹ̀bú, Ìdòko was an ancient kingdom according to Ọba Adéọyè, the Ọlọ́kọ̀ of Ìjẹ̀bú-Musin (personal communication, 1982).

Chapter 7 (Curnow)

This chapter is based on field research conducted in the Warri Kingdom, Nigeria, in 1992, 1993, and 1994, which was partially funded by the National Endowment for the Humanities, the State of Ohio, and Cleveland State University.

I am very grateful to Ogiame Atuwatse II, the Olu of Warri, for granting me research permission and for his kind assistance and encouragement, and to his chiefs, especially the Uwangue, Eson, Iyatsere, and Iye of Warri and the Olaraja of Okere. Many thanks also to my research assistant, Mr. Egert Omoneukanrin; my able photographer, Mr. D. Anthony Mahone; Dr. Mark Ogharaerumi; Mr. J. O. E. Ayomike; Mr. Thomson Kayoh; Mr. Happy Gaja; the entire membership of the Omo Ologbara Cultural Society; and all the *umale* clubs of Warri, Ode-Itsekiri, and Sapele. Special appreciation is also extended to my American colleagues Drs. Martha Anderson, Barbara Blackmun, Joe Nevadomsky, and Philip Peek.

1. There is disagreement over the exact size of the Itsekiri population, although sources agree they are much smaller in number than either the Urhobo or Ijo. P. C. Lloyd estimated there were only about 30,000 in the early 1960s (1963, 209), but the current *Ethnologue* estimate is 510,000 (Grimes 1996), which seems high. Nigerians have repeatedly rejected official censuses, since most citizens feel the numbers have been manipulated for political purposes.

2. As A. F. C. Ryder points out (1969, 28), the word *Huela*, used by Pacheco Pereira, was probably an attempt to spell *Iwere*, the name Itsekiri use for themselves.

3. Itsekiri tradition states that, some time after Ginuwa's journey in the late fifteenth century, a Benin war party came to the Warri region to recover the chiefs' sons who had accompanied him. They were unsuccessful and, fearing their reception in Benin, founded the mainland settlement of Okere.

4. The Itsekiri are actually now on better terms with their parent cultures than they have been for some time. Recent Delta violence in late 1998 and early 1999 led to a formal alliance among the Benin Edo, the Itsekiri, and the Ilaje-Yoruba of Ondo State. This alignment was created in opposition to manifestos (and statements of support) from the Ijo, Urhobo, and Isoko.

5. Derumo, is one of the few pre-nineteenth-century women to be remembered by name in Itsekiri history. Ginuwa's association with her took place at the coast in Ijo territory; he later withdrew with his followers to an inland position at Ijala, not far from Warri and Ode-Itsekiri.

6. For Ijo performance style, I am dependent on Frank Speed's film *Duminea* (Kalabari Ijo), Martha Anderson's Central Ijo footage, Sokari Douglas Camp's Kalabari *Chief! Chief!* and *Alagba* videos, and numerous videos of West and Central Ijo performances broadcast on Delta State's television stations.

7. I base comparisons of size and performance on both published and videotaped versions of Ijo Oki but would be happy to know if other versions and performance styles exist, particularly among the Western Ijo.

8. Olekun should not be confused with Umalokun, the deity who is considered the overall ruler of the sea. Umalokun is analogous (and related to) the Benin and Yoruba deity Olokun, and the Itsekiri consider all water spirits to be mere aspects of Umalokun.

Chapter 8 (Aronson)

This study would not have been possible without the generosity and sensitive insight of Nimi Wariboko, an Abonnema based in the United States. Passionately interested in exploring the many facets of his own culture, he sought answers to my long list of questions about the tortoise while visiting his village in the fall of 1997. I am also indebted to his mother, Grace Wariboko Jack, from Jack's compound, Abonnema, for her generous responses to his many questions. It is to Wariboko and his family that I dedicate this essay.

1. There are three species of the hinge-back in West Africa, the *Kinixys homeana, Kinixys erosa,* and *Kinixys belliana.* In turn, the latter is divided into two subspecies, the *Kinixys belliana belliana* and the *Kinixys belliana nogueyi.* It is on a visual basis and on the advice of Dr. Michael Klemens, a leading expert on hinge-backs, that I have singled out the *Kinixys belliana* species.

2. Tortoises are generally quiet creatures. Only when they are in the act of mating do they tend to vocalize, and some even argue that those sounds may be the grinding of shells or the closing of jaws rather than vocalization itself (Alderton 1988, 57–58). The

"sound" of the hinge-back can be heard on the Web site http://www.tortoise.org.

3. The Ijo are not entirely clear on this distinction. While they identify Ikaki as an *oru* spirit, they are also inclined to characterize him as an *owu* because of his appearance in an *owu*-type masquerade (see below). His marginal affiliation with water may also account for his *owu*-like nature.

4. The text for that song goes as follows:
    In the forest where I live, in the swamp where I love,
    I don't call any child of Kula,
    Kwe kwe kwe, etc.
    Human meat, yum, yum.
    Human bones, yum, yum. [Horton 1967, 226]

5. The name *Kalagidi* is not easily translated. The prefix *kala* suggests "small," and the suffix *agidi* may be a reference to a type of knife (Nimi Wariboko, personal communication, 1998)

6. Not all West African cultures regard the tortoise's shell in so negative a way. For example, the Igbirra conceptualize it as a house and home in the most positive, nurturing sense (John Picton, personal communication, 1998).

7. E. J. Alagoa is cautious to point out that Eastern Ijo trading states are not entirely rooted in the transatlantic trade. Rather, it was a multitude of stimuli that shaped these ruling states (Alagoa 1972, 123). At best, one can say that the Eastern Ijo fine-tuned their trading states to meet the demands of the transatlantic trade.

8. While not discussed in this paper, *ikakibite* is also worn by members of the Sekiapu (Ekine) Society at important masquerade performances. *Ikakibite* with a fishing eagle's feathers (*igo piko*) is the popular and preferred handwear of unmasked Ekine members during masquerade displays (Nimi Wariboko, personal communication, 1987).

9. In Benin, the image of a hand holding a mudfish, itself a symbol of the *oba*'s relationship to the sea god Olokun, evokes the proverb "the one who holds the fish can also let it loose." The egg-in-hand image in Asante culture similarly implies delicacy with which power must be exercised. Loosely translated, the proverb sends the message that should the egg, a symbol of power, be clutched too tightly, it will be crushed. If it is held too loosely, it will slip from the leader's grasp.

10. In addition, an Abonnema family, the Kaladokubo house of the Jack group of houses, is permitted to use the cloth to play Egbelegbe. In 1882, Chief Kaladokubo, who led the Jack group of houses from Elem Kalabari to Abonnema, was granted the right to play the Egbelegbe and use the cloth associated with it (Nimi Wariboko, personal communication, 1997).

Chapter 9 (Kpone-Tonwe and Salmons)

Both authors are highly indebted to Professor E. J. Alagoa for every kind of generous assistance during respective periods of fieldwork. Jill Salmons recognizes the invaluable help provided by Sonpie Kpone-Tonwe's doctoral dissertation. This excellent body of research provided essential insight into the main economic, political, and social structure of Ogoni society, which allowed her to understand the context of Ogoni art and conduct fieldwork accordingly. The authors would also like to thank Sarah Travis Cobb for her assistance in the early stages of the preparation of this essay and for generously sharing photographs taken during her fieldwork among the Ogoni in the 1980s

Jill Salmons is indebted to Jean Paul Barbier for the generous financial support that enabled her to undertake field research in 1992, conducted by kind permission of the Nigerian National Commission for Museums and Monuments. She is grateful to several members of NCMM staff, in particular Dr. and Mrs. Joseph Eboreime and Mrs. Violetta Ekpo and all the staff at Port Harcourt. She wishes to acknowledge the remarkable help given by Gbenetee James Booburah of Kono Boue who worked tirelessly as a research assistant throughout her stay. His knowledge of Ogoni history and customs and wide network of friends helped facilitate a highly productive period of fieldwork in 1992. She also acknowledges the generosity of Gbeneme G. N. K. Giniwa of Korokoro, Tai, who allowed her to stay in his palace during the New Yam festival and M. D. K Tonwe, Mene-bue of Kono Boue, Dr. "Bro," his wife, Rose, and family who helped make her stay in Kono Boue so pleasurable. She also acknowledges the following chiefs, elders, shrine priestesses, potters, and carvers who shared knowledge and apologizes for any incorrect titles or spelling: Mican Gbii and Augustus Karanwa of Kpaen, Nonwu; Gabriel Kpaabe of A-abue Kira; Dick Kali and Mina Menekpoji of Opu-Oko, Nyo-Khana; Thompson Naapa Piagbo of Kono Boue; C. B. S. Nwikina of Kono; the late Edward Kobani; Dr. C. Keibel; Judy Nwanodi; M. L. Viura of Bomo; Mene-bue E. B. Nyone of Lewe; J. Abanee of Kono Boue; A. O. Ngei, One-Eh of Eleme; M. M. N. Akekue of Korokoro; Philip Nnah of Korokoro; Manfred Kue Okpe Gba of Botem; Gbeneme B. A. Mballey of Tai; J. P. Tigiri J. P. of Luyor Gwara; Menebene J. S. Yaadag of Sii; Mene-bue J. B. Subeesua Katah of E-eke; T. K Birinee of Kono; Michael S. Keredee of Bodo; A. Kabaari Tekam of Barrako; M. M. P. Tee of Biara; F. Berebon of Bodo; Gbenemene J. P Bagia of Gokana; S. K. Tigidam of Zaakpon; D. Yorkirika of Kaa; O. B. Nalelo of Biare; E. D. Nwinaabu of Kpaen; Gbeneme M. S. H. Eguru of Ken Khana; Mene-bue C. B. S. Nwikina of Kono; Francis Gberesu of Kegbaradere; Baribor Kpobe; Samuel Mbaki Akpapa and Npolice Koranwii of Ue-eken; Saaro Issac Deekor of Kaa; Neegbo Kpinee, Ue-nee Yor of Bie Gwara; Dormu Kiko of Kpaen; Thankgod Ikperikpe of Kpaen; J. B. Idinee of Kono Boue; Nuke Nwiidag of Pue; Leelou Yoronlee of Kono Boue; Lenu Naagbiwa and Isaac Legbara of Uegwere Boue; Court Fornaa of Nyokwiri Boue; Marie Kone of Nyokwiri Boue; Siniwa Tabarade of Sii; Gabriel Ezemene of Bodo; Kponanyie Tornedeeko of Barako.

She also wishes to thank Keith Nicklin for his help and encouragement in the field and in the writing of this chapter, as well as for despatching her collection of Ogoni carvings from Nigeria to the Horniman Museum, London.

Interleaf K (Nicklin)

Field research conducted in August 1992 was funded by the Horniman Public Museum and Public Park Trust, with kind permission of the Nigerian National Commission for Museums and Monuments. The project would not have been possible without the generous assistance of Dr. N. C. Ejituwu, University of Port Harcourt, as well as many Obolo chiefs, elders, and others.

Chapter 10 (Eicher and Erekosima)

1. Fieldnotes of Joanne B. Eicher, from a personal interview with a Kalabari chief in Buguma, 1988.
2. Generally, Kalabari call these types of deaths "abominations." Da-Wariboko (1991, 150) adds to the ones we have listed: pregnant women, people with communicable diseases, and a "mad person."
3. Not everyone is in agreement with this age definition of "adult." Da-Wariboko defines youths as those from "a day to about thirty years old" and those dying between thirty and fifty as being "young at death" with no expensive wake-keeping (1991, 151–52). Erekosima et al. state: "People of five to fifty years are still regarded as dying young and so their deaths are very sad.... Heavy mourning follows their burial" (1991, 150–51).
4. Isokariari (1983) elaborates on the life of Madame Orupumbu Tariah who was a prominent trader but not a chief.
5. The ultimate and highest authority of women is the formal position of community priestess (egbele ereme), assuming the function of deistic representatives of full age. They differ from the prophetesses (orukuro ereme) who have special skills in providing guidance for Kalabari members of society who seek them out.
6. This period of confinement and attention to the health and well-being of the woman is also called the "fattening" process.
7. We draw from these earlier articles, which will provide additional detail for the interested reader. The 1987 article analyzes the role of the funeral as a celebratory event of life. The 1989 article elaborates upon the art of decorating the funeral bed before and after the funeral, and the 1996 article concentrates on the Indian madras used in the funerals. In addition, the analyses of Erekosima et al. (1991) and Da-Wariboko (1991) provide a general picture of contemporary Kalabari funeral practices. Our formal documentation began when Eicher first observed a funeral in 1980 on the island of Abonnema. She witnessed or participated in more than twenty funerals during eight field trips. Erekosima, a Kalabari man, participated in a countless number of funerals both as a child and as an adult scholar. Because his father was an educator and secondary school principal, Erekosima lived in the Igbo towns of Owerri and Umuahia until his university years in the United States. His family, however, was steeped in Kalabari cultural tradition because of routine travel to Buguma, the birthplace of both his father and mother, for holidays and significant family events, such as funerals.
8. For a more thorough analysis of the Kalabari system, see Eicher and Erekosima (1993) and Eicher and Erekosima (forthcoming).
9. This refers to those relatives studying or working at a significant distance away in Nigeria or elsewhere in Africa, Europe, or America.
10. This number is considered traditional for a woman's house, although some people have included a fourth room, the oyiapu sukubebio, or "men's room," as part of the traditional house (Oruwari and Owei 1989). In addition, the number three is considered an auspicious number in many aspects of Kalabari life. For example, gifts are often given in groups of three at the time of betrothal and marriage; see Wariboko (1999). The general pattern for Kalabari is that a man, who performs the ultimate marriage ceremony (iya) by which the wife and her progeny are effectively transferred to his own lineage, will build a separate house for the wife. This is a part of the dowry package, and he will supply a male and female as housekeepers to maintain this unit; his wife will adopt these housekeepers.
11. Although told that these practices occur daily, Eicher observed that they sometimes happened on alternating days.
12. Women elders guard the family valuables around the clock.
13. Iriabo is singular, iriapu is plural.
14. Eicher conversation with Robin Horton, 1988.
15. This includes bloodline members designated to reach to the fourth generation.
16. Acknowledging their existence in Kalabari cosmology is parallel to acknowledging the existence of airwave bands in an invisible spectrum within our contemporary culture, which projects and transmits radio messages and television images.
17. A pastor until ascending the Kalabari throne, he then became dedicated to upholding the culture's treasured rituals—those from which Christians generally dissociate themselves.
18. A Buguma war-canoe house leader who had rejected Christianity.
19. In these relationship-focused cultures, the capital offenses ranged from adultery as a chief's wife to the mere failure of one man to greet another that he passes on the road. Such suspicious show of unfriendliness was interpreted, in a society that put a premium on social solidarity within the community, as an intent of ill-will toward the other. This could culminate in causing his death, if not the infliction of lesser misfortunes, should it be left unchecked. The loaded meaning of the omitted greeting could lead to an accusation of witchcraft by the offended party. If not effectively resolved locally through vigorous denial by a prescribed ritual response, the matter could end up for arbitration in the court of the Aro oracle.
20. See Alagoa (1972, 141).
21. For usually, as part of the cult operative's secrets, the family members who went on the journey to Aro Chukwu with the accused were shown the blood of goats sprinkled into a stream and told that it belonged to their relative: the result of the deity's mangling when innocence was denied. The verdicts were generally accepted because they were frequently proved to be fair. Unbeknownst to most litigants, the Aro people who settled clusters of their community members in most of these societies, used them as scouts to gather detailed intelligence on almost all cases and pass the information dossier through their secret village-to-village link back to the oracle site. Consequently the verdicts were strongly fact based and reflected experiences within the society.

Conclusion (Anderson and Peek)

1. This stanza from "The Mystic Drum" by Gabriel Okara (see Okara 1978) was reprinted with the kind permission of Andre Deutsch Limited.

References Cited

Adams, Captain John
1823 [1966] *Remarks on the Country Extending from Cape Palmas to the River Congo, with an Appendix Containing an Account of the European Trade with the West Coast of Africa.* London: Frank Cass and Co. Ltd.

Afigbo, A. E.
1969 "The Nineteenth Century of the Aro Slaving Oligarchy of Southeastern Nigeria." *Nigeria Magazine* 1, nos. 10–12: 66–67.

Agberia, John Tokpabere
1998 "Iphri Sculptures as Icon and Images of Religious Worship among the Urhobo People of Nigeria." Ph.D. diss., University of Port Harcourt.

Aidin, Rose
2000 "Heavy Meddle." Article taken from *The Evening Standard* (April 13). "Metal Sculpture at Elephant and Castle: The Mystery is Finally Solved!": http://website.lineone.net/~alexiusp/sculpture.html.

Aimienmwona, Joseph
1997 "Pirates Terrorise Big Time Fishermen," November 15: http://www.postexpresswired.com.

Akuekue, Chief
n.d. Unpublished manuscript on the Tai Region.

Alagba: A Water Spirit Masquerade
1995 Directed and edited by Jane Thorburn. London: After Image, Ltd. Videotape.

Alagoa, E. J.
1964 *The Small Brass City State: A History of Nembe-Brass in the Niger Delta.* Ibadan: Ibadan University Press; Madison: The University of Wisconsin Press.
1967a "Delta Masquerades." *Nigeria Magazine* 93: 145–55.
1967b "Ijo Origins and Migrations (II)." *Nigerian Magazine* 92: 47–55.
1968 "The Western Apoi: Notes on the Use of Ethnographic Data in Historical Reconstruction." *African Notes* 5, no. 1: 12–24.
1970 "Long Distance Trade and States in the Niger Delta." *Journal of African History* 11, no. 3: 319–29.
1971 "The Development of Institutions in the States of the Eastern Niger Delta." *Journal of African History* 12, no. 2: 269–78.
1972 *A Short History of the Niger Delta: An Historical Interpretation of Oral Tradition.* Ibadan: Ibadan University Press.
1973 "Oral Tradition and Archeology: The Case of Onyoma." *Oduma* 2, no. 1: 10–12.
1974 "Ke: The History of an Old Delta Community." *Oduma* 2, no. 1: 4–16.
1975a *King Boy of Brass.* London: Heinemann.
1975b "Terra-cotta from the Niger Delta." *Black Orpheus* 3, no. 2/3: 29.
1976 *A History of the Niger Delta.* Ibadan: Ibadan University Press.
1982 "Owuaya: Mother of Masquerades." In *The Masquerade in Nigerian History and Culture,* edited by Nwanna Nzewunwa, 268–84. Port Harcourt: University of Port Harcourt Press.
1986 "The Slave Trade in Niger Delta Oral Tradition and History." In *Africans in Bondage: Studies in Slavery and the Slave Trade,* edited by Paul E. Lovejoy, 125–35. Madison: University of Wisconsin
1995 *People of the Fish and Eagle: A History of Okpoama in the Eastern Niger Delta.* Lagos and Port Harcourt: Isengi Communications Limited.
forthcoming *Okpu: Ancestral Houses in Nembe and European Antiquities on the Brass and Nun Rivers of the Niger Delta.* Dakar: West African Museums Program; London: International African Institute.

Alagoa, E. J., F. N. Anozie, and N. Nzewunwa, eds.
1988 *The Early History of the Niger Delta.* Hamburg: Helmut Buske Verlag.

Alagoa, E. J., and Fombo, A.
1972 *A Chronicle of Grand Bonny.* Ibadan: Ibadan University Press.

Alagoa, E. J., and Tekena N. Tamuno, eds.
1989 *Land and People of Nigeria: Rivers State.* Port Harcourt: Riverside Communications.

Alawa, Patrick Kpenabe
n.d. *The Concise History of Bodo, Gokana Ogoni.* Port Harcourt: Jollyman's Printers and Stationery Supplies.

Alderton, David
1988 *Turtles and Tortoises of the World.* New York: Facts on File Publications.

Aldred, Cyril
1949 "A Bronze Cult Object from Southern Nigeria." *Man* 47: 38–39.

Allen, Henry A.
1949 "The Jekris...A Tough Race." *The West African Review* 20, no. 262 (July): 757–59.

Allen, William
1840 *Picturesque Views on the River Niger Sketched during Lander's Last Visit in 1832–33.* London: J. Murray.

Allen, William, and T. R. H. Thomson
1848 *A Narrative of the Expedition Sent by Her Majesty's Government to the River Niger in 1841 under the Command of Capt. H. D. Trotter, R.N.* London: Richard Bentley.

Allison, Philip
1988 *Life in the White Man's Grave: A Pictorial Record of the British in West Africa.* New York: Viking.

Amadi, Elechi
1969 The Great Ponds. Heinemann: London.

Amangala, G. I.
1939 *Short History of Ijaw.* Oloibiri: By the author.

Anderson, Martha G.
1981 "Water-Spirit Headdress." In *For Spirits and Kings: African Art from the Tishman Collection,* edited by Susan Vogel, 149–50. New York: The Metropolitan Museum of Art.
1983 "Central Ijo Art: Shrines and Spirit Images." Ph.D. diss., Indiana University.
1987 "The Funeral of an Ijo Shrine Priest." *African Arts* 21, no. 1: 52–57, n. 88.
1997a "From Adumu to Mami Wata: Central Ijo Water Spirit Images." In *The Multi-Disciplinary Approach to African History: Essays in Honour of E. J. Alagoa,* 257–73. Port Harcourt: University of Port Harcourt, Department of History.
1997b "Le Delta." In *Arts du Nigéria: Collection du Musée des arts d'Afrique et d'Océanie,* edited by Jean-Hubert Martin, Etienne Féau, and Hélène Joubert, 119–42. Paris: Réunion des Musées Nationaux.

Anderson, Martha G., and Christine Mullen Kreamer
1989 *Wild Spirits, Strong Medicines: African Art and the Wilderness.* Seattle: Washington University Press with the Center for African Art.

Andersson, Hilary
1998 "Fighting the Oil Firms: Youths Have Been Turning to Ancient Rituals." BBC Online Network, Nov. 6: http://news.bbc.co.uk/hi/english/world/africa/newsid_209000/209441.stm

Anozie, F. N.
1988 "Cultural Prehistory in the Niger Delta." In *The Early History of the Niger Delta,* edited by E. J. Alagoa and F. N. Anozie. Hamburg: Helmut Buske Verlag.

Arnoldi, Mary Jo, and Christine Mullen Kreamer
1995 *Crowning Achievements: African Arts of Dressing the Head.* Los Angeles: UCLA Fowler Museum of Cultural History.

Aronson, Lisa
1980a "History of Cloth Trade in the Niger Delta: A Study in Diffusion." *Textile History* 2: 89–107.
1980b "History of Cloth Trade in the Niger Delta: a Study of Diffusion." In *Textiles of Africa.* Edited by Dale Idiens and K. G. Ponting. Bath: Pasold Research Fund.
1992 "Ijebu Yoruba *aso olona*: A Contextual and Historical Overview," *African Arts* 25, no. 3: 52–63, 101–2.
Forthcoming *The Weaving of History in Southeastern Nigeria from 1750–Present.*

Ashton-Jones, Nick
1995 "Botem-Tai in Ogoniland, Nigeria." *Tropical Agricultural Newsletter* 15, no. 1 (March).

Ayomike, J. O. S.
1988 *A History of Warri.* Benin City: Ilupeju Press.
1990 *The Ijaw in Warri: A Study in Ethnography.* Benin City: Mayomi Publishers.
1992 *Nanna: British Imperialism at Work.* Warri: Mayomi Publishers.

Bacon, Sir Reginald
1887 *Benin: City of Blood.* London: Edward Arnold.

Baker, Geoffrey L.
1996 *Trade Winds on the Niger: The Saga of the Royal Niger Company.* London: The Radcliffe Press.

Baker, Richard St. Barbe.
1954 *Africa Drums.* Oxford: George Ronald.

Balandier, Georges
1974 "Armies." In *Dictionary of Black African Civilization,* edited by Georges Balandier and Jacques Maquet, 23–24. New York: Leon Amiel.

Barbot, John
1732 *A Description of the Coasts of North and South Guinea and of Ethiopia Inferior: Being a New and Accurate Account of the Western Maritime Countries of Africa.* In Churchill Awnsham, *Collection of Voyages and Travels,* vol. 5. London.

Barley, Nigel
1988 *Foreheads of the Dead: An Anthropological View of Kalabari Ancestral Screens.* Washington, D. C.: Smithsonian Institution Press for the National Museum of African Art.
1995 "Figure of a Woman." In *Africa: The Art of a Continent,* edited by Tom Phillips, 399–401, pl. 5.601. London: Royal Academy of Arts.

Barlow, Kathleen, and David Lipset
1997 "Dialogic of Material Culture: Male and Female in Murik Outrigger Canoes." *American Ethnologist* 24, no. 1: 4–36.

Basden, G. T.
1921 [1966] *Among the Ibos of Nigeria.* London: Frank Cass and Co., Ltd.

Bateson, Gregory
1972 *Steps to an Ecology of the Mind.* New York: Ballantine Books.

Bebeke-ola, J. E. I.
n.d. "Bebeke-la (Bebekala)." Unpublished manuscript.

Beier, Ulli
1963 *African Mud Sculpture.* Cambridge: Cambridge University Press.

Ben-Amos, Dan
1967 "Story Telling in Benin." *African Arts* 1, no. 1: 54–59.

Ben-Amos, Paula Girshick
1994 "The Promise of Greatness: Women and Power in an Edo Spirit Possession Cult." In *Religion in Africa,* edited by Thomas D. Blakely, Walter E. A. van Beek, and Dennis L. Thomson, 118–34. London: Curry and Heinemann.

Bentor, Eli
Forthcoming "Spatial Continuities: Masks and Cultural Interactions between the Delta and Eastern Nigeria." *African Arts* 35, no. 1.

Bigelow, Henry, and William C. Schroeder
1953 *Sawfishes, Guitarfishes, Skates and Rays. Fishes of the Western North Atlantic.* Part II, no. 1. Memoir (Sears Foundation for Marine Research). New Haven: Yale University Press.

Bloch, Marc
1961 *Feudal Society.* Translated from the French by L. A. Manyon. Chicago: University of Chicago Press.

Bold, Edward
1823 *The Merchant's and Mariner's African Guide.* Salem: Cushing and Appleton.

Boro, Major Isaac
1982 *The Twelve-Day Revolution.* Edited by Tony Tebekaemi. Benin City: Idodo Umeh Publishers.

Boston, John
1977 *Ikenga Figures among the Northwest Igbo and the Igala.* London: Ethnographica and the Nigerian Federal Department of Antiquities.

Bowen, R. L.
1955 "The Olu of Itsekiri." *Nigeria Magazine* 22: 62–63.

Bradbury, R. E.
1957 *Benin Kingdom and the Edo Speaking Peoples of South-Western Nigeria Together with a Section on the Itsekiri by P. C. Lloyd.* London: I.A.I.
1961 Ézomo's *Ikegobo* and the Benin Cult of the Hand." *Man* 61, no. 165: 129–38.

Brincard, Marie-Therese
1982 *The Art of Metal in Africa.* New York: African-American Institute.

Burdo, Adolphe
1880 *The Niger and the Benueh: Travels in Central Africa.* Translated from the French by Mrs. George Sturge. London: Richard Bentley and Son.

Burton, Richard Francis
1863 *Wanderings in West Africa from Liverpool to Fernando Po. In Two Volumes.* London: Tinsley Brothers.

Chadwick, E. R.
1938 "The 'George Shotton' Hulk." *The Nigerian Field* 7, no. 4: 181–83.

Clark, J. P.
1966 *Ozidi: A Play.* London: Oxford University Press.
1977 *The Ozidi Saga.* Ibadan: Ibadan University Press.

Cobb, Sarah Travis
1995 "The Ogoni of Southeastern Nigeria: An Analysis of Art and Identity." Ph.D. diss., Columbia University.

Cole, Herbert M.
1982 *Mbari: Art and Life among the Owerri Igbo.* Indiana University Press.

Cole, Herbert M., and C. Aniakor
1984 *Igbo Arts: Community and Cosmos.* Los Angeles: Museum of Cultural History, University of California, Los Angeles.

Cosentino, J. Donald
1996   "Tricksters." In *The Dictionary of Art*, vol. 1, 281–84, New York: Grove's Dictionaries, Inc.

Coronel, Michael A.
1979   "Fanti Canoe Decoration." *African Arts* 14, no. 1: 54–59, 99–100.

Croll, Elisabeth, and David Parkin, eds.
1992   *Bush Base: Forest Farm: Culture, Environment, and Development.* London: Routledge.

Crowther, Samuel A., and John Christopher Taylor
1859   *The Gospel on the Banks of the Niger: Journals and Notices of the Native Missionaries Accompanying the Niger Expedition of 1857–1859.* London: Dawsons of Pall Mall.

Curnow, Kathy
Forthcoming   "Cultural Flow and Cultural Breakwaters: Benin and the Delta." *African Arts* 35, no. 2.

Curtin, Philip D.
1970   *The Atlantic Slave Trade: A Census.* Madison: Wisconsin University Press.

Curtin, Philip D., ed.
1967   *Africa Remembered: Narratives by West Africans from the Era of the Slave Trade.* Madison: The University of Wisconsin Press.

Da-Wariboko, R. M. C.
1991   "Kalabari Funeral Rites and the Significance of the Canoe Regatta (poku doku)." In *A Hundred Years of Buguma History in Kalabari Culture,* edited by Tonye V. Erekosima, W. H. Kio Lawson, and O. McJaja. Lagos: Sibon Books Limited.

Daly, Mary Catherine
1984   "Kalabari Female Appearance and the Tradition of Iria." Ph.D. diss., University of Minnesota.
1987   "Iria Bo Appearance at Kalabari Funerals." *African Arts* 21, no. 1: 58–61, 86.

Daly, M. Catherine, Joanne B. Eicher, and Tonye V. Erekosima
1986   "Male and Female Artistry in Kalabari Dress." *African Arts* 19, no. 3: 48–51, 83.

Dapper, Olfert
1688   *Description de L'Afrique.* London.

De Negri, Eve
1968   "Itsekiri Costume." Nigeria Magazine 97: 101–10.

Derefaka, A. A., and F. N. Anozie
Forthcoming   "Economic and Cultural Prehistory in the Niger Delta." *African Arts* 35, no. 1.

Dike, K. O.
1956   *Trade and Politics in the Niger Delta, 1830–1885: An Introduction to the Economic and Political History of Nigeria.* Oxford Studies in African Affairs. Oxford: Clarendon Press.

Donwa-Ifode, Shirley
1983/84   "Is Nigerian Pidgin English Creolising?" *Journal of the Linguistic Association of Nigeria* 2: 199–203.

Douglas, Mary
1975   "Animals in Lele Religious Symbolism." In *Implicit Meanings: Essays in Anthropology,* 27–47. London: Routledge and Kegan Paul.

Douglas Camp, Sokari
2002   http://www.arc.co.uk/sokari/home.html

Drewal, H. J.
1986   "Flaming Crowns, Cooling Waters: Masquerades of the Ìjèbú Yorùbá." *African Arts* 20, no. 1: 32–41, 99–100.
1988a   "Mermaids, Mirrors, and Snake Charmers: Igbo Mami Wata Shrines." *African Arts* 21, no. 2: 38–45, 96.
1988b   "Performing the Other: Mami Wata Worship in West Africa." *The Drama Review* 32, no. 2: 160–85.
1994   "Preface to the Yoruba Entries." In *Visions of Africa: The Jerome Joss Collection of African Art at ucla,* edited by Doran H. Ross, 64–79. Los Angeles: Fowler Museum of Cultural History.
1995   "Face Bell (Umo)." In *Africa: The Art of a Continent,* edited by Tom Phillips, 414, pl. 5.74. London: Royal Academy of Arts.

Drewal, H. J., and M.T. Drewal.
1983   *Gèlèdé: Art and Female Power among the Yorùbá.* Bloomington: Indiana University Press.

Efere, E. E., and Kay Williamson
1989   "Languages." In *The Land and People of Nigeria: Rivers State,* edited by E. J. Alagoa and Tekena N. Tamuno, 42–43. Port Harcourt: Riverside Communications.

Eicher, Joanne
1994   *Textile Trade and Masquerade among the Kalabari of Nigeria.* Videotape. Minneapolis, Minnesota: University of Minnesota.

Eicher, Joanne, and Tonye Erekosima
1981   "Kalabari Cut-Thread and Pulled-Thread Cloth." *African Arts* 14, no. 2: 48–51, 87.
1987   "Kalabari Funerals: Celebration and Display." *African Arts* 19, no. 3: 38–45, 87.
1989   "Kalabari Funeral Rooms as Handicraft and Ephemeral Art." In *Man Does Not Go Naked: Textilien und Handwerk aus Afrikanishen und Andren Landern,* vol. 29, edited by R. Boser-Sarivaxivanus, B. Englebrecht, and B. Gardi, 197–207. Basel, Switzerland: Basler Beitrage zur Ethnologie.
1993   "Taste and Nineteenth Century Patterns of Textile Use among the Kalabari of Nigeria." Paper presented at the Dartmouth College Conference on "Cloth, the World Economy, and the Artisan: Textile Manufacturing and Marketing in South Asia and Africa, 1780–1950," Hanover, N.H.
1996   "Indian Textiles in Kalabari Funerals." In *Asian Art and Culture,* 68–79. Washington, DC: Smithsonian Institution Press.
Forthcoming   *Kalabari Cloth and Culture.*

Eicher, Joanne B., and Tonye V. Erekosima with Otto C. Thieme
1982   *Kalabari Cut-Thread Cloth.* St. Paul: Goldstein Gallery, University of Minnesota.

Ejituwu, N. C.
1991   *A History of Obolo (Andoni) in the Niger Delta.* Oron: Manson Publishing Company.

Ekejiuba, F. I.
1967   "Preliminary Notes on Brasswork of Eastern Nigeria." *African Notes* 4, no. 2: 11–15.

Ekwensi, Cyprian
1964   "We are Here—a Photo Feature on Itsekiri Traditional Dancing." *Nigeria Magazine* 82: 164–72.

Ellis, Alfred B.
1883   *The Land of Fetish.* London: Chapman and Hall.

Environmental Research Foundation
1997   "Crimes of Shell." In *Rachel's Environment and Health Weekly,* no. 546 (May 15, 1997): www.sierraclub.org/jobs/rachel.html.

Erekosima, Tonye V.
1989   "Analysis of a Teaching Resource on Political Integration Applicable to the Nigerian Secondary School Social Studies Curriculum: The Case of Kalabari Men's Traditional Dress." Ph.D. diss., Catholic University of America.

Erekosima, Tonye V., and Joanne B. Eicher
1981 "Kalabari Cut-thread and Pulled-thread Cloth." *African Arts* 14, no. 2: 48–51, 87.
1994 "The Aesthetics of Men's Dress of the Kalabari of Nigeria." In *Aesthetics of Textiles and Clothing: Advancing Multi-disciplinary Perspectives,* edited by Marilyn DeLong and Anne Marie Fiore. International Textiles and Apparel Association Special Publication, no. 7. Monument, Colo.: ITAA.

Erekosima, Tonye V., W. H. Kio Lawson, and O. McJaja, eds.
1991 *A Hundred Years of Buguma History in Kalabari Culture.* Lagos: Sibon Books Limited.

Ereks [Erekosima], Tonye V.
1973 "Kalabari Categories of the Self: A Philosophical Extrapolation in Cultural Dynamism." *Oduma* 1 , no.1: 21–27.

Ezra, Kate
1990 "Review of 'Contemporary African Artists: Changing Tradition' at the Studio Museum in Harlem, New York."*African Arts* 23, no. 4: 79–80.

Fagg, Bernard, and William Fagg
1960 "The Ritual Stools of Ancient Ife." *Man* 60, no. 155.

Fagg, William
1960 *Nigerian Images.* London: Lund Humphries.
1963a *Nigerian Images: The Splendor of African Sculpture.* New York: Frederick A. Praeger.
1963b *Nigerian Tribal Art.* London: Arts Council of Great Britain.

Fischer, Eberhard, and Hans Himmelheber.
1984 *The Arts of the Dan in West Africa.* Zurich: Museum Rietberg.

Fleming, S. J., and K. W. Nicklin
1982 "Analysis of Two Bronzes from a Nigerian Asunaja Shrine." *masca Journal* 2, no. 2: 53–57.

Fombo, Adadonye
1975 *Ibani bibi dawo diri (Studies in the Ibani Dialect of Ijo).* Port Harcourt: University of Port Harcourt, Rivers Readers Project; Rivers State, Nigeria: Rivers State Council for Arts and Culture.

Foss, S. M.
1978 "Urhobo Mats in Praise of Daughters." *African Arts* 12, no. 1: 60–62, 108.
1979 "She Who Sits as King: Celebrations for Young Urhobo Women." *African Arts* 12, no. 2: 45–50, 90–91.

Foss, W. Perkins
1973 "Festival of Ohworu at Evwreni." *African Arts* 6, no. 4: 20–27, 94.
1975 "Images of Aggression: Ivwri Sculpture of the Urhobo." In *African Images: Essays in African Iconology,* edited by Daniel McCall and Edna G. Bay, 132–43. Boston University Papers on Africa 6. New York: Africana Publishing Co.
1976 "The Arts of the Urhobo Peoples of Southern Nigeria." Ph.D. diss., Yale University.
1981 "Water Spirit Mask." In *For Spirits and Kings: African Art from the Paul and Ruth Tishman Collection,* edited by Susan Vogel. New York: The Metropolitan Museum of Art.

Fraser, Douglas
1972 "The Symbols of Ashanti Kingship." In *African Art and Leadership,* edited by Douglas Fraser and Herbert Cole, 137–52. Madison: University of Wisconsin Press.

Freeman, William D.
n.d. *Boundaries and History of Olodiama.* Unpublished manuscript.

Galembo, Phyllis
1993 *Divine Inspiration from Benin to Bahia.* Albuquerque: University of New Mexico Press.

Ganay, Solange de
1987 "Lecture sur une pirogue." In *Ethnologiques: Hommages à Marcel Griaule,* edited by Solange de Ganay et. al., 119–43. Paris: Hermann.

Gibbons, E. J.
1932 Intelligence Report on Ogoni, Opobo Division, Calabar Province, l932 NAE File 28032 CSO26/3 NAE RP. 6378. National Archives, Enugu.

Gleason, Judith, and Chief Allison Ibubuya
1991 "My Year Reached, We Heard Ourselves Singing: Dawn Songs of Girls Becoming Women in Ogbogbo, Okrika, Rivers State, Nigeria, January 1990." *Research in African Literatures* 22, no. 3: 135–48.

Gleason, Judith, and Elisa Mereghetti
1990 *Becoming a Woman in Okrika.* New York: Filmakers Library. Videotape.

Gore, Charles, and Joseph Nevadomsky
1997 "Practice and Agency in Mammy Wata Worship in Southern Nigeria." *African Arts* 30, no. 2: 60–69, 95

Gramont, Sanche de
1975 *The Strong Brown God: The Story of the Niger River.* Boston: Houghton Mifflin Company.

Grey, R. F. A.
1954 "Manillas." *Nigerian Field* 16.

Grimes, Barbara F.
1996 *Ethnologue: Languages of the World.* 13th ed. Dallas: Summer Institute of Linguisitics, Inc. (Electronic version: http://www.sil.org/ethnologue/countries/Nigr.html)

Hamilton, A.
1862 *The River Niger and the Progress of Discovery and Commerce in Central Africa.* London: Dalton and Morgan.

Handelman, Don
1981 "The Ritual Clown: Attributes and Affinities." *Anthropos* 76: 321–70.

Hargreaves, Susan M.
1987 "The Political Economy of Nineteenth Century Bonny: A Study of Power, Authority, Legitimacy, and Ideology in a Delta Trading Community from 1790–1914." Ph.D. diss., University of Birmingham.

Heider, Karl
1970 *The Dugum Dani: A Papuan Culture in the Highlands of West New Guinea.* Chicago: Aldine.

Hodgkin, T.
1960 *Nigerian Perspectives: An Historical Anthology.* London: Oxford University Press.

Horton, Robin
n. d. *Ijo Ritual Sculpture.* Nigeria National Museum, Lagos. Ms. acc. no. 194. Typescript.
1960 *The Gods as Guests: An Aspect of Kalabari Religious Life.* Lagos: Nigeria Magazine Publications.
1962 "The Kalabari World-View: An Outline and Interpretation." *Africa: Journal of the International African Institute* 32, no. 3: 197–220.
1963 "The Kalabari Ekine Society: A Borderland of Religion and Art." *Africa* 33, no. 2: 94–114.
1965a *Kalabari Sculpture.* Federal Republic of Nigeria: Department of Antiquities.
1965b "A Note of Recent Finds of Brasswork in the Niger Delta." *Odu* 2, no. 1: 76–91.
1967 "Ikaki—The Tortoise Masquerade." *Nigeria Magazine* 94: 226–39.
1968 "*Ikpataka Dogi*: A Kalabari Funeral Rite." *African Notes* 5: 52–72.

Hubbard, Rev. John W.
1948   *The Sobo of the Niger Delta.* Zaria: Gaskiya Corp.

Human Rights Watch
1999   *The Price of Oil: Corporate Responsibility and Human Rights Violations in Nigeria's Oil Producing Communities.* New York: Human Rights Watch.

Ibuluya, Allison
1982   "Masquerades in the Rivers State." In *The Masquerade in Nigerian History and Culture: Being the Proceedings of a Workshop Sponsored by the School of Humanities, University of Port Harcourt, Port Harcourt, Nigeria, Sept 7–14, 1980,* edited by Nwanna Nzewunwa, 205–67. Port Harcourt: University of Port Harcourt, Faculty of Humanities.

Ijoma, J. Okoro
1983   "War and Diplomacy in Igboland, West of the Niger in the Pre-colonial Period." *Nigeria Magazine* 145: 10–15.

Ikime, Obaro
1967   "The Western Ijo, 1900–1950: A Preliminary Study." *Journal of the Historical Society of Nigeria* 4, no. 1: 65–87.
1969   *Niger Delta Rivalry.* London: Longman.

Isichei, Elizabeth
1973   *The Ibo People and the Europeans: The Genesis of a Relationship to 1906.* New York: St. Martin's Press.
1976   *A History of the Igbo People.* New York: St. Martin's Press.
1984   *A History of Nigeria.* London: Longman.

Isokariari, Tubonimi J.
1983   *The Legacy of Madame Orupumbo Tariah of Buguma: A Biographical Essay.* B.A. diss., University of Port Harcourt.

Iyalla, B. S.
1968   "Womanhood in the Kalabari." *Nigeria Magazine* 98: 216–24.

Jacobs, J.
1986   "African Art at the Glasgow Art Gallery and Museum." *African Arts* 19, no. 2: 37–38.

Jeffreys, M. D. W.
1930   "Intelligence Report of the Andoni." National Archives, Enugu.
1931   "Intelligence Report on the Ogoni, Opobo Division, Calabar Province, l931." National Archives, Enugu.

Jell-Bahlsen, Sabine
1995   "Dada-Rasta-Hair: The Hidden Messages of Mammy Water in Nigeria." Unpublished paper presented at the Thirty-Eighth Annual Meeting of the African Studies Association, Orlando, Florida, Nov. 3–6.

Jenewari, Charles E. W.
1973   "Owu Aru Sun: Kalabari's Most Colourful Ceremony." *Oduma* 1, no. 1: 27–31.
1980   "The Opongi Masquerade Festival of the Kalabari Ekine Society." *Nigeria Magazine* 130, no. 31: 3–16

Jewett, Alicia Terese
1988   "A Contemporary Ethnography: Change and Continuity among the Ibani of Coastal Nigeria." Ph.D. diss., Queen's College, Cambridge.

Jones, G. I.
1963   *Trading States of the Oil Rivers: A Study of Political Development in Eastern Nigeria.* Oxford: Oxford University Press.
1984   *The Art of Eastern Nigeria.* Cambridge: Cambridge University Press.
1988   "Tribal Distribution," part 2. In *The Background of Eastern Nigerian History* 3. New Haven: Human Relations Area Files.
1989a   *Ibo Art.* Aylesbury: Shire Ethnography
1989b   "A Visit to Ogume in 1937." *African Arts* 22, no. 3: 64–67.

Joselit, David
1990   "Africa Rising." *Art in America* (October): 160–61.

King, John
1822   "Extrait de la rélation inedité d'un voyage fait en 1820, aux royaume de Benin et de Waree." *Journal des voyages, découvertes et navigations modernes* 13: 313–18.

Kingsley, Mary
1897 [1965]   *Travels in West Africa: Congo Français, Corisco, and Cameroon.* 3d ed. London: Frank Cass and Co. Ltd.

Kpone-Tonwe, Sonpie
1987   "The Historical Tradition of Ogoni." M.A. thesis, University of London.
1990   "The Ogoni of the Eastern Niger Delta Mainland: An Economic and Political History from the Earliest Times to about 1900." Ph.D diss., University of Port Harcourt.
1997   "Property Reckoning and Methods of Accumulating Wealth among the Ogoni of the Eastern Niger Delta." *Africa* 67: l, 130–57.

Lander, Richard, and John Lander
1832 [1965]   *The Niger Journal of Richard and John Lander.* Edited and abridged with an introduction by Robin Hallett. London: Kegan Paul. (First published as *Journal of an Expedition to Explore the Course and Termination of the Niger.*)

Law, Robin
1986   "Early European Sources Relating to the Kingdom of Ijebu (1500–1700): A Critical Survey." *History in Africa* 13: 245–60.

Leis, Nancy B.
1964   "Economic Independence and Ijaw Women: A Comparative Study of Two Communities in the Niger Delta." Ph.D. diss., Northwestern University.

Leis, Philip
1962   "Enculturation and Cultural Change in an Ijaw Community." Ph.D. diss., Northwestern University.

Lentz, Carola
1994   "They Must be Dagaba First and Any Other Thing Second… The Colonial and Post-Colonial Creation of Ethnic Identities in North-Western Ghana." *African Studies* 53, no. 2: 57–91.

Leonard, A. G.
1906 [1968]   *The Lower Niger and Its Tribes.* New York: Cass.

Lloyd, P. C.
1956   "Tribalism in Warri." In *Conference Proceedings*, 79–87. Ibadan: Nigerian Institute of Social and Economic Research.
1963   "The Itsekiri in the Nineteenth Century: An Outline Social History." *Journal of African History* 4, no. 2: 207–31.
1967   "Osifekunde of Ijebu." In *Africa Remembered: Narratives by West Africans from the Era of the Slave Trade,* edited by Philip D. Curtin, 217–88. Madison: University of Wisconsin Press.

Lloyd, P. C., and Ryder, A. F. C.
1957   "Dom Domingos, Prince of Warri." *Odu* 4: 27–39.

Loolo, Godwin Namene
1981   *A History of the Ogoni.* N.p.

Lorenz, Carol
1982   "Lower Niger Bronze Bells: Form, Iconography, and Function." In *The Art of Metal in Africa*, edited by M.-T. Brincard, 52–60. New York: African-American Institute.

Loudmer, Guy, and Herve Poulain
1975   *Art Primitif.* Paris: Salon de la Paix.

Lovejoy, Paul E., ed.
1986   *The Ideology of Slavery in Africa.* Beverly Hills: Sage Publications.

Loveridge, Arthur, and Ernest E. Williams
1957 *Revision of the African Tortoises and Turtles of the Suborder Cryptodira.* Bulletin of the Museum of Comparative Zoology at Harvard College 115, no. 6. Cambridge: The Museum.

Luschan, Felix von
1919 *Altertumer von Berlin.* 3 vols. Berlin and Leipzig.

Mackenzie, J. G.
1931 Intelligence Report on Eleme, Opobo Division, Calabar Province. 1931 File EP9595CSE 1/85/48888. National Archives, Enugu.

Manning, Patrick
1981 "Slave Trade, 'Legitimate Trade,' and Imperialism Revisited: The Control of Wealth in the Bights of Benin and Biafra." In *The Ideology of Slavery in Africa,* edited by Paul E. Lovejoy, 203–33. Beverly Hills: Sage Publications.
1990 *Slavery and African Life: Occidental, Oriental, and African Slave Trades.* Cambridge: Cambridge University Press.

Mason, J.
1996 *Olookun: Owner of Rivers and Seas.* Brooklyn: Yoruba Theological Archministry.

McDavitt, Matthew
1996 "The Cultural and Economic Importance of Sawfishes (Family Pristidae)." *Shark News: A Newsletter of the iucn Shark Specialist Group,* no. 8 (Dec.): 10–11.

McEwan, Mike
1997 "Jaws! One Look at This Beast and It's Easy to See Why It's Feared by Man": http://www.aquariacentral.com/fishinfo/fresh/atigerf.htm

McIntosh, R.
1999 "Africa's Storied Past." *Archeology* 52, no. 3: 54–60.

Michelman, Susan O., and Tonye V. Erekosima
1992 "Kalabari Dress in Nigeria: Visual Analysis and Gender Implications." In *Dress and Gender: Making and Meaning in Cultural Contexts*, edited by Ruth Barnes and Joanne B. Eicher. Providence and Oxford: Berg.

Mockler-Ferryman, Augustus F.
1892 *Up the Niger: Narrative of Major Claude MacDonald's Mission up the Niger and Benue Rivers.* London: George Philip.

Moloney, C. M. G.
1889 "Cotton Interests, Foreign and Native in Yoruba, and Generally in West Africa." *Journal of the Manchester Geographical Society* 5: 254–75.

Moore, William
1936 [1970] *History of Itsekiri.* London: Frank Cass & Co.

Murray, Kenneth
n.d. Lagos Museum. Unpublished field notes.

National Museum of African Art, Smithsonian Institution
1988 *Echoes of the Kalabari: Sculpture by Sokari Douglas Camp.* Washington, D.C.: National Museum of African Art, Smithsonian Institution.

Neaher, Nancy
1976a "Bronzes of Southern Nigeria and Igbo Metalsmithing Traditions." Ph.D. diss., Stanford University.
1976b "Igbo Metalsmiths among the Southern Edo." *African Arts* 9: 46–49, 91–2.
1979a "Akwa Who Travel." *Africa* 49, no. 4: 352–66
1979b "Nigerian Bronze Bells." *African Arts* 12, no. 3: 3.

Nevadomsky, Joseph
1984 "Kingship Succession Rituals in Benin, 3: The Coronation of the Oba." *African Arts* 17, no. 3: 48–57, 91–92.
1989 "Preferential Rankings of Ethnic Groups in Southern Nigeria." *Journal of Social Psychology* 129, no. 5: 631–41.

Nicklin, Keith
1982 "The Cross River Bronzes." In *The Art of Metal in Africa,* edited by M.-T. Brincard, 47–51. New York: African-American Institute.
1989 "A Lower Niger Bronze Female Figure." *Important Tribal Art.* Sale Catalog, Monday, July 3, 1989. London: Sotheby's.
1990 "Ekpe in the Rio del Rey." *Tribal Art.* Geneva: Barbier-Mueller Museum.
1995 "Woman Seated on a Stool." In *Africa: The Art of a Continent,* edited by Tom Phillips, 387. London: Royal Academy of Arts.
1999 *Ekpu: The Oron Ancestor Figures of South Eastern Nigeria.* London: Horniman Museum and Gardens and Museu e Laboratório Antropológico da Universidade de Coimbra, Portugal.

Nicklin, K., and S. J. Fleming
1980 "A Bronze 'Carnivore Skull' from Oron, Nigeria." *masca Journal* l, no. 4: 104–5.

Nicklin, Keith, and Jill Salmons
1984 "Cross River Art Styles." *African Arts* 18, no. 1: 28–43.
1997 "Les arts du Nigéria du sud-est: Les Ogoni et les peuples de la Cross River." In *Arts du Nigéria: Collection du Musée des arts d'Afrique et d'Océanie,* edited by Jean-Hubert Martin, Etienne Féau, and Hélène Joubert, 147–68. Paris: Réunion des Musées Nationaux.

Niger Delta Ethnic Nationalities Conference
1999 Niger Delta Communiqué: http://www.sierraclub.com/human-rights/nigercomm.html

Northrup, David
1978 *Trade without Rulers: Pre-Colonial Economic Development in South-Eastern Nigeria.* Oxford: Clarendon Press.

Nwinunu, Degbara Vencent
1982 "Worship of Yogoro Deity in Kpaen, Ogoni." A research project undertaken in partial fulfillment of the requirements for the award of the Nigerian Certificate of Education.

Nzekwu, Onuora
1960 "Masquerade.*" Nigeria Magazine,* Special Independence Issue (October): 134–44.

Nzewunwa, Nwanna
1976 "Bronzes of Southern Nigeria and Igbo Metalsmithing Traditions." Ph.D. diss., Stanford University.
1979 "Awka Who Travel." *Africa* 49, no. 4: 352–66.
1980 *The Niger Delta: Prehistoric Economy and Culture.* Cambridge Monographs in African Archaeology I, B.A.R. International Series 75. Oxford: B.A.R.
1982 *The Masquerade in Nigerian History and Culture: Being the Proceedings of a Workshop Sponsored by the School of Humanities, University of Port Harcourt, Port Harcourt, Nigeria, Sept. 7–14, 1980.* Port Harcourt: University of Port Harcourt, Faculty of Humanities.

Nzimiro, Ikenna
1972 *Studies in Ibo Political Systems.* Berkeley: University of California Press.

Obiomah, D. A.
N.d. *Warri Land, Overlords and Land Rights: Fact, Fiction and Imperialism.* Warri: GKS Press.

Ockiya, D. O.
1988 *My Autobiography.* Edited by T. I. Francis. Port Harcourt.

Odudu, J. N. A.
1970   "A Sociological Research on Okpe Community in Isoko Division." Headmaster's Institute, Benin City. Typescript.

Ogbobine, R. A. I.
1995   *The Foundation of Itsekiri Culture (The Bini Influence).* Benin City: Ruf-Bine Publishing Co.

Ogot, Bethwell A., ed.
1972   *War and Society in Africa: Ten Studies.* London: Frank Cass.

Oguibe, Olu
1997   "Nigeria: Painting and Graphic Arts." In *The Dictionary of Art,* vol 23: 135–39. London: Grove Publications.
1999   "Finding a Place: Nigerian Artists in the Contemporary Art World." *Art Journal* (summer).

Ògunbà, Oyinadé
1967   *Ritual Drama of the Ijebu People: A Study of Indigenous Festivals.* Ph.D. diss., Ibadan University.

Ogunkoya, T.
1956   "The Early History of Ijebu." *Journal of the Historical Society of Nigeria* 1: 48–58.

Ohangbon, M. E.
1979   "Regatta of Bendel State." *Ivie: Nigerian Journal of Arts and Culture* 1, no. 1: 21–23.

Okanta, Ike, and Oronto Douglas
2001   *Where Vultures Feast: Shell, Human Rights, and Oil in the Niger Delta.* San Francisco: Sierra Club Books.

Okara, Gabriel
n.d.   "Izon Culture (A Brief Introduction)." Unpublished manuscript.
1978   *The Fisherman's Invocation.* London: Heinemann.

Okeke, Chika
1995   "The Quest: From Zaria to Nsukka." In *Seven Stories about Modern Art in Africa,* edited by Hane Havell. New York: Flammarion.

Olisa, Chukwuemeka G.
1990   *Ossomari—A Kingdom of the Lower Niger Valley, 1640–1986.* Onitsha: Interlab Ltd.

Omoneukanrin, C. O.
1942   *Itsekiri Law and Custom.* Lagos: Ife-Olu Printing.

Onobrakpeya, Bruce
1988   *Sahelian Masquerades.* Lagos: Ovuomaroro Gallery.

Onwurah, Ngozi
1993   *Monday's Girls.* Produced by Lloyd Gardner for the BBC, Great Britain/Nigeria. Videotape.

Opuogulaya, Chief E. D. W.
1975   *The Cultural Heritage of the Wakirike (The Okrika People).* Port Harcourt: Rivers State Council for the Arts.

Oruwari, Y., and O. Owei
1989   "Community Organization and Architecture." In *Land and People of Nigeria: Rivers State,* edited by T. N. Tamuno and E. J. Alagoa. Port Harcourt: Riverside Communications.

Owode, Henrison Ase
1971   "Wood and Clay Sculpture in Isoko Division." B.A. thesis, Ahmadu Bello University, Zaria.

Owomoyela, Oyekan
1990   "No Problem Can Fail to Crash on His Head: The Trickster in Contemporary African Folklore." *The World & I* 5, no. 4: 625–32.

Owonaro, S. K.
1949   *The History of Ijo (Ijaw) and Her Neighboring Tribes in Nigeria.* Lagos: By the author.

Oyo, Remi
1997   "Nigeria-Politics: Communal Feud Flares on in Oil Region." *IPS.* Lagos, April 21.

Pahl, R. E., ed.
1988   *On Work: Historical, Comparative, and Theoretical Approaches.* Oxford: Basil Blackwell.

Paulme, Denise
1975   "Typologie des contes africains du decepteur." *Cahiers d'études africaines* 15 (4), no. 60: 569–600.

Peek, Philip M.
1976a   "An Ethnohistorical Study of Isoko Religious Traditions." Ph.D. Diss., Indiana University.
1976b   "Isoko Sacred Mud Sculpture." *African Arts* 9, no. 4: 34–39, 91.
1980   "Isoko Bronzes and the Lower Niger Bronze Industries." *African Arts* 13, no. 4: 60–66, 87–88.
1981   "*Ivri.*" In *For Spirits and Kings,* edited by Susan Vogel, 140–43. New York: The Metropolitan Museum of Art.
1983   "The Celebration of Oworu among the Isoko." *African Arts* 16, no. 2: 34–41, 98.
1986   "The Isoko Ethos of *Ivri.*" *African Arts* 20, no. 1: 42–47, 98.
1988   "Ambiguous Sexuality of Isoko Deities." Paper presented at the Eighth Triennial Symposium on African Art, Washington, D.C.
Forthcoming   "Re-Sounding Silences." In *Sounds,* edited by H. F. Stobart and P. Kruth. Cambridge: Cambridge University Press.

Pereira, Duarte Pacheco
1937   *Esmeraldo de situ Orbis.* Translated by George Kimble. London: Haklyut Society.

Pitt-Rivers, Augustus
1900 [1976]   *Antique Works of Art from Benin.* New York: Dover Publications.

Poppi, Cesare
1994   "The Other Within: Masks and Masquerades in Europe." In *Masks and the Art of Expression,* edited by John Mack, 190–215. New York: Harry N. Abrams.

Porter, J. C.
1931   "Oporoma Clan. Intelligence Report." Unpublished manuscript.

Rees, Captain Brabazon
1913   Manchester University Museum Archives. Unpublished manuscript.

Renne, Elisha P.
2001   "'Our Great Mother…Tied This Cloth': *Pelete Bite* Cloth, Women, and Kalabari identity." In *Cloth is the Center of the World: Nigerian Textiles, Global Perspectives,* edited by Susan J. Torntore. St. Paul: The Goldstein Museum of Design, University of Minnesota.

Reuters News Agency
1998   "Squalor amidst the Flow Stations." Oct. 7.

Reyna, S. P.
1990   "Warfare." In *Wars without End: The Political Economy of a Precolonial African State,* 135–48. Hanover, N.H.: New England University Press.

Rivers State Ministry of Information
197?   *Odum.* Port Harcourt. Film.

Roberts, Allen
1995   *Animals in African Art: From the Familiar to the Marvelous.* New York: The Museum for African Art.

Rosen, Norma
1989 "Chalk Iconography in Olokun Worship." *African Arts* 22, no. 3: 44–53, 88.

Rubin, A.
1976 *Figurative Sculptures of the Niger River Delta.* Los Angeles: Gallery K, Inc.

Ryan, James R.
1997 *Picturing Empire: Photography and the Visualization of the British Empire.* Chicago: University of Chicago Press.

Ryder, A. F. C.
1959 "An Early Portuguese Trading Voyage to the Forcados River." *Journal of the Historical Society of Nigeria* 1, no. 4: 294–321.
1969 *Benin and the Europeans,1485–1897.* London: Longman's, Green, and Co.

Sagay, J. O. E.
n.d. [1981] *The Warri Kingdom.* Sapele: Progress Publishers.

Saro-Wiwa, Ken
1992 *Genocide in Nigeria, the Ogoni Tragedy.* London, Lagos, and Port Harcourt: Saros International Publishers.

Schneider, Wolfgang
1990 *Field Guide to the Commercial Marine Resources of the Gulf of Guinea.* Rome: Fao.

Schwimmer, Erik
1979 In *Social Anthropology of Work,* edited by Sandra Wallman, 287–315. London: Academic Press Inc.

Seiber, Roy
1965 "The Insignia of the Igala Chief of Eteh, Eastern Nigeria." *Man* 64: 80–83.
1980 *African Furniture and Household Objects.* Bloomington: Indiana University Press.

Shaw, Thurstan
1970 *Igbo Ukwu: An Account of Archaeological Discoveries in Eastern Nigeria.* 2 vols. London: Faber.

Stevens, Phillips, Jr.
1973 "The Nupe Elo Masquerade." *African Arts* 4, no. 4: 40–43, 94.

Sydow, Eckhart von
1932 "The Image of Janus in African Sculpture." *Africa* 5, no. 1: 14–27.
1954 *Afrikanische Plastik.* Berlin: Gebr. Mann.

Talbot, P. Amaury
1923 *Life in Southern Nigeria.* London: Cass.
1926 *Peoples of Southern Nigeria.* 4 vols. London: Oxford University Press.
1932 *Tribes of the Niger Delta.* London: The Sheldon Press.
1932 [1967] *The Tribes of the Niger Delta.* London: Frank Cass & Co. Ltd.

Tamuno, T. N.
1968 "The Odum Festival." In *Nigeria Magazine* 97: 68–76.

Tasie, G. O. M.
1977 *Kalabari Traditional Religion.* Berlin: Reimer.

Thomas, Northcote W.
1913/14 *Anthropological Report on the Ibo-Speaking Peoples of Nigeria.* London: Harrison and Sons.

Thompson, Robert Farris
1976 *Black Gods and Kings.* Bloomington: Indiana University Press.

Ukadike, Ifeka
1997 "Seven Suspected Sea Pirates Arrested in Delta": http://www.postexpresswired.com. September 24.

Underwood, Leon.
1947 *Figures in the Wood of West Africa.* London: J. Tiranti.

Uya, Okon Edet
1984 *A History of the Oron People of the Lower Cross River Basin.* Oron, Nigeria: Manson Publishing Company.

Vansina, J.
1998 *Art History in Africa.* New York: Longman.

Vogel, Susan.
1974 *Gods of Fortune: The Cult of the Hand in Nigeria.* New York: Museum of Primitive Art.

Wadel, Cato
1979 "The Hidden Work of Everyday Life." In *Social Anthropology of Work,* edited by Sandra Wallman, 365–84. London: Academic Press Inc.

Wallman, Sandra, ed.
1979 *Social Anthropology of Work.* London: Academic Press Inc.

Wariboko, Nimi
1999 *Symbolism in Kalabari Culture: Number Three as a Visible Representation of an Invisible Worldview.* Unpublished manuscript.

Welch, James W.
1936 "The Isoko Clans of the Niger Delta." Ph.D. diss., Cambridge University.

Wéwè, Adétólé
1995 "Oguberiberi Masks: The Ijo Stylistic Traits in Yoruba Speaking Igbobini." *Kurio Africana* 2, no. 1: 34–39.

Whitehouse, A. A.
1905 "An African Fetish." *Journal of the African Society* 4: 410–16.

Wilcox, Rosalinde
Forthcoming "Artistic Traditions and Coastal Interactions: Affinities between the Niger Delta, Coastal Cameroon, and Beyond." *African Arts* 35, no. 1.

Willet, Frank
1967 *Ife in the History of West African Sculpture.* New York: McGraw-Hill.
1971a *African Art: An Introduction.* London: Thames & Hudson.
1971b *African Art.* New York: Praeger Publishers. Inc.

Williams, Denis
1974 *Icon and Image: A Study of Sacred and Secular Forms of African Classical Art.* New York: New York University.

Williamson, Kay
1997 "Defaka Revisited." In *The Multi-disciplinary Approach to African History: Essays in Honour of Ebiegberi Joe Alagoa,* edited by Nkparom C. Ejituwu, 151–83. Port Harcourt: University of Port Harcourt Press.

Williamson, Kay, and Roger Blench
2000 "Niger-Congo." In *African Languages,* edited by Bernd Heine and Derek Nurse. Cambridge: Cambridge University Press.

Worika, U. A.
1982 "The Ogu 'Ogwein' Water Masquerade." In *The Masquerade in Nigerian History and Culture*, edited by N. Nzewunwa, 285–94. Port Harcourt: School of Humanities, University of Port Harcourt.